TREES
STRUCTURE and FUNCTION

TREES
STRUCTURE and FUNCTION

Martin H. Zimmermann
CHARLES BULLARD PROFESSOR OF FORESTRY
AND DIRECTOR OF THE HARVARD FOREST
HARVARD UNIVERSITY

Claud L. Brown
PROFESSOR OF FORESTRY AND BOTANY
UNIVERSITY OF GEORGIA

With a chapter on
irreversible thermodynamics of transport phenomena by
MELVIN T. TYREE
BOTANY SCHOOL, UNIVERSITY OF CAMBRIDGE, ENGLAND

SPRINGER-VERLAG
NEW YORK HEIDELBERG BERLIN
1971

ISBN 0-387-05367-0 Springer-Verlag · New York · Heidelberg · Berlin
ISBN 3-540-05367-0 Springer-Verlag · Berlin · Heidelberg · New York

PREFACE

Trees have the distinction of being the largest and oldest living organisms on earth. Although the herbaceous habit has made unprecedented evolutionary gains since the middle and late Cenozoic, trees still are the most conspicuous plants covering the habitable land surface of the earth. Man has long sought their shelter and protection, utilized their food and fiber, and often exploited them to his own detriment.

Trees have always been of much interest to botanists, and many of the early investigations concerning the structure and function of plants were conducted with trees. At the beginning of the present century the use of trees for basic investigations began to decline. The reasons for this are obvious. Investigations of structure and function began to shift from whole organisms to tissues, then to individual cells, and finally to cellular organelles and subcellular particles. Physiological research became increasingly more detailed and complex, requiring more and more precisely controlled laboratory conditions. Hence, a relatively small number of herbaceous plants, various unicellular algae, fungi, and bacteria have become standard research material in most laboratories.

Because of the unprecedented progress molecular biology has made in recent years, it may, perhaps, seem odd to those who work at the cellular and subcellular levels that some biologists would still choose to work with whole organisms, especially trees! Fortunately, those of us who work with woody plants are constantly reminded that not only do trees perform all the cellular activities of most unicellular and herbaceous plants but, indeed, a good bit more. Where else can one better study the many intriguing problems of water and food transport, dormancy, cambial activity, and differentiation of xylem and phloem than in woody plants?

The present book is devoted largely to those aspects of structure and function which are peculiar to trees. It attempts to close part of the existing gap in our knowledge of organismal plant physiology. No attempt has been made to cover such basic processes as photosynthesis, respiration, metabolism, nutrition, or other topics common to all green plants. These are adequately covered in textbooks of biochemistry and general plant physiology. Problems relating to certain aspects of dormancy and nutrition are discussed along with other functional aspects insofar as they are specifically related to trees; they are not covered as separate entities.

This text emphasizes the relationships between structure and function. The authors hope the reader will gain some knowledge of how trees work, not how a given species reacts under different environments. Our approach is not an ecological one in spite of the current timeliness of the subject. Those interested in the environmental aspects of tree physiology are referred to the excellent texts by Kramer and Kozlowski (1960) and Lyr *et al.* (1967); the citations of these are in this book.

We are indebted to many persons who helped us with the publication of this book. Most of Chapters 1, 2, and 3 were written during the summer and fall of 1968 while one of the authors (CLB) was granted time from teaching and other departmental duties. For this, I wish to express my sincere appreciation to Dean Allyn M. Herrick, School of Forest Resources and Dr. Melvin Fuller, Head, Department of Botany, University of Georgia. I am also indebted to the Georgia Forest Research Council, Macon, Georgia, and to its Director, Mr. Ed Ruark, for continued research support during my tenure at the University of Georgia. I also wish to thank Drs. Paul Kormanik and Donald Hook for their enthusiastic help and comments during the preparation of the manuscript. Special recognition is due Dr. Kormanik for his assistance with most of the illustrations in Chapters 1, 2, and 3.

Parts of Chapters 4, 5 and 7 were written while one of the authors (MHZ) was on sabbatical leave in Zurich, Switzerland, as a Guggenheim fellow. Prof. H. H. Bosshard's hospitality and the generous financial assistance granted by the John Simon Guggenheim Foundation during this time are gratefully acknowledged. Mrs. Barbara McCurda gave valuable help in editorial matters and Miss Monika Mattmüller aided the preparation of many illustrations for Chapters 4, 5 and 7.

We would like to thank those persons who gave much of their time reviewing parts of the book and who offered valuable suggestions for improvement. Drs. William Critchfield, Philip Morey, and Karl Sax read all or portions of Chapters 1, 2, and 3. Professor David Fensom read Chapters 4-7, Dr. Douglas Spanner Chapter 6, Professor Philippe Matile 4, 5 and 6.

Petersham, Massachusetts   MARTIN H. ZIMMERMANN
December 1969

Athens, Georgia   CLAUD L. BROWN
December 1969

CONTENTS

CHAPTER II

SECONDARY GROWTH

Claud L. Brown

CHAPTER III

GROWTH AND FORM
Claud L. Brown

CHAPTER IV

TRANSPORT IN THE XYLEM
Martin H. Zimmermann

CHAPTER V

TRANSPORT IN THE PHLOEM
Martin H. Zimmermann

CHAPTER VI

THE STEADY STATE THERMODYNAMICS OF TRANSLOCATION IN PLANTS

Melvin T. Tyree

CHAPTER VII

STORAGE, MOBILIZATION AND CIRCULATION OF ASSIMILATES

Martin H. Zimmermann

TREES
STRUCTURE and FUNCTION

CHAPTER I

PRIMARY GROWTH

Claud L. Brown

INTRODUCTION

The origin of apical meristems predates the evolutionary development of vascular plants. Land plants evolved as axiate, bipolar structures wholly dependent upon the activity of organized meristems at the tips of shoots and roots. Apical meristems make all primary growth possible by the addition of new cells, they exert complete control over the pattern of cell and tissue differentiation beneath, and also they perpetuate themselves. Thus, we say apical meristems are totipotent because they are autonomous in respect to continued organized development. Their totipotency is clearly shown in experimental studies where excised shoot and root apices supplied with water, mineral nutrients, and a source of carbohydrate can be cultured indefinitely *in vitro*.

All primary growth, including the formation of lateral appendages, results from the activity of distally located apical meristems. Although apical meristems in all vascular plants perform essentially the same function, they differ in their organization among major phylogenetic groups. Even in the nonvascular plants, some of the large complex algae such as *Fucus* grow by the localized activity of a dividing apical cell at the tip of the thallus. In the majority of primitive land plants (mosses, liverworts, horsetails, lycopods, and ferns) primary growth is governed by the activity of a large apical cell, pyramidal in shape, lying at the apex of both shoots and roots. In some of the Lycopsida, no single apical cell is present, and the meristems of both shoot and root consists of an organized group of embryonic cells. A similar but often more complex pattern of organization is found in angiosperms and gymnosperms.

Much attention was given to the organization of apical meristems by botanists in the late 1800's in an effort to delimit certain embryonic regions corresponding to the germ layers zoologists used in describing animal embryology. The histogen

1

theory of Hanstein (1868) was an attempt to accomplish this; however, the origin of different primary tissues, e.g., epidermis, cortex, vascular cylinder, and pith cannot usually be traced to a specific area of "histogen" in the shoot apex.

Although the apical meristems of shoots and roots are alike in many respects, they differ so markedly in others that they will be discussed separately.

1. THE SHOOT APEX

a. Vegetative phase

APICAL MERISTEMS.   The configuration of the apical meristem, though basically alike in angiosperms and gymnosperms, differs somewhat in internal patterns of organization. The tunica-corpus theory of Schmidt (1924) describes a pattern of organization common to many angiosperms. The tunica consists of a mantle or layer of cells extending across the apical dome produced by a preponderance of anticlinal divisions, while the corpus, an interior mass of unlayered cells, is formed by random planes of cell division (Fig. I-1a). In most gymnosperms a layering pattern is absent; therefore, the shoot apex does not conform to the tunica-corpus configuration. Many years ago, Sachs (1878) recognized a pattern of zonation in the shoot apex of *Abies pectinata* DC. that could be compared to a set of parabolic curves with a common focus just below the apex of the meristem. Foster (1938) in studying the pattern of cytohistological zonation in other gymnosperms delimited five rather distinct zones in the *Ginkgo* apex (Fig. I-1b). The apical initial zone gives rise to cells of the central mother cell zone and to the uppermost portion of the peripheral zone, while the "cambium-like" transition zone gives rise to cells on the flanks of the peripheral zone and to the rib meristem beneath. The peripheral zone ultimately gives rise to all lateral appendages, epidermis, cortex, and a good portion of the vascular cylinder. The rib meristem is a zone where cell division occurs predominately at right angles to the

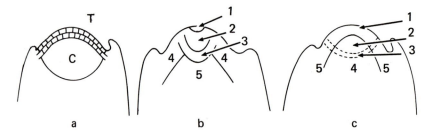

Fig. I–1a, b, c. Diagram of zonation patterns in longitudinal sections of dicotyledon and gymnosperm apical meristems. (a) tunica-corpus organization common to some dicotyledons; T, tunica; C, corpus (after Schmidt, 1924). (b) Cytohistological zonation found in many gymnosperms; 1, apical initial group; 2, central mother cells; 3, transition zone; 4, peripheral zone; and 5, rib meristem zone (after Foster, 1938). (c) Cytohistological zonation pattern applicable to many dicotyledons: 1, mantle layers; 2, central mother cell zone; 3, cambial-like zone (often absent); 4, rib meristem; and 5, peripheral zone (after Popham and Chan, 1950).

shoot axis producing vertical rows of cells. The activity of the rib meristem becomes of much physiological importance in shoot elongation as will be discussed later.

The cytological zonation of the gymnosperm apex can be used, with little modification, to describe the pattern of zonation in many angiosperms (Fig. I-1c) (Popham and Chan, 1950; Clowes, 1961).

The apical meristems of monocotyledons, especially the arborescent monocotyledons, have received much less attention than those of woody dicotyledons and gymnosperms. Readers interested in these plants are referred to the paper by Zimmermann and Tomlinson (1968) and the literature cited therein.

It is apparent from the brief foregoing discussion that the general configuration of the apical meristem proper, as well as the histological zonation within, varies with different species. Apical meristems vary in size, shape, and internal structure not only among species, but also with age, position, and physiological conditions. In fact, during early stages of seedling ontogeny young apical meristems may show little internal cytohistological zonation. Only after a period of growth and development does the apex become sufficiently mature to possess the distinct pattern of zonation common to most gymnosperms (Fig. I-2a, b, and also Fig. I-1b).

Cytohistological zonation of the apex made possible by differences in cell size, shape, vacuolation, stainability, planes of cell division, etc., has led to disagreement among researchers in interpreting the morphogenetic role of these different zones in the shoot apex. Buvat (1952, 1953, 1955) suggests the rather large,

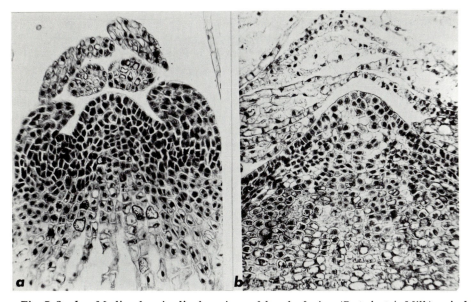

Fig. I–2a, b. Median longitudinal sections of longleaf pine (*P. palustris* Mill.) apical meristems. (a) Ten-day-old seedling without distinct patterns of cytohistological zonation. (b) Mature apex of older tree possessing well-defined cytological zonation.

vacuolated cells comprising the central mother cell zone in gymnosperms and some angiosperms, or comparable cells of the corpus in other angiosperms, are less active mitotically than the surrounding peripheral zones, and form a quiescent area which is "pushed upward" by the mitotic activity and enlargement of the rib meristem zone beneath. Hence in the vegetative apex this distal apical zone, the *meristem d'attente* (the waiting meristem), undergoes few mitoses but is carried along rather passively until the apex shifts into a reproductive state. At this time, according to Buvat (1952) the subjacent peripheral and rib meristem zones become quiescent, and the central mother cells along with the apical initials become quite active and directly contribute to the early development of the inflorescence or flower. This concept, however, has not been widely accepted (see Section 1b).

ORIGIN OF LEAVES.   All leaves arise from apical meristems. A leaf is usually initiated by periclinal divisions (parallel to the surface) in the outer cell layers of the peripheral zone subjacent to the apical dome. In most dicotyledons the first periclinal divisions occur in the second and third cell layer beneath the surface followed by anticlinal divisions (perpendicular to the surface) in the surface layer (see Fig. 5.6, page 107, in Esau, 1965). In some monocotyledons the surface layer also undergoes periclinal divisions giving rise to most tissues of the leaf (Guttenberg, 1960). Therefore, in angiosperms leaves may arise only from the tunica, or from both tunica and corpus cells, depending upon the thickness of the tunica layer. In gymnosperms the leaves arise in the outer layer of cells in the peripheral zone by both periclinal and anticlinal divisions (Guttenberg, 1961).

Leaf primordia first become visible on the side of the shoot apex as small protrusions. The young leaf then grows upward and soon begins to develop into a dorsiventral structure (with a few exceptions, e.g., in some gymnosperms) by the activity of marginal meristems (see Esau, 1965. pp. 448–464). Some leaves of woody plants may develop without interruption depending upon their time of origin, viz. late leaves in some trees of the temperate zones or all leaves in certain trees growing in the tropics. In the majority of trees, however, leaves in various stages of development undergo a period of dormancy in the winter bud and resume growth the following spring (see Section 2).

The precise pattern of leaf initiation by the apical meristem resulting in a rather rigid phyllotaxy has long been the subject of discussion and experimentation. Over a century ago, Hofmeister (1868) proposed that each successive leaf primordium arose in the next largest space available to it. Although such a statement may be valid, it does not explain what actually determines the precise origin of a given primordium at a particular time or place. Some have suggested a causal relationship between the location of the procambial strand and the initiation of a new leaf primordium because in some species, e.g., *Sequoia* and *Ginkgo,* the procambial strands differentiate acropetally into the apical meristem beneath the point of origin of the next leaf primordium (Sterling, 1945; Gunckel and Wetmore, 1946 a). The concept of a stimulus coming from a procambial strand or some other source beneath is not supported by experimental evidence. For example, one may isolate a portion of the meristem from the region beneath by surgical incision without disrupting the normal phyllotaxy.

One of the early attempts to explain why a leaf primordium develops in a certain place was made by Schoute (1913) who proposed that the presence of one primordium tended to inhibit the development of another one near it. This "inhibition hypothesis" apparently involved some sort of correlative growth phenomenon similar to lateral bud inhibition by basipetally transported auxin. Snow and Snow (1948, 1952) have produced some evidence against such an inhibition by removing the youngest visible primordium from the apex of *Lupinus* without causing any change in position of the next formed primordium. It is possible, however, that the inhibition is exerted before the primordium becomes visually differentiated.

Though the available space and inhibition hypotheses advocate different physiological mechanisms of control, they are not diametrically opposed to each other. Both indicate primordia arising upon a common axis should be as far away from immediate neighboring primordia as possible. The maximum distance would occur in plants with opposite phyllotaxy, i.e., 180° apart, with correspondingly smaller angles in those with spiral and whorled phyllotaxies. Students of developmental morphology have long been concerned with the mathematical preciseness of phyllotactic patterns, especially those possessing complex orders of spirality. Many of the mathematical relationships associated with phyllotaxy are discussed in detail by Thompson (1942) and Sinnott (1960).

ORIGIN OF BRANCHES. In seed plants, branches arise in close association with leaves. Although axillary buds appear to arise in the axil of the leaf, they are commonly initiated later than the leaf subtending them. The sequence of appearance of axillary buds varies considerably with species, and for this reason it is difficult to determine if all or part of the bud primordium is directly derived from the apical meristem of the terminal shoot, or partly from the tissue of the internode (Esau, 1965).

The early stage of axillary bud initiation is similar to that of leaf origin. Both anticlinal and periclinal divisions may occur in the superficial layers of the young shoot axis, but the increased growth at greater depths soon causes the young bud to protrude above the surface of the shoot axis. If the young bud continues to develop, its apical meristem gradually becomes organized into the same general pattern as that of the main axis. If the axillary bud elongates or develops into a lateral branch, it produces leaf primordia and second-order axillary buds in the same manner as the parent shoot.

The axillary buds in many woody plants are initiated and become well-formed when the main axis upon which they are borne is still encased in bud scales. In many trees immature lateral buds may be found in the axils of the third or fourth youngest leaf primordium; however, there is considerable species variation in this respect (Gifford, 1951; Garrison, 1955). In Douglas fir, *Pseudotsuga taxifolia*

(Poir.) Britt., the axillary buds are not initiated until the terminal buds begin to elongate in the spring (Sterling, 1947); whereas, in *Ephedra* they may appear above the second youngest leaf primordium (Seeliger, 1954).

In contrast to leaf primordia, axillary buds do not arise in the largest available space between other primordia and the distal apical dome, but in close association with the leaf primordium. If leaves are caused to deviate from their normal phyllotaxy by surgical removal or isolation, the origin of axillary buds follows the pattern of leaf emergence. Also, if incisions are made between the leaf primordium and the apical dome, the axillary bud always occurs on the leaf side rather than the isolated apical dome. This suggests that the leaf primordium itself predetermines the location of the lateral bud. Occasionally, however, the bud primordium giving rise to a flower or inflorescence may appear even before the leaves subtending them (Snow and Snow, 1942). In experimental studies involving the surgical removal and *in vitro* culture of leaf primordia from the fern *Osmunda cinnamomea* L. Steeves and Sussex (1957) found the three youngest primordia developed into radially symmetrical shoots and plants and the older primordia into dorsiventral leaves. Therefore, in its early stage of development, the primordium possesses the potential of developing into either a bud or leaf; but once it reaches a certain size, its fate is determined. In the seed plants, isolated primordia do not develop as buds, but into dorsiventral leaves or radially symmetrical structures with a leaf-like appearance (Sussex, 1955). Therefore, one can infer that the developmental pattern in angiosperm primordia is predetermined at an earlier age than in the vascular cryptogams.

DIFFERENTIATION OF VASCULAR TISSUE.   The process of cell and tissue differentiation begins with the formation of new cells. Differentiation implies change, and all cells, even those of the apical meristem proper, become differentiated to varying degrees. Many intriguing problems in biology today are those associated with differentiation. How, for example, do genetically identical cells lying adjacent to each other differentiate into entirely different cell types possessing various structural and functional roles?

In the shoot apex distinct patterns of cell differentiation occur giving organization to the meristematic cells of the apical meristem proper as shown by cytohistological zonation studies. As growth and development proceed, more obvious patterns of cell and tissue differentiation occur immediately beneath the apical dome. Strands of procambial cells can be traced upward into the apex in a pattern outlining the development of the future vascular system. Because higher plants evolved a highly dissected siphonostele (*eustele*) the procambium giving rise to this type stele develops as a series of strands in association with developing leaves.

Differentiation of procambial strands is generally considered to proceed acropetally from pre-existing strands into the young developing leaf primordia of dicotyledons and gymnosperms. In some of the monocotyledons, especially the arborescent forms, the pattern of procambial differentiation appears to proceed basipetally from the base of the newly formed leaf into the stem where it connects with existing traces (Esau, 1954; Zimmermann and Tomlinson, 1968). Procambial strands may also differentiate basipetally in dicotylendons and gymnosperms beneath adventitious buds, and in the regeneration of vascular tissues following wounding. Sinnott and Block (1945) studied the pattern of basipetal xylem regeneration around severed vascular bundles in *Coleus,* and Jacobs (1952) later demonstrated the role of auxin in promoting the basipetal differentiation of xylary elements in the same species.

Camus (1949) induced the formation of vascular tissue in callus cultures of endive root, *Cichorium endivia* L., by grafting a bud into the upper portion of the callus tissue; and, in a similar study with lilac, *Syringa vulgaris* L., Wetmore and Sorokin (1955) found that shoot apices grafted into the callus parenchyma cells caused differentiation of isolated vascular strands (tracheary elements only) in the callus beneath. The same type of differentiation was obtained by substituting napthalene acetic acid (NAA) in agar blocks for the active apices, which indicates auxin as the factor produced by buds and young leaf primordia inducing the differentiation of xylem tracheary elements.

In later studies, Wetmore and Rier (1963) controlled the position and type of vascular tissue differentiated by varying the level of auxin and sugar in the culture medium. In the absence of auxin, no vascular tissues were formed; whereas, at low sugar levels (2.0 per cent) and increasing auxin levels, xylem elements were formed. If the auxin concentration in the medium was maintained at 2.0 ppm, and the level of sugar increased to 4.0 per cent, then the pattern of vascular differentiation was changed and phloic elements were produced. It is of considerable interest that the relative concentrations of two substances, auxin and sugar, interact in a way to control cellular differentiation. Similar hormonal and nutritional relationships probably exist in intact shoots.

Following the establishment of procambial strands in the active shoot apex certain of the procambial cells begin differentiation into phloem and xylem elements. The first phloic elements, i.e., sieve cells in the gymnosperms and sieve tube members in the angiosperms, usually begin to differentiate acropetally along the outer margin of the procambial strand from the pre-existing phloem elements of the preceding leaf trace. As might be expected from a consideration of nutrition, phloem elements begin to differentiate before those of the xylem. Mobilization of sugars and other nutrients and their upward transport are crucial for the continued high metabolic activity of the shoot apex during this period of growth and development. This pattern may be significantly related to the experimental induction of phloem differentiation in the callus cultures of Wetmore and Rier (1963).

Primary xylem elements initially differentiate on the inner side of the procambial strand, usually near the base of the young leaf. From this point xylem differentiation occurs acropetally into the leaf and basipetally until it connects with the older xylem of the stem. Several vertical tiers of xylem elements may become differentiated as isolated units before becoming continuous with the xylem below. This pattern of tracheary differentiation again may reflect the influence of an initial hormonal induction because the level of auxin, or auxin precursors, are high at the base of young developing leaves. Although the patterns of vascular differentiation do vary somewhat among plant species, and, even within a given apex, depending upon nutritional conditions, these patterns appear to be general for the seed plants. For a more detailed account of the extensive literature one is referred to Esau (1965, pp. 377–393).

b. Reproductive phase

In photoperiodically reactive plants, the transition from an indeterminate vegetative apex to a determinate reproductive apex has been studied cytologically in various species following photoinduction. During the early stage of transition, mitotic activity is usually increased in the distal zones of the apical meristem, with a concomitant decrease in the former highly active peripheral zone. The distal meristematic mantle stains more uniformly for DNA; whereas, in the young reproductive apex, the concentration of RNA and protein increase (Gifford and Tepper, 1962).

It was mentioned earlier that Buvat (1955) and his colleagues suggested that the cells of the corpus or central core of the vegetative apex remained quiescent and were carried along rather passively until the transition to the reproductive state occurred. This concept has not gained widespread acceptance because of conflicting evidence obtained using different approaches to the problem. For example, Gifford and Wetmore (1957) failed to observe any real qualitative differences in the zonation pattern of vegetative and early reproductive apices of several gymnosperms. Only after all the sporophylls are initiated on the reproductive apex does the central mother cell zone become greatly modified or completely disappear. However, the dimensions of this central zone were somewhat smaller in the reproductive apex.

Data obtained by using ^{32}P-labeled phosphate (Partanen and Gifford, 1958) and ^{3}H-thymidine (Gifford, 1960) indicate the central vacuolated mother cell zone is metabolically active and does undergo cell division. Most workers are of the opinion the central mother cell zone is not quiescent during vegetative growth and that the whole apex is involved in reproductive development. A more detailed discussion of these concepts is given by Romberger (1963) and Esau (1965).

2. BUD AND BUD SCALE FORMATION

A bud may be defined as an embryonic shoot possessing an apical meristem and leaf primordia in various stages of development enclosed by bud scales (cataphylls). Bud and bud scale formation have long attracted the attention of plant scientists in all parts of the world. Apparently every region of the world supporting tree growth has some species whose buds are enclosed in bud scales, and the change from the formation of leaf primordia to cataphyll initiation is of special physiological interest.

It is unfortunate in many ways that most of our knowledge of tree growth was first obtained in temperate rather than tropical regions. In temperate regions, buds are prominent structures enclosed by scales on dormant twigs. In tropical regions, some trees never form dormant buds enclosed in scales, although the majority of species do. Between these two extremes are trees possessing intermediate morphological variations in which stipules, leaf blades, or leaf petioles functionally assume the role of bud scales. Even in some species of the north temperate zone, e.g., *Liriodendron tulipifera* L., valvate bud scales have evolved as modified stipules protecting the winter bud from desiccation and still permitting leaf extension until late autumn. Those sub-tropical and tropical species which do not set dormant buds enclosed by bud scales simply cease and resume growth as internal and external conditions permit, and the succulent shoot apex is protected by the young partially extended leaves (see Section 8a). The contents of dormant buds in trees of the temperate zones are highly variable and largely species specific. The morphogenetic complexity of the foliar components contained in the dormant buds of *Pinus* is clearly illustrated in Fig. I-3 from the detailed studies of Doak (1935). Here, for example, the bud scales for the next vegetative bud are preformed at the distal end of the non-elongated dormant bud.

In trees of the temperate zones the internodes between bud scales seldom elongate to any appreciable extent by subapical rib meristem activity, although there are exceptions to this. For example, in some species of *Rhododendron,* the scale internodes partially elongate, whereas, in the tropics, the scale internodes of some trees generally elongate to a greater extent than those separating the true leaves (Koriba, 1958).

The precise physiological mechanism(s) controlling the developmental processes of bud scales and foliage leaves are still obscure. Bud-scale primordia arise on the apical dome in the same way as true foliage primordia, and usually the two cannot be microscopically distinguished until they reach 100 or more microns in size (Foster, 1931, 1935). At this state in *Carya buckleyi* Durand, developmental differences become apparent and the cataphylls undergo a rapid marginal expansion, but the foliar primordia first increase in radial thickness. The cataphylls

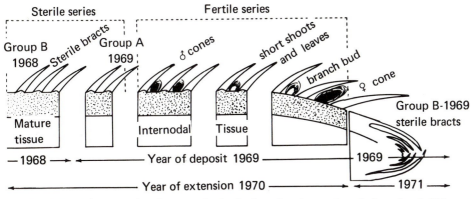

Fig. I-3. Diagram of a dormant bud of pine showing order of deposit of different foliar and reproductive components and their subsequent order of extension. Sterile series refers to bud scales or cataphylls without axillary appendages; fertile series connotes presence of axillary appendages (redrawn from Doak, 1935).

of most species usually mature rapidly and undergo less internal differentiation than foliage leaves. Internally, most cataphylls have a poorly developed mesophyll with the palisade cells often lacking, a meager vascular system, and few, if any, stomates.

In some species there is a wide range of variation in development between cataphylls and leaves and various transitional forms may exist in the same bud (Lubbock, 1889).

As previously mentioned, bud scale formation is a prerequisite of typical bud formation in trees making periodic flushes of growth. Bud scales may be laid down by the apical meristem in spring, summer, or fall depending upon species response; and lateral buds may or may not be formed in the axils of the bud scales. Knowledge about the physiology of these responses is scanty although some experimental control over the development of primordia has been obtained. In those species that respond to photoperiod, short days induce early bud formation and dormancy (Wareing, 1956). Thus, the primordia at the apex which would have developed into foliate leaves under long days were induced morphogenetically to form bud scales. Under natural conditions, however, day length is not necessarily the limiting factor because in many species bud scales are initiated under the longest days of the growing season.

In the lateral buds of *Syringa vulgaris* L., Dostal (1961) found the primordia normally destined to become leaves could be altered in their early stages of development by treating the subtending axillary leaf with gibberellic acid. In other studies, Dostal (1952) removed the outer scales of *Aesculus hippocastanum* L. buds just as the leaf primordia were beginning to develop and caused the reversion to scale formation. Application of auxin to young axillary buds of *Aesculus* also promoted the development of primordia into scales; whereas, the auxin effect could be reversed by the application of 2, 3, 5-triiodobenzoic acid, an anti-auxin. The latter substance promoted the development of primordia into leaves, and, in addition, caused already differentiated scales to undergo renewed elongation and marginal expansion. The bud scales of some species, e.g., beech (*Fagus grandifolia* Ehrh.), naturally undergo elongation at the base during bud expansion in the spring.

Recently Wareing (1964); Eagles and Wareing (1964); and Thomas *et al.* (1965) isolated a growth inhibitor from the leaves of *Betula pubescens* Ehrh. and *Acer pseudoplatanus* L., which they termed "dormin." The application of this inhibitor to seedlings growing under long days induces cessation of growth, formation of bud scales, and dormancy in buds. Apparently "dormin," or abscisic acid as it is now called, is antagonistic to the effects of gibberellic acid (see Section 4c, concerning the interactions of auxins, gibberellins, and cytokinins).

3. THE PHENOMENON OF POLARITY

Polarity is an universally occurring phenomenon resulting in oriented behavior of plants. The first division of the fertilized egg is oriented in that the plane of cell-plate formation establishes the future pattern of axiation in the developing embryo. From this time on, polarity is expressed in the axial develop-

ment of shoots and roots, and it usually cannot be reversed. For example, adventitious buds almost always arise at the apical end of woody stem cuttings, and
roots form at their morphological base. This was demonstrated by Vöchting
(1878) with willow cuttings whether they were left upright or inverted inside a
moist chamber. Roots possess a similar morphological polarity. Root segments
produce buds at their proximal ends and roots at their distal ends whether the
segments are placed horizontally, inverted, or in an upright position (Fig. I-4).

The initiation of new buds and roots on stem or root segments in a polar
manner is commonly attributed to auxin gradients maintained by an inherent
physiological polarity, i.e., the basipetal transport of auxin. As a result of polar

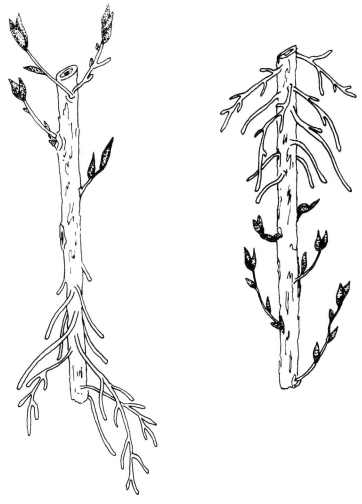

Fig. I–4. Diagram of one-year-old stem segments of eastern cottonwood (*Populus
deltoides* Bartr.) maintained in a moist chamber for several weeks in a normally oriented
position (left) and in an inverted position (right). Note root formation at morphological
basal ends in both stems, and the positive geotrophic curvature of extending shoots in the
inverted segment.

auxin transport, high auxin concentrations are found at the basal end of shoots and the distal end of root cuttings, a condition favoring root initiation. If the distal end of a root segment is repeatedly trimmed off, removing the high level of endogenously transported auxin, shoot primordia begin to form at that end as well as at the proximal end. Conversely, if the proximal end is removed so that very short pieces of root remain, then roots are formed at both ends. That these polarity effects are mediated by auxin is shown by the work of Warmke and Warmke (1950) where root or shoot formation could be induced at either end of root segments by controlling the levels of exogenously applied auxin.

It is sometimes possible to obtain root initiation at the apical end of inverted stem cuttings by centrifugation (Goebel, 1908) or from the pendent branches of weeping willow which because of their normally inverted position may tend to become apolar. Centrifugation of *Populus deltoides* Bartr. stem segments at 1,000 and 5,000 × gravity for 24 hours does not reverse the polarity of the rooting response in this species; however, approximately one per cent of weeping willow cuttings (*Salix babylonica* L.), formed roots at the apical end when inverted in a moist chamber (observations of C. L. Brown).

Another excellent example of the inherent polarity in woody twigs is the inability to obtain graft union by grafting two basal ends of separate twigs together. Even though callus tissue is formed at both ends, a new cambium is not differentiated through the callus to form a graft union. Thus, similar to the like poles of a magnet, the callus at the basal ends of shoots repel each other. There is also a lateral polarity to the cambium because the callus from opposite sides of longitudinally split stems will not knit together to permit the differentiation of a new cambium following grafting.

Vöchting (1878) observed that after removing a ring of bark (girdling) in the middle of woody shoots, roots always formed on the upper side of the girdle and buds or shoots below the girdle just as if the shoot had been severed. He concluded from these and other studies that polarity was an inherent trait of individual cells and once formed was irreversible. Although there are claims of polarity reversal of tissues and organs in higher plants (see Sinnott, 1960, pp. 116–146), such experiments are difficult to repeat with consistent results; hence, Vöchting's basic conclusions still remain valid.

Went (1941) rooted inverted cuttings of *Tagetes* and after they had grown inverted for awhile a new polar auxin transport system developed opposite the one originally present in the normal stem. Thus, two auxin transport systems were present at the same time. The polarity of the original cells was not reversed, rather the cells formed after the stem was inverted developed an opposite polarity, i.e., they transported auxin in a basipetal direction. This would lead one to conclude that gravity has some specific influence on the physical properties of the cell during cell differentiation, perhaps on the properties of the cell membranes, which control the active polar (basipetal) transport of endogenous auxin. Comparative studies of the ultrastructure of cells prior to and after stem inversion might give some insight into the physical basis of polar auxin transport.

In addition to these examples of polarity, the direction of growth is another expression of this phenomenon. In all cases of organized unidirectional growth, the plane of cell plate formation is at right angles to the direction of growth. Transverse divisions are predominant in the rib meristems of extending shoots and roots; whereas, tangential divisions are more prevalent in lateral meristems.

4. PHYSIOLOGY OF SHOOT GROWTH

Up until the 1930's most studies of shoot elongation were concerned with environmental factors affecting the rates and duration of growth. Much emphasis was placed on determining the essentiality of various nutrients and their optimal levels for normal plant development. In addition to nutritional observations, numerous studies were conducted on the effects of temperature, light, and water on such processes as photosynthesis and respiration. In these studies growth was usually analyzed mathematically in terms of the sigmoid growth curve, and variations in the slope or shape of the growth curve of treated versus control plants were accepted as an expression of physiological activity.

With the discovery and chemical identification of a specific growth regulating substance (IAA) in 1934 (Kőgl et al., 1934), the emphasis on control of shoot elongation was shifted from external environmental factors to internal biochemical relationships and their effect on cell elongation. During the next 20 years, hundreds of observations were made on various phases of plant growth and development, and auxin was correlated by some means to almost every physiological process known to occur in higher plants.

Since the 1950's other classes of naturally occurring growth factors, such as the gibberellins and cytokinins, have been discovered to interact with auxin in controlling various developmental processes in plants. In addition to factors which are known to promote growth through cell division and enlargement, there are also other naturally occurring substances which counteract or inhibit the action of one or more growth promotors. Thus, the internal mechanism of growth control becomes exceedingly complex; and the threshold levels of promotors and/or inhibitors acting upon segments of the growth response are important determinants in the pattern of primary growth. Due to shifts in the seasonal levels of promotors and inhibitors, e.g., the initiation and breaking of dormancy, etc., woody plants with their perennial habit have a more complex growth pattern than herbaceous plants.

a. Mobilization

Beginning with a shoot at rest, whether the terminal bud is enclosed in bud scales or not, the shoot apex must become physiologically active prior to resuming growth. Cellular metabolism is shifted from a lower to a higher level of activity and much energy is expended in the process of mobilization.

In the temperate zones, following a period of winter dormancy, we associate the warming days of spring with renewed growth. During the cold season, growth inhibitors which likely brought about the cessation of growth the preceding season have been removed or reduced to lower levels through enzyme activity so that formerly repressed genes can be released for renewed synthesis and growth. One lucid example of the chemical induction of enzyme activity in the process of mobilization is the effect of gibberellin on α-amylase activity in the endosperm of germinating barley seed (Paleg, 1960, 1961). This phenomenon was studied in detail by Varner and Chandra (1964) who found the production of the enzyme to be supported by DNA-dependent RNA synthesis. Thus, in the jargon of the molecular biologist, a repressed gene for the production of amylase is derepressed by its effector, gibberellic acid. The same type of action can be ascribed to the mechanism of bud dormancy. According to Tuan and Bonner (1964) the genome of the dormant potato bud is completely repressed. In the dormant condition, potato buds lack the ability to synthesize RNA at any appreciable rate; in addition, the chromatin isolated from dormant buds fail to support DNA-dependent RNA synthesis in the presence of added polymerase. Dormant potato buds released from dormancy by the application of either gibberellic acid or ethylene chlorohydrin, or buds released naturally with the passage of time can both synthesize RNA *in vivo* and yield chromatin capable of supporting DNA-dependent RNA synthesis. Apparently either ethylene chlorohydrin and/or gibberellic acid can act as an effector, which turns on the synthesis of RNA and proteins, cell division, and other anabolic processes. Bonner (1965) mentions that repressed chromatin may be derepressed to some extent by high temperatures, i.e., at temperatures below the melting point of DNA. He associates the age old practice of breaking dormancy of some buds by soaking them in hot water (50–60° C for several minutes) with the derepression of chromatin. Although the evidence is fragmentary, the idea is worthy of further study.

The universally occurring growth hormone, indoleacetic acid, is essential for cellular elongation, and also seems to be involved in RNA and protein synthesis (Key, 1964; Key and Shannon, 1964). Although the enzymology by which IAA exerts control over growth is still unknown, it does have an effect on DNA-dependent RNA synthesis. As a result of the rapid insights gained in the past decade in the area of molecular biology, we now stand on the threshold of elucidating the precise biochemical mechanisms of control over numerous complex physiological processes.

Once the cells of the shoot apex are released from dormancy, the processes of growth involving protein synthesis, cell division, and cellular elongation proceed under favorable temperatures and available soil moisture. The shoot apices will become centers of intense mobilization requiring high levels of inorganic nutrients, carbohydrates, and organic acids for synthesis of new cellular components.

The process of mobilization involves the translocation and accumulation of substances from a "source" to a "sink" which may occur in several ways. For example, the large accumulation of carbohydrates or fats in storage organs such as fruits, and tubers, results from the enzymatic conversion of soluble, translocatable substances into insoluble forms such as starch or fats, thereby creating a gradient from source to sink for further assimilation (see Chapter V, Section 8).

In addition to accumulation sinks, the flow of materials into regions where they are being rapidly utilized in growth constitutes another type of sink. Young, rapidly developing leaves and stems actively accumulate nutrients against concentration gradients requiring an expenditure of cellular energy in secreting or transporting such substances across cell membranes. The role of auxin in attracting nutrients to centers of growth has long been the subject of debate (Went, 1936); but as pointed out by Thimann (1937), the application of auxin alone to buds or leaves does not result in increased mobilization.

More recently Mothes (1960) and Engelbrecht and Mothes (1962) clearly demonstrated the effect of kinetin (6, furfurylaminopurine) in creating a translocation sink in excised tobacco leaves. Kinetin applied to a localized area of old leaves keeps that portion of the leaf green; and in addition, radioactive glycine is translocated across the leaf and accumulated in the kinetin treated area. The many interesting problems associated with storage and mobilization are discussed in more detail in Chapter VII.

b. Cellular basis of shoot elongation

The process of shoot elongation is illustrated in many texts by a diagram showing three rather distinct zones of primary growth: (1) a zone of cell division at the apical meristem proper, (2) a zone of cell elongation beneath the apical mersitem, and (3) a zone of cell differentiation and maturation toward the base. This concept of stem growth is somewhat misleading because it attempts to compare the pattern of organ growth with that of cell growth. For example, meristematic cells undergo division, the two daughter cells enlarge then one or both, as the case may be, becomes visibly differentiated into a mature cell type. The sequence of events in the extending shoot is not so stereotyped.

In describing stem growth in this manner the most obvious discrepancy is limiting cell division to the apical meristem proper. The majority of new cells in the extending shoot are formed in the subapical region by the activity of the peripheral and ground rib meristems, i.e., the cortical and pith rib meristem respectively. The apical meristem proper does contribute new cells to the subapical region, but by far the largest majority of cells of the primary plant body are produced by the latter. This was clearly shown by Harting (1845) well over a century ago. Most writers of botany texts fail to point out that cell divisions occur not only at considerable distances below the apical meristem, but also in highly vacuolated cells of the pith, cortex, and vascular procambium. Thus we should no longer perpetuate the concept that a typical meristematic cell is a rather small, large nucleated, non-vacuolated cell of the type forming the apical dome, when in fact, these cells are less active mitotically than the more mature, vacuolated cells beneath. The same misconception applies to the root apex, and especially to the vascular cambium where the rapidly dividing cells of the xylem and phloem mother cell zone are highly vacuolated.

Sachs (1965) in reviewing the observations of Harting (1845) for *Tilia parvifolia* Ehrh. points out that cell divisions continue to occur in the pith and cortex as far as 10cm below the apex of the shoot (Fig. I-5). In this 10cm section, the average length of pith cells doubles; whereas, cell number increases over tenfold. Different patterns of histogenesis in different tissues of the stem is illustrated by

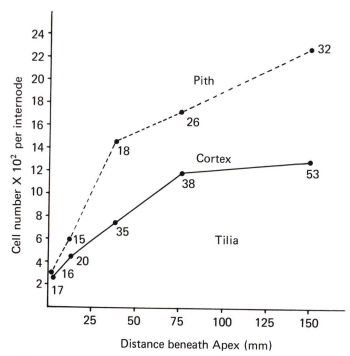

Fig. I–5. Increase in cell number in the subapical pith and cortical tissues of the annual shoot of *Tilia pavifolia* L. The base of each successive internode is plotted at the distance it occurs beneath the shoot apex. The numbers near the experimental points are mean cell lengths (microns) for that internode. Data from Harting (1845), redrawn from Sachs (1965).

the relative rates of cell elongation and cell division, the latter being greater in the cortex than in the pith. A similar pattern of development has been shown by other workers (Sachs, 1965; LeNoir, 1967). In woody plants, Harting (1845) and Moll (1876) found that short internodes contained fewer, rather than shorter, cells than long internodes; and that environmental factors influencing stem length may affect the rate and duration of cell division in the subapical zone. In spite of our considerable knowledge of factors affecting shoot growth and development, such as photoperiod, thermoperiod, water deficits, and so forth, we know little about the relationship of these factors to basic aspects of woody shoot histogenesis. For example, short photoperiods have been shown to induce shorter and fewer internodes and to initiate dormancy in some species (Downs, 1958; Wareing, 1956); however, whether the rate and duration of cell division, or the rate and duration of cellular elongation are influenced most is not known.

The importance of the rib meristems in the shoot must be emphasized because the preponderance of transverse divisions in these zones give rise to files of genetically related cells which ultimately control internodal elongation and total shoot growth. In discussions of shoot growth, the impression usually is conveyed that the rib meristem of the shoot is an ephemeral transition zone merging into the pith, cortical, and provascular tissue beneath. If this were the case, woody shoots would exist essentially as short shoots and extend leaves in the form of a rosette with little or no accompanying internodal elongation. The significance of rib meristem activity is vividly shown by comparing the height growth of a six-year-old longleaf pine (*Pinus palustris* Mill.) with the six-year-old progeny of the hybrid (*P. palustris* Mill. X *P. elliottii* (Fig. I-6a, b.). The former, still in the short shoot or so called "grass-stage" condition, often only attain a height of a few inches because rib meristem activity is inhibited; whereas, the hybrid at the same age may average twenty or more feet in height.

Over 100 years elapsed from the time of Harting's (1845) work before researchers realized that much cell multiplication occurs in vacuolated, subapical cells. Bindloss (1942) pointed out that the prevailing belief 25 years ago was that the primary zone of cell division was confined to an area 60 to 100 microns from the tip of the shoot. Unfortunately the current view in most texts is still the same.

c. Hormonal control of shoot elongation

AUXIN FORMATION AND DISTRIBUTION.   The existence of hormonal influences in plant growth and development were recognized and described many decades before the naturally occurring hormone, indoleacetic acid, was discovered by Went (1928) and identified a few years later by Kőgl *et al.* (1934). Since that time, especially during the 1930's and 1940's, a voluminous amount of work has been done on the distribution of auxin in various groups of plants. Zimmermann (1936) and Avery *et al.* (1937) showed that dormant buds contained little or no diffusible auxin; however, auxin production increased rapidly with bud opening and the extension of internodes. The highest levels of auxin were found in the twigs just prior to the period of most rapid internodel elongation. These workers observed that the sites of auxin production in the expanding terminal bud were associated with the young developing leaves and elongating internodes.

Czaja (1934) was among the first workers to demonstrate the presence of diffusible auxin in the opening buds of several woody plants, viz. species of *Pinus, Picea, Fagus, Quercus* and others. Mirov (1941) studied the yield of diffusible auxin in various parts of the elongating shoots of *Pinus ponderosa* Laws. and *P. torreyana* Parry and found a consistent increase in auxin levels from apex toward the base. The same pattern was observed in various stages of shoot elongation in *Pinus taeda* L. (Brown and Wetmore, 1959; Brown, 1964), and in the elongating shoots of *Liriodendron tulipifera* L. and *Liquidambar styraciflua* L. (Brown *et al.* 1967) as shown in Table I-1. With the onset of internodal elongation, the cells in the rib meristem produce an excess of available auxin which is transported basipetally creating a high concentration gradient in the lower mature portion of the shoot. Zimmermann (1936) also noted that the maximum yields of diffusible auxin from woody shoots do not coincide with maximum regions of growth.

Although the shoot apex, for example, the distal 1.0 cm portion in loblolly pine (*P. taeda* L.) contributes less diffusible auxin than other portions of the shoot, decapitation of this portion causes a rapid decline in yield of diffusible

Fig. I–6a, b. (a) Six-year-old longleaf pine seedlings (*P. palustris* Mill.) showing so called "grass-stage" condition resulting from inhibition of terminal shoot growth. (b) Six-year-old hybrid progeny from a controlled cross of *P. palustris* Mill. X *P. elliottii* Engelm. showing the effect of the latter parent in stimulating early and rapid height growth of the seedling progeny.

TABLE I–1

Yields of diffusible auxin from 2.0 cm sections of terminal and lateral shoots of *Liriodendron tulipifera* L. and *Liquidambar styraciflua* L. (from Brown, *et al.,* 1967).

| | Yellow poplar | | Sweetgum | |
	Terminal	Lateral	Terminal	Lateral
	Degrees Avena Curvature [a]			
Apex	8.8 [b] ± 0.4 [c]	5.1 ± 0.5	6.3 ± 0.7	4.3 ± 0.5
Mid-point	12.1 ± 0.9	9.9 ± 0.7	10.6 ± 1.1	6.4 ± 0.8
Base	19.3 ± 1.2	11.2 ± 1.3	15.1 ± 2.0	10.0 ± 0.9

[a] All curvatures corrected to the same sensitivity on successive test days by known IAA standards. The yields of diffusible auxin from the plant material at different positions were corrected and standardized on the basis of fresh weight of the stem segments diffused.

[b] Yields expressed as means of three Avena tests made biweekly during active growth in May and June with three replications per test. Each value is the mean of 108 individual Avena plant curvatures.

[c] Standard error of the mean.

auxin in the internodes beneath, so that 24 hours later the amount of auxin obtained from any portion of the shoot is nil (unpublished data of C. L. Brown). Even though the shoot apex proper contributes less auxin than the elongating or mature basal internodes, the apex somehow exerts control over the production of growth hormones beneath. During the early stages of shoot elongation in pine, removal of the young developing needle bundles also lowers the level of diffusible auxin in all parts of the shoot within 24 hours, but not to the same extent as removal of the distal portion of the shoot. Removal of the young leaves in *Ginkgo* also causes a decrease in auxin production in the stem, although the leaves themselves produce only a negligible amount of auxin (Gunckel and Thimann, 1949).

In all woody shoots examined thus far more diffusible auxin appears to be produced in the rib meristems of elongating internodes than by the young developing leaves as in most herbaceous plants.

In recent years there seems to be some doubt that indoleacetic acid is the most prevalent naturally occurring growth hormone to be found in all groups of plants (see review by Romberger, 1963, pp. 126–127; 132–133). Fransson (1953, 1959) reported the occurrence of a growth promoting substance in shoots of *Pinus sylvestris* L. which failed to chromatograph identically with synthetic IAA. The substance was referred to by Fransson as pine auxin (Pinus I). Wodzicki (1968) recently showed that oleoresins interfere in the proper identification of IAA by paper chromatography. Using improved purification techniques Wodzicki showed the presence of a growth promoting substance in extracts from the same species (*P. sylvestris* L.) corresponding to that of synthetic IAA.

APICAL DOMINANCE. One of the first physiological processes to be recognized as linking the inhibition of growth in one part of a plant to a hormone produced in another part was that of apical dominance. The simplest expression of this phenomenon is the general observation that lateral buds along an elongating stem do not usually develop in the presence of an active shoot apex. Removal of the apex of an actively growing shoot releases one or more of the lateral buds beneath; whereas, decapitation of the apex followed by the application of auxin to the cut surface holds the lateral buds in check. The demonstration of this principle by Thimann and Skoog (1933, 1934) led to the concept that basipetally transported auxin exerts a direct inhibitory effect on the buds along the shoot. This rather simple pattern in which auxin produced in the shoot apex inhibits lateral buds lower down the shoot has been challenged from time to time by various workers who cite instances of bud release patterns differing from that just described.

For example, Snow (1937, 1940) pointed out that in some plants buds farthest from the apex are inhibited more than those nearest the apex, this does not seem logical if auxin coming from the terminal bud is the inhibitor. However, this is the pattern one might expect if the concentration of endogenous auxin increases toward the base of the shoot (see Section 4c, on auxin formation and distribution).

Went (1936, 1939) and Van Overbeek (1938) suggested the action of auxin was indirect, because inorganic nutrients and foods are translocated to the terminal shoot which is high in auxin content and undergoing rapid growth. No one questions that the rapidly growing apex with its young developing leaves are mobilization sinks; yet, in some woody species, the lateral buds escape inhibition just beneath the apex in the region of most rapid growth and development (Champagnat, 1954, 1961; Brown *et al.,* 1967).

Gregory and Veale (1957) express the viewpoint that purely nutritional factors, such as the supply of available carbohydrates and nitrogen, control the degree of apical dominance and bud inhibition. They suggest that auxin is only indirectly involved by inhibiting the formation of vascular tissue into axillary buds which affects their ability to compete for nutrients and prevents them from growing.

The fact that lateral buds do occasionally escape inhibition and develop into lateral shoots near the middle or upper portion of rapidly elongating terminal shoots where endogenous auxin levels are high (cf Champagnat, 1954, 1961), coupled with the observation that the second-order lateral buds on these first-order lateral branches are completely inhibited in some species under lower levels of diffusible (polarly transported) auxin as shown by Brown *et al.* (1967) would lend support to the concept of Gregory and Veal (1957) that nutritional factors exert the primary effect on bud inhibition. On the contrary, one cannot ignore the observation that decapitation of the apex of these lateral branches will release one or more of the inhibited second-order lateral buds beneath. Because auxin is present, and because decapitation of the apex does have an immediate effect in lowering the content of diffusible auxin in all parts of the shoot beneath (see Section 4c on auxin formation and distribution) one must conclude that auxin *per se* is somehow directly involved in the initial process of lateral bud inhibition. The direct inhibitory effect of indoleacetic acid in physiological concentrations on the growth of buds has been repeatedly demonstrated in a wide variety of plants and there is no reason to doubt that it can directly inhibit the growth of lateral buds. Some of the objections to the concept of direct auxin inhibition discussed above are, in fact, conditions which relate to the *release of buds from inhibition* and not to the actual mechanism or the different viewpoints now held on the mechanism of correlative inhibition. The sensitivity of buds to release from inhibition is not only a function of overall vigor and nutrition but also involves the interaction of other growth factors such as cytokinins and possibly gibberellins as discussed in the remainder of this section.

In woody plants some of the growth responses normally interpreted as incisive expressions of apical dominance are not related to *apical dominance* in the sense that Thimann and Skoog (1933, 1934) first used the term to denote the inhibition of lateral buds by an actively growing apex in the herbaceous plant *Vicia faba*. The discrepancy lies in the fact that lateral buds on the previous year's twig following a period of winter dormancy or rest are no longer under the auxin inhibition of the terminal bud; rather some of the uppermost lateral buds usually release synchronously with the terminal bud and often suppress its continued development. These and other effects commonly interpreted in terms of apical dominance are discussed in Chapter III, Section 2a).

RELEASE OF BUDS FROM INHIBITION. Even though the phenomenon of apical dominance is some way mediated by the action of IAA, the initial step releasing buds from inhibition seems to involve naturally occurring cytokinins (Sachs and Thimann, 1967). Kinetin has been known for some time to be antagonistic to auxin in releasing buds from inhibition (Wickson and Thimann, 1958). Although there is no proof to substantiate the direct auxin inhibition hypothesis of Thimann (1937), an initially high level of basipetally transported auxin in the proximity of developing lateral buds may repress the "gene" that enzymatically controls the levels of cytokinins in the distal apical region of the inhibited lateral bud. The removal of the source of inhibition, i.e., the decapitation of the actively elongating terminal shoot, might possibly release the gene for cytokinin production; hence, the lateral bud becomes active. This could explain how auxin in the terminal shoot can inhibit lateral bud growth under one set of conditions; whereas, localized auxin production could promote growth of the same bud once it is activated under a different set of conditions. Thus, sensitivity to auxin action is probably mediated through interacting levels of different growth factors.

In woody shoots and perhaps in herbaceous ones, the degree of inhibition changes with time, and the pattern of bud release varies considerably with species. For example, decapitation of the apex of an elongating shoot normally results in the release of one or more of the lateral buds beneath. If, however, the distal part of the shoot is removed in many angiosperms (notably, *Carya, Fraxinus,* and *Acer*) after shoot elongation has ceased, but while conditions for growth are still optimum (e.g. in mid-June in the latitude of Athens, Georgia) the inhibited lateral buds on the current year twig *are not* released from inhibition. Rather such buds must usually undergo a period of winter dormancy before beginning active growth the following spring. Therefore, in some species the natural reduction of auxin levels concomitant with cessation of growth and the formation of a new terminal bud brings with it a stronger degree of inhibition requiring the removal of foliage in some cases, or a period of winter rest. Goebel (1880) recognized the inhibitory influence of leaves on axillary bud growth almost a century ago, and Wareing (1964) recently extracted the active inhibitor from the leaves of *Acer pseudoplatanus* L. grown under short photoperiods.

In contrast to the complete inhibition just described in some angiosperms, the short shoots of various pines (*P. taeda* L., *P. elliottii* Engelm., *P. echinata* Mill.) of the Southeastern United States can be released from inhibition by decapitation of the shoot apex even during the late summer months long after shoot extension has ceased. In addition, almost all of the short shoots occurring on the last two flushes of extension growth in loblolly pine (*P. taeda* L.) seedlings can be initially released by feeding approximately 10 ml of a 10 ppm kinetin solution into the transpiration stream of a severed lateral branch (Fig. I-7), (observations of C. L. Brown). The prominently swollen and well-developed short shoot buds fail to develop into long shoots apparently because of insufficient levels of other growth factors to trigger rib meristem activity. This assumption is based on the proposed role of auxin in inducing internodal elongation of buds after their initial release from inhibition following the application of kinetin (Sachs and Thimann, 1967). Gibberellin could also be involved in inducing cell division in the rib-meristem and play a subsequent role in cell elongation by its interaction with auxin (see following section on role of gibberellins in stem elongation).

ROLE OF GIBBERELLINS IN STEM ELONGATION.   The gibberellins as a class of growth promoting substances were recognized as early as 1926 by Kurosawa, a Japanese researcher, when a fungus filtrate applied to rice seedlings promoted their growth (Stowe and Yamaki, 1959). During the early 1950's gibberellin research was stimulated in the Western Hemisphere and today approximately 27 substances, all with a similar terpenoid structure and all naturally occurring, have been isolated and identified (Crozier *et al.*, 1970). Although closely related in structure, they induce different developmental responses in various plants (Paleg, 1965; Van Overbeek, 1966). Gibberellic acid (GA_3) is the one most often produced commercially from fermentation of fungal cultures, as well as the most effective one in promoting internodal elongation of certain dwarf varieties of corn, peas, and other plants.

Gibberellins, like auxins, promote the irreversible enlargement of cells in the internodes of the plants they effect; however, their specific action appears to be different from that of auxin. For example, one current view is that auxin must be present in the cell before gibberellin can exert its effects on enlargement. In some plants, externally applied gibberellin and auxin act synergistically, i. e., the final growth response is greater than the sum of the growth induced by either substance acting alone. In those cases where cells, tissues, or organs do not respond to applied gibberellin it is assumed that the levels of naturally occurring gibberellins are already optimum so that other factors limit the growth response. Several suggestions have been made on the role of gibberellin in promoting cell elongation in the presence of auxin. For example, in auxin induced cell elonga-

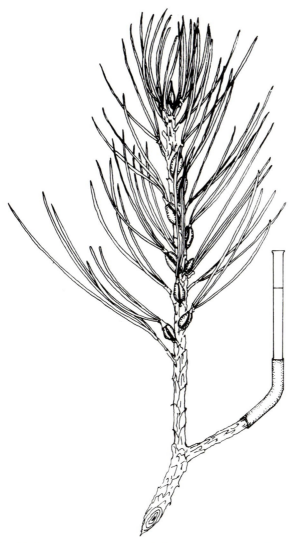

Fig. I–7. Twig of two-year-old loblolly pine (*P. taeda* L.) seedling 30 days after injection of 10 ppm kinetin (10 ml) into the transpiration stream through a severed lateral branch beneath. Note pronounced swelling of needle fascicles enclosing well-developed short shoot buds.

tion the osmotically active material within the cell does not increase, but the cell wall is weakened to permit the rapid uptake of water. Gibberellins appear to induce the formation of enzymes that weaken cell walls; therefore, they may play a direct role in the elongation process. Gibberellins may also stimulate auxin synthesis by inducing the formation of proteolytic enzymes which effect the release of tryptophan, a precursor of IAA. Furthermore, gibberellin promotes α-amylase activity which hydrolyzes starch to sugars, thereby increasing the level of osmotically active material in the cell sap to maintain osmotic concentration during cellular elongation. Thus, gibberellin may interact with auxin in any or all of these activities to bring about the growth response. Van Overbeek (1966) has presented an excellent review of interactions between gibberellins, cytokinins, and auxin in regulating plant growth.

There is ample evidence that gibberellins are produced in regions of cell division and/or elongation such as developing buds, young leaf primordia, developing fruits and seeds, and in growing shoot tips. They are rapidly transported from place to place; but in contrast to auxin they do not show polar movement.

Gibberellin synthesis appears to be very sensitive to photoperiodic control in many plants. For example, many rosette plants when grown under short days remain as rosettes and possess a low gibberellin content. If, however, they are transferred to long photoperiods, the endogenous levels of gibberellin may increase and they undergo internodal elongation to form normal long shoots. In many instances, those plants that respond favorably to long photoperiods also respond to gibberellin when applied as a foliar spray. In either case, the increased level of gibberellin promotes cell division in the sub-apical region of the shoot causing a shift from the short to long shoot habit of growth (Sachs et al., 1959). In these rosette plants, as well as in certain types of genetic dwarfs, gibberellin appears to be the limiting factor (growth hormone) in controlling shoot growth through its specific effect on rib meristem activity. In species not stimulated to undergo increased cell divisions in the rib meristems by externally applied gibberellin, e. g., the short shoot apex of longleaf pine seedlings (Brown, 1964), the level of one or more interacting growth factors may be limiting, or some inhibitor may be present in sufficient concentration to counteract or suppress the action of gibberellin. It may also be that the applied hormone does not reach the site of inhibition in sufficient concentration, or that some form of gibberellin other than gibberellic acid (GA_3) would be more effective in eliciting the growth response.

Various growth responses have been obtained in woody plants by the application of gibberellin to leaves, stems, and buds. Foliar application increases internodal elongation in some woody angiosperms; but has little or no effect in others. Conifers in general do not respond as readily as angiosperms which may reflect a sufficient endogenous supply of gibberellin in their cells and tissues. The conifers are rich in terpenoid substances and gibberellin may seldom become limiting because of a readily available supply of these precursors, although this is purely speculative.

In several species of woody plants (e. g., *Fagus sylvatica* L., *Camellia japonica* L., *Weigela florida* L.) photoperiodically induced dormancy can be broken by the application of gibberellic acid (GA_3). The first interpretation of this response was that short photoperiods resulted in a deficiency of gibberellin because of decreased synthesis. The explanation became more complex, however, when Wareing and his co-workers (Wareing, 1964; Eagles and Wareing, 1964; and Thomas et al., 1965) isolated a growth inhibitor from the leaves of *Betula pubescens* Ehrh. and *Acer pseudoplatanus* L. growing under short days. They appropriately termed this inhibitor "dormin." This substance when extracted from leaves and applied to seedlings elongating under long-day conditions, brings about cessation of growth and the formation of dormant buds. Subsequently, Cornforth *et al.* (1965) isolated crystalline dormin from the leaves of English sycamore, *Acer pseudoplatanus* L. and found it to be identical with abscisin II, characterized by Ohkuma *et al.* (1965) as a methylated cyclohexane. To avoid confusion in terminology the term abscisic acid is now used by most workers to replace this earlier nomenclature.

It now appears that abscisic acid may be involved in various physiological responses primarily through its action as a gibberellin antagonist *in vivo* (Thomas *et al.*, 1965). Additional observations on the interaction of auxins, gibberellins and cytokinins are discussed in the following section on long and short shoots.

5. LONG AND SHORT SHOOTS

Two morphologically distinct shoots commonly referred to as long and short shoots occur in many woody plants. In the early literature the short shoots of conifers were often called dwarf shoots and those of deciduous trees, especially fruit trees, were termed spur shoots. The terms are still used interchangeably today by many researchers.

The degree of genetic control over the short shoot habit is highly variable among species. For example, in the genera *Pinus* and *Larix* short shoot distribution is highly predictable, and most of the foliage is borne on them. In *Ginkgo*, their pattern of distribution is somewhat variable, but still usually predictable on older trees. A wider range in expression of the short shoot habit seems to exist in decidious than in coniferous trees. In some genera (e.g. *Malus, Prunus, Pyrus, Citrus, Crataegus,* etc.) short shoots are produced in rather consistent patterns along the twigs; whereas, in other genera (e.g., *Fagus, Betula,* and *Acer*), their pattern of distribution on any given twig is less predictable, although their frequency usually increases with age (Fig. I-8). Wilson (1966) finds that over 90 per cent of the shoots on red maple (*Acer rubrum* L.) trees 30 years of age or older are short shoots.

The physiological factors controlling the short shoot habit of growth have attracted researchers for many years, and many observations have been made on the occurrence and general growth habits of short shoots (Büsgen and Münch, 1929, pp. 21–25). Areschoug (1877) was of the opinion that short shoots could not persist indefinitely without occasionally reverting to the long shoot habit. He termed such reversions "regeneration shoots" and noted that the reversion from short shoot to long shoots and vice versa was prevalent among many species (Fig. I-9a, b).

During the past two decades several detailed anatomical and physiological studies have been conducted on the short shoots of several species. Gunckel and Wetmore (1946 a, b) made a thorough study of bud development in *Ginkgo* and found no qualitative differences between the apical meristems of long shoots and short shoots. The primary differences between the two types of shoots were

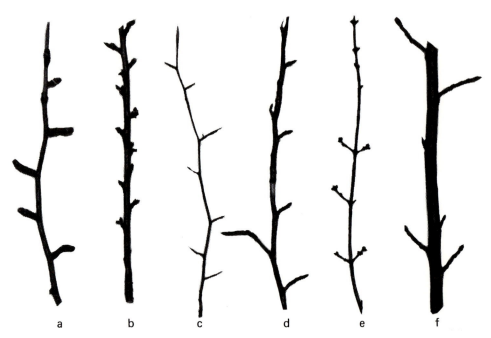

Fig. I–8. Short shoots along the twigs of various tree species. a, *Ginkgo;* b, *Prunus;* c, *Fagus;* d, *Liquidambar;* e, *Acer;* and f, *Liriodendron.*

quantitative ones in respect to the activity of the subapical rib meristem zone. In short shoots the rib meristem fails to become active upon opening of the buds so that little or no internodal elongation occurs. The putative long and short shoot buds in *Ginkgo* are identical, but the two buds are morphologically dissimilar in *Larix decidua* because of differences in development which occur during the preceding season (Frampton, 1960).

In addition to a wide range in the pattern of distribution of short shoots along the twigs of many trees, certain species of pine (*P. palustris* Mill., *P. tropicalis, P. montezumae,* and *P. michoacana*) of the southern United States, Cuba, and Mexico undergo a period of juvenile development in which the main axis (terminal bud) of the plant exists as a short shoot for several years following seed germination. Seedlings of longleaf pine (P. *palustris* may remain in the "grass-stage" from 2 to 15 years or more depending upon competition and vigor (cf Fig. I-6a). Various aspects of the short shoot habit in this species, including genetic observations of F_1 and F_2 seedling progenies have been studied in depth by Brown (1964).

The auxin physiology of the short shoot habit in *Ginkgo* was studied by Gunckel and Thimann (1949) and Gunckel *et al.* (1949) relative to yields of diffusible auxin during different stages of shoot development. The yield of diffusible auxin from either long or short shoot buds increased during the period of bud swell, but declined upon bud opening. In those buds developing as short shoots, i.e., extending leaves without any accompanying internodal elongation,

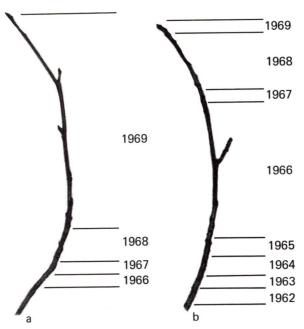

Fig. I–9a, b. Lateral twigs of *Liquidambar styraciflua* L. showing alternating patterns of short shoot and long shoot growth. (a) Reversion from the short shoot to long shoot habit. (b) Reversion from the short shoot to long shoot habit and again to the short shoot habit in successive years. Lines indicate terminal bud scale scars and the distance between them the amount of growth during any given year.

the auxin levels continued to decline. In contrast, those buds developing into long shoots showed a surge in production of diffusible auxin as the rib meristems of the internodes became active (Fig. I-10).

In young vigorous *Ginkgo* seedlings, decapitation of the terminal long shoot buds normally resulted in the release of one or more putative short shoot buds on the stem beneath; whereas, decapitation followed by the application of high concentrations of naphthaleneacetic acid (5000 ppm in lanolin paste) prevented the uppermost buds from developing into long shoots (Gunckel *et al.*, 1949). Upon the basis of these observations, these workers concluded that diffusible auxin coming from an elongating terminal bud determined whether or not a lateral bud would develop into a long shoot or remain as a short shoot. In older trees the development of long shoots in response to decapitation was more variable, and appeared to be highly correlated with the inherent vigor of individual branches.

The short shoot habit of longleaf pine seedlings appears to be more complex, and under more rigid genetic control, than the short shoots of *Ginkgo*. In the former, the main shoot grows as a short shoot which produces numerous needle bearing short shoots spirally arranged and closely compacted around the stem. This gives rise to the unique condition of numerous short shoots being borne upon a short shoot axis.

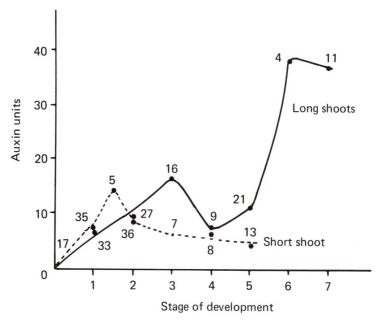

Fig. I–10. Yield of diffusable auxin from long and short shoot buds of *Ginkgo biloba* L. Stage of bud development is indicated by: 0, dormant winter buds; 1, buds tight, but swelling; 2, buds showing first green; 3, bud scales opening; 4, petiole elongation; 5, leaf blades expanding; 6, internodes apparent in long shoots; 7, long shoots. Stages 0–4 represent putative short shoots or long shoots; stages 5–7 are definite for short and long shoots respectively. Figures near plotted points on curves represent number of buds used in each determination. Data adapted from Gunckel and Thimann (1949).

The short shoot habit in the seedlings of longleaf pine is so rigidly controlled (i.e., the inhibition of rib meristem activity is so complete) that no single treatment or combination of treatments such as vernalization; photoperiod; application of gibberellin, kinetin, or indoleacetic acid in foliar sprays or by injection; or growing excised embryos on a variety of media, have any appreciable effect in stimulating internodal elongation (Brown, 1964). Grafting the young 30-day-old shoot apex into the apex of older loblolly pine (*P. taeda* L.) seedlings failed to release the inhibition. Also, in contrast to other pine species, decapitation of the terminal bud fails to release one or more short shoots (needle fascicles) to form a new leader(s).

The swelling or opening terminal buds of the short shoot apex in longleaf pine, unlike the buds of *Ginkgo,* fail to yield any diffusible auxin; however, they do produce ether or alcohol extractable indoleacetic acid during this early stage. The excised shoot apex of this species is apolar with respect to auxin transport, and such apices will take up IAA by diffusion when applied to either distal or proximal cut surfaces of the shoot apex. Applied IAA is neither inactivated nor metabolized by the shoot apex of longleaf pine as long as it retains the short shoot habit. Thus, the mechanism of the inhibition in the rib meristem of this species appears to be quite different from that suggested for the short shoots of *Ginkgo;* obviously, it cannot be attributed to apical dominance, i.e., the inhibitory effect of diffusible auxin coming from an elongating terminal bud. These observations indicate that rib meristem activity in the short shoots of longleaf pine is inhibited by either 1) the presence of a true inhibitory substance which inhibits the action of auxin, gibberellin, or cytokinin, or 2) the lack of a threshold level of one or more of these interacting growth promoting factors. Some of the complexities and interactions involved in the hormonal regulation of growth in higher plants is discussed by Galston and Davies (1969).

Sachs and Thimann (1967) suggests that cytokinin is the factor which initially releases a bud from the auxin inhibition of apical dominance, whereas subsequent internodal elongation of the released bud is affected by the level of auxin produced in the rib meristem. If one attempts to relate this mechanism to the physiology of short shoots, it appears that the first step of cytokinin mediated release is met because the buds do become active and extend new leaves; whereas, the second step, that of auxin production in the individual short shoot rib meristem, is inhibited.

One has to use considerable caution in relating the mechanism of lateral bud release from apical dominance in herbaceous plants to the release of short shoots in trees which have undergone a period of rest, and which are no longer under the direct control of the terminal leader. For example, it is difficult to reconcile why short shoots exist in one species because of an auxin inhibition from the terminal leader at the beginning of the second season's growth when many of the uppermost lateral buds in the majority of trees release to form long shoots following a period of rest. It seems illogical to suggest that the sensitivity of *Ginkgo* buds to auxin inhibition is still high the following season, when, in fact, the short shoot buds do open and form leaves but the rib meristem remains inhibited. Such behavior appears to be associated with a lack of auxin rather than an auxin inhibition.

In the case of longleaf pine apices it appears that the phenomenon of cell and tissue polarity is imminently associated with the inhibition of the rib meristem; certainly, the histological patterns of cell size and shape confirm this possibility. The majority of cells in the subapical zones of short shoots increase radially in size becoming almost spherical in shape rather than vertically elongate with respect to the shoot axis as in normal long shoots (Fig. I-11a, b). This expression of cell form appears causally related to apolar auxin transport in longleaf pine apices because cells of the rib meristem zone *do become* vertically elongated and polar with respect to basipetal auxin transport whenever the seedlings begin to make height growth. The polarity of the shoot apex in the short shoots of *Ginkgo,* has apparently not been checked, although the cytohistological observations are quite similar to those in longleaf pine.

The problem of rib meristem inhibition is complex, and involves more than a direct auxin inhibition in buds having undergone a period of rest.

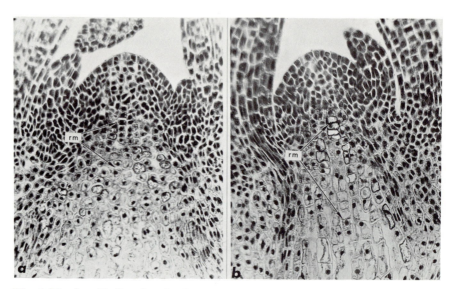

Fig. I–11a, b. Median longitudinal sections of 30-day-old pine apices. (a) Typical short shoot apex of longleaf pine (*P. palustris* Mill.) with a relatively inactive rib meristem (rm) and radially enlarged cells beneath. (b) Long shoot apex of loblolly pine (*P. taeda* L.) possessing an active rib meristem and vertically elongated cells beneath resulting in internodal elongation.

6. ADVENTITIOUS BUDS

Many woody plants have the inherent potentiality of producing buds in parenchyma tissues not directly associated with apical meristems and in places not dictated by their normal phyllotactic pattern. Buds arising in this manner are termed *adventitious*.

The formation of adventitious buds on stems of woody plants is not as prevalent as many people think; and of those species producing adventitious buds, by far the largest majority are produced on lateral roots. In many cases, following pruning or wounding of fruit or shade trees and woody ornamentals, the proliferation of rapidly growing shoots is not due to the formation of adventitious buds at all, but to the release of preformed suppressed buds embedded in the periderm of the stem (see Section 7).

In shoots, adventitious buds may arise in any tissue exterior to the xylem capable of undergoing renewed meristematic activity. Adventitious buds in herbaceous plants often arise along the margin of leaves, on cut petioles, or in association with the leaf veins. In fact, many ornamental plants, such as begonia (*Begonia rex.* L.), African violets (*Saintpaulia*), and others, are normally propagated in this way.

Although it is possible to obtain organized apical meristems in proliferating epidermal or cortical cells of young shoots, most adventitious buds in woody stems form in the cork cambium (phellogen), phloem parenchyma, or ray initials of the vascular cambium. In many trees, adventitious buds arise in response to wounding following proliferation of callus cells of one of the above-mentioned tissues. Adventitious buds in undisturbed shoots are of exogenous origin, that is, they arise in superficial tissues near the surface of the stem such as exterior cortical or phellogen cells which normally proliferate in connection with lenticel formation.

Soon after their formation, apical meristems on primary shoots or roots must make connection to the existing vascular system in order to develop into a bud. The vascular connection of the new bud to the main axis has received attention from several workers (see Esau, 1965, p. 383). The procambial strands connecting the bud with the main axis may develop acropetally to become continuous with the procambium of the main shoot, or in some cases procambial strands produced at the base of young leaf primordia differentiate basipetally to make connection with the vascular strands of the shoot.

Most adventitious buds in woody plants arise from the superficial tissues of stems or roots where much secondary growth has already occurred. In such cases the differentiation of procambial strands is basipetal from the leaf primordia of the new bud to the secondary vascular tissue (Dermen, 1959).

The work of Skoog and Tsui (1948, 1951) concerning the effects of adenine on the induction of buds in tobacco stems and callus grown *in vitro* was a significant contribution to our knowledge of the factors involved in bud initiation. In later studies, Skoog and Miller (1957) clearly demonstrated the role of kinetin (6, furfurylaminopurine), a derivative of DNA, in initiating bud formation in callus cells of tobacco. With the proper level of kinetin and auxin (IAA) they could induce either bud or root formation separately or both at the same time. High levels of kinetin and low levels of auxin induced bud formation; whereas, reverse levels induced root formation. The exact mechanism by which kinetin promotes bud initiation is not known; however, the substance has been isolated (Miller *et al.*, 1955) and identified (Miller *et al.*, 1955, 1956) as a specific factor for cell division. In addition to promoting bud formation, Wickson and Thimann (1957) found it to be antagonistic to auxin in releasing buds from apical dominance (see Section 4c in this chapter). Also, kinetin replaced the red light effect in releasing lettuce seeds from dormancy, and as previously discussed stimulates the mobilization of nutrients in leaves. For a more detailed discussion of these effects see Leopold (1964, pp. 133–143).

Various developing tissues of plants, especially developing buds, fruits, and seed endosperm, are unusually rich in natural cytokinins. In experimental studies one of the commonly used sources of cytokinin is coconut milk, the liquid endosperm of the coconut palm, which Steward *et al.* (1958) used so effectively in bringing about the formation of organized apical meristems and plantlets from carrot tissue grown *in vitro*. The practical significance of these studies lies in the utility they offer in the vegetative propagation of valuable genetic selections or hybrids of commercially important forest trees. By using tissue culture techniques it has been possible to grow haploid cells from both the pollen and female gametophyte of *Ginkgo* (Tulecke, 1957, 1964) and from the pollen of another gymnosperm *Ephedra* (Konar, 1963). Nitsch and Nitsch (1969) have recently accomplished the remarkable feat of obtaining haploid plantets from tobacco pollen grown *in vitro*. Using these same techniques it seems very probable that homozygous diploids may soon be produced in woody plants. This would be a valuable asset to the forest geneticist in producing homozygous lines by bypassing lengthy periods of inbreeding and it could have much basic and practical utility in the future. Some of these possibilities as they relate to forest tree improvement have been previously discussed by Brown (1967).

All buds on roots are adventitious in origin, and most arise exogenously from tissues exterior to the stele; however, there are instances where they appear to arise endogenously from the pericycle as do lateral roots. The question often arises as to whether young meristems giving rise to lateral roots can shift morphogenetically to form buds. In studying the origin of young root primordia in horseradish roots (*Rorripa armoracia* L.), Dore (1955) found that most organized meristems occurred in the phellogen of the main root in close association with scars of older lateral roots, and that such meristems could develop into either buds or roots depending upon the physiological conditions prevalent at the time. Under high levels of auxin, the ratio of roots to buds increased; whereas, under lower auxin levels more of the apparently neutral primordia developed into buds.

Most adventitious buds develop into shoots the same season they are formed; hence, they do not normally undergo dormancy. This is the pattern, for example, in the initiation of root suckers in certain species of *Populus, Robinia,* and *Rhus*. In sweetgum (*Liquidambar styraciflua* L.), however, numerous buds are initiated either endogenously or exogenously, in young or old roots respectively, which may become dormant and exist as suppressed buds embedded in the periderm of the root for several years before being released to form root suckers (Fig. I-12a, b, c) (Kormanik and Brown, 1967). In view of this observation, other woody species may also produce suppressed buds which exist for varying periods of time before being released to form root suckers.

The pattern of bud release along the roots of sweetgum is of much physiological interest. Heretofore, the formation of root suckers in aspen has been attributed, in part, to disturbances of the parent tree such as wounding or detopping, or senescence of older trees. Because of the presence of numerous performed suppressed buds in sweetgum, the pattern of release is somewhat different. Vigorous 15 to 40-year-old sweetgum trees release numerous root buds in successive years to form root suckers without any apparent injury to the parent trees (Fig. I-13). Exposing lateral roots to light has a pronounced effect on releasing suppressed buds; and the degree of competition for water, nutrients, and light under field conditions determines the successful development of root suckers. For example, in sweetgum trees growing around the edge of mixed pine-hardwood stands in the Georgia Piedmont, more than 90 per cent of the root suckers formed are on the side where the lateral roots extended relatively free of competition into the open field.

Because so many suppressed buds are released in young sweetgum trees still possessing strong apical control, it seems that factors coming from the stems or proximal portion of the roots would be unlikely to exert control over bud re-

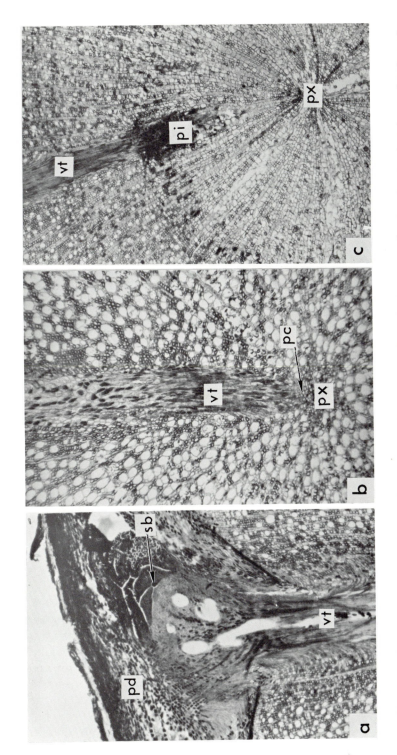

Fig. I-12a, b, c. Tranverse sections of lateral roots of sweetgum (*Liquidambar styraciflua* L.) showing location and points of origin of suppressed buds. (a) Suppressed bud lying in periderm with vascular trace extending inward. (b) Central portion of an 8-year-old root showing origin of bud trace from the former pericycle zone. (c) Origin of bud and its vascular trace at a point of previous injury in secondary tissues. (pd, periderm; sb, suppressed bud; vt, vascular trace; pc, pericycle; pi, point of injury; and px, primary xylem) (from Kormanik and Brown, 1967).

Fig. I-13. A stand of root sprouts from a single 40-year-old sweetgum tree. The sprouts range in age from one to 15 years and some are over five inches in diameter at breast height (from Kormanik and Brown, 1967).

lease. Yet in every case where lateral roots are girdled, buds are always released on the distal side, i.e. on the side of the girdle farthest from the parent tree, indicating that some type of correlative inhibition over bud release is operative. This is the same pattern obtained when a girdle is placed along the bole of sweetgum. Suppressed buds are released beneath the girdle giving rise to epicormic branches (see Section 7).

Another interesting aspect of the release of buds on the roots of sweetgum is the subsequent pattern of root development near the shoot-root junction. In every instance there is a very rapid and pronounced hypertrophy of root development on the distal side of the root sucker (Fig. I-14). If the root sucker has its origin some distance from the tree, the proximal portion of the lateral root usually dies within 5 to 10 years. This type of development is another manifestation of the strict polarity of development in plants, and in this case it undoubtedly involves the basipetal and distal transport of growth factors and foods coming from the newly developing root sucker inducing this pattern of growth and development. The question also arises what initial effect the parent tree has on the growth rate of the young root sucker. During periods of high moisture stress or summer

Fig. I–14. Enlarged, overdeveloped portion of lateral root distal to point of sprout origin in sweetgum. Proximal portion of root leading to parent tree is now undergoing senescense and will soon die.

drought, to what degree do tensions established in the upper crown of an 80-foot-high parent tree affect the water balance in a 3-foot sprout attached to the same root system (see Chapter IV, Section 6b).

7. SUPPRESSED BUDS AND EPICORMIC BRANCHES

Forest-grown trees released by thinnings or partial cuttings often form numerous epicormic shoots along their bole (Fig. I-15). This eruption of previously formed buds is more prevalent in some species than others and is of much concern to forest managers because it lowers the quality of lumber and other forest products.

Quite an extensive literature is available concerning the origin of embedded buds and the formation of epicormic branches in various species (cf. Bűsgen and Műnch, 1929, pp. 70–72). In the older literature buds embedded in the periderm of branches and stems are referred to as dormant buds. Such buds, however, are active during much of the growing season in laying down new leaf and scale primordia and in keeping pace with the radially expanding cambium. For this reason, we prefer to use the term suppressed buds, instead of dormant buds, to indicate varying degrees of seasonal meristematic activity.

Suppressed buds originate in different ways among species. In some trees, a single axillary bud remains inhibited and becomes embedded in the bark within a few years by the radially expanding secondary tissues. In other trees the axillary buds may produce additional buds in the axils of their basal bud scales which

Fig. I–15. Release of suppressed buds and formation of epicormic branches along the bole of 15 to 20-year-old forest grown trees of *Liquidambar styraciflua* L. following removal of adjacent trees.

become embedded in the periderm to exist as suppressed buds (Fig. I-16). In such cases the original axillary bud may develop into a lateral branch, or it may eventually abort leaving behind one or more embedded scale buds. In still other trees supernumerary buds at different nodes may remain inhibited long enough to become enveloped by the expanding periderm. Occasionally, but rarely, adventitious buds resulting from localized injury or die-back of small branches may remain inhibited and become embedded in the bark. Nests of such buds have been observed in water oak (*Quercus nigra* L.) in association with profilerated ray cells in the cambial zone (Fig. I-17).

Once buds are embedded in the periderm, they may give rise to additional buds in the axils of their bud scales. In some species the apical meristem of the suppressed bud may abort or become damaged releasing one or more of the axillary scale buds resulting in a forking of the initial vascular trace (Fig. I-18a, b). Thus, a single supressed bud on the primary twig may become the progenitor of numerous suppressed buds as the stem increases in size with age. In one study more than 60 suppressed buds were traced to four parent buds in a two-foot portion of a *Liquidambar styraciflua* stem only ten inches in diameter (Kormanik and Brown, 1964).

The almost complete inhibition of rib meristem activity in suppressed buds is usually attributed to the inhibitory effect of basipetally transported auxin in the phloem or cambium. Girdling the stem by removing a band of bark or cutting into the stem to sever the phloem and cambium usually releases the suppressed buds from inhibition below the girdle or wound. This response is usually accepted as evidence that the inhibition has been removed by blocking the downward movement of auxin. This explanation is perhaps too simple. For example, Kormanik (1968) found that girdling stems just before bud break in early spring (before the cambium became highly active and presumably while the levels of diffusible auxin were low) was more effective in releasing the suppressed buds of sweetgum, green ash, and several oaks than by applying the treatment in late spring after full leafing out. Also, girdles applied in late summer were usually less effective than those applied in spring. These results indicate that a stronger inhibition develops in embedded buds during the season which may require a period of winter rest to overcome.

One wonders, following the application of a bark girdle, if bud promoting substances such as cytokinins are increased in the uppermost bark tissues immediately beneath the girdle accompanying the decrease in auxin concentration at this point. It may be that the abrupt shift in the ratio of auxin and cytokinin subjacent to the girdle triggers the rib meristem into activity causing the suppressed buds to develop into long shoots.

In addition to seasonal effects in the release of suppressed buds following girdling, striking differences occur in the pattern of release between certain ring- and diffuse-porous trees. In sweetgum, yellow poplar, and red maple (all diffuse-porous), the suppressed buds are released for only a short distance below a girdle; whereas, in the ring-porous oaks and ashes a single girdle releases the buds over a much greater distance along the bole (Kormanik, 1968). The activation of

Fig. I–16. Transverse section of a one-year-old lateral branch in sweetgum showing the position of two basal scale buds which remain inhibited and will later become embedded in the periderm of the main stem to exist as suppressed buds.

Fig. I–17. Portion of transverse section of water oak (*Quercus nigra* L.) possessing nests of adventitious buds associated with earlier stem injury and the proliferation of rays.

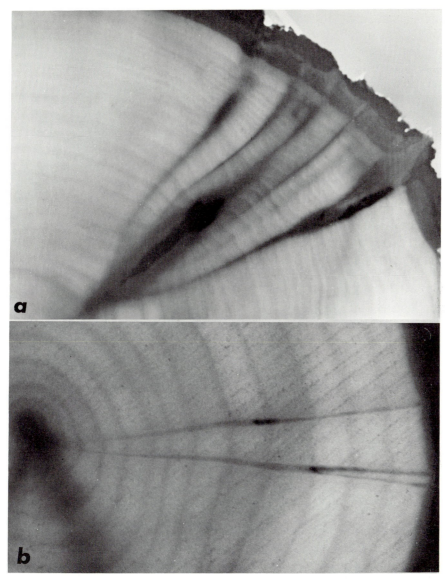

Fig. I–18a, b. Portion of transverse sections of (a) sweetgum (*Liquidambar styraciflua* L.) and (b) green ash (*Fraxinus pennsylvanica* Marsh.) stems showing branching of vascular traces.

inhibited buds, like the initiation of cambial activity, may be more rapid in ring-porous than in diffuse-porous trees so that a greater distance along the bole is affected immediately following application of a girdle.

Gravity may also influence the release of suppressed buds. Whenever trees are displaced from their normal upright position to a horizontal one, numerous suppressed buds are usually released all along the upper side of the stem. The pattern of release is in contrast to the rather restricted distance buds are released beneath a girdle. The effect of gravity on the release of suppressed buds, like the tropistic responses of primary shoots and roots, is explained by an auxin mediated mechanism. Apparently a lateral redistribution of auxin occurs in horizontally placed stems as a result of differences in rate of transport between the dorsal and ventral sides (Leech and Wareing, 1967). The effect of gravity on apical dominance and other developmental processes in trees is discussed in Chapter III, Section 5b).

8. PATTERNS OF PRIMARY SHOOT GROWTH

a. Variation in tropical and temperate regions

Intermittent rather than continuous shoot growth is typical of most woody plants. In the majority of trees, periods of rapid stem elongation alternate with periods of little or no elongation even under environmental conditions favorable for continuous growth. One may easily explain why trees growing in regions of alternating warm and cold or wet and dry periods evolved a pattern of growth adapted to withstand seasonal environmental stress. But it is more difficult to explain why the majority of trees in tropical areas where rainfall is evenly distributed and mild temperatures prevail conform to distinct cyclic patterns of growth.

Similar patterns of primary growth have probably arisen in different parts of the world in the past independently of each other. For example, under a favorable temperature and rainfall regime the growth pattern of woody plants might vary from continuous growth to long periods of growth interrupted by short periods of rest or to shorter periods of alternating growth and rest. Conversely, in the temperate zones and at high altitudes in the tropics, or under alternating wet and dry conditions, one would only expect to find trees with an intermittent growth habit because of the selection pressure of the environment. The characterization of different growth patterns is further complicated by the ocurrence of intermediate types between the tropics and temperate zones which may or may not have undergone selection pressures of a seasonal environment. Genetic variation among species, climatic changes in the geologic past, and the migration of taxa from the tropics to temperate regions and vice versa has led to an array of growth patterns difficult to categorize under any scheme of classification.

The complexity of the problem may be reduced somewhat if we consider the patterns of growth which may occur under two distinctly contrasting climates. One can contrast the growth patterns of trees growing in a tropical environment such as that of Singapore (1°18′N) where the temperature is non-seasonal and the rainfall adequately distributed with a mid-latitude north temperate region such as that found in the vicinity of Philadelphia, Pennsylvania (40°N) where the length of the frost-free season is approximately 185 days and the seasonal distribution of rainfall is adequate.

First, if we look at the composition of trees growing in these two regions with respect to only the evergreen or deciduous habit, we find approximately 95 per cent of the trees in the Singapore area are evergreen. The arboresent monocots, cycads, conifers, and tree ferns account for about 20 per cent of the total number of the evergreen taxa (Koriba, 1958). In the Philadelphia area this distribution of taxa is reversed, i.e., approximately 90 per cent of the woody taxa are deciduous, the remaining 10 per cent consists of evergreen conifers and angiosperms. Of particular interest is the relatively low percentage of evergreen angiosperms in the uniform environment of Singapore that grow continuously forming new leaves throughout the year. According to Koriba (1958) of all evergreen species less than 20 per cent have continuous growth. Therefore, even under an uniform environment more than 80 per cent of the woody species have some type of intermittent growth.

To better understand the diverse patterns of primary growth under uniform conditions, Koriba grouped the trees of the Singapore area into three major types with reference to the growth habit of individual shoots as follows: 1) evergrowing, 2) intermittent, and 3) manifold.

In the evergrowing types the apical meristem of the twig grows constantly forming new leaves throughout the year. Leaf size and length of the internodes are fairly uniform. The apical meristem is protected by outer developing leaves, petioles, or stipules. In some trees the young leaves may be covered by hairs or secrete a gummy resin to form a protective sheath around the apical meristem.

In the intermittently growing trees, true resting buds enclosed in bud scales are formed at the end of each period of shoot extension. In these species leaf size and internode length are variable, bud scale scars are evident, and differences in appearance of successively formed twigs are apparent due to the abruptness of cork formation on older twigs. This pattern conforms to recurrent flushes of growth in trees of the temperate zones, where the periodicity of flushing may not conform to any seasonal pattern; it may occur only once a year in some species and more frequently in others. The resting buds may be essentially naked or covered tightly by modified petioles, stipules, or leaves.

In evergreen trees with intermittent growth the older leaves fall off after new leafing out, as in evergreen trees of temperate regions. But a few evergreen species (ca. five per cent in Malaya) shed their leaves just prior to new shoot growth thus becoming deciduous in habit for only a short period of time.

In most tropical trees possessing intermittent growth the branches of the entire tree are commonly synchronized with respect to release and cessation of growth; some intermittent trees leaf out from one to three times each year, twice being the most common in the Singapore area. Other species, however, may leaf out from three to five times each year, their growth being correlated with slight changes of weather, mostly rainfall. Still, other trees leaf out with no apparent yearly periodicity, and some possessing the deciduous habit may not extend new shoots for periods of over a year. It is little wonder, therefore, that we know so little about the factors controlling the growth of tropical trees. The patterns of growth are not incomprehensible; rather, they have not been given adequate study. The periodicity of radial growth and growth ring formation in tropical trees and its correlation with primary growth is even less poorly understood (see Chapter 11, Section 2a).

The manifold habit of growth is non-synchronous growth among individual branches during a given period. Some branches are growing while others are resting; other branches may either abort their shoot apex, produce an inflorescence, or revert to a short shoot, thereby releasing one or more lateral buds. The manifold habit is especially noticeable in old trees where positional effects of the branches in the crown create nutritional and hormonal differences because of light, nutrient, and water availability. Koriba (1958) points out that many woody plants of the temperate zones, such as *Magnolia, Pyrus,* and *Vaccinium* when transferred to an uniform environment develop the manifold habit of growth.

A similar manifold growth habit occurred in a 15-year-old loblolly pine (*P. taeda* L.) transplanted to a large specially constructed greenhouse at the A. J. Hodge Gardens near Many, Louisiana. In this particular instance several other species of pines were grafted onto the lateral branches of this loblolly pine which grew continuously for several years under the relatively uniform greenhouse conditions (observations of C. L. Brown). The tree soon became a "showcase" for visitors to the gardens. While some branches were undergoing vegetative growth, others were producing pollen or maturing female cones, and still others remained completely dormant.

The ability of some trees of temperate regions to revert from the intermittent to the manifold habit of growth under uniform environments shows the wide range of genetic plasticity among woody plants. Conversely, there are many temperate-zone species possessing such a rigid cold requirement for breaking bud dormancy, both vegetative and reproductive buds, that they could not long survive in tropical or sub-tropical regions. Furthermore, many trees of the temperate zones would be unable to reproduce successfully in the tropics because of an inherent cold requirement for seed germination.

In the temperate zones all tree growth is intermittent. Numerous observations have been made in the past correlating the periodicity of tree growth with variations in climatic factors such as daylength and temperature. Although in many species valid correlations do exist between photoperiod and cessation of tree growth, they do not necessarily apply to most trees of the temperate zones. In fact, many trees in temperate regions complete extension growth during the longest days of the summer while temperature and soil moisture is optimum for growth. In the higher latitudes, however, cessation of shoot growth of certain trees may be highly correlated with daylength, e.g., in *Populus trichocarpa* shoot growth ceases whenever the daylength reaches a critical period either naturally or experimentally (Pauley and Perry, 1954). These trees when moved southward cease growth earlier than they would have in their native habitat unless the daylength is artificially extended. Cessation of growth in such ecotypes is controlled by photoperiod and not by an inherent adaptation to length of the growing season. In some cases adverse effects can occur when trees are transplanted from lower to higher latitudes because of the longer photoperiods preceding the autumn equinox. For example, many pine species of the southern United States transplanted to the latitude of Massachusetts in mid-summer will continue to grow late into the season, fail to harden off, and thus be killed by early frosts. The same species could withstand the low winter temperatures had they become dormant several weeks prior to being exposed to freezing temperatures.

Even though photoperiod can have pronounced effects on cessation or prolonging the growth of some trees especially those of the higher latitudes, it does not appear to be the major controlling factor in the cessation or initiation of extension growth of trees over most forested regions of the world. Also, as pointed out by Alvim (1964) subtle changes in the microclimate (e.g., water stress, light intensity, or temperature) may be an adequate stimulus to shift the hormone/inhibitor ratio causing either renewed activity or cessation of growth.

The growth pattern of the intermittently growing cacao tree (*Theobroma cacao* L.) was intensively studied by Alvim (1956) in the tropical lowlands of Costa Rica. Bi-weekly data were collected on the growth of 400 branches from 80 cacao trees (five branches per tree) for 26 consecutive months. Correlation coefficients were obtained between climatic factors (rainfall, daily hours of insolation, mean daily maximum and minimum temperature, mean daily temperature, and mean diurnal range of temperature) and the percentage of flushing and dormant shoots. Bud bursting was highly correlated with the mean diurnal temperature range (thermoperiod). Maximum temperature and total insolation were also positively correlated with flushing, but heat alone did not seem to be a major factor because the most intensive flushing occurred at the beginning of spring (March) and again at the beginning of fall (September-October) and not during the warmest months from May to September.

Alvim (1964) points out that as one moves either north or south of the equator the bud bursting appears to be correlated with increasing day lengths. For example, cacao in Bahia, Brazil (15°S) flushes 4 or 5 times from September to April during the longer photoperiods and not at all during the shorter photoperiods from May to August. A similar pattern of flushing is observed in cacao in Costa Rica (10°N) where less flushing occurs during the shorter days from November to January.

There is also the interesting observation of Alvim (1960) concerning the periodicity of flowering in coffee (*Coffea*) whose growth alternates with the wet and dry seasons. Coffee often flowers gregariously following rainfall after a short dry period. This response has often been attributed to a "cooling shock" by the indirect effect of rainfall on temperature. Alvim found, however, that the flower buds of coffee growing along the desert coast of Peru remained dormant for several months if the plants were irrigated at weekly intervals. But if the irrigation were suspended for a period of 3 to 5 weeks subjecting the plants to a short period of drought, then they flowered abundantly about 10 days following the next irrigation. Thus, in some tropical plants drought may have the same effect in breaking dormancy as that of a cold period in the temperate zones.

From the foregoing discussion it is apparent that much inherent variation exists among trees of any region with respect to the control environmental factors exert over bud bursting and cessation of primary growth. In some trees, an external factor such as photoperiod exerts primary control over internal hormonal systems controlling growth, in others, photoperiod clearly interacts with thermoperiod. Whereas, in still other trees the growth of individual branches seems to be under the autonomous control of inherent rhythms not clearly related to any specific factor of the environment. Although we have accumulated much information about the experimental control of growth of tree seedlings in the temperate zones, and to a lesser degree that of older trees, we still have much to learn about the control of growth in sub-tropical and tropical trees..

b. Intermittent growth in temperate regions

Although all trees of the temperate zones show intermittent growth, the manner in which primary growth occurs among species is highly variable. The rates and duration of growth of many young coniferous and deciduous trees have been studied in detail (cf. Kramer and Kozlowski, 1960, pp. 26–32).

The pattern of primary growth, i.e., the way in which shoot extension occurs, has a profound effect upon nutritional relationships as well as patterns of bud release and crown form. The pattern of shoot extension of intermittently growing trees may be grouped into four categories: (1) a single flush of terminal growth followed by formation of a resting bud, (2) recurrent flushes of terminal growth with terminal bud formation at the end of each flush, (3) a flush of growth followed by shoot-tip abortion, and (4) a sustained flush of growth extending late-formed leaves prior to terminal bud formation. The terminal bud of some trees in the last category may also abort, e.g. *Betula*.

Many trees of the temperate zones make only a single flush of growth in early spring or summer and form distinct terminal buds while environmental conditions are optimum for continued growth. To this group belong trees such as oaks, hickories, ashes, and many conifers. Because some of the pines normally make only one distinct seasonal flush of growth separating each season's lateral buds and branches to form a whorled appearance, their pattern of growth has been termed "uninodal." Uninodal in this usage is a misnomer.

Trees which make one rather rapid flush of growth usually contain all of their leaf primordia preformed in the resting bud, although some of the last-formed primordia may be little more than small mounds of tissue just beneath the apical dome. Lateral buds may or may not be present in a rudimentary form in the preformed terminal bud. In pines and some angiosperms the bud scale primordia for the next terminal bud are already preformed in the resting winter bud (see Section 2). In the older literature, it is often implied that all cells of the next season's growth are contained in the resting terminal bud. This is not the case, however, because numerous cell divisions occur in the subapical rib meristems of the elongating shoot (see Section 4b).

The rate of shoot extension in trees making one flush of growth may be rapid and the duration of growth may be extremely short, as in Georgia buckeye (*Aesculus georgiana* Sarg.) where total growth is completed in 10-12 days following bud break. In other species such as tulip poplar, *Liriodendron tulipifera* L., growth may extend for a period of 150 days or more (Fig. I-19).

Many young trees belonging to the first group mentioned above especially oaks and maples, may make more than one flush of growth under exceptionally vigorous conditions, e.g., stump sprouts, and heavily fertilized seedlings. Occasionally older trees receiving excessive rainfall following periods of summer drought make an additional flush of growth. The latter are often referred to as lammas shoots in the English and Johannistriebe in the German literature. Other species such as mockernut hickory (*Carya tomentosa* Nutt.) and Georgia buckeye (*Aesculus georgiana* Sarg.) seldom, if ever, form lammas shoots in their native habitat.

In the second category, i.e., those trees which normally make recurrent flushes of growth each season, do so by the repeated formation and release of currently

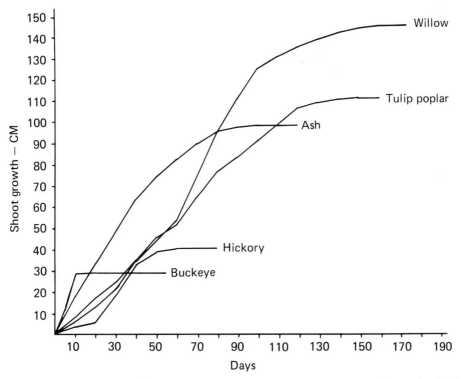

Fig. I–19. Rate and duration of shoot growth among several woody species in the Georgia Piedmont. Measurements of shoot elongation were made biweekly on 9 trees ranging from 8 to 15 years in age. Buckeye (*Aesculus georgiana* Sarg.); Hickory, (*Carya tomentosa* Nutt.); ash (*Fraxinus pennsylvanica* Marsh.); tulip poplar (*Liriodendron tulipifera* L.); and willow (*Salix nigra* Marsh.).

formed terminal buds. This habit of growth is frequent among the pines of the southern and southeastern United States (e.g., *P. taeda* L., *P. elliottii* Engelm., *P. virginiana* Mill.). It is the most prevalent habit of growth among most evergreen and deciduous trees of the subtropics and tropic regions.

The environmental conditions under which the successive terminal buds are produced determines the number and extent of new leaves to be extended in the next flush of growth. Apparently the interval of time between the formation and subsequent release of successive buds has a profound effect on the number of nodes to be extended and the total length of the shoot. In young pine seedlings growing in the greenhouse under rather uniform temperature and photoperiod, each successive flush of growth becomes smaller until the seedlings undergo a period of rest. Older trees growing under natural conditions follow the same pattern. Tropical trees possessing the recurrent growth habit may not show the same degree of reduction in successive flushes if the time interval between the formation of new buds and shoot extension is of sufficient duration to permit the formation of numerous leaf primordia.

In the third category of shoot extension the shoot apex aborts following extension of the pseudo-terminal or last-formed lateral bud of the previous season. In some species such as beech (*Fagus grandifolia* Ehrh.) the shoot tip aborts soon after extension of the preformed leaves; whereas, in black willow (*Salix nigra* Marsh) and mimosa (*Albizzia julibrissin* Dur.) the apical meristem continues to produce additional leaves until late in the growing season before the apex aborts. The distinct contrast in numbers of leaves produced by these species in Georgia and the date of apex abortion is shown in Table I-2. The phenomenon of shoot tip abortion has been recognized for over a century (cf. Romberger, 1963, pp. 62–65). It is common in the genera *Ulmus, Betula, Salix, Corylus, Ostrya, Syringa, Tilia, Robinia, Cercidiphyllum, Rhamnus, Carpinus, Platanus, Gleditsia, Diospyros, Catalpa* and occasionally found in *Fagus* and many tropical genera.

The physiological mechanism controlling shoot tip abortion is not clearly known, although in the late 1800's Wiesner (1889) discovered that the abortion of the shoot apex of *Rhamnus cathartica* L. could be prevented by the timely removal of lateral buds. The same response was reported for *Cercidiphyllum japonicum* L., (Titman and Wetmore, 1955) and for vigorous shoots of *Syringa*

TABLE I–2

A comparison of leaf number contained in the winter buds (pseudo-terminal buds) and number of leaves produced during the growing season prior to shoot tip abortion. Data collected in the vicinity of Athens, Georgia.

Species	Mean Number of Leaves [a]	
	In Dormant Bud	Along Shoot at Time of Tip Abortion
Albizzia julibrissin Dur.	7.8	23.2 (120 days)
Fagus grandifolia Ehrh.	7.1	9.0 (100 days)
Salix nigra Marsh.	8.3	66.6 (165 days)

[a] Means based on single bud or shoot counts of 15 individual trees.

vulgaris L. (Garrison and Wetmore, 1961). Klebs (1917) also prevented abortion of the apex in *Robinia pseudoacacia* L. seedlings for periods up to 10 months by placing them under continuous light. He concluded that removal of leaves or lateral buds was not necessary. Several years later Wareing (1954) and Downs (1958) essentially came to the same conclusion, viz., that long photoperiods delay shoot tip abortion and short photoperiods hasten it in *Robinia* and *Catalpa*.

From these observations some type of inhibitor appears to be formed in axillary buds and/or leaves, and it is translocated acropetally to cause shoot-tip abortion. One might speculate that short photoperiods would enhance the production of an inhibitor such as abscisic acid, whereas, long photoperiods might promote a higher level of gibberellin synthesis to counteract the inhibitory effect. However, under natural conditions shoot tip abortion in some species, similar to growth cessation and terminal bud formation, often occurs during the longest days of the growing season.

An interesting morphological feature of twigs which abort their apices is their sympodial or zig-zag pattern of growth (Fig. I-20). Why this trait should be so perfectly correlated with the ultimate senescense and death of the apex is not known, but it may reflect some peculiar physiological influence of the apex over the structure of the developing twig beneath. Sinnott (1960, pp. 309) mentions that some herbaceous plants with the zig-zag pattern of growth, form straight shoots when placed in the dark. It would be of interest to determine the influence of light on this characteristic in woody plants.

The fourth category of shoot extension includes those trees which make sustained growth for varying periods producing new primordia which develop as late leaves and end the season with the formation of a distinct terminal bud. These species are not as numerous as those in the first and third categories previously discussed; however, they are fairly well distributed throughout the temperate zones. Two species possessing this type growth which have been studied in the vicinity of Athens, Georgia, are tulip poplar (*Liriodendron tulipifera* L.) and sweetgum (*Liquidambar styraciflua*. L.). Both species have a long growing season and produce about the same number of late leaves during the season as those preformed in the terminal bud. In sweetgum there is a distinct leaf dimorphism related to the sequence of leaf formation, i.e., early versus late-formed leaves (Fig. I-21). Surprisingly enough, only a few examples of leaf dimorphism have been reported on adult twigs in woody plants and these are related to the formation of early or late leaves in *Populus* (Critchfield, 1960) and *Betula* (Clausen and Kozlowski, 1965), to lammas shoot formation (Späth, 1912), or to leaves borne on short shoots as *Circidiphyllum* (Titman and Wetmore, 1955). In many trees there are no distinct differences in early and late-formed leaves, or those formed on lammas shoots or short shoots.

One could cite numerous examples of heterophylly or dimorphism in leaves and shoots of juvenile versus adult forms, a condition referred to as heteroblastic development by Goebel (1928) (see Sinnott, 1960 pp. 206–215). A reversion to the juvenile leaf form occurs in some trees on adventitious shoots, epicormic branches, and root suckers. (see Chapter III, Section 3b).

HONEY LOCUST

Fig. I–20. Zig-zag pattern of shoot growth common to honey locust (*Gleditsia triacanthos* L.) and other woody species which abort their shoot tips during or near the end of the growing season.

Critchfield (1960) concluded from his studies of heterophylly in *Populus* that in many instances a relationship existed between the conditions present during early leaf ontogeny and ultimate leaf form. That nutritional levels are involved in determining leaf form during development is clearly shown by the effects of sucrose levels on leaf shape in the fern *Todea* (Wetmore, 1953). Also, the typical lanceolate shape of *Populus trichocarpa* Torr. and Gray leaves can be modified

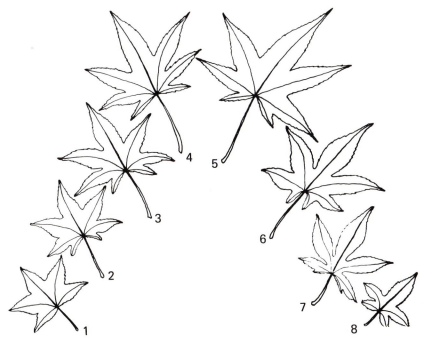

Fig. I–21. Leaf dimorphism in sweetgum (*Liquidambar styraciflua* L.). The first formed leaves which over-winter in the terminal bud (early leaves) are less deeply lobed than those formed during the growing season (late leaves). Note also differences in blade size and petiole lengths associated with the sigmoid growth pattern of the elongating shoot.

to a cordate form by feeding isolated stem segments low levels of inorganic nutrients and three per cent sucrose before bud break in early spring. Thus, the form of leaves which overwinter in dormant axillary buds can be modified under high levels of nutrition (observations of C. L. Brown in Prof. R. H. Wetmore's laboratory, Harvard University, 1956).

The cessation of growth in species growing late into the season may be influenced by photoperiod because the apex stops producing new leaf primordia and begins production of cataphylls in several trees in early August in the vicinity of Athens, Georgia (34°N). Other species such as tulip poplar, may continue to extend leaves very slowly up until mid-October or later so that in some seasons the last formed, small, succulent leaves are killed by the early frost. Bud formation in this species is similar to that of sub-tropical or tropical trees with intermittent growth. The stipules of each leaf completely encases the next youngest leaf, and the apical meristem is always protected by a series of stipules acting as bud scales. In the dormant terminal buds of young, vigorous tulip poplar trees in the Athens area one may find as many as 14 to 17 preformed leaves each separately encased by a subtending pair of stipules.

c. Diurnal variation in shoot growth

Under favorable temperatures shoot elongation is usually more rapid at night than during the day. Reed (1939) followed the daily shoot extension of loblolly and shortleaf pines in North Carolina between 6:30 A.M. and 6:30 P.M. for over a period of three weeks in early summer. He found almost twice as much growth occurring at night as during the day. The average growth during the day was 6.4 mm and 4.8 mm for loblolly and shortleaf pine; while at night they averaged 12.5 mm and 8.3 mm respectively. These differences probably reflect a reduction in water stress at night, alternating with higher periods of stress during the day.

In the higher latitudes at the beginning of the growing season, shoot extension may be practically nil at night due to low temperatures. Kienholz (1934) found that shoot growth of certain conifers was negligible when the night temperature dropped below 5.5°C. Rapidly extending shoots of loblolly pine seedlings (ca. 2.0 cm per day) can be abruptly stopped in 24 hours by placing them in a cold room at 5°C. They will resume growth very slowly even at this temperature, elongating 0.5 to 1.5 cm during a period of 30 to 45 days. If transferred back to greenhouse temperatures of 28 to 30°C, they will resume rapid growth and complete the initial phase of interrupted shoot extension (observations of C. L. Brown).

d. The significance of intermittent shoot growth

One of the questions arousing the interest of tree physiologists is why the intermittent pattern of primary growth evolved as the predominant type even under the uniform climate of certain tropical regions. Although it is recognized that the continuous pattern of growth in the tropics often fluctuates with periods of high and low activity; it is nevertheless true that the majority of species possess distinct cyclic periods of growth and rest.

In looking at the fossil record a continuous short-shoot habit of growth appeared to be highly successful and prevalent during the Carboniferous, a period of relatively mild and uniform climate supporting luxuriant growth. Some of the largest and most successful Lycopods existed during this period, e.g., *Lepidodendron* and *Sigillaria,* along with massive tree ferns and other Pteridophytes. The short-shoot habit was still highly successful in the Bennettitales through the Permian and into the Mesozoic Era, the period often referred to as the "Age of Cycads." Even today the Cycads as a group exemplify the short shoot habit of growth throughout their entire life cycle. New leaves (fronds) are produced in a continuous manner under favorable conditions, or their formation may be seasonal in monsoon-type climates. In such plants the majority of energy expended in growth is in the formation of leaves rather than in their separation by extending internodes; hence, growth in height is extremely slow. A specimen of *Dioon edule* L. is known to be 1000 years old and only 1.5 meters in height (Chamberlain, 1935 p. 63). Many arborescent monocotyledons, e.g., most palms, also possess the typical short-shoot habit of growth.

Although the long-shoot habit of growth (or transition toward this habit) can be traced back to the Cordaitales of the Upper Devonian and Carboniferous Periods and to the Coniferales from the Carboniferous to the present, this habit of growth became worldwide in distribution with the sudden rise of the angiosperms in the Cretaceous. Not only does the rapid extension of internodes followed by periods of rest have adaptive significance to periods of environmental stress, but it also provides a wide range in vertical stratification and permits association of diverse species on the same site. In addition, concomitant with the evolution of the angiosperm leaf, the separation and orientation of these structures to take advantage of solar radiation and free gas exchange undoubtedly became of adaptive significance.

A combination of the short- and long-shoot habit has also been highly successful in many woody species. In several genera of gymnosperms, e.g., *Pinus, Larix, Ginkgo,* and in numerous angiosperm genera, e.g., *Pyrus, Malus, Citrus, Acer, Fagus,* etc. the majority of foliage leaves in the former and a mixture of foliage leaves and flowers in the latter are borne on short shoots. As many angiosperm trees become older and more massive in size, the leaves are evenly dispersed around the outer periphery on numerous short shoots, another trait of adaptive significance.

These differences in inherent patterns of growth serve to point out the wide array and diversified patterns of primary growth made possible by recurring evolutionary variation. Many of the growth patterns discussed are adapted to specific ecological situations. The pattern of rapid extension growth followed by alternate periods of energy storage and rest is more universally competitive, even in the tropics, than a slower, sustained pattern of growth. In any event, these differences in rates and types of growth have made possible the successful association of numerous woody and herbaceous species under a wide variety of ecosystems.

9. THE ROOT APEX

a. Configuration

The root apex differs in several respects from that of the shoot. The apical meristem not only gives rise to all primary tissues of the root but also produces cells in a distal direction to form the root cap. In contrast to the shoot apex, no lateral organs are produced near the apical meristem of the root; therefore, there are no rhythmic changes in its configuration during growth. Extension growth of the root is confined to a narrow region at the apex rarely exceeding two or three millimeters in length, and lateral roots arise endogenously in the pericycle some distance behind the zone of elongation.

In the lower vascular plants different tissues of the root can be traced either to a single apical cell or to a tier of several initials. The organization of the meristematic region in gymnosperms and angiosperms is variable and complex. At least four different patterns of apical meristem organization other than the single apical cell type have been described for the seed plants (see Esau, 1965, pp. 116–124).

b. Cellular activity and extension growth

Numerous physiological studies have been conducted with roots because of the longitudinal sequence of cell and tissue differentiation proximal to the apical meristem. Analytical studies of nucleic acid metabolism, protein synthesis, and enzyme activity along the root axis have been performed in an attempt to correlate biochemical activities with patterns of differentiation. Torrey (1967) has summarized much of this work as follows: (1) The cells of the root cap differentiate very rapidly in a distal direction. Those cells lying within a short distance from the apical initials show an increase in content of total carbohydrate, stored starch, and DNA. (2) The apical initials (the so-called quiescent center of Clowes, 1956 and 1958) show very low metabolic rates. These cells are lower in dry weight, contain less total and protein nitrogen, and nucleic acids than surrounding cells. (3) Just proximal to the quiescent zone, two phases of cell enlargement can be recognized. First, most of the cells undergo a radial enlargement especially those giving rise to future cortical and xylem elements. Secondly, these cells begin to elongate longitudinally accompanied by a rapid increase in metabolism.

The role of growth factors such as auxins, gibberellins, and cytokinins in controlling cell division and elongation in roots are much less understood than their various effects on shoot growth. This, in part, is due to the extremely low concentrations of these hormones in roots and their sensitivity in response to different levels of exogenously applied growth factors such as auxin. For example, a concentration of externally applied auxin (IAA) which produces optimal stem elongation in isolated stem segments of many plants (ca. 10^{-5} M) results in almost complete inhibition of root elongation of the same species. Only at concentrations of less than 10^{-9}M is there is no inhibition, and concentrations as low as 10^{-10} or 10^{-11} M have been shown to stimulate root elongation in some plants.

The role of gibberellins in root elongation is also poorly understood, but in general, externally applied gibberellins tend to inhibit growth at levels which promote shoot growth.

There are conflicting reports in the older literature concerning the nature of the auxin transport system in primary roots. Some workers have reported a basipetal polar movement of auxin from the tip; whereas, others found an appreciable acropetal movement into the tip. Recent studies by Wilkins and Scott (1968) using ^{14}C labeled IAA give strong evidence of the presence of an acropetal polar movement of auxin in excised root tips of several herbaceous plants. This acropetal movement of auxin is dependent upon metabolic energy and occurs in decapitated root tips as well as non-decapitated ones (Scott and Wilkins, 1968; and Wilkins and Scott, 1968). Therefore, in primary roots the current evidence favors an acropetal polar transport system which is opposite to the polar basipetal movement of auxin in elongating shoots.

c. Differentiation of primary tissues

Researchers in morphogenesis have long studied the orderly patterns of tissue differentiation in roots in an attempt to understand how these patterns are controlled. Because tissue differentiation is acropetal and continuous from pre-existing differentiated tissues beneath, some workers maintain that certain morphogenetic substances, i.e., growth factors, nutrients, or metabolites, coming from these mature tissues impose a given pattern of differentiation on the newly formed cells produced by the apical meristem. Thus, the pattern already present pre-determines the pattern to be produced. Others hold the viewpoint that the control of differentiation lies in the meristem itself through its production and regulation of certain morphogenetic substances correlating development. Similar viewpoints are held by researchers studying differentiation of shoot apices (cf Section 1a).

Some interesting insights have been gained into the pattern of tissue differentiation in roots from the experiments of Torrey (1955, 1957). Excised root tips of *Pisum* about 0.5 mm in length without any differentiated vascular tissue were grown in nutrient solutions containing inorganic nutrients, sugar, and vitamins. Under these conditions many of the pea roots produced a diarch or even monarch pattern of xylem differentiation rather than a triarch primary xylem characteristic of the species. As the roots continued to grow, however, the pattern of xylem differentiation ultimately shifted to the triarch condition. Furthermore, whenever the roots were decapitated and allowed to regenerate new meristems in culture, the pattern of vascular differentiation could be significantly modified by varying the concentration of auxin (IAA) in the medium (Torrey, 1957). For example, the normally occurring triarch xylem in the pea root could be changed to a hexarch pattern with a high concentration of IAA (10^{-5}M); whereas, upon transfer to lower auxin concentrations the pattern of xylem differentiation would change to a pentarch or tetrarch condition. These studies support the viewpoint that the apical meristem of the root controls the pattern of vascularization beneath, and weakens the opposing view of an acropetal induction from pre-existing tissues. Torrey concluded from his studies that if the diameter of the central cylinder of the root meristem is changed by some hormonal or nutritional means, then the subsequent pattern of vascular differentiation is also changed. Wilcox (1962) also observed that the diameter of the root and of the central cylinder effects the number of protoxylem strands in incense cedar (*Libocedrus decurrens* Torr.).

d. Origin of lateral roots

Unlike the origin of leaves and axillary buds on the surface of the shoot apex, lateral roots arise some distance from the apical meristem deep within the tissues of the root; i.e., they arise endogenously. Lateral roots commonly have their origin in the pericycle of the stele, and grow outward by rupturing the exterior primary tissues. By the time the new lateral root emerges from the parent root it possesses a highly organized apical meristem and root cap. Although the root cap is commonly thought to be a distinguishing feature of all roots, it is absent or weakly defined in the short lateral roots of pine (Kramer, 1949).

The lateral roots of many plants arise with some degree of regularity in association with the radially extending xylem poles of the stele. Experimental studies concerning the origin of lateral roots indicate that the physiological factors affecting the initiation of apical meristems are complex. Undoubtedly, the concentration of growth factors, carbohydrates, vitamins, and inorganic nutrients are important in determining the location and distribution of lateral roots. Because lateral roots arise some distance from the apex indicates the apical meristem may exercise some inhibitory control over root initiation (Thimann, 1936). That nutrition and vigor play an important part in lateral root initiation is shown by Wilcox (1962) in the roots of *Libocedrus*. The lateral roots are more widely spaced and originate a greater distance from the apex in rapidly growing roots than in slowly growing ones.

10. PERIODICITY OF ROOT GROWTH

Over two hundred years ago the French philosopher, Duhamel du Monceau (1760) made the observation that tree roots grew during the winter months whenever soil temperatures were favorable. He also found that the roots of some trees commenced growing in spring before bud break and continued to grow after autumn leaf fall. Since this time, numerous workers have used various techniques to observe root growth and have come to the same general conclusions as Duhamel (see review by Romberger, 1963 pp. 166–171).

In studying the patterns of root growth and development in trees, one has to be careful in making generalizations concerning physiological mechanisms because of differences in species response. This is especially true when seedlings, instead of older trees, are used as experimental material. Seedlings are more responsive to the environment because of the close proximity of shoots to roots and the rather immediate effect of one upon the other. Thus physiological concepts based on seedlings may not be applicable either to other seedling species or to older trees. For example, Richardson (1958) found root growth of *Acer saccharinum* L. seedlings completely inhibited after autumn leaf fall until a chilling requirement of the buds had been met. In contrast, Wilcox (1962) in studying root dormancy in *Libocedrus decurrens* Torr. found neither a dependent relationship between shoot and root growth or evidence for chilling requirement of the buds. Root growth ceased near the end of December in seedlings kept in a heated greenhouse which Wilcox suggested might be related to the short photoperiod. However, seedlings grown under favorable temperatures and a 17-hour photoperiod from September to May still showed very little root growth from December to March.

In trees of the temperate zones there is a seasonal periodicity of root extension with peaks usually occurring in the spring and fall, although individual roots may undergo alternating periods of growth and rest independent of seasonal activity. One may question then, whether roots ever go dormant in the sense that buds do; i.e., once elongation of an individual root ceases does it require a period of rest before growth can be resumed? If so, this would imply that some endogenous substance imposes a physiological dormancy within the root tip itself, and that such a substance must be biochemically altered to permit resumption of growth. Most observations on the periodicity of root growth indicates that a type of quiescense is induced by environmental factors such as temperature, drought, aeration, etc. Lyford and Wilson (1966) found temperature to be the controlling factor in root extension of older forest grown trees during the winter months if the roots were well aerated and supplied with adequate moisture. In these studies a building was constructed over a bulldozed trench in the forest, and exposed lateral roots were placed in trays covered with soil and kept moist by frequent watering. The temperature around the roots was controlled by heating the individual trays or by controlling the air temperature of small insulated rooms within the building. Lyford and Wilson found the day to day variation in growth rate of red maple roots to be highly sensitive to temperature. The growth of roots in unheated trays closely paralleled the fluctuation in daily mean temperature outside the building. Roots in trays with controlled temperatures grew at almost constant rates independent of outside temperatures surrounding the parent trees. During the winter months the soil temperature outside where the tree stems were located was often less than 1°C, yet some roots in the heated insulated rooms grew throughout the winter. The rate of root elongation during the summer months was also highly correlated with the temperature of the root tips and not the temperature of the parent stem.

Ladefoged (1939) also observed the independent relationship between shoot and root growth in that the roots of stumps of felled larch and fir trees began growing at the same time as those of neighboring intact trees.

It would be of interest to study the pattern of cambial activation in roots artificially stimulated to grow during the winter months or the roots of recently felled trees, because the hormonal stimulus for activation of the cambium is supposedly transmitted basipetally from the actively growing stem (see Chapter II, Section 6a).

The periodicity of root growth may be summarized as follows: (1) Not all roots of a tree grow at any one time; while some roots are growing, others are quiescent. (2) In many angiosperms and gymnosperms of the temperate zones, there is a peak period of active root growth in spring which may begin before, during, or after shoot growth. This activity is followed by a reduction of growth during summer in both rate and number of roots produced. In the fall, there may be another peak of activity after which the majority of roots become quiescent with the onset of winter and low soil temperatures. (3) Individual roots show cyclic periods of growth indicating some endogenous mechanism of control; however, this control may be modified by changes in the external environment. Seedlings are more responsive to environmental change than older trees.

11. FORM AND EXTENT OF ROOTS

Many woody plants possess a characteristic pattern of root development even if grown under different environmental conditions. Inherent differences in patterns of root development are especially noticeable during early seedling growth; but root systems often become greatly modified in later years by environmental influences such as soil texture, water availability, and overall nutrition. For these reasons the depth and extent of lateral roots is highly variable even within the same species. Contrary to what many laymen believe, the bulk of the root system of most trees growing on medium textured soils (loams and clay-loams) is within three feet of the surface. The majority of the smaller absorbing roots lie in the upper six inches of the forest soil. Density of spacing or competition among individual trees has a pronounced effect on the extension of lateral roots; therefore, generalized statements on the extent of lateral root development have little meaning. In open-grown trees it is common to find lateral roots extending out two to three times beyond the radius of the crown, although the majority of the absorbing roots may lie within the area circumscribed by the periphery of the crown. More specific data on the form and extent of root systems in trees are found in Kramer and Kozlowski (1960), Toumey (1929), and Büsgen and Münch 1929).

a. Direction of root growth

Young extending primary roots are highly sensitive to gravity, and under natural conditions they show a strong positively geotropic response. Lateral roots also respond to gravity but to a lesser degree depending upon the amount of branching and the positioning effect exercised by the parent root. The plagiotropic response of roots, i.e., the controlling effect exerted by the primary root tip in positioning lateral roots, is similar to the influence of the terminal leader over lateral branches (see Chapter III, section 5a). In young tree seedlings, removal of the tap root often results in the downward vertical growth of one to several lateral roots which formerly grew obliquely or even perpendicular to the primary root axis. As root systems become more massive through repeated branching, the influence of the parent root over the higher order lateral roots is finally lost. Furthermore, each successive generation of lateral roots becomes less and less responsive to gravity, and other factors including available soil moisture and temperature often influence and control the direction of root growth. Even the strong positively geotropic response of primary roots in germinating seeds can be overcome if moisture is supplied from above. This causes the roots to grow upward into the moist substrate instead of downward.

Mechanical forces also have much influence on the direction of growth and the final form of roots. Both primary and lateral roots will grow around an impenetrable object after which the root tips tend to re-orient to their original direction of growth. Wilson (1967) made some interesting observations on the direction of growth of lateral roots in red maple and their re-orientation (exotropy) following growth around barriers slanted at varying degrees.

12. NUTRIENT ABSORPTION BY WOODY ROOTS

The complex process of ion absorption by vascular plants has been discussed in several recent reviews and no attempt will be made to cover current concepts in this important area of physiology. Because of the extensive and perennial nature of tree roots, questions frequently arise concerning the relative importance of entry of ions and water through older suberized roots (Kramer, 1946; Kramer and Kozlowski, 1960). Actively growing, succulent root tips including either the root hair zone or the mycorrhizal associations common to most woody plants constitutes zones of active ion uptake and accumulation. Furthermore, evidence is accumulating that a significant amount of inorganic nutrients move passively with water through the apoplast of suberized roots undergoing secondary growth (Kramer, 1969 pp. 114–117).

In the roots of herbaceous plants the endodermis supposedly blocks the movement of ions in the apoplast because of the suberin deposits in the matrix of the radial and transverse cell walls. Ions moving across the endodermis into the stele and ultimately into the xylem would have to pass through living membranes by a mechanism requiring the expenditure of metabolic energy, viz. energy from respiration. Ion accumulation within the vacuoles of all actively metabolizing root cells is another energy requiring process; but this process is only indirectly, if at all, involved with the movement of ions into the vascular system. In other words, the ions secreted into the vacuole and kept there by an expenditure of energy are not the ones translocated to other parts of the tree.

Although there is no question about the importance of active ion uptake and accumulation in cells of the growing root tips, one should remember that in the perennial roots of woody plants the endodermis and cortical tissues are usually ruptured a short distance proximal to the actively absorbing root tips. This rupture of primary tissues, especially the endodermis, opens pathways for water and ion movement directly into the vascular tissues via the cell walls.

In a study designed to show the effects of transpiration rates on the uptake and transport of ^{45}Ca by slash pine (*P. elliottii* Engelm.) seedlings, Helseth (1968) clearly showed a transpiration-dependent movement of calcium into the shoots. The importance of this mass flux of ions into the woody root and eventually upward in the xylem sap has yet to be properly quantified and evaluated under natural field conditions. Undoubtedly as Kramer (1946, 1969) suggests, mass movement of water and nutrients through suberized roots accounts for an appreciable amount of salt uptake in woody plants.

13. MYCORRHIZAL ASSOCIATIONS

The importance of mycorrhizal associations in the inorganic nutrition of forest trees has been recognized for many years. Hatch (1936) working with mycorrhizal and non-mycorrhizal white pine (*P. strobus* L.) seedlings in prairie soils free of mycorrhizal fungi found outstanding differences in the increased absorption of nitrogen, phosphorous, and potassium by the mycorrhizal plants. Uninoculated seedlings growing in the non-mycorrhizal prairie soils did not obtain sufficient nutrients to maintain normal growth. The beneficial effects of mycorrhizal associations is usually attributed to the increase in absorbing surface created by the hyphae and rhizomorphs extending into the soil (Hatch, 1937).

Mycorrhizal roots are classified as two basic types 1) ectotrophic and 2) endotrophic. The roots of some trees may possess both types of mycorrhizae and are sometimes referred to as ectendotropic. The ectotrophic types are commonly associated with the short roots of trees in the Abietineae, Betulaceae, Fagaceae, and Salicaceae. Such roots are usually less than 0.5 cm in length, have no root

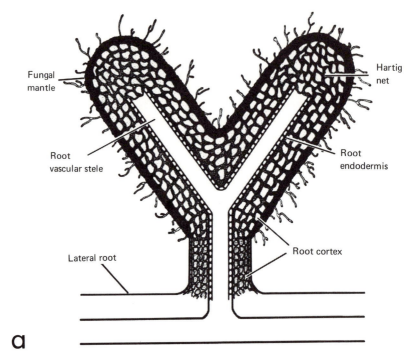

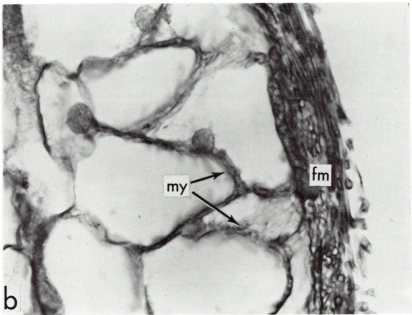

Fig. I–22a, b. Ectotrophic mycorrhizae associated with short roots of woody plants. (a) Diagram of a mycorrhizal association inducing dichotomy of a short root in pine. (b) Outer portion of a transverse section of shortleaf pine (*P. echinata* Mill.) root showing outer fungal mantle (fm) and mycelia (my) penetrating the primary walls of the cortex forming the so called "Hartig-net" (photographs courtesy D. H. Marx, USFS, Athens).

cap, and possess a monarch stele. The fungal hyphae penetrate the cell walls of the cortex and cover the outside of the short root to form a mantle or the so-called Hartig net (Fig. I-22a, b). The infected short roots become swollen, are often forked, and sometimes form groups of corralloid clusters (Fig. I-23).

The endotrophic type is associated with the finely divided roots in trees of the Aceraceae, Ulmaceae, Oleaceae, Magnoliaceae, and Juglandaceae. The mycelium develops intracellularly in the cortical cells and does not cause the same degree of swelling or forking as the ectotrophic forms. The endotrophic associations appear less prevalent in some localities than the ectotrophic types, e.g., Jackson and Driver (1969) observed the ectotrophic type in seven out of eight hardwood species in the Georgia Piedmont. Two of the species (*Liriodendron tulipifera* L. and *Carya pallida* (Ashe) Engl. and Graebn.) possessed both ectotrophic and endotrophic associations; while one, *Nyssa sylvatica* Marsh only had the endotrophic type.

Substantial evidence indicates that mycorrhizal roots accumulate more nutrients per unit of dry weight than non-infected roots (Kramer and Wilbur, 1949; Hodgson, 1954; and Harley, 1956). Melin and Nilsson (1950, 1955) and Melin *et al.,* (1958) have shown that radioactive phosphorous and calcium applied to the mycorrhizae mycelium is absorbed and translocated to the shoots of pine seedlings. In addition to the probably beneficial role of mycorrhizae in absorption of nutrients, Zak (1964) suggested that antibiotic substances produced by

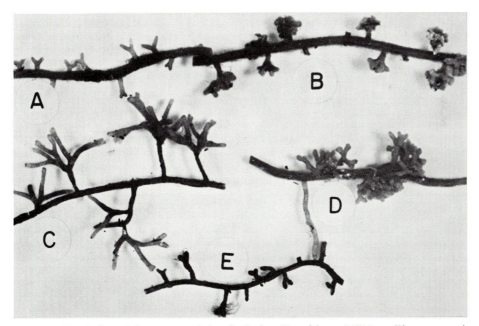

Fig. I–23. Infected short roots of shortleaf pine (*P. echinata* Mill.) seedlings grown in shortleaf pine humus for six months in the greenhouse. Five distinct morphological associations are often evident on individual seedlings (A, B, C, D, and E). From Marx and Davey (1969).

the mycorrhizal fungi protect the young roots from parasitic organisms in the soil. In recent studies, Marx and Davey (1969) demonstrated the resistance of naturally occurring mycorrhizae to infections by *Phytophthora cinnamomi* Rands., a pathogenic root fungus of shortleaf (*P. echinata* Mill.) and loblolly (*P. taeda* L.) pines.

Although mycorrhizal associations are undoubtedly beneficial to trees growing under natural conditions, and perhaps even essential to some in soils with low nutrient supplying capacity, they are not required for normal growth and development of seedlings supplied with adequate nutrients (Hatch, 1937; Hacskaylo and Palmer, 1957). In fact, in nutrient-sand cultures, seedlings of *Pinus taeda* L. and *P. echinata* Mill. lost most of their visible mycorrhizal associations in a period of six months under high levels of mineral nutrition (Brown, 1954).

LITERATURE CITED

ALVIM, P. DE. T. 1956. In "VI Reuniao Comite Tecnico Interam. Cacau", pp. 117–125. Bahia, Brazil.—ALVIM, P. DE T. 1960. Moisture stress as a requirement for flowering of coffee. Sci. 132: 354.—ALVIM, P. DE T. 1964. Tree growth periodicity in tropical climates. In: *"The Formation of Wood in Forest Trees."* Ed. M. H. Zimmermann. Academic Press. N.Y. pp. 479–495.—ARESCHOUG, E. 1877. Beiträge zur Biologie der Holzgewächse. Lund Univ. Arsskrift XIII Ludd. Quoted from Büsgen and Münch, 1929. pp. 21.—AVERY, G. S., P. R. BURKHOLDER, and H. B. CREIGHTON. 1937. Production and distribution of growth hormone in shoots of *Aesculus* and *Malus,* and its probable role in stimulating cambial activity. Amer. Jour. Bot. 24: 51–58.

BINDLOSS, E. 1942. A developmental analysis of cell length as related to stem length. Amer. Jour. Bot. 29: 179–188.—BONNER, J. 1965. *The molecular biology of development.* Oxford Univ. Press. 155 pp.—BROWN, C. L. 1954. The response of shortleaf and loblolly pines to micronutrient deficiencies of zinc, boron, manganese, and copper. MS Thesis. University of Georgia. 63 pp.—BROWN, C. L. 1964. The seedling habit of longleaf pine. Ga. Forest Research Council. Report No. 10. Macon, Ga. 68 pp.—BROWN, C. L. 1967. The application of tissue culture techniques to various problems in forest tree improvement. Proc. Ninth Conf. Forest Tree Improv. #28. Macon, Ga. pp. 108–110.—BROWN, C. L., R. McALPINE, and P. KORMANIK. 1967. Apical dominance and form in woody plants: A reappraisal. Amer. Jour. Bot. 54: 153–162.—BROWN, C. L. and R. H. WETMORE. 1959. Auxin transport in the long shoots of pine. Amer. Jour. Bot. 46: 586–589.—BÜSGEN, M., and E. MÜNCH. 1929. *The Structure and Life of Forest Trees.* Trans. Thompson. John Wiley and Son. N.Y. 436 pp.—BUVAT, R. 1952. Structure, evolution et fonctionnement du méristème apical de quelques dicotyledones. Ann. des Sci. Nat. Ser. XI Bot. 13: 199–300.—BUVAT, R. 1953. L'apex de *Triticum vulgare*; modalités de reprise des mitoses lors de la germination et du fonctionnement végétatif Paris Acad. des Sci. Compt. Rend. 236: 1989–1991.—BUVAT, R. 1955. Le méristème apical de la tige. L'Année Biol. Sér. 3, T 31 (59 Ann.): 595–656.

CAMUS, G. 1949. Recherches sur le rôle des courgeons dans les phenomènes de morphogenèse. Rev. Cyt. Biol. Veg. 11: 1–195.—CHAMBERLAIN, C. J. 1935. Gymnosperms Structure and Evolution. University of Chicago Press, Chicago, Ill. 484 pp.—CHAMPAGNAT, P. 1954. Recherches sur les "rameaux anticipés" des Végétaux. Rev. Cytol. Biol. Veg. 15: 1–54.—

CHAMPAGNAT, P. 1961. Dominance apicale. Tropisms, épinastie. Encycl. Plant Physiol. 14: 872–886. Springer-Verlag, Berlin.—CLAUSEN, J. J., and T. T. KOZLOWSKI. 1965. Heterophyllous shoots in *Betula papyrifera*. Nature. 205: 1030–1031.—CLOWES, F. A. L. 1956. Localization of nucleic acid synthesis in root meristems. Jour. Exper. Bot. 7: 307–312.—CLOWES, F. A. L. 1958. Protein synthesis in root meristems. Journ. Exper. Bot. 9: 229–238.—CLOWES, F. A. L. 1961. Apical meristems. Bot. Monog. 2. 217 pp. Oxford: Blackwell.—CORNFORTH, J. W., B. V. MILBARROW, G. RYBACK, and P. F. WAREING. 1965. Chemistry and physiology of "dormins" in Sycamore. Nature. 205: 1269–1270.—CRAFTS, A. S. 1943 a. Vascular differentiation in the shoot apex of *Sequoia sempervirens*. Amer. Jour. Bot. 30: 110–121.—CRAFTS, A. S. 1943 b. Vascular differentiation in the shoot apices of ten coniferous species. Amer. Jour. Bot. 30: 382–393.—CRITCHFIELD, W. B. 1960. Leaf dimorphism in *Populus trichocarpa*. Amer. J. Bot. 47: 699–711.—CROZIER, A., C. C. KUO, R. C. DURLEY, and R. P. PHARIS 1970. The biological activities of 26 gibberellins in nine plant bioassays. Can. J. Bot. 48: 867–877.—CZAJA, A. T. 1934. Der Nachweis des Wuchsstoffes bei Holzpflanzen. Ber. Deutsche. Bot. Ges. 52: 267–271.

DERMEN, H. 1959. Adventitious bud and stem relationship in apple. Jour. Wash. Acad. Sci. 49: 261–268.—DOAK, C. C. 1935. Evolution of foliar types, dwarf shoots, and cone scales of *Pinus*. Ill. Biol. Monog. 13(3): 106 pp.—DORE, J. 1955. Studies in the regeneration of horseradish. Ann. Bot. 19: 127–137.—DOSTAL, R. 1952. Experimental morphogenesis of buds in the horsechestnut (*Aesculus hippocastanum* L.) Moravskoslezske Akad. ved Prirodnich, Prace 24: 109–146. (In Czech with English summary)—DOSTAL, R. 1961. Gibberellinsäure und Knospenbildung bei *Syringa vulgaris*. Naturwiss. 48: 139–140.—DOWNS, R. J. 1958. Photoperiodic control of growth and dormancy in woody plants. In: *The Physiology of Forest Trees*, Ed. K. V. Thimann. Ronald Press, N.Y. pp. 529–537.—DUHAMEL DU MONCEAU, M. 1760. Des semis et plantations des arbres, et de leur culture. 383 pp. Paris: Guerin Delatour.

EAGLES, C. F., and P. F. WAREING. 1964. The role of growth substances in the regulation of bud dormancy. Physiol. Plant. 17: 697–709.—ENGELBRECHT, L., and K. MOTHES. 1962. "Überwindung der Knospenruhe durch Kinetin (6-Furfurylaminopurine). Naturwiss. 49: 427.—ESAU, K. 1954. Primary vascular differentiation in plants. Cambridge Phil. Soc. Biol. Rev. 29: 46–86.—ESAU, K. 1965. *Plant Anatomy* 2nd Ed. John Wiley and Sons, Inc. N.Y. 767 pp.

FOSTER, A. S. 1931. Investigations on the morphology and comparative history of development of foliar organs. II. Cataphyll and foliage leaf form and organization in black hickory (*Carya buckleyi* var. Arkansana). Amer. Jour. Bot. 18: 864–887.—FOSTER, A. S. 1935. Comparative histogenesis of foliar transition forms in *Carya*. Calif. Univ. Pub. Bot. 19: 159–185.—FOSTER, A. S. 1938. Structure and growth of the shoot apex in *Ginkgo biloba*. Torrey Bot. Club Bull. 65: 531–556.—FRAMPTON, C. V. 1960. Some aspects of the developmental anatomy of the long shoot in *Larix decidua* Mill., with particular reference to seasonal periodicity. New Phytol. 59: 175–191.—FRANSSON, P. 153. Studies on auxin in young stem parts of *Pinus silvestris*. Physiol. Plant. 6: 544–550.—FRANSSON, P. 1959. Studies on shoot and root cell elongation stimulator in *Pinus silvestris*. Physiol. Plant. 12: 188–198.

GALSTON, A. W., and P. J. DAVIES. 1969. Hormonal regulation in higher plants. Sci. 163: 1288–1297.—GARRISON, R. 1955. Studies in the development of auxiliary buds. Amer. Jour. Bot. 48: 789–795.—GARRISON, R., and R. H. WETMORE. 1961. Studies in shoot tip abortion: *Syringa vulgaris*. Amer. Jour. Bot. 48: 789–795.—GIFFORD, E. M. JR. 1951.

Ontogeny of the vegetative axillary bud in *Drimys winteri* var. *chilensis*. Amer. Jour. Bot. 38: 234–243.—GIFFORD, E. M. JR. 1960. Incorporation of H³ -thymidine into shoot and root apices of *Ceratopteris thalictroides*. Amer. Jour. Bot. 47: 834–837.—GIFFORD, E. M. JR. and H. B. TEPPER. 1962. Histochemical and autoradiographic studies of floral induction in *Chenopodium album*. Amer. Jour. Bot. 49: 706–714.—GIFFORD, E. M. JR. and R. H. WETMORE. 1957. Apical meristems of vegetative shoots and strobili in certain gymnosperms. Nat. Acad. Sci. Proc. 43: 571–576. GOEBEL, K. 1880. Beiträge zur Morphologie und Physiologie des Blattes. Bot. Zeit. 38: 801–815, 817–826, 833–845.—GOEBEL, K. 1908. Einleitung in die experimentelle Morphologie der Pflanzen. Teubner, Leipzig and Berlin. 260 pp.—GOEBEL, K. 1928. Organographie der Pflanzen. 3rd. ed. Fischer. Jena. 642 pp.— GREGORY, F. G., and J. A. VEALE. 1957. A re-assessment of the problem of apical dominance. Soc. Expt. Biol. Symp. 11: 1–20.—GUNCKEL, J. E., and K. V. THIMANN. 1949. Studies of development in long shoots and short shoots of *Ginkgo biloba* L. III. Auxin production in shoot growth. Amer. Jour. Bot. 36: 145–151.—GUNCKEL, J. E., K. V. THIMANN, and R. H. WETMORE. 1949. Studies of development in long shoots and short shoots of *Ginkgo biloba*. L. IV. Growth habit, shoot expression, and the mechanism of control. Amer. Jour. Bot. 36: 309–318.—GUNCKEL, J. E. and R. H. WETMORE. 1946 a. Studies of development in long shoots and short shoots of *Ginkgo biloba* L. I. The origin and pattern of development of the cortex, pith, and procambium. Amer. Jour. Bot. 33: 285–295.—GUNCKEL, J. E., and R. H. WETMORE 1946 b. Studies of development in long shoots and short shoots of *Ginkgo biloba* L. II. Phyllotaxis and the organization of the primary vascular system; primary phloem and primary xylem. Amer. Jour. Bot. 33: 532–543.—GUTTENBERG, H. VON. 1960. Grundzüge der Histogenese höherer Pflanzen. I. Die Angiospermen. In: Handbuch der Pflanzenanatomie. Band 8. Tiel 3. 315 pp. Berlin.— GUTTENBERG, H. VON 1961. Grundzüge der Histogenese höherer Pflanzen. II. Die Gymnospermen. In: Handbuch der Pflanzenanatomie. Band 8. Teil 4. Berlin.

HACSKAYLO, E. and J. G. PALMER. 1957. Effects of several biocides on growth of seedling pines and incidence of mycorrhizae in field plots. Plant Dis. Rep. 41: 354–358.— HANSTEIN, J. 1868. Die Scheitelzellgruppe im Vegetationspunkt der Phanerogamen. Festchr. Niederrhein. Gesell. Natur und Heilkunde, Bonn. 1868: 109–143.—HARLEY, J. L. 1956. The mycorrhiza of forest trees. Endeavour. 15: 43–48.—HARTING, M. G. 1845. Recherges micrométriques sur le dévélopment des parties élémentaires de la tige annuelle des plantes dicotyledonées. Ann. Sci. Nat. Bot. 3e Ser. 4: 210–279.—HATCH, A. B. 1936. The role of mycorrhizae in afforestation. Jour. For. 34: 22–29.—HATCH, A. B. 1937. The physical basis of mycotrophy in *Pinus*. Black Rock Forest Bull. 6. 168 pp. Harvard Univ. —HELSETH, F. 1968. The effect of oxygen tension and transpiration on uptake and transport of calcium in intact plants. Ph.D. dissertation. Univ. of Georgia. Athens, Ga.— HODGSON, R. A. 1954. A study of the physiology of mycorrhizal roots on *Pinus taeda* L. M.A. thesis. Duke Univ., N.C.—HOFMEISTER, W. 1868. Allgemeine Morphologie der Gewächse. Handb. der Physiol. Bot. 1: 405–640.

JACKSON, L. W. R., and C. H. DRIVER. 1969. Morphology of mycorrhizae on deciduous forest tree species. Castanea 34: 230–235.—JACOBS, W. P. 1952. The role of auxin in differentiation of xylem around a wound. Amer. Jour. Bot. 39: 301–309.

KEY, J. L. 1964. Ribonucleic acid and protein synthesis as essential processes for cell elongation. Plant Physiol. 39: 365–370.—KEY, J. L. and J. C. SHANNON. 1964. Enhancement by auxin of RNA synthesis in excised soybean hypocotyl tissue. Plant Physiol. 39: 360–364.—KIENHOLZ, R. 1934. Leader needle, cambial, and root growth of certain conifers and their relationships. Bot. Gaz. 96: 73–92.—Klebs, G. 1917. Über das Verhältnis von Wachstum und Ruhe bei den Pflanzen. Biol. Zbl. 37: 373–415.—Kögl, F., A. J. Haagen-Smit, and H. Erxleben. 1934. Über ein neues Auxin ("Heteroauxin") aus Harn. XI. Mitteilung. 2. Physiol. Chem. 228: 90–103.—Konar, R. N. 1963. A haploid tissue from the pollen of *Ephedra foliata* Boiss. Phytomorphology 13: 170–174.—Koriba, K. 1958. On the periodicity of tree growth in the tropics. Singapore Garden Bul. 17: 11–81.—Kormanik, P. P. 1968. Suppressed buds and epicormic branches in sweetgum (*Liquidambar styraciflua* L.) Ph.D. thesis. University of Georgia. 108 pp.—Kormanik, P. P. and C. L. Brown. 1964. Origin of secondary dormant buds in sweetgum. SE Forest Expt. Sta. Research Note. U.S.F.S. SE-36. 4 pp.—Kormanik, P. P., and C. L. Brown. 1967. Root buds and the development of root suckers in sweetgum. For Sci. 13: 338–345.—Kramer, P. J. 1946. Absorption of water through suberized roots of trees. Plant Physiol. 21: 37–41.—Kramer, P. J. 1949. *Plant and Soil Water Relationships*. McGraw-Hill, New York, N.Y. 347 pp.—Kramer, P. J. 1969. *Plant and Soil Water Relationships: A Modern Synthesis*. McGraw-Hill Book Company. New York, N.Y. 482 pp.—Kramer, P. J., and T. T. Kozlowski. 1960. *Physiology of Trees*. McGraw-Hill, N.Y. 642 pp.—Kramer, P. J. and K. M. Wilbur. 1949. Absorption of radioactive phosphorous by mycorrhizal roots of pine. Sci. 110: 8–9.

Ladefoged, K. 1939. Untersuchungen über die Periodizität im Ausbruch und Längenwachstum der Wurzeln. Fosttl. Forsogsv. Danmark 16: 1–256.—LeNoir, W. 1967. The effect of light on the cellular components of polarized growth in bean internodes. Amer. Jour. Bot. 54: 876–886.—Leech, R. W. A., and P. F. Wareing. 1967. Distribution of auxin in horizontal woody stems in relation to gravimorphism. Nature 214: 1025.—Leopold, A. C. 1964. *Plant Growth and Development*. McGraw-Hill Book Co. N.Y. 1964. 466 pp.—Lubbock, J. 1899. Buds and stipules. London: Paul, Trench, Trübner and Co. 239 pp.—Lyford, W. H., and B. F. Wilson. 1966. Controlled growth of forest tree roots: technique and application. Harvard Forest Paper No. 16. Harvard Univ. Petersham, Mass.

Marx, D. H. and C. B. Davey. 1969. The influence of ectotrophic mycorrhizal fungi on the resistance of pine roots to pathogenic infections IV. Resistance of naturally occurring mycorrhizae to infections by *Phytophthora cinnamoni*. Phytopathology 59: 559–565—Melin, E.. and H. Nilsson. 1950. Transfer of radioactive phosphorous to pine seedlings by means of mycorrhizal hyphae. Physiol. Plant. 3: 88–92.—Melin, E., and H. Nilsson. 1955. Ca^{45} used as an indicator of transport of cations to pine seedlings by means of mycorrhizal mycelium. Svensk. Bot. Tidskr. 49: 119–122.—Melin, E., H. Nilsson, and E. Hacskaylo. 1958. Translocation of cations to seedlings of *Pinus virginiana* through mycorrhizal mycelium. Bot. Gaz. 119: 243–246.—Miller, C. O., F. Skoog, F. S. Okumara, M. H. von Saltza, and F. M. Strong. 1955. Structure and synthesis of kinetin. Amer. Chem. Soc. Jour. 77: 2662–2663.—Miller, C. O., F. Skoog, F. S. Okumara, H. von Saltza, and F. M. Strong. 1956. Isolation, structure, and synthesis of kinetin, a substance promoting cell division. Amer. Chem. Soc. Jour. 78: 1375–1380.—Mirov, N. T. 1941. Distribution of growth hormone in shoots of two species of pine. Jour. Forestry. 39: 457–464. —Moll, J. W. 1876. De invloed celdeeling en celstresking op den groei. In Tammes, T. Verhandel. Koninkl. Ned. Akad. Wetenschap., Sect. II. 9: 1–146. 1903.—Mothes, K. 1960. Über das Altern der Blätter und die Möglichkeit ihrer Wiederverjungung. Naturwiss. 47: 337–350.

Nitsch, J. P. and C. Nitsch. 1969. Haploid plants from pollen grains. Sci. 163: 85–87.

Ohkuma, K. F. T., Addicott, O. E. Smith, W. E. Thiessen. 1965. The structure of abscisin II. Tetrahedron Letters 2529–2535.

PALEG, L. G. 1960. Physiological effects of gibberellic acid. II. Plant Physiol. 35: 902–906.—PALEG, L. G. 1961. Physiological effects of gibberellic acid. III. Plant Physiol. 36: 829–837.—PALEG, L. G. 1965. Physiological effects of gibberellins. Ann. Rev. Plant Physiol. 15: 291–322.—PARTANEN, C. R., and E. M. GIFFORD, JR. 1958. Application of autoradiographic techniques to studies of shoot apices. Nature 182: 1747–1748.—PAULEY, S. S., and T. O. PERRY. 1954. Ecotypic variations of the photoperiodic response in *Populus*. Jour. Arnold Arboretum, 35: 167–188.—POPHAM, R. A., and A. P. CHAN. 1950. Zonation in the vegetative stem tip of *Chrysanthemum morifolium* Bailey. Amer. Jour. Bot. 37: 476–484.

REED, J. F. 1939. Root and shoot growth of shortleaf and loblolly pines in relation to certain environmental conditions. Duke Univ. School of Forestry Bull. 4.—RICHARDSON, S. D. 1958. Bud dormancy and root development in *Acer saccharinum*. In: *The Physiology of Forest Trees* Ed. K. V. Thimann. Ronald Press, New York. N.Y.—ROMBERGER, J. A. 1963. *Meristems, Growth, and Development in Woody Plants*. U.S.D.A. Tech. Bulletin #1292. U.S. Gov. Printing Office. 214 pp.

SACHS, J. 1878. Über die Anordnung der Zellen in jüngsten Pflanzentheilen. Arb. Bot. Inst. Würzburg 2: 46–104.—SACHS, R. M. 1965. Stem elongation. Ann. Rev. Plant Physiol. 16: 73–96.—SACHS, R. M., C. BRETZ, and A. LANG. 1959. Cell division and gibberellic acid. Expt. Cell Res. 18: 230–244.—SACHS, T., and K. V. THIMANN. 1967. The role of auxins and cytokinins in the release of buds from dominance. Amer. Jour. Bot. 54: 136–144.—SCHOUTE, J. C. 1913. Beiträge zur Blattsstellungslehre. I. Die Theorie. Rec. Trav. Bot. Néerl. 10: 153–325.—SCHMIDT, A. 1924. Histologische Studien an phanerogamen Vegetationspunkten. Bot. Arch. 8: 345–404.—SCOTT, T. K., and M. B. WILKINS. 1968. Auxin transport in roots. II. Polar flux of IAA in *Zea* roots. Planta 83: 323–334.—SEELINGER, I. 1954. Studien am Sprossvegetationskegel von *Ephedra fragilis* var. *campylopoda*. Stapf. Flora. 141: 114–162.—SINNOTT, E. W. 1960. *Plant Morphogenesis*. McGraw-Hill. N.Y. 550 pp.—SINNOTT, E. W., and R. BLOCK. 1945. The cytoplasmic basis of intercellular patterns in vascular differentiation. Amer. Jour. Bot. 32: 151–156.—SKOOG, F., and C. O. MILLER. 1951. Growth substances and the formation of buds in plant tissues. pp. 263–298. In: *Plant Growth Substances*, (Ed.) F. Skoog. Univ. Wisconsin Press. Madison, Wis.—SKOOG, F., and C. MILLER. 1957. Chemical regulation of growth and organ formation in plant tissues cultured *in vitro*. Symp. Soc. Exptl. Biol. 11: 118–131.—SKOOG, F., and C. TSUI. 1948. Chemical control of growth and bud formation on tobacco stem and callus cultured *in vitro*. Amer. Jour. Bot. 35: 782–787.—SNOW, M., and R. SNOW. 1942. The determination of axillary buds. New Phytol. 41: 13–22.—SNOW, M., and R. SNOW. 1948. On the determination of leaves. Soc. Expt. Biol. Symp. 2: 263–275.—SNOW, M., and R. SNOW. 1952. Minimum areas and leaf determination. Proc. Roy. Soc. London, B. 139: 545–566.—SNOW, R. 1937. On the nature of correlative inhibition. New Phytol. 36: 283–300.—SNOW, R. 1940. A hormone for correlative inhibition. New Phytol. 39: 177–184.—SPÄTH, H. L. 1912. Der Johannistrieb. 91 pp. Berlin: Parey.—STEEVES, T. A. and I. M. SUSSEX. 1957. Studies on the development of excised leaves in sterile culture. Amer. Jour. Bot. 44: 665–673.—STERLING, C. 1945. Growth and vascular development in the shoot apex of *Sequoia sempervirens* (Lamb.) Endl. II. Vascular development in relation to phyllotaxis. Amer. Jour. Bot. 32: 380–386.—STERLING, C. 1947. Organization of the shoot of *Pseudotsuga taxifolia* (Lamb.) Britt. II. Vascularization. Amer. Jour. Bot. 34: 272–280.—STEWARD, F. C., M. O. MAPES, and K. MEARS. 1958. Organization in cultures grown from freely suspended cells. Amer. Jour. Bot. 45: 705–708.—STOWE, B. B. and T. YAMAKI. 1959. Gibberellins: Stimulants of plant growth. Sci. 129: 807–816.—SUSSEX, I. M. 1955. Morphogenesis in *Solanum tuberosum* L: Apical structure and development pattern of the juvenile shoot. *Phytomorphology* 5: 253–273.

THOMAS, T. H., P. F. WAREING, and P. M. ROBINSON. 1965. Action of the sycamore 'Dormin' as a gibberellin antagonist. Nature: 205: 1270–1272.—THOMPSON, D'ARCY. 1942. *On Growth and Form*. 2nd Ed. Cambridge Univ. Press. 1116 pp.—THIMANN, K. V. 1936. Auxins and the growth of roots. Amer. Jour. Bot. 23: 561–569.—THIMANN, K. V. 1937. On the nature of inhibitors caused by auxin. Amer. Jour. Bot. 24: 407–412.—THIMANN, K. V., and F. SKOOG. 1933. Studies on the growth hormone of plants. III. The inhibiting action of the growth substance on bud development. Nat. Acad. Sci. Proc. 19: 714–716.— THIMANN, K. V., and F. SKOOG. 1934. On the inhibition of bud development and other functions of growth substance in *Vicia faba*. Roy. Soc. London Proc., Ser. B. 114: 317–339. —TITMAN, P. W., and R. H. WETMORE. 1955. The growth of long and short shoots in *Cercidiphyllum*. Amer. Jour. Bot. 42: 364–372.—TORREY, J. G. 1955. On the determination of vascular patterns during tissue differentiation in excised pea roots. Amer. Jour. Bot. 42: 183–198.—TORREY, J. G. 1957. Auxin control of vascular pattern in regenerating pea root meristems grown *in vitro*. Amer. Jour. Bot. 44: 859–870.—TORREY, J. G. 1967. *Development in Flowering Plants*. McMillan and Co., New York. 184 pp.—TOUMEY, J. W. 1929. Initial root habit in American trees and its bearing on regeneration. Proc. Internatl. Cong. Plant Sci. 1: 713–728. Ithaca, N.Y., G. Banta Publ. Co., Manasha, Wis.— TUAN, D. and J. BONNER. 1964. Dormancy associated with repression of genetic activity. Plant Physiol. 39: 768–772.—TULECKE, W. 1957. The pollen of *Ginkgo biloba:* In vitro culture and tissue formation. Amer. Jour. Bot. 44: 602–608.—TULECKE, W. 1964. A haploid tissue culture from the female gametophyte of *Ginkgo biloba* L. Nature. 203: 94–95.

VAN OVERBEEK, J. 1938. Auxin distribution in seeedlings and its bearing on the problem of bud inhibition. Bot. Gaz. 100: 133–166.—VAN OVERBEEK, J. 1966. Plant hormones and regulators. Sci. 152: 721–731.—VARNER, J. E., and R. G. CHANDRA. 1964. Hormonal control of enzyme synthesis in barley endosperm. Proc. Nat. Acad. Sci. U.S. 52: 100–106.— VÖCHTING, H. 1878. Über Organbildung im Pflanzenreich. Max Cohen, Bonn. 258 pp.

WAREING, P. F. 1954. Growth studies of woody species. VI. The locus of photoperiodic perception in relation to dormancy. Physiol. Plant. 7: 261–277.—WAREING, P. F. 1956. Photoperiodism in woody plants. Ann. Rev. Plant Physiol. 7: 191–214.—WAREING, P. F. 1958. Interaction between indoleacetic acid and gibberellic acid in cambial activity. Nature 181: 1744–1745.—WAREING, P. F. 1964. Proc. Intern. Bot. Congress. Edinburgh. Abst. 017.—WARMKE, H. E., and G. L. WARMKE. 1950. The role of auxin in differentiation of root and shoot primordia from root cuttings of *Taraxacum* and *Cichorium*. Amer. Jour. Bot. 37: 272–280.—WENT, F. W. 1928. Wuchsstoff und Wachstum. Réc. Trav. Bot. Néerl. 25: 1–116.—WENT, F. W. 1936. Allegmeine Betrachtungen über das Auxin-Problem. Biol. Zbl. 56: 449–463.—WENT, F. W. 1939. Some experiments on bud growth. Amer. Jour. Bot. 26: 109–117. WENT, F. W. 1941. Polarity of auxin transport in inverted *Tagetes* cuttings. Bot. Gaz. 103: 386–890.—WETMORE, R. H. 1953. Carbohydrate supply and leaf development in sporeling ferns. Sci. 118: 578.—WETMORE, R. H., and J. P. RIER. 1963. Experimental induction of vascular tissues in callus of angiosperms. Amer. Jour. Bot. 50: 418–530.—WETMORE, R. H., and S. SOROKIN. 1955. On the differentiation of xylem. Jour. Arnold Arboretum. 36: 305–317.—WICKSON, M., and K. V. THIMANN. 1958. The antagonism of auxin and kinetin in apical dominance. Physiol. Plant. 11: 62–74.—WIESNER, J. 1889. Der absteigende Wasserstrom und dessen physiologische Bedeutung. Bot. Ztg. 47: 1–9.— WILCOX, H. 1962. Growth studies of the root of incense cedar, *Libocedrus decurrens*. II.

Morphological features of the root system and growth behavior. Amer. Jour. Bot. 49: 237–245.—Wilkins, M. B., and T. K. Scott. 1968. Auxin transport in roots. III. Dependence of the polar flux of IAA in *Zea* roots upon metabolism. Planta 83: 335–346.— Wilson, B. F. 1966. Development of the shoot system of *Acer rubrum* L. Harvard Forest Paper No. 14. Harvard University. Petersham, Mass.—Wilson, B. F. 1967. Root growth around barriers. Bot. Gaz. 128: 79–82.—Wodzicki, T. J. 1968. The occurrence of indole-acetic acid in *Pinus sylvestris* L. Amer. Jour. Bot. 55: 564–571.

Zak, B. 1964. Role of mycorrhizae in root disease. Ann. Rev. Phytopathol. 2: 377–392. —Zimmermann, M. H. and P. B. Tomlinson. 1968. Vascular construction and development in the aerial stem of *Prionium* (Juncaceae). Amer. Jour. Bot. 55: 1100–1109.— Zimmermann, W. A. 1936. Untersuchungen über die räumliche und zeitliche Verteilung des Wuchsstoffes bei Bäumen. Z. Bot. 30: 209–252.

CHAPTER II

SECONDARY GROWTH

Claud L. Brown

INTRODUCTION

The evolution of vascular plants possessing structural modifications capable of withstanding the stress of terrestrial habitats was one of the most significant evolutionary advances to occur in the plant kingdom. The rate at which evolutionary changes occurred from the appearance of the first primitive vascular plants in the Upper Silurian-Lower Devonian to the luxuriant and varied flora of the Carboniferous, a span of approximately 100 million years, is surpassed only by the rapid rise of the angiosperms in the Cenozoic.

In the fossil record of the Lower Devonian vascular plants, there is no evidence of the existence of a vascular cambium. The plants which existed during this period were relatively small and consisted of a single protostele without much cortex. The fossil record indicates that plants of this type probably never exceeded two meters in height. It was only with the evolution of the vascular cambium that truly tree-like forms arose (Barghoorn, 1964).

The vascular cambium probably had its origin in the Middle Devonian, some 300 million years ago. During this period the genus *Schizopodium* formed radially aligned xylem elements around the periphery of a lobed xylem core which appears to reflect primitive cambial activity. From the Middle Devonian on, however, cambial activity became common place, and by the Upper Devonian extensive secondary activity is found in all phyletic lines which make up the rich flora of the Carboniferous (Barghoorn, 1964). One of the enigmas of paleobotany is the wide-spread occurrence in the Upper Devonian of *Callixylon,* a tree of massive size (ca. 20 meters tall with trunks over one meter in diameter) possessing tracheids with bordered pits and truly an ancestoral type of modern gymnosperms.

Although several arborescent lycopods arose in the late Devonian and early Carboniferous, the internal structure of the genera *Lepidodendron* and *Sigillaria* is of particular interest because of their heights. In contrast to *Callixylon* these genera attained heights of 40 meters or more, but they developed relatively little secondary xylem. The vascular cylinder was seldom more than several centimeters in diameter, but there was a massive development of secondary parenchyma and periderm. This small ratio of water conducting tissue in the stem may partly account for the extinction of these arborescent Lycopods during the Permian, a period of abrupt climatic changes accompanied by intervals of high moisture stress. *Callixylon,* having a massive woody cylinder and less external parenchymatous tissue, may have given rise to other phyletic lines capable of surviving the harsh climatic stresses of the Permian.

Of further interest in the evolutionary development of land plants is the diversity in patterns of cambial activity and the high degree of anatomical specialization found in modern angiosperms. Yet, as Barghoorn (1964) points out in the evolution of angiosperms from the Cenozoic to the present time the suppression and ultimate loss of cambial activity is one of the most outstanding features of evolution in this group. Undoubtedly much survival value is placed upon the small size of herbaceous plants and shortness of their reproductive cycle. Thus, with the increasing selection pressures of adverse climates in the middle and higher latitudes since the Miocene, the more primitive woody forms have suffered serious losses in numbers. An interesting graphic scheme (Fig. II-1) clearly shows these trends and relationships.

1. THE VASCULAR CAMBIUM

Researchers have not always agreed upon what constitutes the radial dimensions of the vascular cambium. Theodor Hartig (1853) came to the conclusion that the cambium was a biseriate layer of cells in which two initials lay adjacent to each other so that one produced xylem cells in one direction and the other produced phloem cells in the opposite direction. Several years later Sanio (1873) suggested that the cambium itself consisted of only a single layer of cells. Each time a division occurred in the cambial initial, one of the daughter cells remained as the cambial initial, while the other cell became a xylem or phloem mother cell. These mother cells usually divide once or more before their derivatives differentiate and mature into xylem or phloem cells.

When one views a radial section of stem during the height of cambial activity it is difficult, if not impossible, to point out the exact location of the cambial initials because of frequent cell divisions on either side by the xylem and phloem mother cells. Hence from time to time objections have been raised concerning the validity of assuming the cambium to be only one cell in thickness. Bailey (1923) pointed out, however, that if the cambium were not uniseriate the radial continuity of differentiating xylem and phloem cells across this lateral meristem could not long exist. For example, if a xylem mother cell rather than a cambial initial underwent a pseudotransverse division to increase the girth of the cambium, then there would be no phloem counterpart, and new tiers of discontinu-

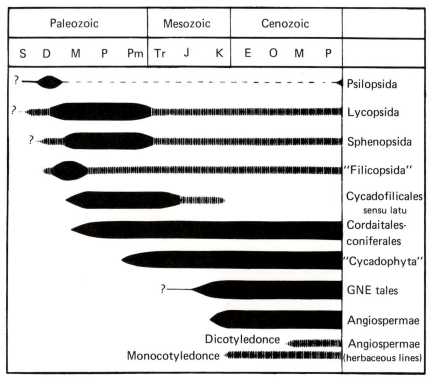

Fig. II–1. Graph showing the occurrence of cambial activity and its persistence during geologic time in the major groups of vascular plants. Secondary growth is indicated by the broad black bars and loss of secondary activity by the narrow interrupted bars. Note loss of cambial activity in the various groups of the lower vascular plants during late Paleozoic and Mesozoic and the origin of herbaceousness among dicotyledons during the middle and later Cenozoic (after Barghoorn, 1964).

ous cells would arise on the xylem side of the cambium. Bannan (1957) found such divisions occurring occasionally in the xylem mother cell zone of conifers but not in a ratio high enough to cause serious radial discontinuity.

Most workers today consider the cambium as a functionally uniseriate layer, but the width of the xylem and phloem mother cell zone varies with seasonal activity, vigor, and cycle of periclinal divisions, i.e., divisions that increase the number of cells in each radial file. Frequently the term cambial zone is used to describe the entire radial width of the actively dividing xylem and phloem mother cells including the layer of cambial initials. The concept of a functionally uniseriate cambium does not require the cambial initials to be tangentially aligned. That is, adjacent cambial initials may be radially offset according to their immediate state of mitotic activity. A standardized and useful terminology for describing various cell types and tissues associated with secondary activity is suggested by Wilson, *et al.* (1966) and is given in Fig. II-2.

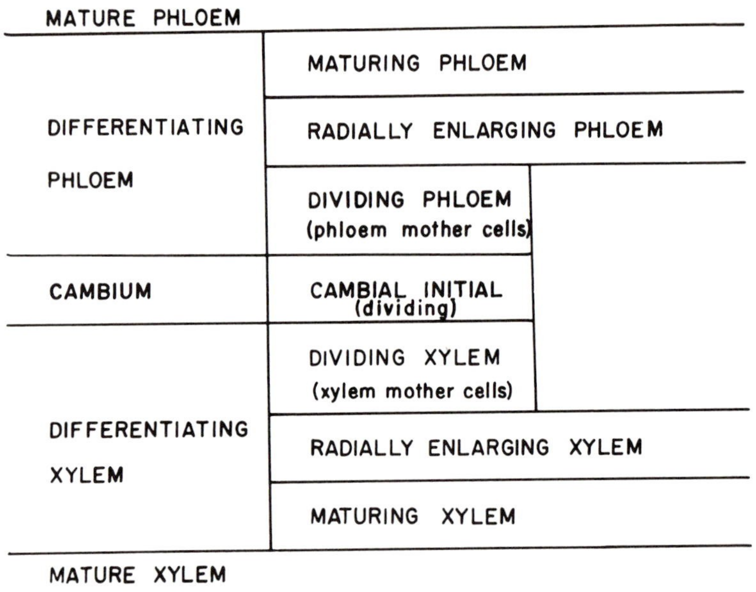

MATURE PHLOEM		
DIFFERENTIATING PHLOEM	MATURING PHLOEM	
	RADIALLY ENLARGING PHLOEM	
	DIVIDING PHLOEM (phloem mother cells)	
CAMBIUM	CAMBIAL INITIAL (dividing)	
DIFFERENTIATING XYLEM	DIVIDING XYLEM (xylem mother cells)	
	RADIALLY ENLARGING XYLEM	
	MATURING XYLEM	
MATURE XYLEM		

Fig. II–2. Chart giving useful terminology for describing cell types and tissues associated with secondary activity (after Wilson, *et al.* 1966).

a. Cambial origin and cell types

The vascular cambium is initially derived from procambial cells which differentiate acropetally from pre-existing strands into the apex of the elongating primary shoot. Here, strands of vertically elongated procambial cells can be traced upward into the young leaves and into or near the base of the apical meristem proper in a pattern outlining the development of the future vascular system. Following the maturation of the primary xylem and phloem the central portion of the vascular bundle remains meristematic and functions as the vascular cambium. The cambium becomes a continuous circular sheath in the maturing portion of the elongating woody shoot by the tangential differentiation of new cambial initials through the ground meristem connecting the separate vascular bundles.

The vascular cambium is made up of two cell types: 1) *fusiform initials,* and 2) *ray initials.* The former are elongated cells with tapering ends whereas the ray initials are much smaller and almost isodiametric in shape. Although the fusiform initials may appear to be only four to six-sided to the inexperienced observer, Dodd (1948) finds those of Scots pine (*P. sylvestris* L.) to have an average of 18 different faces. The configuration of fusiform initials in other conifers is similar but it varies among species. Because the fusiform initials give rise to all the vertical elongate elements of the xylem and phloem, their initial and final dimensions, and the many physiological factors affecting these dimensions are of much importance to the kind and quality of wood produced. The dimensions and volume of the fusiform initials show a wide range in variation within the same tree with age and location, as well as among species. This was first clearly elucidated by Sanio (1872) in Scots pine, and substantiated by numerous workers in both gymnosperms and angiosperms since that time (Spurr and Hyvarinen, 1954).

For example, the lengths in millimeters of fusiform initials in the following species were recorded by Bailey (1920a): *P. strobus* L., 3.20; *Ginkgo,* 2.20; *Myristica,* 1.31; *Populus,* 0.49; *Fraxinus,* 0.29; and *Robinia,* 0.17.

In tangential view two types of cambia may be distinguished, viz. storied and non-storied (Fig. II-3a, b). In the storied type the fusiform initials are relatively short and occur in horizontal tiers so that their end walls form essentially straight rows. In the non-storied type, the end walls overlap, a common feature of species with long fusiform initials. The non-storied type is more primitive than the storied type, being a common feature of the fossil pteridophytes and gymnosperms. It is also present in all living gymnosperms and primitive angiosperms

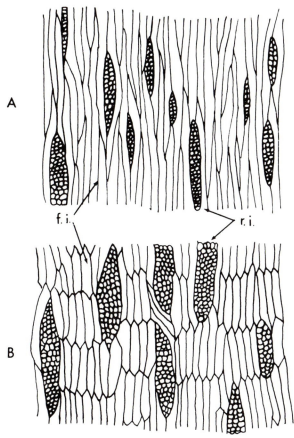

Fig. II–3a, b. Diagram of two cambia types: (A) nonstoried cambium with overlapping fusiform initials (fi) common to many dicotyledons and conifers, and (B) storied cambium found in some of the more modern dicotyledons such as *Robinia pseudoacacia* L. or *Diospyros virginiana* L. Ray initials (ri).

(Bailey, 1923). The storied type cambium is restricted to the more highly specialized dicotyledons.

b. Pattern of cell division

The process of cell division in the highly vacuolate fusiform initials of the cambium was first adequately described by Bailey (1920a, b). The ellipsoidal nucleus, usually near the center of the cell, undergoes mitosis with the two daughter nuclei remaining relatively close together in the narrow elongate cell. The cell plate begins to form between the daughter nuclei by the phragmoplast, an extension of the spindle fibers at telophase. In radial longitudinal sections the phragmoplast is seen to extend in opposite directions, the two sets of fibers extending the cell plate to the ends of the fusiform initial (Fig. II-4). These tangential (periclinal) divisions not only occur in the cambial initials, they also frequently occur in the xylem and phloem mother cells on either side making up a rather wide zone of actively dividing cells during the peak of cambial activity.

Because of these continued divisions, laying down new xylem derivatives on the inside of the cambium, the circumference of the axis continually increases. The cambial initials do not increase in tangential diameter to keep pace with this activity, so they obviously must undergo longitudinal radial divisions to

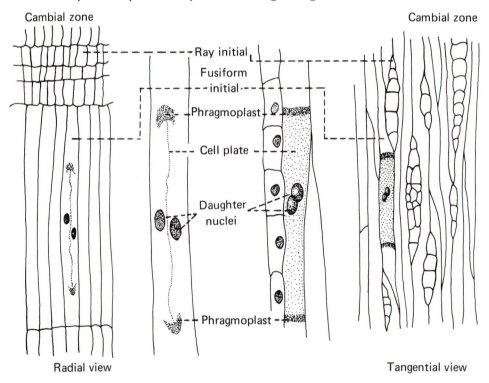

Fig. II–4. Diagram of tangential (periclinal) division of a fusiform initial in radial and tangential views. This type of division gives rise to radial rows of xylem and phloem derivatives.

increase the girth of the cambium *per se*. In storied cambia, this is accomplished by radial divisions in the same way as the tangential ones just described. In non-storied cambia, however, the initial cell divides by the formation of an obliquely radial (pseudotransverse) wall, followed by elongation of the cells at their apices (apical intrusive growth) until each daughter cell is as long as, or longer than, the original mother cell (Fig. II-5) (Bailey, 1923).

The careful and extensive work of Bannan (1954, 1955, 1956, 1957) in white cedar (*Thuja occidentalis* L.) has shown how the rate and distribution of pseudo-transverse divisions in the cambium changes with time and how these changes in turn affect the ultimate length of the initials and the mature tracheids derived from them. For example, during the first few years of rapid diameter growth pseudotransverse divisions are frequent and occur throughout the growth ring. The frequency of these divisions, accompanied by a high survival rate, normally results in the formation of short fusiform initials, and consequently short tracheids. With increasing age, the frequency of pseudotransverse divisions is reduced, the survival rate of newly formed initials declines, and such divisions are restricted to the latewood zone within successive growth rings. In mature trees most of the pseudotransverse divisions are restricted to the last formed late-wood, where survival of the daughter initials may be low, so that the surviving cells rapidly elongate filling the spaces created by the aborted initials. Hence, longer fusiform initials and tracheids are gradually produced until a maximum

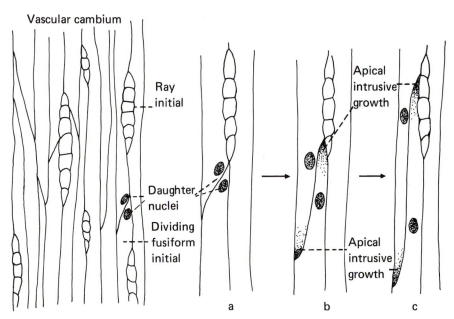

Fig. II-5. Tangential view of vascular cambium showing (a) pseudotransverse division of fusiform initial followed by later stages of elongation by apical intrusive growth (b) and (c). This type of cell division gives rise to two daughter fusiform initials thereby increasing the girth of the cambium.

size is reached for a given species, after which, yearly fluctuations appear in tracheid length reflecting the many subtle and complex growth responses of the vascular cambium.

c. Ray formation

The increasing circumference of the tree bole also requires that the number of ray cells be continually increased if the relationships between distribution of rays and vertical elements be maintained. The origin of new rays in gymnosperms has been studied in detail by Bannan (1934, 1951) and Barghoorn (1940a) and in angiosperms by Barghoorn (1940b, 1941).

A new ray frequently arises from a short segment cut out of the radial face of a fusiform initial where the nucleus migrates prior to cell division, or it may arise from the end of a fusiform initial by a transverse division. The ray then increases in height by transverse division of the cell, and in width by radial divisions (Bannan 1951, 1954). The process of ray initiation and extension in the cambium seems to vary considerably with species. Some of the fusiform initials are lost completely whereas others are broken up into ray cells by several divisions.

Detailed studies of cellular differentiation in woody rays by Braun (1964, 1967) indicate little correlation between the type of ray cells produced and the organizational pattern of the wood. In the early stages of ray-cell differentiation in the gymnosperms and primitive angiosperms the parenchyma cells of the rays are in direct contact with tracheids and vessels by conspicuous pitting on their radial walls. In more advanced angiosperms newly-formed cells of small rays also make contact by pitting to vessels and tracheids, but as the rays extend in height to form five or six cell layers, a segregation of function becomes apparent. The contact cells are to be found only at the top and bottom of the rays (in some species these are upright cells); whereas in the middle tier, cells have no pits to vessels and are referred to as isolation cells. These cells likely play an important role in the lateral movement of water and solutes especially during periods of mobilization (see Chapter VII, Section 3a).

In addition to the formation of new ray initials numerous developmental changes constantly occur in the actively dividing cambium. For example, in producing new cambial initials apparently more cells are formed than is necessary, and numerous fusiform initials are eliminated. Bannan (1960) found in rapidly growing *Thuja occidentalis* L. the survival rate of new initials to be about 20 per cent; whereas, in slow growing trees it was nearer 50 per cent. Evert (1961) observed a comparable loss of fusiform initials in *Pyrus communis* L. One factor in the survival pattern of new fusiform initials is their apparent contact or proximity to ray cells. Apparently the initials are supplied with carbohydrates and nutrients almost exclusively by the rays, hence if they become too far removed from the source of nutrition they either die or undergo division to form new ray initials. As suggested by Ziegler (1964), this may be a very effective feedback mechanism for regulating the arrangement and distribution of ray cells. This regulation is so constant, i.e., species specific, it permits taxonomic identification and separation of many woods. Obviously here is a morphogenetic pattern of differentiation worthy of considerable more study.

RAY AND PHLOEM DILATATION. In the non-conducting phloem the rays may become dilated because of an increase in the circumference of the stem or root (Fig. II-6). This response is brought about by radial anticlinal divisions of ray cells followed by their tangential enlargement. In some species the divisions are confined to the median portion of the ray, and the cells give the appearance of a meristem (Holdheide, 1951; Schneider, 1955). Not all phloem rays become dilated. Some retain the same dimensions they possessed at the time of origin in the vascular cambium (cf. Fig. II-6).

In some species, dilatation of the phloem occurs by the division of phloem parenchyma cells forming wide wedges of tissues in the non-conducting phloem (Chattaway, 1955) (Fig. II-7).

A more generalized type of phloem dilatation occurs in certain pines. For example, in young longleaf pine seedlings still in the grass stage (see Chapter I, Section 5) the phelloderm and phloem parenchyma cells scattered throughout the non-conductive phloem divide to form an extensive storage tissue. In most instances of ray or phloem dilatation the older sieve tubes or sieve cells are crushed or displaced by the expanding parenchyma cells (cf. Brown, 1964).

d. Correlation of primary with secondary growth

Perhaps no single physiological process in trees has been studied more than the periodic reactivation of the vascular cambium. Even today, with our knowledge of hormonal regulation of growth, there are many questions yet to be answered about the initiation of cambial activity.

In the temperate regions of the world the resumption of cambial growth each spring is correlated with the renewed activity of buds and the development of leaves. In tropical and sub-tropical regions, however, the initiation of cambial activity in some species is less well defined because the sequence of developmental events during the year are not clearly separated by pronounced periods of intense activity and rest. In some tropical trees, the cambium may remain active the year around with peak periods of activity corresponding with periods of rapid shoot extension. Certainly, we know much less about the patterns of cambial activity in tropical trees, including both initiation and cessation of growth, than those of the temperate zone because so few detailed studies have been conducted with different species in tropical regions. Even less is known about the patterns of early- and late-wood formation in tropical trees. (see Section 3 of this chapter). Therefore, most of our discussions on secondary growth will be confined to observations on conifers and dicotyledonous trees of the temperate zones, because unfortunately, most of the research on cambial activity has been restricted to the trees of these regions.

The activation of the cambium in early spring has long been associated with the renewed activity of buds. Theodor Hartig (1853), in studying the behavior of willow cutting, made the observation that not only did cambial activity begin

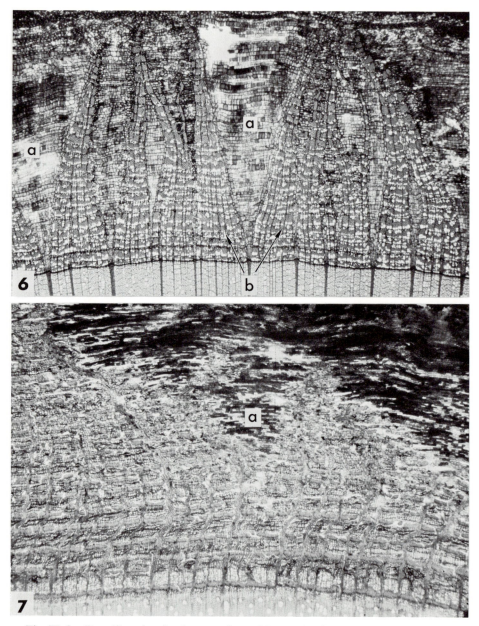

Fig. II–6. Ray dilatation in the secondary phloem of *Tilia americana* L. resulting in wedge shaped intrusions (a). Nondilated rays still predominate in the phloem (b).

Fig. II–7. Phloem dilatation in *Acer pensylvanicum* L. Note displacement of rays by enlargement of phloem parenchyma (a).

at the base of the terminal bud and spread downward, but that a similar activity began in a wedge shape under each actively expanding lateral bud and spread laterally as it moved down the twig. Even when the cuttings were inverted the pattern was still the same, i.e., a polar, basipetal activation of the cambium occurred beneath the buds. Priestley (1930) noted that there had never been any record of an upward movement of cambial activity from the bud in a distal direction. Sledge (1930) reported, however, that in dormant hardwood cuttings cambial activity could proceed slowly upward from the basal wound callus before the buds began to extend; however, at bud break normal basipetal cambial activation occurred throughout the stem beneath the buds. Hartig (1853) had also made this observation, but apparently it went unnoticed. Some 30 years later Jost (1891, 1893) confirmed Hartig's earlier association of cambial activity with the growth of buds. Because he was interested in the food or nutritional aspects of growth, Jost placed twigs in the dark and followed their pattern of cambial activation. In all cases, he found renewed cambial growth only beneath the elongating lateral shoots, with a lack of cambium activity throughout the stem because of a limiting food supply. Jost also made the observation that in late summer the premature forcing of buds to form "Johannistriebe" or lammas shoots was often accompanied by the formation of a new layer of thin-walled, earlywood type cells for some distance down the twig giving rise to an additional growth ring.

Coster (1928) also observed that the activity of the cambium in many evergreen tropical dicotyledonous trees possessing intermittent growth was correlated with bud activity. It is of interest, however, that cambial activity will resume at the base of the petiole in evergreen leaves when such leaves are taken as cuttings. Jost regarded this as the only clear-cut example of cambial growth being initiated without the presence of buds, and in organs situated on the same axis above the place where cambial activity is normally manifested. It is of interest that over half a century later several researchers came to the same conclusion that leaves could stimulate cambial activity.

e. Seasonal pattern of cell division in the cambial zone

The resumption of cambial activity in trees of the temperate zones has long been associated with the phenomenon of bark peeling or slipping with the warmer temperatures of spring. For years it was assumed that cell divisions in the cambium was a prerequisite for bark slippage. However, it is known from the observations of Huber (1948), Ladefoged (1952), Wilcox et al. (1956) that it may precede cambial divisions for periods of 2 to 4 weeks depending upon the inherent nature of the species and existing environmental conditions. During the early stages of cambial reactivation the cells expand radially due to the increase in water uptake; their radial walls become thinner, and the cytoplasm becomes less dense occupying a thin parietal layer around the large central vacuole (Bannan, 1955). With this renewed physiological activity the bark may be easily peeled. These changes first appear below the buds and move basipetally along the branches and stem. In spruce, Huber (1948) found the downward movement of this process to occur at a rate of about 1.0 meter per day in warm weather; whereas, in a ring-porous oak the rate of movement was so rapid that it was difficult to detect a difference in peelability between the twigs and the base of the truck.

Once the cambium becomes physiologically active, the question arises, where do the first cell divisions occur in this meristem? The older concept presented in most general botany texts is that the cambial initials are the first cells to undergo renewed cell division following a period of rest. The conifers have been studied more extensively than angiosperms in this respect. The initiating layer, i.e. the cambium *per se*, is usually not the first cell to divide upon resumption of growth in the spring; rather, the last formed xylem mother cells which over-wintered in the stem are normally the first cells to undergo division, followed by divisions in the initials themselves until a peak rate of cell production is reached a few weeks later (Bannan, 1954, 1955, 1962; Wilson, 1964; Wilson and Howard, 1968). In white pine, for example, the number of cells in the cambial zone in winter is at a minimum (4–8) but in the spring it reaches 10–15 in fast growing trees, and then gradually decreases again until at the end of the summer the dormancy level of 4 to 8 cells is again reached (Wilson, 1964).

The first few divisions in the cambial zone take place slowly and a period of 3 to 4 weeks may elapse between the first 3 or 4 divisions. Once the cambium is highly activated cell divisions occur more rapidly. In white cedar (*Thuja occidentalis* L.) the time between successive xylem mother cell divisions during rapid earlywood formation ranges from 4 to 6 days in the Toronto area. This period of time is much longer than the interval between divisions in the rib-meristems of the primary shoot which is on the order of 8 to 18 hours. Apparently the relatively slow division of cambial cells is reflected by the length of time required for the phragmoplasts to reach the tips of the long cambial derivatives. The synthesis of cellular proteins and cell wall components over the large area occupied by the cambial zone is also a factor involved in successive divisions as suggested by Bannan (1962).

Apparently only two quantitative studies have been made showing the distribution of mitoses across the cambial zone and both (*Thuja occidentalis* L. and *Pinus strobus* L.) show a peak frequency in the center of the zone (Bannan, 1955; Wilson, 1964). In late spring and early summer during the period of most frequent cell divisions, the radial enlargement of the xylem mother cells is rapid but only slight, reaching 10 to 15 microns before they divide. Cells that reach the phase of enlargement do not divide further, and they may reach radial diameters of 40 to 50 microns. The final radial diameter depends largely on the seasonal growth pattern or environmental conditions imposed upon the trees during this period. A diagram of how cambial activity might proceed in early spring is presented in Fig. II-8a, b.

On the phloem side of the cambium in conifers, phloem mother cells are cut off periodically from the initiating layer at a slower rate than the xylem mother cells. Bannan (1955) found that in white cedar each phloem mother cell usually divides once to produce two cells, the outer of which generally differentiates into

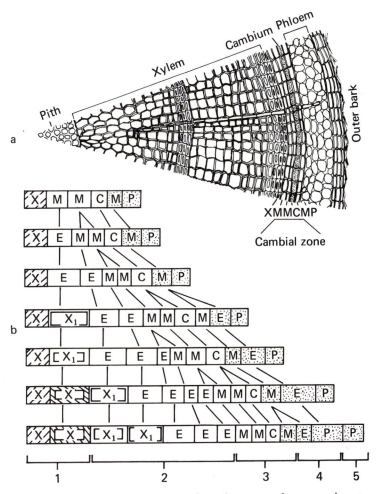

Fig. II–8. (a) Portion of a transverse section of a young dormant pine stem showing arrangement of tissues. The cambial zone consists of four tiers of radially aligned cells which give rise to new xylem and phloem elements during the growing season. Cambial initials (C) are stipuled. Cells to the left and right of the cambial initial are xylem and phloem mother cells (M) respectively; these are bordered by the previous season's mature xylem (X) and mature phloem (P) elements.

(b) Diagramatic presentation of how cambial activity might proceed in early spring showing a theoretical sequence of xylem and phloem formation by cells of the cambial zone. Stipuled cells to the right of the cambial initials (C) indicate phloem derivatives; cells undergoing enlargement are labeled (E); cell wall thickening is occurring in xylem cells (X_1). Numerals indicate various regions of development: (1) mature xylem; (2) differentiating xylem; (3) cambial zone; (4) differentiating phloem; and (5) mature phloem. (Fig. II–8b modified from Wilson and Howard, 1968).

a sieve cell, and the inner into a parenchyma cell or fiber depending on the previous pattern of differentiation. The number of phloem mother cells produced during the season is much less than those produced on the xylem side, and usually the first division in the phloem mother cells lag behind that on the xylem side by a period of 3 to 6 weeks. For example, in one season in the Toronto area the first cell divisions in the xylem mother cells occurred in white cedar around April 15, whereas the first division in the phloem mother cells was 5 to 6 weeks later at the end of May. The number of new phloem cells produced by the end of May in this species is usually 2 to 4, whereas at this time there may be as many as 30 to 60 new xylem derivatives produced. By the end of August an average of 12 to 16 new phloem cells had formed; whereas, a 100 or more new xylem elements may be produced in vigorously growing trees. Obtaining data of this nature is extremely painstaking and time-consuming and even more difficult to clearly present because of the dynamic three-dimensional aspects of cambial development. Wilson (1964) and Wilson and Howard (1968) in a series of extensive studies on cell divisions in the cambial zone of white pine (*P. strobus*) developed a model for cell production in which many variables affecting the components of radial growth can be mathematically treated. Undoubtedly such models will be very useful in future studies of radial growth and development.

Although the pattern of cell division accompanying the resumption of growth in white cedar as described by Bannan (1955, 1962) may be the general pattern for many conifers, a distinctly different one occurs in *Pyrus*, a diffuse-porous dicotyledon studied by Evert (1960, 1963). In this species, the first divisions occurred in the overwintering phloem mother cells as early as 4 to 6 weeks before divisions in the xylem mother cells. This pattern may hold true for most angiosperms because the functional phloem is normally restricted to the innermost increment, and the early differentiation of immature sieve elements from the previous season is necessary for effective mobilization and redistribution of food reserves accompanying the renewed surge of rapid growth following a period of rest (see Chapter VII, Section 4b).

In view of Evert's observations in *Pyrus*, one wonders if the pattern of phloem development significantly differs between diffuse- and ring-porous hardwoods in a manner similar to that of xylem development. In the latter group new earlywood vessels are commonly differentiated in advance of bud breaking and leafing out in early spring (see Chapter IV, Section 7c). It may be that the ring-porous hardwoods resemble the conifers in this respect, and the first divisions occur on the xylem mother cell side of the cambium to facilitate the early differentiation of large earlywood vessels essential for current year water conduction.

f. Variations in the pattern of cambial activation between ring- and diffuse-porous species

Over the years several workers have reported seemingly conflicting patterns of cambial reactivation in hardwoods and conifers. Some maintain, for example, that the cambium first becomes active just beneath the buds and the activity extends downward into the twigs and trunk. Others indicate that the cambium may become active in the trunk independently of the branches and the reactivation may then extend both upward and downward. Priestley and Scott (1936) were the first to make a clear distinction between the pattern of cambial activation in diffuse- and ring-porous angiosperms. They noted that in the diffuse-porous group the cambium became active at the base of swelling and extending buds and activity proceeded rather slowly down the twigs into the trunk toward the base of the tree. In some diffuse-porous trees a period of two to four weeks or longer may elapse between the time of cambial activation in the twigs and the resumption of radial growth at the base of the trunk. In contrast, the cambium of ring-porous trees appears to become activated so rapidly throughout the twigs and trunk, that activation appears to occur almost simultaneously throughout the whole stem. Therefore, in many ring-porous species the bark may slip several days before noticeable bud swell occurs in early spring, and by the time the buds break and young leaves begin to extend, newly formed xylem vessels are already functional. This rapid cambial activation and xylem formation in the ring-porous group obviously has survival value in providing new channels of water transport each spring because of embolisms developing in the large vessels of the previous season (see Chapter IV, Section 7c).

Because of these differences in cambial activation, questions often arose concerning the essential role of buds or young leaves in activating the cambium each spring. The prevalent theory being that a hormonal stimulus, probably IAA, coming from the young expanding buds and leaves, is the physiological mechanism triggering the activation of the cambium (see Section g). Thus, some workers argued that in the ring-porous group if the cambium became active before visible activity in the buds, perhaps a hormonal stimulus from the buds was unnecessary or even lacking. This possibility was studied by Wareing (1950, 1951) in a series of debudding and ringing experiments with both ring- and diffuse-porous species.

Young ring-porous trees of *Fraxinus, Quercus, Robinia,* and *Castanea* were completely debudded above ground in late winter before any bud activity had begun, and their stems sampled periodically during the spring to compare the initiation of cambial activity with untreated controls. In all cases, abundant wide vessels were found throughout the trunks of the young debudded trees, although they were more numerous at the base than in the upper portions of the tree. In distinct contrast, debudded diffuse-porus species of *Acer* and *Tilia* showed no cambial activity whatever, except for a short distance below strong adventitious buds.

Because the debudded ring-porous species showed some new xylem formation, Wareing (1951) performed additional ringing experiments on debudded and intact trees to determine if there was any movement of the cambial stimulus from specific "foci" in such trees. Cambial activity was again present above the girdle in both debudded and untreated trees, but not immediately below the girdle, indicating that a basipetal stimulus was blocked by the ringing. In sectioning the stem segments some distance below the ring, however, he found renewed cambial activity had occurred, and by stripping away the bark it became clear that the newly formed vessels could be traced to old leaf scars and the site of adventitious buds previously present or still hidden in the bark. Therefore, Wareing (1951) concluded that even in the ring-porous trees, a hormonal stimulus came from minute adventitious buds and was transported basipetally activating the cambium beneath. The primary difference in cambial activation between debudded ring- and diffuse-porous species is due to differences of degree or sensitivity rather than different modes of physiological activity. A small amount of bud growth triggers cambial activity over considerable distances in the ring-porous group; whereas, in diffuse-porous species the slight activity of similar buds is ineffective in initiating the same degree of cambial activity. Wareing (1951) interpreted these observations to mean that a reserve auxin-precursor was present in the cambium of ring-porous species which makes possible the rapid spread of vessel formation throughout the tree at an early stage of bud development. Whether this is actually the case, or whether the levels of other growth factors such as gibberellin or cytokinins are also involved in eliciting this early and rapid difference in response remains to be demonstrated. At the time this work was done, it was generally thought that auxin alone was *the* causal factor in the initiation of cambial activity (see Section g).

Observations on the pattern of cambial initiation in conifers is even more conflicting. Priestley (1930) stated that in many conifers cambial activity may be resumed independently in the main stem and branches, but in either case the activity can be traced to the base of breaking buds and moves basipetally along the shoot. In a series of debudding and defoliating experiments with young white pines (*P. strobus* L.) Münch (1938) found that debudding had little effect on the initiation of cambial growth in the branches and stems beneath, whereas complete defoliation resulted in little or no cambial activity (see Chapter III, Section 4b). Münch (1938) was of the opinion, therefore, that both the young and old leaves in coniferous evergreens contributed the hormonal stimulus to activate the cambium. From these and other observations it appears that cambial activity in conifers begins near the base of active buds and young leafy twigs in early spring at the time of, or even preceding active shoot extension, and moves rapidly throughout the branches and main stem in much the same manner as in the ring-porous hardwoods previously described. Certainly, the basipetal progression of activity is more rapid in the conifers than in the diffuse-porous hardwoods.

g. Hormonal control of cambial activity

Well over a hundred years have passed since Theodor Hartig (1853) made the pertinent observation that radial growth usually began at the base of expanding buds and spread downward into the branches and trunk. Although the rate at which cambial activity moves basipetally from the uppermost shoot tips to the basal portion of the trunk significantly varies with species, the causal mechanism has long been associated with a hormonal stimulus. Even before the turn of the present century, Jost (1891) postulated that the stimulus which activated the cambium was hormonal in nature and in no way was it directly related to the then prevalent nutritional theory of cambial growth. Later, Jost (1907) abandoned his correlation theory and stated that the formation of new leaves and xylem were dependent upon common factors and that correlative (hormonal) effects were not involved. In the years to follow, however, Kastens (1924) and Coster (1927, 1928) revived the original ideas of Jost, and postulated again that the stimulus was hormonal in nature. Up until the 1930's the strongest evidence that the stimulus was hormonal was obtained from numerous debudding and ringing experiments (girdling), which confirmed the role of buds and leaves in producing some substances(s) translocated downward which was removed, or whose downward movement was blocked by these treatments.

During the late 1920's and early 1930's the discovery and isolation of natural growth promoting substances in plants, followed by the identification of the physiologically active substance, indole-3-acetic acid (IAA) led to the formulation of the theory that naturally occurring and basipetally transported IAA, produced in active buds and elongating shoots was the hormonal stimulus activating the cambium in the spring (Zimmermann, 1936; Avery *et al.,* 1937, Söding, 1937).

Although some workers conclude that auxin, i.e., IAA is the primary stimulus activating the cambium in early spring, considerable evidence is accumulating that substances other than IAA (promoters and inhibitors) are involved in this complex process. For example, the periodicity of cambial activity is not solely a function of auxin level. In early spring following a period of overwintering, the dormant cambium is much more responsive to a given level of applied IAA in decapitated branches than it is later in the season, or in dormant branches before a period of winter rest (Reinders-Gouwentak, 1941). This would indicate that inhibitory substances have accumulated during the previous growing season which must be removed during a period of rest before IAA can exert its effect on cambial activity. It may also be that the levels of other growth promoting substances such as gibberellins and cytokinins which interact with natural inhibitors and native auxin are so low that the latter cannot exert its full effect.

Furthermore, in contrast to the hypothesis that buds must always be present to activate the cambium of deciduous trees (Wareing, 1951; 1958), it should be recalled from the experiments of Münch (1938) with white pine (*P. strobus* L.) that activation of the cambium was inhibited only when the shoots were debudded and defoliated simultaneously. Thus in evergreen conifers the stimulus can apparently be derived from older, as well as young developing leaves. In other experiments with white pine, Münch (1938) found cambial activity to be completely inhibited just beneath a bark girdle, but a short distance beneath, the cambium became more active than in non-girdled stems (see Chapter III, Section 4b). Such studies indicate that the initiation of cambial activity in conifers may be less dependent on actively growing buds and leaves than in the more evolutionary advanced angiosperms. They also suggest that once the cambium is activated it may supply its own source of auxin and other growth factors quite independently of a continuous basipetal flow from the developing or mature shoots in the crown. Jacquiot (1950) using cambial explants of several woody species was also able to obtain cambial activity *in vitro* for periods of 6 to 8 weeks without an exogenous source of auxin.

In more recent experiments with diffuse- and ring-porous hardwoods, Wareing (1958), Wareing, *et al.* (1964) have shown the interacting role of IAA with gibberellic acid (GA) in activating the cambium and controlling the pattern of differentiation in the newly formed derivatives. In the completely disbudded control shoots of *Acer pseudoplatanus* L., *Populus robusta* (a hybrid), and *Fraxinus excelsior* L. there was no evidence of renewed cell division in the cambium, whereas in both IAA and GA treated stems new cambial derivatives were formed. When IAA was applied alone, new xylem elements were formed in discontinuous groups around the periphery of the stem with little evidence of any cell division occurring between the groups. In the shoots treated with GA alone, cell divisions occurred throughout the cambium producing an inner continuous layer of xylem derivatives which failed to undergo further differentiation into normal xylem elements. If, however, IAA and GA were applied together to the disbudded shoots a wide zone of newly formed xylem was formed which was differentiated into normally thickened and lignified vessels, fibers, and tracheids. Thus, IAA and GA together not only stimulated more total cambial activity but resulted in the formation of normally differentiated xylem.

In these studies Wareing and his associates found IAA alone failed to stimulate the production of new phloem derivatives, whereas gibberellic acid did cause an increase in the amount of phloem parenchyma. As in the case of xylem formation, a combination of IAA and GA brought about more phloem formation than GA alone; however, few if any sieve tube members or companion cells were formed indicating basic differences in the pattern of cellular differentiation between these contiguous tissues, i.e. xylem and phloem.

DeMaggio (1966) found gibberellic acid to stimulate the differentiation of sieve cells in explants of dormant white pine (*P. strobus* L.) when applied by micropipette to the cambial zone at concentrations of 10 or 100 parts per million. Cells of the cambial zone, as well as the phloem parenchyma, became noticeably enlarged, although apparently little, if any, cell divisions occurred in the cambium in response to the application of gibberellic acid. Thus, a comparable role of gibberellin in stimulating cell division in the cambial zone of gymnosperms, especially in conifers has not been clearly demonstrated. Most conifers have been largely unresponsive to applications of GA in respect to shoot elongation, and, in fact, concentrations or levels of GA which promote internodal elongation of various angiosperms, tend to inhibit or have no growth promotion effect on conifers (Nelson, 1957; Westing, 1959; and Kraus and Johansen, 1960). It may be that the conifers as a group already possess a supra-optimal level of gibberellin or gibberellin-like substances since the structure of these compounds is not far removed from other terpenoids so plentiful in this group of plants. This is purely speculative, however, and a precise quantitative study of the seasonal levels of IAA, GA, and cytokinins at different distances along the bole of woody plants is urgently needed to elucidate the pattern of hormonal control over the important process of cambial activity.

All of the recent studies relating to cambial physiology indicate, that the activation and continued activity of the cambia in woody plants involves more than just the presence of IAA coming from expanding buds. In fact, the work of Wareing, *et al.* (1964), as well as numerous other studies on differentiation of xylary elements, shows that IAA plays a prominent role in the differentiation of mature xylem elements, perhaps even more so than it does in cell divisions *per se.* Although IAA has some effect on cell divisions in the cambium (likely in the presence of cytokinin), GA appears to have a much greater effect in this capacity; while it exerts little or no apparent effect upon the process of xylem differentiation and maturation of normal xylary elements. In view of what is presently known about naturally occurring inhibitors, the initiation of cambial activity is a complex interaction between these substances and the levels of more than one type of growth promotor (IAA and GA, and perhaps the cytokinins). Such inhibitors may be either counterbalanced by a high concentration of growth promotors or somehow reduced to a lower level during a period of winter rest.

As Wareing *et al,* (1964) point out, debudded woody stems contain small quantities of auxins and other growth factors, so that the exogenous application of one may be sufficient to bring about cambial cell division in the presence of low concentrations of the others. This point may be clearly demonstrated by observing differences in species response of dormant internodal stem segments using a liquid sterile culture technique. This technique, recently discussed by Brown and Wodzicki (1969) for studying cambial activity, was used earlier to observe the effects of sucrose, IAA, and Kinetin (6, furfurylaminopurine) on the activation of the cambium in several diffuse- and ring-porous hardwoods and a conifer (*P. strobus* L.), (Brown, 1962). Briefly, some of the species studied produced new cambial derivatives on the xylem side in 10 to 21 days without a source of exogenous IAA, whereas other species failed to undergo any cell divisions in the cambium even when IAA or kinetin was applied separately or in combination over a range of physiological concentrations. It is likely that exogenously applied gibberellin would have elicited a more favorable response, especially in combination with IAA, although such tests were not performed in this study.

h. Cessation of cambial activity

The seasonal pattern of cambial activity varies within and among species growing on the same site at various latitudes. Almost a century ago, Robert Hartig (1885) noted differences in the initiation and cessation of diameter growth in spruces on the north slopes versus those on the warmer sunny south slopes in central Germany. Trees on the latter sites had completed one-fourth of their annual increment 30 days or more before any cambial activity could be detected in those only a 100 paces away on the cooler north slopes. There is also an age effect on the periodicity of cambial activity in many species. Büsgen and Münch (1929) report differences in both initiation and cessation of diameter growth in conifers; the younger trees normally began activity earlier and extend later into the season than older ones.

There is apparently less variation in the north temperate zones in the initiation and cessation of growth than in the lower latitudes. For example, Eggler (1955) found in southern Louisiana a three-month interval between the time certain tupelo gum trees (*Nyssa aquatica* L.) on the same site began diameter growth. A similar spread was found in the time of cessation of cambial activity within the same trees. Jackson (1952) reports the diameter growth of different species on the same site varied from 70 to 209 days in the Georgia Piedmont. In these cases it is obvious that internal physiological mechanisms rather than environmental conditions *per se* govern cambial activity. What then brings about the cessation of cambial activity in individual trees?

Several workers have proposed that the cessation of cambial activity was highly correlated with the period of shoot extension or height growth. Although the initiation of cambial activity is, under normal conditions, closely related to the swelling and bursting of buds, height growth in most woody species ceases long before diameter growth. This is especially true of those species which make only one rapid flush of extension growth in early spring but continue to grow in diameter until late summer or early fall. Table II-1 illustrates this general pattern of growth for several tree species of the temperate zones.

TABLE II-1

Differences in duration of height and diameter growth in several diffuse-porous species (data from Reimer, 1949).

Species	Height Growth Period	Duration (weeks)	Amount (mm)	Diameter Growth Period	Duration (weeks)	Amount (mm)
Prunus	Apr. 14–June 4	8	92.0	May 26–Sept. 30	19	2.30
Acer platanoides	Apr. 7–May 26	8	39.7	June 17–Aug. 4	8	1.42
Acer saccharum	Apr. 14–May 26	7	42.3	June 10–Aug. 25	12	1.46
Tilia	Apr. 21–June 17	9	48.8	June 17–Sept. 22	15	1.58
Fagus	Apr. 7–May 26	8	87.2	May 19–Aug. 25	15	1.79

Most workers agree that the cessation of cambial activity in individual trees, especially in open-grown vigorous trees, occurs first in the uppermost twigs and gradually proceeds downward to the lower trunk and finally into the roots (Swarbrick, 1927; Lodewick, 1928; Studhalter *et al.* (1963); Büsgen and Münch (1929, p. 102) make the statement, however, that in closed stands cambial activity ceases first in the basal and middle portion of the weaker lower branches and then sometime later in the uppermost vigorous shoots. Also, in very old trees or in trees of poor vigor the cambium may cease dividing on the lower bole before it does in the upper portion of the stem.

The observation that the cambium normally ceases activity first in the uppermost twigs of healthy, vigorous trees sometime after shoot elongation stops has been interpreted as evidence that a continuous source of diffusible auxin from young elongating shoots and leaves is essential for continued cambial activity, i.e., that the cambium, once triggered into activity, cannot continue to supply its source of auxin and other hormones autonomously. One could just as easily argue, however, that some inhibitory substance(s) produced by mature leaves later in the season is transmitted downward from the upper crown bringing about the cessation of cambial activity (see Section 3b).

So little is known about the cessation of cambial growth in tropical and sub-tropical species that generalizations have little meaning at the present time. Because of the wide variations in patterns of shoot growth among trees growing in the same environment, one would expect to find similar variations in the periodicity of cambial activity. Although peaks of high cambial activity alternate with periods of low activity or quiescence in many tropical trees, it is difficult to determine precisely when cambial activity ceases because of the multiplicity of growth layers produced in some trees and the poor demarcation of growth rings in others. In such trees, secondary growth may occur intermittently or almost continuously and the number of observations required to elucidate clearly the patterns of cessation in individual trees are yet to be made. Even in the lower Coastal Plain of the southeastern United States one- and two-year-old nursery grown pine seedlings (*P. taeda* L. and *P. elliottii* Engelm) grow in diameter intermittently during warm periods in mid-winter while the terminal buds remain visibly dormant. The stem diameters of such seedlings often double from November to February without visible shoot elongation, indicating that the physiology of seedling growth is quite different than that of older trees.

Thus, it is seen that the pattern of cessation of cambial activity can vary widely among and within species as a result of interactions between internal hormonal and nutritional balances, age, and environmental conditions affecting various physiological processes. Additional research on this problem will likely show that the ratio of growth promoting factors to natural inhibitors shifts during shoot extension and leafing out, so that cyclic patterns of acivity usually exist even under the most favorable environmental conditions.

2. THE CORK CAMBIUM

Quite a bit is known about the origin and morphology of cork cambia, but few workers have directed their attention to the physiology of this secondary meristem. Most texts state that the cork cambium or *phellogen* gives rise to cork cells or *phellem* to the exterior, and occasionally to one or more layers of interior cells, the *phelloderm,* which resembles cortical parenchyma. All three tissues are collectively referred to as the *periderm,* an outer protective tissue of secondary origin.

The periderm is not synonymous with the term bark. Bark usually refers to all tissues exterior to the vascular cambium. In fact, when the bark is peeled from trees during active growth the vascular cambium is also removed, hence from a practical viewpoint bark would include everything exterior to the outer ring of secondary xylem. Sometimes the terms *inner* and *outer bark* are used. In common usage the term *inner bark* refers to the vascular cambium and the living portion of conducting and non-conducting phloem; the *outer bark* consists of the periderm and all tissues of the axis isolated by its formation (Fig. II-9a). The technical term used to describe the outer bark is *rhytidome* as used by DeBary (1884).

The majority of woody plants possess a periderm which replaces the epidermis as the young stems and roots increase in girth. The formation of the periderm may occur very early in the young stems and roots of some species, whereas in others it may be delayed for longer periods of time. In some woody genera a periderm never develops although there may be a yearly increase in stem thickness (Esau, 1965). Thus in certain species of *Ilex, Acer, Citrus, Eucalyptus,* and *Acacia* the cortical tissue and epidermis keep pace with the enlarging vascular cylinder by continued cell division and enlargement as long as the plant lives.

The first phellogen may originate at varying depths along the axis. In some species the epidermal cells give rise to the phellogen (some members of *Rosaceae, Salix, Nerium*) but in most cases it is differentiated from the outer cortical cells, or still deeper from the inner layers of the cortex or outer phloem. In some trees the first formed phellogen may remain functional for years, e.g., *Fagus, Carpinus, Acer, Abies,* which accounts for the smooth external features of the bark even in old age as witnessed by the presence of lovers' initials carved there many years ago. In most forest species, however, the original phellogen is replaced from time to time by the subsequent differentiation of new ones in successively deeper tissues of the cortex or secondary phloem.

One of the most interesting aspects about the origin of the cork cambium is the way in which a continuous layer of cells may differentiate *de novo* in older mature cells of the cortex or in the nonconducting tissue of the phloem. Hence, completely differentiated cells of a mature tissue, redifferentiate to become embryonic or meristematic in a continuous manner to form a cambial layer. The differentiation of the phellogen in young stems just beneath the epidermis or beneath a wound is often explained on the basis of some physiological gradient, such as differences in gas exchange, water stress, or levels of wound hormones, but the successive formation of lens-shaped or crescent-shaped phellogens in the typical rhytidome formation of most trees (cf. Fig. II-9a) is difficult to explain by any surface gradient phenomena (see Section 5).

After the phellogen is formed, the majority of cell divisions are periclinal giving rise to radial files of cells by repeated tangential wall formation. Anticlinal divisions also frequently occur in young continuous phellogens increasing its girth to keep pace with the even increasing circumference of the inner vascular cylinder.

In contrast to the vascular cambium, the cork cambium of most trees produces many more external derivatives (cork cells) than inner phelloderm cells. The phellogen of some species produces no phelloderm cells at all. In others it normally produces only one or two layers during a given season; while the number of cork cells produced may become extensive as in the cork oak (*Quercus suber* L.). In some woody plants, however, the phellogen may produce several layers of phelloderm calls which function in a storage capacity similar to that of the phloem parenchyma. Such is the case in young seedlings of longleaf pine (*P. palustris* Mill.) (Fig. II-9b).

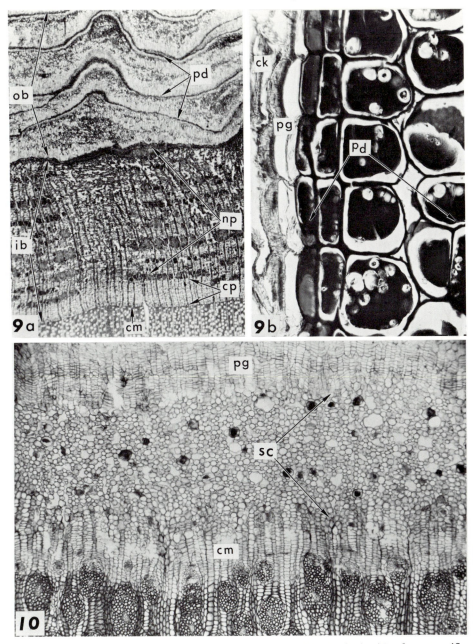

Fig. II–9a, b.   (a) Transverse section of outer stem and bark of *Liquidambar styraciflua* L. showing successive layers of periderm (pd); inner bark (ib) comprising the vascular cambium (cm), conducting phloem (cp), and non-conducting phloem (np); and the outer bark (ob) or rhytidome comprising all tissues set aside by the last formed periderm. (b) Transection of portion of longleaf pine, *P. palustris* Mill., stem showing several layers of phelloderm (pd) containing starch grains, phellogen (pg), cork (ck).

Fig. II–10.   Transverse section of stem of *Cordyline indivisa* Kunth, an arborescent monocotyledon, showing secondary tissues. Phellogen (pg); secondary cortex (sc) and vascular cambium (cm). From Tomlinson and Zimmermann (1969).

The outer protective tissue in the arborescent monocotyledons varies as to origin and type but cork cambia in the sense just described for dicots and gymnosperms are present only in species with secondary growth. In many monocots, such as the bamboos, the epidermis remains throughout life and becomes extremely hard by sclerification of the walls. In other species e.g., many palms the ground parenchyma beneath the stem surface merely becomes suberized to form a protective outer covering and part of the cortex may even erode in older stems.

In those monocotyledons which increase in diameter by secondary growth, an outer protective tissue is formed by repeated divisions of a phellogen near the periphery of the stem followed by suberization of the outermost cells. By repeated periclinical divisions, several tangential tiers of cells are formed which become suberized and differentiate as cork cells. Because cork cells are often produced in tangential bands, the outer layer thus formed is referred to as *storied cork*. Occasionally, non-suberized, parenchyma cells of the ground meristem become trapped and embedded between the files of cork cells giving rise to a tissue analogous to the rhytidome of dicots as in *Yucca, Cordyline,* and *Dracaena* (Fig. II-10).

The protective nature of the periderm in trees is derived from the physical nature of the cork cells. At maturity these cells are dead and highly suberized. Being devoid of contents they serve as poor conductors of heat, and being suberized they are less pervious to water and water vapor. The cork layer is usually much thinner on roots than on stems, and the fleshy part of roots exterior to the xylem imbibe large quantities of water similar to the action of a sponge. Although it is commonly stated that suberin is resistent to the enzymes of microorganisms and cork is not readily decayed, the environmental conditions of the soil either retard the formation of cork or speed up its degradation. The former seems more plausible since cork is often a constituent of plant fossils.

The cork cells may begin to deposit suberin during development and after they reach maturity before the protoplasts undergo senescence (Bowen, 1963; Mader, 1954). The suberin is deposited in the form of lamallae over the primary cellulose cell wall as an adcrustation. Electron micrographs of suberized cork cells appear layered apparently because of alternating deposits of suberin and waxes (Falk and El-Hadidi, 1961). The middle lamella and the cellulosic part of the cell wall often take a phoroglucinal stain and thus appear to be lignified. The cell walls are not pitted but Sitte (1955) reports the presence of plasmodesmatal pores in studies with the electron microscope. Sitte (1957) reports that suberin contains unsaturated fatty acids and is partially permeable; whereas, the layers of wax contribute most to the impervious nature of cork cells.

Virtually nothing can be said about the seasonal pattern of activation and cessation of cell divisions in the phellogen of woody perennials. Few, if any, comparative studies have been made correlating the initiation of cambial and phellogen activity in trees. In those trees with a single continuous phellogen, one wonders if cell divisions in this meristem occur before, simultaneously with, or after divisions in the vascular cambium. Furthermore, one may ask what stimulus activates the cork cambium to divide. Does it depend upon some hormonal stimulus transmitted basipetally from buds and leaves, or does some stimulus move laterally from active cells of the vascular cambium and phloem causing the cells to resume activity? Of even more interest, is the process that controls the pattern of new phellogen differentiation each spring in the deeper lying tissues of the phloem. This pattern results in the formation of such specific morphological traits that the trained observer can easily identify most forest trees by the external features of the bark.

3. GROWTH RING FORMATION

a. Occurrence of growth rings

Almost everyone is familiar with the concentric markings on the cross-sections of tree stumps or stems of felled trees. Growth rings are discernible to the naked eye or under the microscope because of differences in the physical properties of the xylem elements produced during cyclic growth. The manner in which these differences arise varies with species. For example, in conifers the wood is more or less uniformly composed of tracheids and the growth ring is distinguished by differences in both cell size and cell wall thickness between elements produced during the early and late part of the growing season (Fig. II-11).

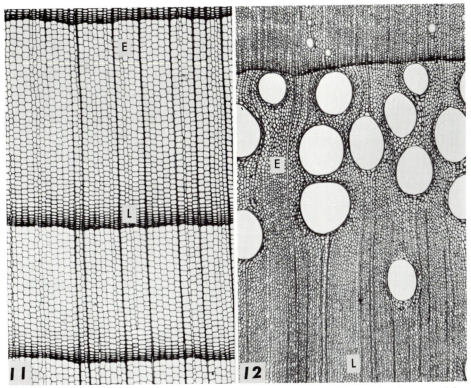

Fig. II–11. Transverse section of wood of *Pinus ponderosa* Laws. showing transition in size and shape of earlywood (E) and latewood (L) tracheids in successive growth rings.

Fig. II–12. Transverse section of wood of a ring-porous oak (*Quercus velutina* Lam.) showing extremely large vessels in the first formed earlywood (E) and the preponderence of fibers in the latewood (L).

In dicotyledonous trees, the demarcation of successive growth rings may be very distinct or hardly noticeable depending upon the inherent characteristic of the species. In the ring-porous trees such as oaks, ashes, hickories, etc., the rings are very evident to the eye because of the formation of a rather narrow band of large earlywood vessels, followed by the production of a more compact latewood composed of smaller vessels and an increase in fibers and fiber tracheids (Fig. II-12).

In the diffuse-porous angiosperms the growth rings are not always clearly recognized by the unaided eye, especially in those species where the only demarcation between successive layers is a radial flattening of the last few elements formed (Fig. II-13). Many diffuse-porous trees, however, produce more fibers than vessels near the end of the growth period and these rings are clearly seen with the naked eye (Fig. II-14). A detailed account of these basic differences in wood structure of gymnosperms and angiosperms and the many interesting integrada-

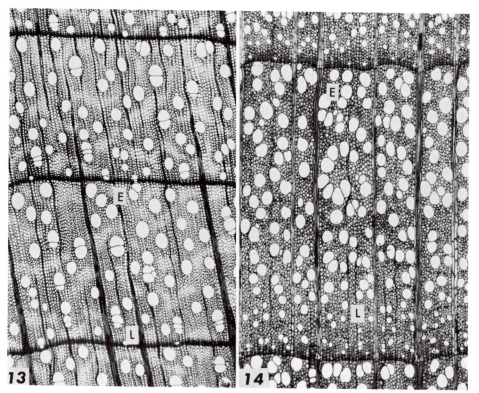

Fig. II–13. Transverse section of a diffuse-porous hardwood (*Liriodendron tulipifera* L.) showing fairly uniform distribution of vessels throughout the growth ring and radial flattening of the last formed latewood elements.

Fig. II–14. Transverse section of a diffuse-porous hardwood (*Fagus grandifolia* Ehrh.) showing a higher proportion of vessels in the earlywood (E) than in the latewood (L) and a correspondingly increase in the proportion of thick-walled fibers in the latter.

tions which exist in the latter group may be found in Panshin *et al.* (1964) and Record and Hess (1943).

Braun (1962, 1963), has studied in considerable depth the anatomical relationships among various tissue systems in wood and how these are related to the physiology of water movement within and between growth rings. Observations on the wood of various gymnosperms, primitive, intermediate, and modern angiosperms led to a classification of 14 types of wood construction based on such characteristics as 1) extent and distribution of ground tissue (tracheids and fibers), 2) position and size of vessels and the nature of their cross walls, 3) contact between ground tissue and vessels, 4) position of xylem parenchyma, and 5) intercellular spaces between ground tissue.

From a functional viewpoint these patterns of tissue organization show an evolutionary trend from the more primitively combined conduction-mechanical function of tracheids in the gymnosperms to a more specialized separation of mechanical tissues (fibers) and conducting elements (vessels) in the advanced angiosperms.

In the more primitive woods the tracheids and fiber tracheids maintain functional contact with each other through bordered pits on the radial walls, and also by pits on the tangential walls of the late wood cells providing lateral contact between successive growth rings. In many angiosperms the vessels form a complex network within the ring, and in some woods they make contact with parallel vessels in adjacent rings through pitting on the tangential walls. In other angiosperms the vessels are isolated within the tracheid matrix so that only the latter formed vessels make contact across adjacent growth rings. In some woods the vessels may also be completely surrounded by living cells (paratracheal parenchyma) within the ring but still make contact with other parallel vessels at the boundry of successive growth rings. These studies by Braun point out the complex nature of the organization of the hydrosystem in trees.

The periodicity of growth ring formation varies with species, age, and growing conditions. Thus, it is difficult to make broad generalizations about the seasonal pattern of formation. In the older literature the term growth ring and annual ring were used synonymously because most observations on their formation had been made with trees of the North temperate zones where only one ring is normally produced each year. As more species were studied, especially the angiosperms, it was found that multiple rings often formed during the same season, or conversely certain rings could be missing completely along some portion of the tree axis. Multiple rings may occur in trees of the temperate zones which form lammas shoots in late summer, or following defoliation and leafing out after insect attacks, fire, or wind damage during the growing season.

Multiple rings are quite common in sub-tropical and tropical trees possessing intermittent shoot growth, and a new growth ring often forms corresponding to each new flush of growth. The pattern of growth ring formation in trees possessing the manifold habit of growth (see Chapter I, Section 8a) is highly variable in different parts of the tree because of the non-synchronous growth habit of individual branches. Whether the cambium along the main bole of these trees grows continuously producing indistinct and discontinuous growth rings, or whether it produces numerous multiple rings is not currently known.

Some trees in the tropics never form distinct concentric growth rings, although the cambium may show peak periods of activity alternating with quiescent ones (Antevs, 1917). Apparently the cambia of such trees can begin and cease activity (cell division) without interrupting the processes of cell differentiation so that no differences occur in cell size, cell wall thickness, or cell type during cyclic periods of growth. Whether such trees have never acquired the genetic potentiality of producing growth rings, or whether they have secondarily lost this potential is not presently clear. It is known, however, that cyclic growth is a primitive evolutionary trait and growth rings are characteristic of the wood of *Callixylon* in the Upper Devonian and of many woody species during the Permian.

Most mature trees of the temperate zones which undergo a period of rest produce only one distinct growth layer per season on the lower bole, even though the uppermost shoots may flush more than once. In case of lammas shoot formation or recurrent flashes of growth the young shoots or upper bole near the crown may show multiple rings, but the rings often do not extend the length of the bole. As one would expect, therefore, young trees are more prone to produce multiple rings than older ones because of their vigor and tendency to produce multiple flushes of shoot growth.

Unfortunately much of the physiological research on the mechanism of growth ring formation has been done on seedling trees which are very responsive to various experimental conditions. For example, one can rather easily control the extension growth of young coniferous seedlings by varying the photoperiod, i.e., short vs. long days, whereas, similar treatments on older trees (35–50 yrs.) in the field has little or no effect on shoot extension or growth ring formation (Van Buijtenen, 1955). Coster (1927, 1928) also pointed out that typically deciduous species retained their foliage throughout the year during seedling and sapling stages, but as they became older the leafless period of rest is gradually lengthened. Koriba (1958) and Richards (1942) reported similar observations. The same is frequently observed, in various deciduous trees of the southern United States, especially the juvenile forms of water oak (*Q. nigra* L.) and willow oak (*Q. phellos* L.) which tend to remain evergreen, undergoing multiple flushes of growth during the long growing season.

From these general observations it is possible to recognize three general patterns of growth ring formation in mature trees: 1) those that form only one ring each season under normal conditions of growth; 2) those that commonly form more than one ring each year (multiple rings); and 3) a limited number of species that fail to form distinct growth rings at all. Trees in category one obviously occur most frequently in temperate regions. Those in group two are more prevalent in the sub-tropics and tropics; whereas, the latter group occur mostly in tropical regions possessing a uniform environment and in those trees making continuous growth.

b. Physiology of growth ring formation

One of the early attempts to explain the cause of growth ring formation was made by DeVries (1872, 1875), who believed that an increase in bark pressure during the growing season brought about the mechanical thickening and radial flattening of the cambial cells in summer to produce latewood. DeVries supposedly released the pressure by placing longitudinal slits in the bark in late summer which caused the cambium to revert to the production of thin-walled cells of the earlywood type. In contrast, the application of external pressures to the bark by winding a rope around the tree early in the season caused the formation of xylem resembling latewood. DeVries' arguments seemed so logical that the famous German physiologist Julius von Sachs (1882) devoted a most interesting section to summerwood formation in his *Lectures on the Physiology of Plants* based on these experiments which he considered conclusive.

Krabbe (1882) refuted the ideas of DeVries by showing that the bark pressure was less in summer during latewood formation than during the rapid period of earlywood formation. Moreover, as pointed out by Krabbe, the rapid transition of the wood elements to the last-formed flattened ones is so abrupt in some species that it would be difficult to explain how a sudden pressure could develop to bring about such flattening. He also demonstrated that external pressures of 3–5 atmospheres were required to reduce the radial growth of conifers, which far exceeds the natural bark pressure (Krabbe, 1884). Thus, Krabbe concluded that DeVries' artificially induced "springwood" and "summerwood" were pathological results of injury rather than causal factors in growth ring formation.

After these early observations of DeVries and Krabbe, and for many years to follow, most physiologists held the viewpoint that the environment in which the tree was growing, especially water stress had a direct effect upon what type of wood the tree produced. For example, the seasonal water content of various species usually shows a spring maximum correlated with bud burst and renewed cambial activity; whereas, increased water stress later in the season may often be correlated with cessation of shoot growth and latewood formation. The production of "false" rings, i.e., an additional ring formed in summer following a wet period gave further support to the concept that soil moisture relationships directly affected growth ring formation. Priestley (1930) put forth a rather strong argument that a decreasing water supply and increasing carbohydrate levels brought about the shift to latewood formation and the cessation of cambial activity in dicotyledons. Priestly also noted in ring-porous trees that wide vessels of the earlywood type were normally formed during extension growth, and that smaller vessels along with other elements were formed after the cessation of extension growth.

Most experimental observations on growth ring formation have been conducted with coniferous seedlings mainly because of the simplicity of the xylem, i.e., only one major cell type, the tracheids, need to be studied for changes in lumen size and cell wall thickness.

Experimental control over the sequence of developmental events leading to growth ring formation in conifers, i.e., production, differentiation, and maturation of tracheids has been achieved by such factors as photoperiod and drought. The result of these studies have led several researchers to conclude that the two variables, radial cell diameter and cell wall thickness are independent of each other, although in nature they are commonly associated in growth ring formation (Wodzicki and Witkowska, 1961; Larson, 1962; Zahner and Oliver, 1962). That this is true, may be clearly shown by manipulating photoperiod, light intensity, and water stress so that one can produce tracheids, at least in seedlings and young trees, possessing almost any combination of radial diameter and wall thickness.

During the past decade a considerable body of evidence has accumulated supporting the hormonal control of growth ring formation (Larson, 1960, 1962; Wareing, 1958). This concept relates the production of high levels of diffusible and basipetally transported auxin (IAA) associated with shoot extension and leaf development with the formation of large diameter cells (earlywood) and the cessation of shoot growth accompanied by reduced levels of diffusible auxin with the initiation of latewood formation. Thus, any environmental effect such as drought or temperature would affect growth ring formation indirectly through its more direct effect on shoot growth and leaf extension and the subsequent levels of IAA.

In studying the physiology of growth ring formation in 5-year-old red pine (*P. resinosa*, Ait.) seedlings Larson (1960) used photoperiod as a tool in controlling terminal growth to relate periods of shoot activity with growth and differentiation in the xylem beneath. Under long days (18 hours) he found that shoot growth was prolonged and large diameter cells of the earlywood type continued to be produced. Auxin bioassays showed that the period of rapid shoot growth was also a period of high auxin production. Whenever long-day plants were placed under short-day conditions (8 hours) shoot extension ceased, accompanied by a marked decrease in auxin production, and a transition to the production of xylem cells of the latewood type.

Larson was also able to produce false rings in the xylem by interposing a series of short days into a long day cycle. It is of interest that the false ring could not be induced to form unless an active bud was present; trees decapitated during the short day cycle continued to produce latewood type cells even when returned to long day conditions. If, however, IAA was exogenously applied to the decapitated tips of short day plants, the cambium responded by producing a new zone of earlywood-type cells, even without the subsequent long day stimulus. These correlations between shoot growth, auxin levels, and the type of wood produced are interpreted by Larson (1960, 1962) as direct evidence for hormonal control of growth ring formation.

One of the apparent anomalies of the auxin concept of growth ring formation is that the transition from large diameter earlywood tracheids to flattened latewood tracheids first occurs near the base of the tree and moves acropetally either under natural or experimental conditions; whereas, cessation of cambial activity (cell division) apparently occurs in the reverse direction. Larson (1964) explains the decrease in cell size on auxin gradients along the bole corresponding with developmental stages of shoot and needle extension. For example, during the early surge of growth reactivation in spring, i.e., bursting of buds and rapid shoot elongation, a high level of auxin is present along the entire bole and large diameter earlywood cells are produced. As shoot extension slows down and ceases, the levels of transported auxin begin to decrease so that the cells farthest from the source are affected first, hence the transition to narrow lumen cells begins at the base and extends acropetally as auxin levels decline. For a period of time following the cessation of shoot growth, the needles on the current shoot continue to elongate and this elongation apparently produces enough diffusible auxin to keep the current twigs and upper portion of the bole producing earlywood like cells during most of the season. This would account for the production of juvenile wood with poor growth ring differentiation some distance beneath the crown, a characteristic type of wood found throughout the central core of the tree bole which progresses upward as the tree grows in height. Hence, the cells produced late in the season in the upper bole are more like earlywood than latewood with respect to lumen size or radial diameter. Finally upon maturation of the current needles, the auxin levels drop even lower and cambium activity ceases. Under such a scheme, however, the cambium lower down the bole would have to produce a low but sufficient level of auxin autonomously to continue the formation of latewood, if, as most studies indicate cambial activity (cell divisions) cease first in the twigs and proceeds basipetally. This pattern of activity supports the concept that some type of inhibitor may be produced in the foliage which, when translocated downward, interacts with the levels of auxin, gibberellins, and perhaps other growth factors in bringing about the formation of latewood and the cessation of radial growth. It should be recalled that in the studies of Wareing (1958) and Wareing et al. (1964) that gibberellin had a greater effect in the initiation of cambial activity than auxin (IAA) alone, and it probably continues to play a major role in the process of cell division throughout the season.

It is also of interest that cell-wall thickening, another feature of latewood formation, normally begins at the base of the tree and moves upward although it is not necessarily synchronized with the pattern of cell enlargement previously described. If, however, this aspect of latewood formation is related to net assimulation or reshuttling of photosynthate from the crown to the bole, then one might expect a reverse pattern of cell-wall thickening in older and larger trees. For example, those cells nearest the site of photosynthate production i.e., in the lower crown and upper bole should logically be the first to assimilate this carbohydrate into cell wall material.

Wodzicki (1964, 1965) in studying the formation of latewood in *Larix decidua* Mill., suggests that wall thickness is mediated by the formation of an inhibitor in the foliage during seasonal development. Cell-wall thickening is a function of the rate and duration of cellulose deposition during the process of tracheid differentiation and maturation, and Wodzicki found the levels of water soluble inhibitors in the leaves and cortex of larch and Scots pine (*P. sylvestris* L.) to be more highly correlated with the maturation of xylem cells than decreasing levels of auxin during seasonal development.

Balatinecz and Kennedy (1967) have also followed the seasonal pattern of indolic compounds in 40-year-old European larch *Larix decidua* Mill. in Ontario. They obtained high levels of auxin activity along the bole in spring corresponding with earlywood formation and lower levels during the season accompanied by an increased concentration of a phenolic growth inhibitor and latewood formation. They support the concept that endogenous growth substances control the mechanism of growth ring formation translating the effects of physical environmental factors into biochemical mechanisms of control.

In general, the hormonal and nutritional aspects of growth ring formation as envisioned by several researchers, may be summarized as follows: any condition that enhances bud break, rapid shoot growth, and continued leaf development, results in high levels of auxin production and large diameter cells of the earlywood type. Conversely, low temperatures, drought, or short photoperiods which adversely affect shoot extension and leaf development, lowers the levels of diffusible auxin, and brings about the formation of smaller or radially flattened tracheids of the latewood type. The increase in cell wall thickening usually accompanying, but causally unrelated to cell diameter, may be explained in terms of seasonal assimilation. Environmental factors such as light intensity and temperature through their effects on photosynthesis and respiration directly affect net assimilation and the synthesis of cell wall material.

Although the foregoing summary concerning the physiology of growth-ring formation may logically fit the observed sequence of events in seedlings or young coniferous trees, it seems much too simplified to account for the complicated patterns of cellular differentiation in older trees and especially in angiosperms that produce multiple rings or no rings at all. Auxin is undoubtedly involved in the process of cell enlargement, yet it is difficult to relate the radial flattening of cells throughout the massive boles of mature trees, some of which exceed 100 meters in height, to auxin produced in the elongating shoots or developing leaves of the crown and transported basipetally in proper concentrations along relatively constant gradients. It becomes increasingly more obvious that the seasonal levels of several types of growth promoters, viz. auxin, gibberellins, and cytokinins, operating in the presence of different levels of natural inhibitors, about which we know so little, control the complex physiology of xylem differentiation and growth ring formation.

4. REACTION WOOD

a. Presence and distribution

The orientation of elongating stems in space is brought about by differential longitudinal growth on opposite sides. These tropistic responses, both geotropic and phototropic, have been studied in many plants. In woody plant parts, where secondary growth has begun, such tropistic movements obviously cannot occur because extension growth has ceased. Hence, the orientation of branches and stems possessing secondary tissues must be brought about by some mechanism involving the process of bending.

Whenever young actively growing woody plants are displaced from their normal vertical position, a rapid negative geotropic response occurs in the elongating twig just beneath the apex, followed by a more gradual progressive upward bending of the previous year's growth where stem elongation can no longer occur. In examining the cross-sectional area of such stems, one usually finds a pattern of eccentric growth accompanied by the presence of reaction wood. In general, this eccentric growth is towards the upper side in leaning stems and branches of dicotyledons, but on the lower side in gymnosperms. Because of these differences in position of occurrence, reaction wood in angiosperms is referred to as tension wood; in gymnosperms it is called compression wood.

Anatomically the cellular characteristics of tension wood and compression wood are distinctly different. Compression wood in gymnosperms results from a differential growth response of the cambium, and the tracheids are considerably shorter and more rounded than normal tracheids. Because of their roundness intercellular spaces are formed and the cells develop thicker secondary walls possessing a higher lignin to cellulose ratio (Fig. II-15).

In the initial stages of tension wood formation, the fibers appear normal until an inner gelatinous, unlignified layer of the secondary cell wall begins to differentiate. The protoplast in tension wood fibers continues to lay down a thick gelatinous wall, often convoluted in form, until oftentimes the lumen of the cell is almost completely filled (Fig. II-16). The increase in gelatinous fiber formation is usually accompanied by a marked reduction in the number and size of vessels produced in tension wood (Wardrop, 1964).

Although tension wood may form in some angiosperms without an increase in cambial activity and an accompanying stem eccentricity, an active cambium is essential to reaction wood formation. For example, Wardrop (1956) found that whenever stems of *Eucalyptus* were bent into a horizontal position and the cambium removed from the upper side, reaction wood failed to form beneath the wound and recovery of the stem did not take place. If, however, the cambium were damaged on the lower side of the stem, the stem would recover its normal position. Similar results were obtained with Monterey pine (*P. radiata* D. Don.) if the cambium was damaged or removed on the appropriate side, i.e., compression wood was formed only on the lower side if the cambium was left intact.

b. Causes of reaction wood formation

The differential growth of stems and branches which usually accompanies reaction-wood formation led several early workers to conclude that reaction wood develops as a response to mechanical stress (Metzger, 1908). This viewpoint undoubtedly came about from the observations that the cambium was stimulated into greater activity on the lower side of leaning coniferous stems and on the upper side of horizontally displaced dicotyledonous stems. In either case it was

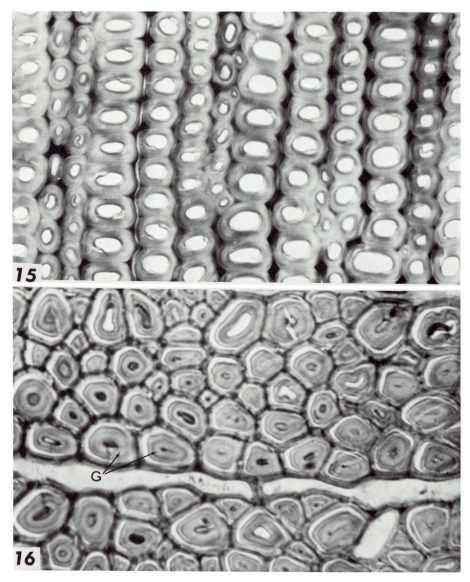

Fig. II–15. Transverse section of compression wood tracheids in *Pinus elliottii* Engl. Note their round shape, thick walls, and frequency of intercellular spaces.

Fig. II–16. Tension wood fibers in transverse section of red maple (*Acer rubrum* L.) stem. Note thickness of the gelatinous layers (G) and its loose attachment to the first formed portion of the secondary cell wall.

assumed that the new change in position of the stem placed the cambium under tensile or compressive forces.

In reality, the weight of displaced stems or horizontal branches is an indirect manifestation of gravitational forces and several workers have long expressed the idea that the formation of reaction wood is a reaction to the influence of gravity rather than tissue stress (Jaccard, 1919; Ewart and Mason-Jones, 1906). Several types of experiments have been performed which substantiate this viewpoint. Jaccard (1938) bent vertical stems into complete loops and observed that the reaction wood always formed on the upper side of the loops irrespective of whether that portion of the stem was under tension or compression (Fig. II-17). Additional evidence that reaction wood is formed under the influence of gravity was obtained

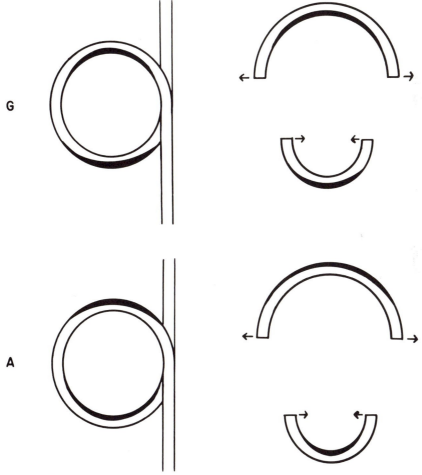

Fig. II–17. (Left) Diagram of the formation of reaction wood in looped stems of gymnosperms (G) and angiosperms (A). (Right) Severed loops of such stems illustrating the direction of movement brought about by compressive and tensile forces established during reaction wood formation. (After Jaccard, 1938).

by Jaccard by placing plants vertically on the perimeter of a horizontally rotating disc. Under slight centrifugal force, the plant stems curved toward the center of the disc. In gymnosperms compression wood formed on the outer side of the stem; in angiosperms tension wood formed on the inner side of the stems. Thus, whenever gravitational forces were replaced by continuous centrifugal forces reaction wood was formed by the upright stems.

Further evidence that gravity is a predominant factor in reaction-wood formation has been obtained by slowly rotating both conifers and angiosperms on horizontal klinostats. Neither compression nor tension wood forms in such experiments (Wershing and Bailey, 1942; Wardrop 1964).

Wardrop (1964) conducted a simple but very clever experiment to show that mechanical stresses were not causally involved in reaction-wood formation by bending the stems of *Tristania conferta* at right angles prior to placing them on a horizontal klinostat. Even after bending, reaction wood was not formed, clearly demonstrating that gravity, and not mechanical stress, was effective in inducing the formation of reaction wood. This is a classic example of how a simply designed yet ingenious experiment solved a controversy of half a century.

A rather unique case of tension-wood formation has been observed in the aerial roots of the sub-tropical fig tree (*Ficus benjamina* L.) by Zimmermann, *et al.* (1968). Aerial roots produced by the branches extend downward to the ground and once anchored begin secondary growth. Initially, and up until the roots reach 10–15 millimeters in diameter, they produce tension wood, after which time normal wood is formed. The aerial roots contract appreciably while producing tension wood as shown by planting the roots in pots during the free hanging stage. During subsequent development they often lift the pot from the ground. The type of tension wood formed by these unusual structures is identical in every respect to the tension wood produced along the upper side of lateral branches.

The vertical upright stems of many dicotyledons (e.g., *Acer rubrum* L.) also produce tension wood without any apparent displacement from their vertical position. The formation of tension wood in such cases does not result from differential growth of the cambium or the apparent influence of gravity on the lateral displacement of auxin. These plants offer an excellent source of material for future investigations on causes of reaction wood formation.

c. The role of hormones in reaction wood formation

As in the case of numerous other growth responses in woody plants, auxin has been postulated either directly or indirectly as the causal factor in controlling the formation of reaction wood. The evidence for the induction of compression wood by IAA in conifers is more direct than the formation of tension wood in the angiosperms. Wershing and Bailey (1942) showed that the asymmetrical application of IAA to the stem of white pine seedlings (*P. strobus* L.) induced the formation of compression wood. Onaka (1949) observed that eccentric growth did not occur in bent stems if the apex was removed or if the stem was completely ringed by an incision. Neither would the stems recover their normal position.

Wardrop (1956) also observed that if a stem was bent out of its vertical position for a period of time and recovery started, it would continue to recover if the apex was removed; however, if the apices were removed prior to bending then the stems would not recover. These experiments suggest that basipetally transported auxin (IAA) coming initially from actively elongating shoots is laterally displaced and accumulates on the lower surface of displaced or bent stems to bring about increased cambial activity and the formation of compression wood. Once the endogenous auxin has moved laterally under the influence of gravity, apparently enough auxin can be produced autonomously by the cambium to bring about recovery of the stem even if the terminal shoot is decapitated. This is the common interpretation of reaction-wood formation in branches under natural conditions, although apparently no good quantitative auxin determinations have been made in this respect.

Nečesaný (1958) studied the distribution of growth substances in artificially bent stems of *Populus alba* L., and found a higher concentration of auxin on the lower side. Wareing *et al.* (1964) were unable, however, to confirm Nečesaný's results in detecting consistent differences in growth promoters (or inhibitors) in extracts from the upper or lower side of poplar or willow branches.

Wareing *et al.* (1964) were able to show that cambial activity *per se* was always stimulated on the upper side of isolated, horizontally-placed stem segments of *Populus* and *Fraxinus* when exogenous IAA, alone, or in combination with gibberellic acid (GA), was applied to the lower half of the stems. Just the opposite response was obtained with stem segments of *Pseudotsuga* and *Larix*. These workers interpreted their results to mean that auxin was somehow redistributed to the upper side of angiosperm stems and to the lower side of gymnosperm stems on the basis of increased cambial activity and the upward re-orientation of xylem elements in the angiosperm stem segments. They did not, however, study the stem segments anatomically for the formation of tension or compression wood corresponding to increased cambial activity.

Wardrop (1964) points out that ring width or the eccentricity of growth in angiosperm twigs does not always correlate with the formation of tension wood. In fact, in some observed cases cambial activity may be greater on the lower side of the twig and typical tension wood still produced on the upper side. In gymnosperms, however, the formation of compression wood is apparently always associated with increased localized cambial activity. Compression wood is often found throughout the vertical stems of conifers in conjunction with spiral grain. Although the actual mechanism of spiral grain formation is still obscure it may, in fact, be highly correlated with increased localized cambial activity causing redistribution of auxin and compression-wood formation.

The concept that low auxin concentration on the upper side of angiosperm stems leads to tension-wood formation is substantiated by the observations of Nečessaný (1958) that the application of IAA to the upper side of twigs suspresses tension-wood formation in *Populus alba* L. Casperson (1963, 1965) also reported that the application of IAA or 2,4-D unilaterally to the erect epicotyls of *Aesculus hippocastanum* L. induced the formation of tension wood on the side opposite the site of application. Thus, he suggested that tension wood is induced in response to an auxin gradient across the stem, and in that portion possessing the lowest auxin concentration. This concept is also supported by the observations of Cronshaw and Morey (1965) that triiodobenzoic acid (TIBA), an auxin antagonist which suspends polar auxin transport, promotes the formation of tension wood when applied to upright twigs of red maple (*Acer rubrum* L.). In other studies by Morey and Cronshaw (1968a, 1968b) where gibberellic acid and TIBA were applied simultaneously to maple stems, the former greatly stimulated cambial activity and more tension wood was formed. If, however, auxin (IAA or NAA) were applied with TIBA and GA the differentiation of tension wood was markedly inhibited. It seems, therefore, that the physiological mechanism for explaining reaction-wood formation is hormonal in nature and is directly related to the relative amounts or balance of auxin on the upper and lower sides of stems. In both angiosperms and gymnosperms gravity somehow affects the distribution of auxin causing a greater accumulation on the lower side of the branch so that these observations are in accord with the experimental evidence that high auxin levels in gymnosperms promotes compression-wood formation, and in angiosperms low auxin levels promote tension-wood formation. It is also pertinent that the distribution of high peroxidase activity in the differentiating xylem elements on the upper side of angiosperm twigs as reported by Wardrop and Scaife (1956) is also found in the walls of differentiating tension wood fibers following their induction by the application of TIBA (Cronshaw and Morey, 1965).

Wareing *et al.* (1964) in studying the intensity of cambial activity on upper and lower sides of isolated stem segments suggested that differential cambial activity may not necessarily be due to a redistribution of auxin, but rather to a differential sensitivity of the cambium on opposite sides. They supported the viewpoint that auxin may move in opposite directions in dicots and conifers on the basis of observations by Hartmann (1942) and Sinnott (1952) that compression wood could form on either upper or lower surfaces of pine branches depending upon the way they were displaced from their normal lateral position. If such branches are moved downward more compression wood is formed on the underside which tends to reorient them to their original position. If similar branches are moved upward, however, compression wood now forms on the upper side of the branch and forces it downward to its original position. A similar but opposite response occurs in angiosperms, i.e., if the branch is pulled up tension wood develops on the lower side; if it is pulled down tension wood develops on the upper side (Wardrop, 1956) (Fig. II-18). The repositioning of a branch pulled up however, requires the presence of a vertically-growing stem in which an epinastic effect is transmitted downward from the dominant apex, so that the balance of auxin, and perhaps other factors, on the upper and lower sides of the lateral branch at any given time are operative in controlling the position of that particular branch. The positioning effect of lateral branches in respect to the main leader is termed *plagiotropism* and has been extensively studied by Münch (1938). It involves both an epinastic control by the dominant apex tending to force the lateral branches downward, and a counter-acting negatively geotropic

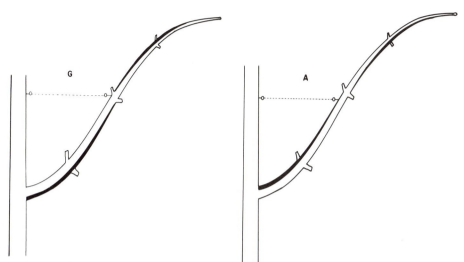

Fig. II–18. Diagram of the repositioning of lateral branches in gymnosperms (G) and angiosperms (A) when pulled upward and held in place by guy wires. In both cases reaction wood forms on the side opposite its normal position due to the epinastic effect exerted by the vertically growing main stem.

effect of the branch which tends to position it towards the vertical (see Chapter III, Section 5a). Thus, the opposite redistribution of auxin as proposed by Wareing *et al.* (1964) for dicots and conifers in isolated stem segments is not comparable to the redistribution of auxin in intact lateral branches still under epinastic control by an actively growing terminal apex. Conversely, the theory of high auxin levels and compression wood formation, or low auxin levels and tension wood formation is, in fact, in accord with the observations of Sinnott (1952) and Wardrop (1956) with dicotyledons. Whenever a branch is pulled upward a higher ratio of auxin accumulates on the upper side because of the epinastic effect, and induces compression wood in conifers on the *upper* rather than lower side, but in angiosperms tension wood forms in the opposite position, i.e., on the lower side as it is supposed to where the auxin concentration is now lower. Although this explanation appears logical from all supporting evidence, the actual proof of such a physiological balance in auxin under natural conditions has not yet been adequately quantified or clearly demonstrated.

5. REGENERATION OF SECONDARY TISSUES

Trees have a remarkable capacity for regenerating lost or damaged parts. This inherent potentiality can be traced to the proliferative ability of parenchymatous cells in various secondary tissues, especially those of the cambial zone and its immediate derivatives. Although any parenchyma cell is theoretically totipotent and capable of de-differentiating to become meristematic, some cells within the cambial zone as well as those undergoing differentiation to form new xylem and phloem elements, are more responsive to treatment than others. For example, the xylem ray cells and vertical xylem parenchyma only a few cells removed centripetally from the xylem mother cell zone are usually refractory to treatment either *in vivo* or *in vitro;* whereas, almost all of the phloem ray cells and vertical parenchyma centrifugal to the cambium will readily proliferate under favorable moisture and temperature conditions. Therefore, the manner in which secondary tissues regenerate following wounding depends largely upon what tissues are exposed to the environment and the external conditions under which regeneration takes place (Noel, 1968). One would expect variations in the pattern of wound healing on debarked stems of different species depending upon where the separation of tissues occurred at the time of wounding or debarking. The pattern of healing even on the same tree trunk may vary during the season for the same reason, e.g., in early spring and summer the bark may separate in the xylem mother cell zone but later in the growing season the separation may occur in the cambial zone or even in the phloem mother cell zone leaving part or all of the cambium attached to the xylem side. Thus, the subsequent patterns of regeneration would differ.

a. Bark regeneration on exposed xylem surfaces

Whenever the bark is removed from the bole of various hardwoods and conifers during the height of cambial activity, the separation often occurs in the xylem mother cell zone leaving the vascular cambium attached to the bark (Fig. II-19). If the tangentially exposed xylem surface is kept moist by covering it with aluminum foil or polyethylene plastic film a relatively uniform wound callus will

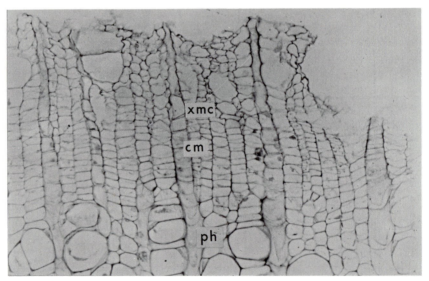

Fig. II–19. Transverse section of bark segment of *Populus trichocarpa* Torr. and Gray removed from the main stem during height of cambial activity. The irregular separation took place in the xylem mother cell (xmc) zone and differentiating xylem leaving the vascular cambium (cm) intact along with the inner phloem (ph) of the bark segment.

rapidly form across the entire surface of the wood. The majority of the callus cells are derived from the proliferating ray cells of the xylem although some of the partially differentiated xylem elements may septate by transverse divisions and contribute some cells to the newly formed callus (Sharples and Gunnery, 1933) (Fig. II-20).

After a period of two to three weeks, depending upon species response, environmental conditions, etc., the callus on the exposed xylem surface may become

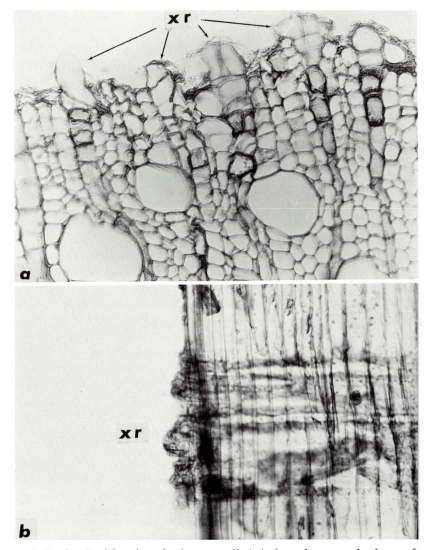

Fig. II–20a, b. Proliferation of xylem ray cells (xr) along the exposed xylem surfaces of a dicotyledon and a conifer. (a) Transverse section of red maple (*Acer rubrum* L.) 48 hours after bark removal; (b) radial section of slash pine (*Pinus elliottii* Engelm.) xylem five days after bark removal. Pine photograph courtesy of E. G. Beck, University of Georgia.

one-two millimeters in radial thickness accompanied by suberization of the outer-most two-three layers of cells which undergo senescence and die. Accompanying these changes, a new cork cambium starts to differentiate at the periphery of the callus in association with the pre-existing cork cambium in the undisturbed bark. Just beneath the newly differentiating cork cambium a new vascular cambium begins to form around the outer periphery of the callus as a continuation of the existing undisturbed vascular cambium. Thus, in viewing the tangentially exposed xylem surface both cork and vascular cambia continue to differentiate centri-petally from the outer margin of the wound until continuity of the cambia is restored throughout the callus.

The newly differentiating vascular cambium becomes recognizable in the callus by the initiation of oriented patterns of cell divisions. Thus, in radial sections one may observe the formation of a narrow zone of meristematic cells which divide periclinally giving rise to radial rows of xylem and phloem mother cells. The cells on either side of the newly differentiated cambium begin to dif-ferentiate into xylary and phloic elements on the inner and outer sides respec-tively.

The first-formed xylem and phloem elements are usually short and abnormal in appearance resembling in size and shape the callus parenchyma cells from which the first cambial cells differentiate (Fig. II-21 a, and b.). Later, as the cambium becomes more highly organized into ray and fusiform initials the ele-ments produced are more elongated and eventually normal xylem and phloem characteristic of the species is produced.

Several hypotheses have been put forth to explain the physiology of cambial regeneration (see review by Wilson and Wilson, 1961). Many researchers have attributed the pattern of cambial differentiation in wound tissue to a hormonal stimulus coming from the existing cambium because in most instances of natural regeneration the newly formed cambium forms adjacent to, and in continuity with the existing undisturbed cambium. If, however, at the time of wounding or debarking, the surface of the xylem around the periphery of the wound is scraped or chiseled out leaving an inner isolated undisturbed wood surface to form a callus, a new cork and vascular cambia will form *de novo* beneath the callus sur-face as observed in *Trema orientalis* (Noel, 1968). A similar pattern of regenera-tion has been observed in *Quercus coccinea* Muenchh., *Acer rubrum* L., *Prunus serotina* Ehrh. and *Pinus echinata* Mill. (unpublished observations of C. L. Brown).

It is apparent, therefore, that the stimulus for the differentiation of cambia in an exposed callus, if hormonal in nature, does not have to be supplied by the existing intact cambium. Wilson and Wilson (1961) proposed a more generalized theory concerning the origin and positioning of regenerating cambia by suggest-ing that some kind of gradient, whether nutritional or hormonal, is established across the callus which determines the exact depth at which the cells will become meristematic. Although the proposal offers little in the way of elucidating the mechanism of cambial differentiation, it provides some objectivity in viewing the concept that auxin, if involved in blocking out the pattern of cambial dif-ferentiation, does not have to come from a pre-existing cambium.

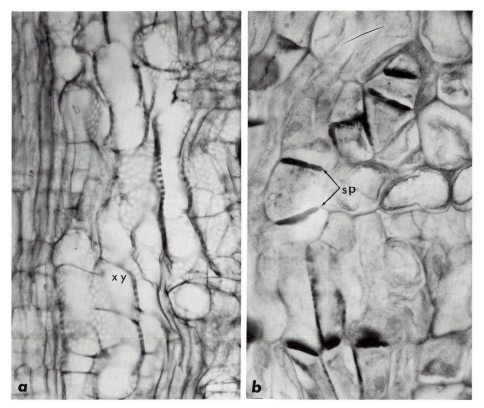

Fig. II–21a, b. Differentiation of (a) xylem and (b) phloem elements in callus tissue adjacent to a newly differentiating cambium as seen in longitudinal section. Note shortened and contorted xylem elements (xy) in (a) and differentiation of sieve plates (sp) with definitive callose along the end walls of the callus parenchyma cells in (b). Callose stained with resorcin blue.

The regeneration of new cambia on exposed or damaged xylem surfaces is of practical value in the care and maintenance of shade or ornamental trees. If, for example, a surface wound on the tree bole is immediately wrapped or covered by polyethylene film, lanolin, or some non-toxic substance, a new bark will regenerate in many species the same season. On the other hand, if the wound is painted or left uncovered the newly exposed parenchyma cells of the xylem are either killed by toxic materials in the paint or die from desiccation. Consequently, healing of the wound proceeds slowly from callus tissues formed from the existing cambial zone around the outer periphery until the yearly centripetal growth of the callus completely covers the exposed xylem (Fig. II-22a).

HEALING OF SEVERED LATERAL BRANCHES. Unfortunately, in pruning limbs from trees, the older ray and xylem parenchyma cells on the exposed transverse surface will not proliferate even if kept moist; therefore the pattern of healing begins by the formation of a callus at the cambial zone around the periphery of the severed branch. The callus then begins to grow centripetally until the branch

Fig. II–22a, b. (a) Healing of surface wound on bole of hickory (*Carya tomentosa* Nutt.). Note how wound callus has become spindle shaped due to more rapid growth of the callus tissue along the longitudinal or vertical axis. (b) Healing of severed lateral branch on bole of pecan (*Carya illinoensis* (Wangenh.) K. Koch). Note also more rapid growth of the callus along the longitudinal axis.

scar is covered. Initially the wound callus formed around a branch is uniform in size and concentric, as the callus continues to grow in successive seasons a vertical polarity is established presumedly under the influence of materials transported in the phloem. Henceforth, the callus on the lateral flanks of the wound grows more rapid than that at the top and bottom resulting in the formation of a spindle-shaped scar tissue (Fig. II-22b).

The differences in the pattern of wound healing between exposed tangential surfaces along the bole and transverse surfaces of severed branches is of interest to the morphogeneticist. The ray and vertical xylem parenchyma cells centripetal to the cambial zone age so quickly that even those cells just centripetal to the xylem mother cell zone fail to proliferate under optimal conditions for growth. In many hardwoods and conifers the ray cells rapidly form secondary cell walls which explains their early loss of proliferative ability, but even in certain conifers where the ray cells do not form secondary cell walls they do not proliferate to form a callus except within or immediately adjacent to the cambial zone. Numerous attempts to obtain proliferation of the older ray cells in xylem explants of one- and two-year-old twigs grown *in vitro* failed in *Acer rubrum* L., *Salix nigra* Marsh, *Populus deltoides* Bartr., *Pinus elliottii* Engelm., *P. palustris* Mill., and *P. strobus l.* Only those ray cells along the exposed tangential surface of the twigs and living pith cells proliferate to form a healthy green callus (unpublished observations of C. L. Brown). How general these observations extend to other genera is not known. The medullary ray parenchyma cells near the pith of a 50-year-old basswood stem (*Tilia americana* L.) were grown in culture by Barker (1953); however, the ray cells along any other portion of the xylem failed to proliferate to form a callus. Ray and vertical parenchyma cells of the phloem, in distinct contrast to those of the xylem, usually retain the ability to proliferate as long as they remain alive.

b. Effects of pressure on differentiation of secondary tissues

The effects of mechanical pressure and spatial relationships on cell proliferation and regeneration of secondary tissues along the inner surface of bark strips have been studied by Brown and Sax (1962). Longitudinal strips of bark (approximately 1.5 cm wide and 8.0 cm long) in *Populus trichocarpa* Torr. and Gray and *Pinus strobus* L. were separated from the tree and left attached at the upper end, encased in a thin-gauge polyethylene bag to prevent desiccation, and either 1) left suspended free, or 2) returned back to their original slot and placed under a membrane pressure of 0.5–1.0 atm. In strips left hanging free, the exposed ray cells in the xylem mother cell zone rapidly proliferated to give rise to most of the callus along the inner bark surface (Fig. II-23a, b). Within 10–20 days the outer cells of the callus became suberized and a new cork and vascular cambium began to differentiate at the outer margins of the strips adjacent to and in continuity with the existing cambia (Fig. II-24). The newly differentiating cambia extended tangentially through the callus from both sides of the strip until continuity of the cambial ring was restored (Fig. II-25). The first formed xylem and phloem elements produced by the original cambium following bark separation, as well as the first elements formed by the newly differentiated cambium, were abnormally short and malformed, but within three to four weeks both tissues became more normal in appearance. Thus, beginning with a thin longitudinal strip of bark separated from the tree and kept moist, a pattern of tissue regeneration occurs which eventually restores a pattern of radial symmetry leading to the development of a new stem. In *Populus,* adventitious buds and roots can be induced to form on such regenerated bark segments giving rise to a new plant.

In those bark strips separated by a layer of polyethylene and placed back against the tree under pressure, the exposed ray cells and some of the vertical elements in the differentiating xylem mother cell zone initially proliferate to form a thin layer of callus along the inner surface of the strip. This proliferation continues until the free spaces along the undulating bark surface are filled with cells. As soon as the callus cells come under mutual pressures cell division ceases, and the elements start to lay down secondary cell walls which become lignified. The original vascular cambium continues to set aside xylem derivatives which

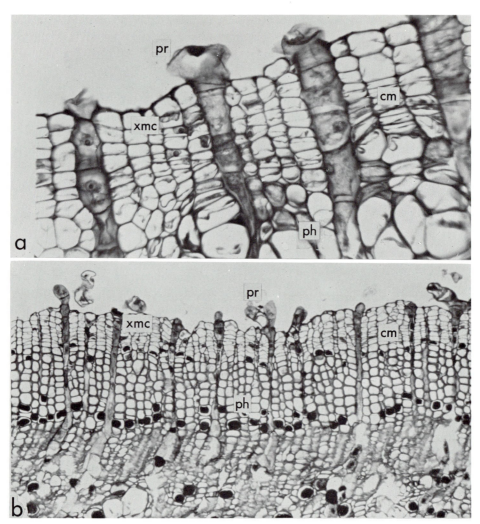

Fig. II–23a, b. Transverse sections of longitudinal bark strips of (a) *Populus tricho-carpa* Torr. and Gray and (b) white pine (*P. strobus* L.) separated from the bole wood but left attached to the parent tree at the upper end for periods of 48 and 72 hours respectively. Note rapid extension and initial proliferation of ray cells (pr) upon release of pressure. Xylem mother cells (xmc), cambial zone (cm), phloem (ph). (From Brown and Sax, 1962).

differentiate as shortened, malformed elements until mutual pressures are restored, after which time normal xylem organization is restored (Fig. II-26).

Some bark strips were allowed to proliferate for 7–10 days prior to placing them back against the tree under pressure. When this is done the applied pressure stops the tangential differentiation of cambia in the callus, and many of the callus cells begin to lay down a thick secondary cell wall which later becomes lignified (Fig. II-27). It is of interest that mechanical pressures of the magnitude

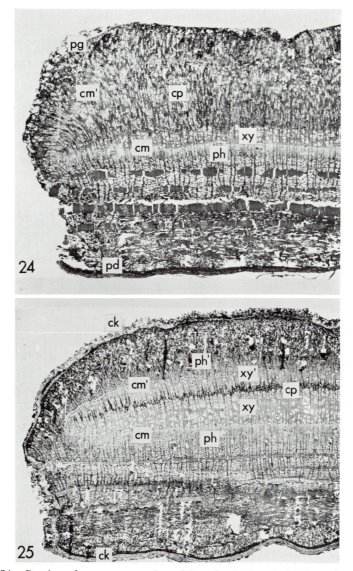

Fig. II–24. Portion of transverse section of *Populus* bark strip 21 days after separation from the bole showing development of extensive callus pad (cp) along inner surface, and the tangential differentiation of a new cambium (cm′) extending from the existing original cambium (cm). Newly differentiated phellogen (pg), xylem (xy) produced after separation from the bole, conducting phloem (ph), and periderm (pd).

Fig. II–25. Portion of transverse section of *Populus* bark strip 60 days after separation from the bole showing continuity of the cambial ring and restoration of a flattened, but radially symmetrical, essentially normal stem. Cork (ck), phellogen (pg), newly differentiated cambium (cm′); original cambium (cm), xylem and phloem respectively produced by the original and newly differentiated cambium (xy, xy′ and ph, ph′), callus parenchyma (cp) trapped in center resembling pith.

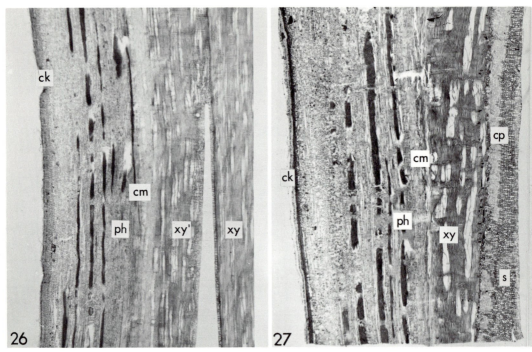

Fig. II–26. Longitudinal section of *Populus* bark strip separated from bole and then placed again under pressure for 30 days. Polyethylene plastic film inserted at zone between xy and xy′ separating bole wood xylem (xy) from xylem formed after bark separation (xy′). Cambial zone (cm), phloem (ph), and cork (ck).

Fig. II–27. Longitudinal section of *Populus* bark strip separated from the bole for 14 days to form a callus pad (cp) and then placed under pressure against the tree bole for an additional 30-day period. Note influence of pressure on differentiation of thick secondary cell walls (s) in the formerly thin-walled parenchyma cells of the callus. Xylem formed after bark separation (xy), cambial zone (cm), phloem (ph), cork (ck).

0.5–1.0 atm. so readily influence the patterns of cellular differentiation, especially when one often observes the upheaval of sidewalks or rupture of building foundations by pressures created through the radial growth of roots and stems.

It is also noteworthy that the vascular cambium along the inner surface of bark strips left attached to the tree does not proliferate, but remains functional as a lateral meristem. One might attribute this to the presence of an outer protective layer of xylem mother cells; however, when similar bark strips are placed on a culture medium containing 2.0 per cent sucrose, major and minor elements, and a low physiological concentration of auxin (0.5 ppm, IAA) the fusiform and ray initials rapidly proliferate disrupting all subsequent organized growth. These same concentrations of nutrients and auxin do not cause loss or proliferation of the cambium when fed to intact stem segments *in vivo* indicating that spatial relationships, pressures, nutrition and growth factors are all involved in maintaining cambial activity and normal differentiation of its derivatives.

6. RADIAL GROWTH OF ROOTS

Information on the seasonal distribution of radial growth in roots is scanty. Although many studies have been made on secondary growth of roots, they have been somewhat sporadic and often subordinate to similar studies on stems. Only recently has a good portion of this information been brought together and amplified by the researches of Fayle (1968).

a. Cambial activation in roots

Most observations concerning the activation of the cambium in tree roots indicate that it proceeds downward from the stem and outward to the root tips. The root tips may have already started extension growth prior to the re-activation of the cambium because the roots of some trees undergo extension growth throughout the winter months (see Chapter I, Section 10). This pattern of cambial activation into the root is of interest because the hormonal stimulus moves acropetally toward, rather than basipetally from, the actively growing tip as it does in stems. Therefore, in contrast to the shoot apex, the root apex apparently exerts little control over the activity of the cambium and the differentiation of secondary tissues proximal to it. One might expect this pattern of activation because the polarity of transport in secondary roots appears to be a continuation of that established in the stem. Although severed lateral roots may continue extension growth for a time, they usually do not undergo secondary growth unless they are connected to other roots by natural grafts or unless root buds are released to supply the root with a source of carbohydrate and growth hormones.

Some workers have occasionally noted that the radial growth of roots may occur sporadically or irregularly if certain environmental conditions are altered. For example, whenever lateral roots are subjected to more favorable temperatures in localized soil areas, the cambium may become active at this point if reserve carbohydrates and endogenous growth factors are adequate. In these instances, however, radial growth proceeds slowly and becomes relatively unimportant because the normal seasonal pattern of growth quickly over-rides such isolated areas of cambial activity.

b. Distribution of growth

The distribution of radial growth at the base of stems and roots leading to the formation of prominent butt swell near the ground line has received the attention of several researchers. Hartig (1891) suggested that foods accumulated at the base of trees because the cambial activation of the roots came later than that of the stem. Von Mohl (1869) was of the opinion that food material accumulated near the base because of the abrupt angles formed between stem and roots at this point, and because roots were subjected to pressures by the soil which impeded rapid movement of assimilates. Other workers have attributed the cambial stimulation and wider growth rings in the root collar zone to stimulation of the cambium because it is under greater mechanical stress at this point.

The width of the growth layer in lateral roots usually tapers from the base of the root toward the apex. This reduction in ring width is often very rapid near the base but decreases more gradually toward the tip. The growth layer at the stem-root junction in most trees is eccentric; the upper portion of the ring is usually thicker than the lower side probably because of the direct continuity of phloem transport on the upper side and the accompanying enhanced nutrition. Beyond the zone of rapid taper near the root base no regular pattern of growth eccentricity occurs. Contrary to what is commonly believed, the growth layer on the lower side of lateral roots is not generally greater than the upper side (Fayle, 1968). Eccentricities in growth distribution along different parts of the root are common because of pressures imposed by the soil and other roots, growth around objects, and the state of vigor of individual roots.

Many interactions occur between shoots and roots affecting ring width and the distribution of growth. Mechanical stresses transmitted to the roots by the weight of the aerial portion, stimulation by swaying (see Chapter III, Section 6a, and Fayle, 1968, pp. 43–45) and the amounts of photosynthates translocated to the roots greatly affect ring width. Local environmental conditions especially those affecting the extension of roots into new soil areas affects the overall vigor of individual trees through increased nutrient and water uptake. One might ask why some lateral roots grow more rapidly in diameter than neighboring roots of the same age. Do the roots with the widest growth layers pull material to them from the stem because of a feed-back mechanism involving mobilization at the root tips, or is their increased size a fortuitous result of a position effect with the stem involving more direct channels of transport?

Whenever portions of lateral roots are exposed to the external environment their growth usually increases because of changes in environmental conditions which enhance cambial activity. For example, soil pressures are decreased whereas aeration, temperature, and light are increased. The latter two seem to have a greater influence on increased radial growth than the first two, and of these, exposure to light seems to exert the most stimulating effect. Although chlorophyll develops in the inner bark upon exposure to light, it is unlikely that localized photosynthate production accounts for the increase in diameter growth. It is likely that some photomorphogenetic reaction occurs bringing about an increase in production of growth factors and a localized mobilization of food reserves. In a few observations by Fayle (1968), light quality had a rather pronounced effect on the root diameter growth of *Pinus sylvestris* L. and *P. banksiana* Lamb. In both species the response to red light was greater than to blue light when applied at essentially the same intensity. Light also has a pronounced effect on the anatomical features of roots (see Section c, below).

From this brief discussion it is obvious that the distribution of growth in root systems and along individual roots depends upon many interacting factors of the shoot and root environment. Internally the relative distribution of growth depends upon carbohydrate supply and food reserves coming ultimately from the stem, water and nutrients supplied by the roots, and regulation of growth by the interaction of exogenously transported growth substances with those produced endogenously by the root.

c. Anatomical observations

Numerous studies concerning the anatomical features of roots may be found in the older literature, and several generalizations can be made contrasting the anatomy of roots with stems. The most striking differences are: (1) pith is absent in the roots of dicotyledonous trees and gymnosperms; (2) the ratio of parenchyma to trachlary elements in the xylem is usually higher in roots and consequently the number of vessels per unit area in hardwoods is usually less; (3) growth rings usually contain less cells than those of the stem and the boundry between successive rings is usually less clearly defined; (4) cells in the root are generally larger, have thinner walls, are less lignified, and possess more pits than those of the stem. The increase in size of root cells including length, as well as radial and tangential diameters, applies to all elements of the xylem, i.e., vessels, fibers, tracheids, and parenchyma (see review by Fayle, 1968).

Because of these structural differences the root wood of hardwoods is much lighter than stem wood, but in conifers the differences in density are not as pronounced. Some of the greatest differences in wood structure between stems and roots occur in the ring-porous angiosperms. The roots of these trees tend to become diffuse-porous with increasing distance from the base.

CELLULAR DIFFERENCES IN LATERAL ROOTS. In general, cell length and diameter, both radial and tangential, increase in a given growth layer from the base of the root toward the tip. The increase in cell size occurs rapidly at the base of the root followed by a gradual increase toward the distal end where a reduction in size often occurs in some roots. Cell-wall thickness decreases along the root with increasing distance from the stem. Thus, with an increase in cell size and a decrease in cell wall thickness the growth layers become less pronounced with distance away from the stem.

These general observations concerning cell dimensions in roots are difficult to explain in terms of auxin gradients along the root. In stems, for example, large cell diameters are commonly associated with high levels of auxin in spring and early summer and smaller diameters with decreasing auxin levels in mid- or late summer (see Section 3b). Therefore, a basipetally decreasing auxin gradient along the stem during summer supposedly brings about the radial flattening of latewood cells. The decrease in cell size occurs first at the base of the stem and then extends upward because a gradual seasonal decline in auxin levels in the crown first affects those cells fartherest away from the source. Because the levels of auxin in the root are apparently maintained by transport from the stem one might expect smaller cell sizes in roots than in stems especially when the level became limiting in late summer. One could argue, however, that the sensitivity of the cambium and its derivatives to auxin is greater in roots than stems as is the case in tropistic responses; hence, the lower levels of auxin that reach the root promotes cellular enlargement. This explanation presents difficulties, however, because of the radial and tangential increase in cell sizes from the base of the root toward the tip. To explain these cellular differences in terms of an auxin mechanism, one would have to propose that the level of auxin in the basal portion of roots is inhibitory and causes a reduction in cell size (although the cells are still larger than those of the stem); whereas, a decreasing auxin gradient toward the root tip becomes optimum for the gradual acropetal increase in cell size. It is likely that factors in addition to auxin levels are operative in controlling cell size and differentiation in roots as well as in stems.

Observations on buried stems and exposed roots make it quite clear that photomorphogenetic mechanisms are involved in the differentiation of cambial derivatives. Buried stems of both hardwoods and conifers rapidly become root-like and exposed roots become stem-like in many anatomical and morphological features. In most instances the changes in anatomy are more pronounced in exposed roots than in buried stems (Fayle, 1968). One particular example will illustrate this point. The wood of ring-porous lateral roots tends to become diffuse-porous under natural conditions, but whenever the roots are exposed to light radial growth is stimulated and the ring-porous condition is restored. This is of particular interest to the morphogenetist because light usually causes a lateral displacement of auxin to the darkened side of a shoot and theoretically the lower level of auxin should cause a diminution in cell size on the light exposed side. In the case of roots however, there is an initial increase in vessel size to restore the ring-porous condition. This, one could argue is again due to the greater sensitivity of roots to IAA, and at lower concentrations the xylem derivatives become larger. It is likely that the causal mechanism is more complex, and it deserves more critical study.

d. Cessation of cambial activity in roots

Observations on the cessation of cambial growth in roots are not always in agreement. Many researchers are of the opinion that the cessation of radial growth is a continuation of the process in stems progressing downward from the shoot apex to the root tip. One of the difficulties in generalizing about the cessation of diameter growth in roots in the existing patterns of variation in root growth from the higher latitudes to the tropics. It has been noted earlier that roots of many trees grow throughout the winter months in the middle and lower latitudes while shoots are at rest or in a quiescent state. In fact, the roots of many hardwoods growing in the south temperate zones and sub-tropics hardly cease diameter growth before the next cycle of radial growth begins; whereas, the roots of other sub-tropical and tropical trees grow continuously with intermittent peaks of high and low activity. Therefore, one should be surprised if the pattern of cessation of cambial activity were the same in all species the world over.

Some workers have reported the cessation of radial growth from the root tip toward the base (Wight, 1933; Onaka, 1950). In such trees the cessation of cambial activity in both stems and roots is basipetal, but opposite in direction, and radial growth ceases last somewhere along the proximal portion of the root. Undoubtedly this pattern of growth cessation exists in some trees. Most workers agree that the cessation of cambial activity is basipetal in stems and whether it extends distally into the root tip apparently varies with species.

LITERATURE CITED

Avery, G. A. Jr., P. R. Burkholder, and H. B. Creighton. 1937. Production and distribution of growth hormone in shoots of *Aesculus* and *Malus,* and its probable role in stimulating cambial activity. Amer. Jour. Bot. 24: 51–58.—Antevs, E. 1917. Die Jahresringe der Holzgewächse und die Bedeutung derselben als klimatischer Indicator. Progressus Rei Bot. 5: 285–386.

Bailey, I. W. 1920a. The cambium and its derivative tissues. II. Size variations of cambial initials in gymnosperms and angiosperms. Amer. Jour. Bot. 7: 355–367.—Bailey, I. W. 1920b. The cambium and its derivative tissues. III. A reconnaissance of cytological phenomena in the cambium. Amer. Jour. Bot. 7: 417–434.—Bailey, I. W. 1923. The cambium and its derivative tissues. IV. The increase in girth of the cambium. Amer. Jour. Bot. 10: 499–509.—Balatinecz, J. J., and R. W. Kennedy. 1967. Mechanism of earlywood-latewood differentiation in *Larix decidua.* Proc. Fourth Forest Biology Conf. TAPPI Pointe Claire, Quebec. 36–55.—Bannan, M. W. 1934. Origin and cellular character of xylem rays in gymnosperms. Bot. Gaz. 96: 260–281.—Bannan, M. W. 1951. The annual cycle of size changes in the fusiform cambial cells of *Chamaecyparis* and *Thuja.* Can. Jour. Bot. 29: 421–437.—Bannan, M. W. 1954. Ring widths, tracheid size and ray volume in stem wood of *Thuja occidentalis.* Can. Jour. Bot. 31: 466–479.—Bannan, M. W. 1955. The vascular cambium and radial growth in *Thuja occidentalis.* L. Can. Jour. Bot. 33: 113–138.—Bannan, M. W. 1956. Some aspects of the elongation of fusiform cambial cells in *Thuja occidentalis.* Can. Jour. Bot. 34: 175–196.—Bannan, M. W. 1957. The relative frequency of the different types of anti-clinal divisions in conifer cambium. Can. Jour. Bot. 35: 875–884.—Bannan, M. W. 1960. Ontogenetic trends in conifer cambium with respect to frequency of anti-clinal divisions and cell length. Can. Jour. Bot. 38: 795–802. —Bannan, M. W. 1962. The vascular cambium and tree-ring development. In: *Tree Growth,* Ed. T. T. Kozlowski. Ronald Press, N.Y. pp. 3–21.—Barghoorn, E. S. 1940a. Origin and development of the uniseriate ray in the Coniferae. Bull. Torrey Bot. Club. 67: 303–328.—Barghoorn, E. S. 1940b. The ontogenetic development and phylogenetic specialization of rays in the xylem of dicotyledons. I. The primitive ray structure. Amer. Jour. Bot. 27: 918–928.—Barghoorn, E. S. 1941. The ontogenetic development and phylogenetic specialization of rays in the xylem dicotyledons. II. Modification of the multiseriate and uniseriate rays. Amer. Jour. Bot. 28: 273–282.—Barghoorn, E. S. 1964. Evolution of cambium in geologic time. In: *Formation of Wood In Forest Trees,* Ed. M. H. Zimmermann. Academic Press, N.Y. pp. 3–17.—Barker, W. G. 1953. Proliferative capacity of the medullary sheath region in the stem of *Tilia americana.* Amer. Jour. Bot. 40: 773–778.—Bowen, W. R. 1963. Origin and development of winged cork in *Euonymus alatus.* Bot. Gaz. 124: 256–261.—Braun, H. J. 1962. Die Organisation des Hydrosystems im Stammholz der Bäume und Sträucher. Ber. Deutsch. Bot. Ges. 75: 401–410.—Braun, H. J. 1963. *Die Organisation des Stammes von Bäumen und Sträuchern.* Wissensch. Verlagsges. Stuttgart.—Braun, H. J. 1964. Zelldifferenzierung im Holzstrahl. Ber. Deutsch. Bot. Ges. 77: 355–365.—Braun, H. J. 1967. Entwicklung und Bau der Holzstrahlen unter dem Aspekt der Kontakt-Isolations-Differenzierung gegenüber dem Hydrosystem I. Das Prinzip der Kontakt-Isolations-Differenzierung. Holzforschung 21: 33–37.—Brown, C. L. 1962. Initiation of cambial activity in diffuse- and ring-porous hardwoods. Proc. Assoc. Sou. Agric. Workers. Jacksonville, Fla. p. 226.—BROWN, C. L., and K. SAX. 1962. The influence of pressure on the differentiation of secondary tissues. Amer. Jour. Bot. 49: 683–691.— BROWN, C. L., and T. J. WODZICKI. 1969. A simple technique for investigating cambial activity and the differentiation of cambial derivatives. For. Sci. 15: 26–29.—BÜSGEN, M. and E. MÜNCH. 1929. *The Structure and Life of Forest Trees.* 3rd ed. Translated by T. Thompson. John Wiley and Sons, Inc., New York.

CASPERSON, G. 1963. Ueber die Bildung der Zellwand beim Reaktionsholz II. Zur Physiologie des Reaktionsholzes. Holztechnologie 4: 33–37.—CASPERSON, G. 1965. Ueber endogene Faktoren der Reaktionsholzbildung I. Wuchsstoffapplikation an Kastanienepikotylen. Planta 64: 225–240.—CHATTAWAY, M. M. 1955. The anatomy of bark. VI. Peppermints. boxes, ironbarks, and other eucalypts with cracked and furrowed bark. Austral. Jour. Bot. 3: 170–176.—COSTER, C. 1927, 1928. Zur Anatomie und Physiologic der Zuwachsszonen und Jahresringbildung in den Tropen. Ann. Jard. Bot. Buitenzorg 37: 49–160. 38: 1–114.—CRONSHAW, J. and P. R. MOREY. 1965. Induction of tension wood by 2,3,5-Triiodobenzoic acid. Nat. 205: 816–818.

DEBARY, A. 1884. *Comparative Anatomy of the Vegetative Organs of Phanerogams and ferns.* Oxford, Clarendon Press.—DEMAGGIO, A. 1966. Phloem differentiation: induced stimulation by gibberellic acid. Sci. 152: 370–372.—DODD, J. D. 1948. On the shapes of cells in the cambial zone of *Pinus silvestris* L. Amer. Jour. Bot. 35: 666–682.

EGGLER, W. A. 1955. Radial growth in nine species of trees in southern Louisiana. Ecology 36: 130–136.—ESAU, K. 1965. *Plant Anatomy.* 2nd ed., John Wiley and Sons, Inc., New York.—EVERT, R. F. 1960. Phloem structure in *Pyrus communis* L. and its seasonal changes. Calif. Univ. Public. Bot. 32: 127–194.—EVERT, R. F. 1961. Some aspects of cambial development in *Pyrus communis.* Amer. Jour. Bot. 48: 479–488.—EVERT, R. F. 1963. The cambium and seasonal development of the phloem of *Pyrus malus.* Amer. Jour. Bot. 50: 149–159.—EWART, A. C. J. and A. G. MASON-JONES. 1906. Observations on the formation of compression wood. Ann. Bot. 20: 201–208.

FAYLE, D. C. F. 1968. Radial Growth in tree roots. Tech. Report No. 9. Faculty of Forestry, University of Toronto, Toronto, Quebec. 183 pp.—FALK, H. and M. N. EL-HADIDI. 1961. Der Feinbau der Suberinschichten verkorkter Zellwände. Ztschr. f. Naturf. 16b: 134–137.

HARTIG, T. 1853. Ueber die Entwickelung des Jahrringes der Holzpflanzen. Bot. Ztg. 11: 553–560, 569–579.—HARTIG, T. 1862. Ueber die Bewegung des Saftes in den Holzpflanzen Bot. Zeit. 20: 73–76, 81–87, 97–100, 105–109.—HARTIG, R. 1885. Holz der deutschen Nadelwaldbäume. Berlin. (quoted from Büsgen and Münch, 1929, p. 100).— HARTIG, R. 1891. Lehrbuch der Anatomie und Physiologie der Pflanzen. J. Springer, Berlin. 308 pp.—HARTIG, R. 1892. Ueber Dickenwachstum und Jahrringbildung. Bot. Zeit. 50: 176–180, 193–196.—HARTMANN, F. 1942. Das statische Wuchsgesetz bei Nadel- und Laubbäumen. Neue Erkenntnis über Ursache, Gesetzmässigkeit und Sinn des Reaktionsholzes. Springer, Vienna. 111 pp.—HOLDHEIDE, W. 1951. Anatomie mitteleuropäischer Gehölzrinden. In: Handbuch der Mikroskopie in der Technik. Band 5. Heft 1. 193–367. Frankfurt am Main, Umschau Verlag.—HUBER, B. 1948. Physiologie der Rindenschälung bei Fichte und Eichen. Forstwiss. Centbl. 67: 129–164.

JACCARD, P. 1919. Nouvelles recherches sur l'accroissement en epaisseur des arbres. Memoire primé et publié par la Fondation Schnyder von Wartensee a Zurich, Switzerland. —JACCARD, P. 1938. Excentrisches Dickenwachstum und anatomisch-histologische Differenzierung des Holzes. Ber. Schweiz. Botan. Ges. 48: 481.—JACKSON, L. W. R. 1952. Radial growth of forest trees in the Georgia Piedmont. Ecology. 33: 336–341.—JACQUIOT, C. 1950. Contribution a étude des facteurs determinant le cycle d'activité du cambium chez quelques arbres forestièrs. Rev. Forst. Franc. 2: 605–619.—JOST, L. 1891. Über Dickenwachstum und Jahresringbildung. Bot. Ztg. 49: 482–499.—JOST, L. 1893. Über die Beziehungen zwischen der Blattentwickelung und der Gefässbildung in der Pflanze. Bot. Ztg. 51: 89–138.—JOST, L. 1907. Lectures on Plant Physiology. Oxford Univ. Press, Oxford. Translated by R. J. H. Gibson.

KASTENS, E. 1924. Beiträge zur Kenntnis der Funktion der Siebröhren. Mitt. Inst. Allg. Bot. Hamburg. 6: 33–70.—KORIBA, K. 1958. On the periodicity of tree growth in the tropics. Garden Bull. Straits Settlements. 17: 11–81.—KRABBE, G. 1882. Sitzber. d. Berliner Akad., LI, p. 1093. (Quoted from Büsgen and Münch, 1929, p. 180).)—KRABBE, G. 1884. Sitzber. d. Berliner Akad. (Quoted from Büsgen and Münch, 1929, p. 181).)—KRAUS, J. F. and R. W. JOHANSEN. 1960. A test of gibberellic acid on longleaf pine. Jour. For. 58: 194.

LADEFOGED, K. 1952. The periodicity of wood formation. Copenhagen. Biol. Skr. 7 (3) : 98 pp.—LARSON, P. R. 1960. A physiological consideration of the springwood-summerwood transition in red pine. For. Sci. 6: 110–122.—LARSON, P. R. 1962. Auxin gradients and the regulation of cambial activity. In: *Tree Growth*. Ed. T. T. Kozlowski. pp. 97–117. Ronald Press, N.Y.—LARSON, P. R. 1964. Some indirect effects of environment on wood formation. In: *Formation of Wood in Forest Trees*. Ed. M. H. Zimmermann. Academic Press, N.Y. pp. 345–365.—LODEWICK, J. E. 1928. Seasonal activity of the cambium in some northeastern trees. N.Y. State Col. Forestry Tech. Publ. 23, 52 pp. Syracuse, N.Y.

MADER, H. 1954. Kork. Handb. der Pflanzenphysiol. 10: 282–299.—METZGER, K. 1908. Konstruktionsprinzip des sekundären Holzkörpers. Naturw. Z. Forst. u. Landwirtsch. 6: 249.—MOHL, H. VON. 1869. Ein Beitrag zur Lehre vom Dickenwachstum des Stammes der dicotylen Bäume. Bot. Ztg. 27: 1–15.—MOREY, P. R. and J. CRONSHAW. 1968a. Developmental changes in the secondary xylem of *Acer rubrum* induced by various auxins and 2,3,5-tri-iodobenzoic acid. Protoplasma 65: 287–313. MOREY, P. R. and J. CRONSHAW. 1968b. Developmental changes in the secondary xylem of *Acer rubrum* induced by gibberellic acid, various auxins and 2,3,5-tri-iodobenzoic acid. Protoplasma 65: 315–326.—MÜNCH, E. 1938. Untersuchungen über die Harmonie der Baumgestalt. Jahrb. f. wiss. Bot. 86: 581–673. (English translation of this paper available on microfilm from: Translation center, John Crerar Library, 35 West 33rd St., Chicago, Ill. 60616) .

NEČESANÝ, V. 1958. Effect of β-indoleacetic acid on the formation of reaction wood. Phyton, Buenos Aires. 11: 117–127.—NELSON, T. C. 1957. Early responses of some southern tree species to gibberellic acid. Jour. Forestry. 55: 518–520.—NOEL, A. R. A. 1968. Callus formation and differentiation at an exposed cambial surface. Ann. Bot. 32: 347–359.

ONAKA, F. 1949. Studies on compression and tension wood. Bull. of the Wood Research Institute, Kyoto Univ., Japan. 1: 1–83.—ONAKA, F. 1950. The effects of such treatments as defoliation, debudding, girdling, and screening of light on growth and especially on radial growth of ever-green conifers. Kyoto Univ. For. Bull. 18: 55–95.

PANSHIN, A. J., C. DE ZEEUW, and H. P. BROWN. 1964. Textbook of wood technology. Vol. 1, 2nd ed. McGraw-Hill Book Company, New York, N.Y. 643 pp.—PRIESTLEY, J. H. 1930. Studies in the physiology of cambial activity III. The seasonal activity of the cambium. New Phytol. 29: 316–354.—Priestley, J. H. and L. I. Scott. 1936. A note upon summer wood production in the tree. Proc. Leeds Phil. Lit. Soc. 3, Pt. 4, 235–248.

Record, S. J. and R. W. Hess. 1943. Timbers of the New World. Yale Univ. Press. New Haven, Conn.—Reimer, C. W. 1949. Growth correlations in five species of deciduous trees. Butler Univ. Bot. Studies 9: 43–59.—Reinders-Gouwentak, C. A. 1941. Cambial activity as dependent on the presence of growth hormone and the non-resting condition of stems. Proc. Ned. Akad. Wetensch. Amst. 44: 654–662.—Richards, R. W. 1942. The Tropical Rain Forest. Cambridge Univ. Press, London. 450 pp.

Sachs, J. von. 1882. Lectures on the Physiology of Plants. Translated by H. M. Ward. Oxford, Clarendon Press. 836 pp.—Sanio, K. 1872. Ueber die Grösse der Holzzellen bei der gemeinen Kiefer (Pinus sylvestris). Jahrb. wiss. Bot. 8: 401–420.—Sanio, K. 1873. Anatomie der gemeinen Kiefer (Pinus silvestris L.) Jahrb. wiss. Bot. 9: 50–126.— Schneider, H. 1955. Ontogeny of the lemon tree bark. Amer. Jour. Bot. 42: 893–905.— Sharples, A. and H. Gunnery. 1933. Callus formation in Hibiscus Rosa-sinensis L. and Hevea brasiliensis Müll. Arg. Ann. Bot. 47: 827–840.—Sinnott, E. W. 1952. Reaction wood and the regulation of tree form. Amer. Jour. Bot. 39: 69–78.—Sitte, P. 1955. Der Feinbau verkorkter Zellwände. Mikroskopie 10: 178–200.—Sitte, P. 1957. Der Feinbau der Kork-Zellwände. In: Die Chemie der Zellwand. E. Treiber. Berlin, Springer-Verlag.— Sledge, W. A. 1930. The rooting of woody cuttings, considered from the standpoint of anatomy. Jour. Pomology and Hort. Sci. 8: 1–22.—Söding, H. 1937. Wuchsstoff und Kambiumtätigkeit. Jahrb. wiss. Bot. 84: 639–670.—Spurr, S., and H. Hyvarinen. 1954. Wood fiber length as related to position in tree and growth. Bot. Rev. 20: 561–575.— Studhalter, R. W., W. S. Glock, and S. R. Agerter. 1963. Tree Growth. Bot. Rev. 29: 245–365.—Swarbrick, T. 1927. Studies in the physiology of fruit trees. I. Seasonal starch content and cambial activity in one- to five-year-old apple branches. Jour. Pomology and Hort. Sci. 6: 137–156.

Tomlinson, P. B. and M. H. Zimmermann. 1969. Vascular anatomy of monocotyledons with secondary growth—an introduction. J. Arnold Arb. 50: 159–179.

Van Buijtenen, H. 1955. Summerwood formation in loblolly pine. Ph.D. dissertation. Agric. and Mechanical College of Texas. College Station, Tex. 82 pp.—Vries, Hugo de. 1872. Über den Einfluss des Druckes auf die Ausbildung des Herbstholzes. Flora. 30: 241–246.—Vries, Hugo de. 1875. Über den Einfluss des Rindendruckes auf den anatomischen Bau des Holzes. Flora. 33: 97–102.

Wardrop, A. B. 1956. The distribution and formation of tension wood in some species of Eucalyptus. Australian Jour. Bot. 4: 152–166.—Wardrop, A. B. 1964. The reaction anatomy of arborescent angiosperms. In: Formation of Wood in Forest Trees. M. H. Zimmermann, Ed. pp. 405–456. Academic Press, New York.—Wardrop, A. B. and E. Scaife. 1956. Occurrence of peroxidase in tension wood of angiosperms. Nature 178: 867.—Wareing, P. F. 1950. Extension and radial growth in trees. Nature 166: 278.— Wareing, P. F. 1951. Growth studies in woody species. IV. The initiation of cambial activity in ring-porous species. Physiol. Plant 4: 546–562.—Wareing, P. F. 1958. The physiology of cambial activity. Jour. Inst. Wood Sci. 1: 34–42.—Wareing, P. F., C. E. A. Haney, and J. Digby. 1964. The role of endogenous hormones in cambial activity and xylem differentiation. In: The Formation of Wood in Forest Trees. Ed. M. H. Zimmermann. 323–344. Academic Press, N.Y.—Wershing, H. F. and I. W. Bailey. 1942. Seedlings as experimental material in the study of "redwood" in conifers. Jour. Forestry. 40:

411–414.—Westing, A. H. 1959. Effect of gibberellin on conifers: Generally negative. Jour. Forestry 57: 120–122.—Wight, W. 1933. Radial growth of the xylem and the starch reserves of *Pinus sylvestris:* a preliminary survey. New Phytol. 32: 77–96.—Wilcox, H., F. J. Czabator, G. Girolami, D. E. Moreland, and R. F. Smith. 1956. Chemical debarking of some pulpwood species. Tech. Pub. N.Y. State Col. Forestry, Syracuse Univ. 77.—Wilson, B. F. 1964. A model for cell production by the cambium of conifers. In: *Formation of Wood in Forest Trees,* Ed. M. H. Zimmermann. 19–36. Academic Press, N.Y.—Wilson, B. F. and R. A. Howard. 1968. A computer model for cambial activity. For. Sci. 14: 77–90.—Wilson, B. F., T. J. Wodzicki, and R. Zahner. 1966. Differentiation of cambial derivatives: proposed terminology. For. Sci. 12: 438–440.—Wilson, J. W., and P. M. W. Wilson. 1961. The position of regenerating cambia—A new hypothesis. New Phytol. 60: 63–73.—Wodzicki, T. J. 1964. Photoperiodic control of natural growth substances and wood formation in larch *(Larix decidua* D. C.) J. Exp. Bot. 15: 584–599.—Wodzicki, T. J. 1965. Annual ring of wood formation and seasonal changes of natural growth-inhibitors in larch. Acta. Soc. Bot. Poloniae 34: 117–151.—Wodzicki, T. J. and L. Witkowska. 1961. On the photoperiodic control of extension growth and wood formation in Norway spruce *(Picea abies* (L.) Karst). Acta. Soc. Bot. Poloniae 30: 755–764.

Zahner, R. 1962. Terminal growth and wood formation by juvenile loblolly pine under two soil moisture regimes. For. Sci. 8: 345–352.—Zahner, R. and W. W. Oliver. 1962. The influence of thinning and pruning on the dates of summerwood initiation in red and jack pines. For. Sci. 8: 51–63.—Ziegler, H. 1964. The storage, mobilization, and distribution of reserve material in trees. In: *Formation of Wood in Forest Trees.* Ed. M. H. Zimmermann. 303–320. Academic Press, N.Y.—Zimmermann, M. H., A. B. Wardrop, and P. B. Tomlinson. 1968. Tension wood in the aerial roots of *Ficus benjamina* L. Wood Sci. and Tech. 2: 95–104.—Zimmerman, W. A. 1936. Untersuchungen über die räumliche und zeitliche Verteilung des Wuchsstoffes bei Bäumen. Ztschr. f. Bot. 30: 209–252.

CHAPTER III

GROWTH AND FORM

Claud L. Brown

INTRODUCTION

Trees, because of their perennial habit, massive size, and morphological diversity, present many intriguing problems of growth and development. They are of special interest to the physiologist due to the many correlations existing between leaves and buds, buds and stems, and stems and roots. From an organizational and functional viewpoint, trees must be considered as much more than an aggregate of twigs and branches attached to a common axis. No one cell, tissue, or organ can influence another without in some way having influenced itself. Such physiological "feed-back" is inherent in the organization of multicellular plants; and trees, because of their continued growth in height and breadth, have been the subject of many interesting morphogenetic studies.

Growth, as we have seen in the previous chapters, does not proceed equally in all directions. Beginning with the very first divisions of the fertilized egg, a specific, inherent polarity is established which leads to continued organized development throughout the life of the plant. Thus, the vascular plant becomes an axiate bipolar structure, with the shoot apex at one end giving rise to leaves and buds in an inherent phyllotaxic pattern, and the root apex at the other producing lateral roots in a manner often peculiar to the species. In this chapter we will look at the many ramifications of growth and form in woody plants in an attempt to gain a better insight into the physiological processes controlling these developmental responses.

1. INHERENT PATTERNS OF GROWTH AND FORM

a. Trees and shrubs

The easily recognized differences between redwoods and mesquite or live oaks and blueberries are so apparent to the casual observer that a discussion of what constitutes a tree or shrub may at first seem pedantic. Yet, there are several distinctions of physiological importance to be made concerning basic differences between these two patterns of growth habit.

Theophrastus, a student of Aristotle, in the third century B.C. attempted a natural system of plant classification based upon trees, shrubs, and herbs. Since that time botanists and foresters have arbitrarily separated trees from shrubs by assigning certain sizes and dimensions to each. In the discussion to follow, we are more concerned with the physiological and morphological relationships resulting in a particular form than we are in establishing criteria to delineate one from the other.

To say that the main differences between trees and shrubs is genetic does not explain the physiological basis for these differences. When one looks at the many different types of woody shrubs, it becomes apparent that their ultimate size and habit of growth may be controlled or modified by vastly different physiological processes or environmental conditions. One cannot generalize by stating that shrubs are smaller than trees because of an initially slower growth rate. In fact, some species of short-lived woody shrubs can successfully compete with, and even outgrow, certain tree species at an early age only to become subordinate a few years later because of a rapid decline in growth rates. In distinct contrast, other shrubs initially possess an extremely slow rate of growth which is maintained throughout their life span.

The shrubby habit of growth has arisen in various ways and may be associated with different physiological mechanisms. Conceivably, either an initially slow rate of growth or a decline in growth at an early age may in some way be linked to fundamental problems of transport in either xylem or phloem, or in both. For example, transport in either tissue could be seriously impaired by the hormonal control of cambial activity resulting in a reduction of xylem and phloem formation. A reduction in phloem transport capacity from leaf to root could limit root extension causing a decrease in water and nutrient uptake with a concomitant reduction in photosynthate so that the potential for height growth is reached at a very early age. One can also think of specific factors that might lead to the shrubby habit in other species. For example, the timing between extension growth and the formation of adequately lignified secondary xylem for mechanical support may result in the formation of drooping or semi-prostrate forms (Fig. III-1). Once a terminal or upright shoot bends out of the vertical, the influence of gravity on rates of transport of growth factors and food is changed. This in turn affects the release of buds from apical dominance (see Section 5b). A continued repetition of this growth pattern causes a sprawling shrubby appearance rather than the upright tree habit.

Other woody plants become shrubby early in life because they sprout profusely near the root collar or produce root suckers at closely spaced intervals along their lateral roots (Figs. III-2, III-3). In these species not only does the genetic potential exist for the formation of numerous adventitious buds, but also the shoot apex loses control over these buds at an early age releasing them from inhibition to form numerous upright stems which successfully competes with the

Fig. III–1. Drooping habit of winter honeysuckle (*Lonicera fragrantissima* Lind. and Paxt.) common to many woody shrubs.

Fig. III–2. Crepe myrtle (*Lagerstroemia indica* L.), a woody ornamental which sprouts profusely from the root collar.

Fig. III–3. A clone of sassafras (*Sassafras albidum* (Nutt.) Nees) formed by the growth of root suckers from lateral roots.

original mother shoot. In due time the later formed shoots give rise to additional sprouts until sizable clumps or clones of woody shrubs are established.

Occasionally the shrubby habit arises by mutation among our common forest trees. A typical example of reversion to a dwarf shrubby habit is shown by the mutant form of sweetgum (*Liquidambar styraciflua* L.) in Fig. III-4a. In this particular case the base of the young plant branched profusely near the root collar giving rise to a network of predominately short shoots comprising most of the crown. Occasionally a short shoot reverts to an intermediate long shoot which grows several inches during one season, then reverts again to the typical short shoot habit. Some of the lateral twigs may extend to a length of only 10–15 cm in 6–8 years (Fig. III-4b). Of particular interest in such mutant forms is the physiological mechanism causing this reversion to the short shoot habit. The physiology of short shoots is eminently associated with auxin and other growth factors; in addition, inhibitors are probably involved. The balance of growth factors and inhibitors at any given locus determines whether a short shoot will remain a short shoot that season or revert to a long shoot for one or more seasons. Dwarf varieties such as the sweetgum shown above should prove very valuable in making comparative studies to determine what histological and physiological differences might account for this expression of form.

Many types of woody shrubs near the timber line are adapted to protection by snow cover in the severe winter months, so that their ultimate size is limited by the depth of snow and severity of winter winds.

Before leaving the subject of trees and shrubs, one can recall that the growth habit of some shrubs can be readily altered by judicious pruning and training of the stems so that small trees or tree-like forms can be maintained for long periods

Fig. III–4a, b. Dwarf mutant form of sweetgum (*Liquidambar styraciflua* L.). (a) Propagule from the original parent tree less than 9 feet tall at 25 years of age. (b) Twigs 10–15 cm in length ranging from 3–8 years of age possessing varying degrees of the short shoot growth habit.

of time. The limitation imposed here is one of genetic potential, because it is obvious that growth can only be enhanced to a certain level even under the most optimal environment. The opposite condition can be environmentally induced by dwarfing normal tree species through repeated pruning, or growing them under severe environmental stress. Many examples can be cited in which trees, when grown out of their normal geographic range or ecological niche, acquire a shrubby or semi-dwarf habit because their genetic potential is limited by the new environment. White spruce (*Picea glauca* L.) that makes a well-formed, valuable timber tree in New Hampshire may well become a shrub at the timber line in northern Canada; whereas, wild cotton (*Gossypium* spp.) which grows as a woody perennial in South America can exist only as a semi-woody annual in the southern United States.

The most vivid examples of induced dwarfism in woody plants is the age-old practice of culturing the Bonsai trees of China and Japan. In such practice an extreme reduction of shoot growth is induced by the careful restriction and confinement of the root systems. Of practical commercial importance, many fruit trees including apples, peaches, pears, and plums, are now dwarfed to varying degrees by grafting or budding the desired variety onto genetically dwarfed rootstocks inducing a shrub-like appearance. This practice restricts vegetative growth and promotes the production of flowers and fruits apparently by holding high reserves of carbohydrates in the above-ground portion of the small trees (Sax, 1962).

b. Leaf arrangement and crown form

The origin of leaves and axillary buds and their arrangement into alternate, opposite, and whorled patterns has been discussed in Chapter I. We mention bud arrangement again at this point because it may significantly contribute to the pattern of growth and form of individual branches and the overall appearance of the tree crown. For example, the repeated forking or false dichotomy of maple and ash crowns usually has a diagnostic value in species recognition because it is at once associated with the opposite arrangement of leaves and buds (Fig. III-5a). Many botanists and foresters are unaware, however, that an almost identical crown appearance can also arise from alternately arranged leaves and buds in certain species (Fig. III-5b). Another anomaly is the distinguishing whorled appearance of the branches in many gymnosperms which nevertheless arise in a very precise alternate pattern (cf. Fig. III-13). Therefore, it is important to recognize that the final form and shape of tree crowns result from many inherent and environmental influences, and similar forms can develop in more than one way by modification of the initial branching habit. This enormous range in the response of trees to their environment makes it difficult to classify or categorize each species on the basis of overall crown appearance, although the growth habit of some trees is so rigidly controlled genetically that they always possess a characteristic shape and form.

Fig. III–5a, b.   Similarity in crown form between certain trees with opposite and alternately arranged leaves and buds. (a) Crown of green ash (*Fraxinus pennsylvanica* Marsh.) showing repeated forking associated with the opposite arrangement of branches. (b) Repeated forking in the crown of pecan (*Carya illinoensis* cv. *Stuart* (Wangenh.) K. Koch) caused by the inhibition and frequent dieback of terminal shoots releasing the alternately arranged branch buds.

2. APICAL CONTROL OF GROWTH AND FORM

a. Columnar, excurrent, and decurrent forms

The form of woody plants is determined by the differential elongation of buds and branches, and the expression of a particular growth habit is commonly associated with the phenomenon of apical dominance. For example, the absence of vegetative lateral buds in most arborescent monocotyledons leads to the columnar growth habit where unbranched stems simply terminate in a tuft of leaves (Fig. III-6a). In most coniferous species and in some dicotyledons the main stem or leader outgrows the lateral branches beneath giving rise to cone-shaped crowns and a clearly defined central bole (Fig. III-6b). This pattern of branching is termed excurrent. In the majority of dicotyledonous trees, notably the oaks, hickories, maples, elms, and many others, the lateral branches grow as fast as, or faster than, the terminal shoot, giving rise to the decurrent or deliquescent growth habit where the central stem eventually disappears from repeated forking to form a large spreading crown (Fig. III-6c).

Fig. III-6a, b, c. The columnar, excurrent, and decurrent growth habit of trees illustrated by (a) the royal palm [*Roystonea alata* (Bartr.) Harper], (b) loblolly pine (*P. taeda* L.) and (c) black walnut (*Juglans nigra* L.)

Most foresters and botanists assume the excurrent branching habit to be an expression of strong apical dominance because the terminal leader maintains control over the branches beneath. Likewise, the decurrent or deliquescent branching habit is usually explained on the basis of weak apical dominance because of the profusely branched crown. Brown *et al.* (1967) pointed out that the physiological mechanism controlling these patterns of growth is more complex than formerly realized, and cannot be simply explained in terms of strong or weak apical dominance as in herbaceous plants. For example, in the excurrent forms most of the uppermost lateral buds on the current year terminal leader are only partially inhibited by the actively growing apex (Fig. III-7a), whereas, in the profusely branched decurrent forms almost all of the lateral buds on the current year shoots are completely inhibited (Fig. III-7b). In the decurrent and deliquescent forms during the second season, after a period of dormancy or occasionally during the current season if lammas shoots are formed, one or more of the uppermost lateral buds elongate as rapidly as, or more rapidly than, the terminal bud giving rise to repeatedly branched stems (Fig. III-8a, b).

The interpretation of crown form on the basis of apical dominance undoubtedly came about by attempting to relate the classical work of Thimann and Skoog (1933, 1934) with *Vicia faba* L. to woody plants without having studied the patterns of bud inhibition on individual tree branches. Because decapitation of bean seedlings leads to branching and the bushy habit of growth, it was assumed that trees with the decurrent or deliquescent branching habit must have lost apical dominance. The disparity between the release of lateral buds on herbaceous plants following decapitation and the natural release of inhibited lateral buds on twigs after over-wintering or following periods of drought is obvious, so the relationship between bud inhibition and form in woody plants is not nearly as simple as it might first appear.

The problem of crown form is confounded because of the time sequence involved in the formation and release of lateral buds. For example, we have recently observed that most axillary buds which undergo a period of winter dormancy in the terminal bud fail to elongate during the following growing season. Usually they remain completely inhibited on the current year's shoot, and it is not until the second spring, following another period of winter dormancy, that some of the most vigorous buds in the uppermost position of the shoot elongate. This observation seems to hold true for all decurrent trees in the temperate zones making one rapid flush of growth early in the growing season and forming new terminal buds which become dormant even under the most optimal external conditions for growth. It is of interest that even in the excurrent angiosperms, such as sweetgum (*Liquidambar styraciflua* L.) and yellow poplar (*Liriodendron tulipifera* L.), the preformed lateral buds overwintering in the terminal bud remain completely inhibited during leader extension the following spring. It is those buds laid down by the apical meristem during the current growing season (late leaves and buds, see Chapter I, Section 2) that elongate immediately beneath the active shoot apex.

There are also decurrent species which grow late into the season producing

Fig. III–7a, b.   Terminal leader of current year's growth in (a) an excurrent conifer, *Taxiodium distichum* var. *nutans* (Ait.) Sweet, and (b) a decurrent dicotyledon, *Quercus rubra* L. Note the extension of almost all lateral buds in the former and the complete inhibition of lateral buds in the latter.

Fig. III–8a, b.   Branched stems of (a) red maple (*Acer rubrum* L.) and (b) pecan (*Carya illinoensis* (Wangenh.) K. Koch) due to the release of the uppermost lateral buds in spring. Note inhibition and suppression of vegetative terminal shoots.

Fig. III–9a, b.   Repeated forking of (a) *Rhus glabra* L. and (b) *Aesculus georgiana* Sarg. due to formation of terminal inflorescenses at an early age.

new leaves and lateral buds which fail to elongate, so that all lateral buds formed during the current and previous season remain completely inhibited. All ring-porous hardwoods we have observed in the temperate zones possess the decurrent branching habit because all of their lateral buds are completely inhibited during shoot extension and leaf development. If growth of these trees occurs late into the season it is by repeated flushes, i.e., the extension of newly formed terminal buds (Lammas shoots), rather than by the continuous formation of late leaves and axillary buds. In contrast, diffuse-porous hardwoods may possess either the excurrent or decurrent branching habit, but the excurrent habit appears to be restricted to those species producing late leaves and buds.

We may briefly summarize our concepts of apical dominance and form in woody plants by stating that the term apical dominance is misleading when applied to tree crowns and that its usage should be restricted to the pattern of bud inhibition on currently elongating individual shoots as originally applied to herbaceous plants. If by definition, the term apical dominance connotes bud inhibition by an active apex on currently elongating shoots, then form in trees must be explained in a manner that will be consistent with the original meaning of the term. Another term, *apical control,* seems better suited for describing the physiological condition governing the excurrent or decurrent pattern of growth. One could then explain the excurrent pattern of growth in terms of strong *apical control* made possible by the initial expression of weak apical dominance or incomplete bud inhibition, so that the terminal leader always maintains complete control over the partially suppressed branches below. Only by this pattern can truly conical shaped crowns arise and be indefinitely maintained. Conversely, strong apical dominance resulting in the complete inhibition of lateral buds on the current year's shoots gives rise to the decurrent habit of growth. The release and rapid growth of two or more uppermost lateral buds the following spring tends to suppress the terminal leader so that apical control is lost and repeated forking occurs in the crown. Although this terminology, viz., *strong apical control* versus *weak apical dominance* and vice versa, may at first seem contradictory, it is consistent with our observations and the general pattern of growth and form in woody plants.

3. MODIFICATION OF FORM WITH AGE

In the preceding section we discussed the general branching habits of trees, i.e., excurrent versus decurrent forms, and their relationship to the phenomenon of apical dominance and the sequence of lateral bud release on individual branches. Although these basic patterns of growth and stem form are inherently controlled by the tree's genetic potential, one must realize that trees are continually exposed to a wide range of environmental conditions during phasic development from juvenility to maturity, modifying crown form in various ways during different stages of development.

For example, *all* forest trees initially possess the excurrent habit of growth for some period during their early development, otherwise none would exist with an unbranched bole for any period of time. The shift from the excurrent to the decurrent form varies in time with species; nevertheless, vigor, competition (open-grown versus densely-grown), and reproductive patterns play important roles in determining at what time the uppermost lateral buds will develop rapidly enough to suppress or outgrow the terminal leader. In some species the shift comes early and abruptly because of the formation of terminal inflorescenses as in sumac (*Rhus glabra* L. and *Aesculus georgiana* Sarg.) (Fig. III-9a and b); whereas, in other species there appears to be a gradual shift in declining vigor of the terminal leader accompanied by a gradual yearly increase in the vigor of the uppermost competing lateral buds as shown in young cottonwood trees (*Populus deltoides* Bartr.) (Fig. III-10).

The shift of excurrent trees to a decurrent form, can also be brought about at an early age whenever such trees are grown on service sites, especially where available moisture becomes limiting for tree growth (Fig. III-11). Also, in overmature conifers, especially in some species of *Pinus,* the crowns become flat-topped and decurrent because of an apparent loss in vigor associated with their massive size, increased competition among branches, and stresses in long range transport of water, nutrients, and food (Fig. III-12). Twigs from the crowns of old trees grafted onto young rootstocks usually "rejuvenate" rapidly with respect to increased growth and vigor, however, they retain the morphological features of old trees with respect to stem size, coarseness of foliage, and reproductive habits (Fig. III-13).

a. Branch angles and crown form

One of the most striking features of tree crowns is the change in orientation of individual branches from the apex toward the base. With few exceptions, one may observe progressive changes in branch angles and position from acutely oriented branches in the upper crown, through horizontally oriented ones near mid-crown, to the lower, less vigorous, drooping branches at the base. Thus, it is seen that the position of individual branches may change considerably during ontogeny, especially during the early stages of rapid growth, so that during the course of tree development a given branch occupies different angles with the vertical axis. If one follows these changes from the beginning of lateral-branch formation, the initial angle of divergence may be rather acute, even in excurrent species where a strong epinastic response is usually operative (see Section 5a). As the branch extends in length it bends downward so that the angle becomes less acute, while the ends being more responsive to light and gravity tend to turn upward again in many species. Burtt (1899) termed the angle produced during the middle course of growth "angle of inclination" and the angle formed by the turned up tip of the branch "geotropic angle."

Büsgen and Münch (1929) discuss the importance of crown from in the distribution of run-off water from precipitation in and around individual trees. Trees having branches with acute angles of inclination collect run-off water toward the center of the crown and near the main bole; those with more horizontal branches favor the movement of water toward the outside of the crown. There-

Fig. III-10. Gradual shift to the decurrent growth habit by a young cottonwood tree (*Populus deltoides* Bartr.) growing in an open field. Note uppermost lateral branches strongly competing with terminal leader which will result in early forking of the main bole.

Fig. III-11. A 35-year-old tulip poplar (*Liriodendron tulipifera* L.) growing on a dry, severe site. Note the early shift to the decurrent growth habit and the repeated forking of lateral branches.

Fig. III-12. Shift from the excurrent to decurrent growth habit of shortleaf pine (*P. echinata* Mill.) associated with age and site limitations.

Fig. III–13. Eight-year-old slash pine *(P. elliottii* Engelm.) clonal seed orchard established by grafting scions from older trees onto two-year-old seedling root stock. Note swelling or over-growth of the root stock at the point of graft union. (Photograph courtesy James Wynens, Georgia Forestry Commission).

fore, in young, small trees with acute angles of inclination much of the intercepted water would stay near the developing root system; whereas, in older trees with spreading crowns the water would be channeled further outward to the zone of finer, absorbing roots.

In excurrent species, branch angles are usually less acute than in decurrent forms. This tendency toward horizontal positioning of lateral branches can be interpreted in terms of strong apical control whereby the terminal leader exerts a pronounced epinastic response to counteract the negative geotropic response of the branch. For this reason the lateral branches of most coniferous species tend to develop perpendicular to the vertical axis (cf. Fig. III-7a).

In decurrent trees where the terminal leader is often suppressed, its epinastic effect is lost and the lateral branches tend to grow upward at more acute angles (see Figs. III-8a, b). Two co-dominant lateral branches growing upward at acute angles tend to exert a mutual epinastic effect on each other. If either is removed by pruning, the remaining leader will assume the vertical position (Fig. III-14).

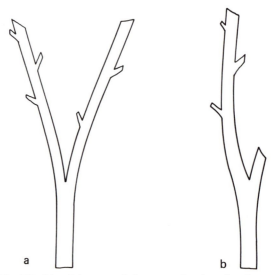

Fig. III–14.   Diagram of the mutual epinastic effect exerted
by lateral branches (a) and the loss of this effect upon removal
of one of the branches (b).

In the profusely branched decurrent trees, many of the uppermost branches, long free from apical control of the main stem at an earlier age, compete with each other for light and growing space and tend to become vertically oriented across the summit of the crown (Fig. III-15). A somewhat exaggerated expression of this condition may be seen in older trees that have been severely pruned (pollarded) which causes the simultaneous release of numerous suppressed or adventitious buds to form an array of upright shoots (Fig. III-16).

Occasionally genetic variants known as fastigiate forms arise in various species in which all branches are formed and tend to persist at acute angles to the vertical axis (Fig. III-17). Such fastigiate variants show a high degree of genetic control over this trait and these forms are often prized as ornamental. However, in selecting superior coniferous phenotypes forest geneticists prefer trees with wide, rather than narrow, branch angles because of the relationships between branch angle and wood quality. Conifers with narrow or acute branch angles are inclined to prune less readily, produce larger knots, and result in greater formation of reaction wood.

b. Juvenile versus adult forms

Many morphological and physiological changes occur in trees during their ontogeny. Plants undergo phasic development in essentially the same way as animals; i.e., they pass through stages of embryonic growth, juvenility, adolescence and maturity, followed by senescence and death. In woody plants these stages are often very pronounced because of their long life cycle. The juvenile stage in trees has received much attention in the past because of the many distinct morphological and physiological changes which occur in the transition from juvenility to sexual maturity. Schaffalitzky de Muckadell (1959) has described

Fig. III–15. Open-grown tree of white oak (*Quercus alba* L.) illustrating the strong negative geotropic response of individual twigs in becoming vertically oriented across the summit of the crown.

Fig. III–16. The release of numerous buds following pruning of a 65-year-old red oak (*Quercus falcata* Michx.). Not how each shoot tends to express dominance and essentially functions as a young individual tree on a common root stock.

Fig. III–17. The Lombardy poplar (*Populus nigra* var. *italica* Muenchh.) with its fastigiate, columnar form is cultivated widely as an ornamental tree.

many of the morphological traits associated with the juvenile habit such as differences in leaf shape and phyllotaxy, growth habit, bark appearance, production of spines or thorns, and retention of leaves by the lower and inner portion of tree crowns Fig. III-18).

Two of the more common physiological traits associated with juvenility are the non-flowering response and rootability of cuttings. Of particular interest is the general observation that each of the traits mentioned so far may be transmitted by vegetative propagation. Although vegetatively propagated offspring from the juvenile stage normally proceed to the adult stage in their normal ontogeny, the duration of the juvenile stage in some trees may persist for 50 years or more (Sax, 1962). Apparently some conifers remain in the juvenile stage for

Fig. III–18. Retention of leaves during the winter months on lower branches of scarlet oak (*Quercus coccinea* Muenchh.), a juvenile trait common to many deciduous hardwoods.

Fig. III–19. A five-year-old tulip poplar (*Liriodendron tulipifera* L.) growing on a dry, severe site in the Georgia Piedmont. This species normally makes strong excurrent growth up until 35–50 years of age on average to better than average sites even in open-grown situations. Note the shift to the decurrent habit during its second and third growing season.

their entire life, such as the "Retinospora" forms of *Thuja* (Beissner, 1930). Woyciki (1954), however, in attempting to produce the "Retinospora" forms from cuttings taken from the juvenile portion of *Thuja, Chamaecyparis,* and *Biota,* found that the juvenile foliage did not persist. He concluded that the "Retinospora" forms arose by somatic mutations in the seedlings or young shoots. Although some controversy may exist over the duration of the juvenile period in these forms, the juvenile condition can be maintained for long periods of time in several plants by vegetative propagation.

Molisch (1930) used the term *topophysis* in describing those cases in which cuttings taken from a certain part of the tree retain the characteristics of that portion of the tree for extended periods of time but which do not involve a genetic change. Thus, in the strictest sense, any juvenile trait which persists for any length of time after grafting or propagation that happens to be related to position, can be termed a topophysis phenomenon. One of the often used examples of a true topophysis effect, not necessarily related to a juvenile characteristic, is the persistence of the flattened, dorsiventral habit of lateral branches from *Araucaria* trees (see Fig. III-26) when grafted into a terminal position. Such branches fail to gain apical control and continue to grow in a horizontal position with respect to gravity. This example is rather atypical, however, because the lateral branches of most trees when grafted onto young rootstock do develop as normal plants.

To foresters the physiological aspects of aging in trees often become of more interest than morphological ones because they directly involve sexual reproduction and rootability. Although it has been claimed by Braddick (1822) that scions from seedling trees can be induced to flower early by grafting them onto older flower bearing branches, many attempts to hasten flowering in fruit trees and forest species have failed (Sax, 1962). The reverse effect has been claimed by Michurin (1949); i.e., that adult flowering branches when grafted onto seedlings promote earlier flowering. These observations have not been widely observed, however, and they remain controversial for the present.

The rooting response of woody plants in relation to juvenility was noted by Goebel (1898) in conifers and has since been confirmed by numerous workers. Most woody plants can be rooted from seedlings, but the ability to form roots seems to decrease rapidly with increasing age. In fact, it is almost impossible to root some conifers even at five years of age, and some fail to root at all even with the application of so-called "rooting hormones" under optimal conditions for propagation where light, humidity, and temperature are controlled.

In some species, cuttings from lateral branches root more easily than those from the upper part of the tree (Thimann and Delisle, 1939); however, this generalization cannot be applied to most adult trees. In young trees the lower branches may retain some degree of physiological juvenility, but in older trees they usually lose vigor and root with difficulty or not at all. The early observations of Knight (1795) that the basal part of the tree retains its juvenility appears, in general, to hold true, and numerous trees that cannot be propagated from the lower lateral or terminal branches can be perpetuated by using stump or root sprouts. In many species these sprouts can be induced to form by partial or complete girdling of the main stem near the ground. There is also some indication that suppressed buds along the lower portion of the bole, when released by girdling to form epicormic branches, retain their juvenile condition with respect to ease of rooting (Kormanik and Porterfield, 1966).

Moorby and Wareing (1963), in reviewing certain aspects of aging in woody plants, referred to these relatively stable (graft transferable) morphological and physiological characteristics as *maturation,* whereas they used the term *aging* in a more restricted sense to describe certain reversible physiological changes occurring during the life of the tree. Some of the changes they studied were reduced annual growth increment, decrease in geotropic responses, and loss of apical dominance. All of these conditions are easily reversible by grafting older scions onto young seedlings.

The results of various pruning experiments conducted on young trees of Scots pine (*Pinus sylvestris* L.) and Japanese larch (*Larix leptolepis,* Sieb. and Zucc.) led Moorby and Wareing (1963) to conclude that these aging processes were directly related to competition for nutrients among individual branches and that apical dominance played an important role in the distribution of available nutrients. Their conclusions were supported by tracing the accumulation of ^{32}P in different aged twigs on 3-year-old branches in association with the pruning treatments.

Although competition for available nutrients is involved in loss of vigor of subordinate twigs and branches, the distribution and availability of water may be just as important in large trees growing under natural conditions. In fact, each of the physiological traits studied by Moorby and Wareing is easily induced even in young plants grown under high soil-moisture stress (Fig. III-19). As mentioned in our discussion on apical control of growth and form, the shift from the excurrent to decurrent branching habit in older trees is associated with massive increases in size; therefore, competition for water and nutrients, coupled with problems of long-distance transport in both directions, undoubtedly influences the vigor and growth patterns of individual shoots. The fact that competition among branches is a significant factor in determining crown form is clearly shown by the higher ratio of short shoots to long shoots with increasing age in tree crowns. Wilson (1966), in a quantitative study of bud and branch distribution in red maple (*Acer rubrum* L.), found that over 90 per cent of the buds in older trees developed as short shoots.

Hence, aging in woody plants involves both permanent and temporary changes in relation to time and position, and these changes can ultimately be traced to the cells of the meristems. What causes these changes in apical and lateral meristems? Some support the viewpoint that the aging of meristems is determined by the materials supplied to it by the rest of the plant. That is, the cells of the meristem themselves do not change or age during the life of the plant, rather the morphological and physiological differences observed between juvenile and adult stages, or in different locations, result from the quality and quantity of the substances reaching the different meristems as the tree grows older and more massive. The distribution of inorganic nutrients, carbohydrates, amino acids, and various growth substances, are known to be influenced by water stress and competition, and some researchers maintain that it is the balance of these factors which determines the various aging phenomena.

Other workers assume that the meristems themselves age; i.e., they undergo change during the life of the plant so that there are young meristems and adult meristems on the same plant. The response of each meristem is still affected by the substances brought to it from the other part of the plant, but the response to any substance may differ because the meristems themselves are different. Evidence can be presented to support either of these viewpoints because some aging traits are readily reversible when the meristems are treated in certain ways, whereas others are stable.

The latter viewpoint appears to be more consistent with the concept of phasic development of plants in which different genes are turned "on" and "off" with varying degrees of difficulty or ease. In adult meristems, the genes controlling form seem more stable than those controlling certain physiological mechanisms, and once "turned on" cannot be reversed to the perhaps less stable juvenile condition. Even some physiologically controlled processes, such as the flowering response, a typical adult trait, are exceedingly stable. Once the genes for the production of "florigen" are turned on, they apparently are difficult to reverse.

The problems of aging in trees are complex and much remains to be learned about the causal mechanisms involved. One might ask, why some cells remain functional for years; whereas others, even in the same plant, exist for only a few hours. Or why the seeds of some trees such as the poplars and willows are short-lived, while those of certain legumes may remain viable for a hundred years or more? The biochemical processes associated with aging, senescense, and death constitute one of the many fascinating areas of biology today.

4. GROWTH CORRELATIONS AND FORM

a. Types of stimulatory and inhibitory responses

The massive size obtained by woody plants is made possible by correlations between extension and radial growth. Extensive shoot and root development can only occur in gymnosperms and dicotyledons if secondary tissue is formed to give mechanical support while providing a bi-directional pathway for long-distance transport of water, nutrients, and foods.

It is clear that growth in one part of a plant affects what occurs in another part and that each must in some way be integrated into an organized whole. This integration is accompanied by various types of physiological correlations in higher plants. Some correlations may be purely nutritional, in which the growth of one part is dependent upon food produced in another. For example, root growth is completely dependent upon food and certain growth factors (vitamins and hormones) produced by the leaves. Similar nutritional correlations are readily observed between leaf area and fruit size, or crown size and stem growth.

Another type of nutritional correlation which involves more than just the transfer of foods and nutrients from one part to the other, can be shown by the removal of mobilization centers. Goebel (1928) described growing organs (shoots, leaves, fruits, etc.) as "attraction centers," which under normal conditions draw to them ions, carbohydrates, and nitrogenous compounds needed for synthesis. If such centers are removed, the growth of remaining meristematic centers is enhanced. This response is referred to as a *compensatory correlation* because of the compensatory increase in the growth of the remaining structures. Horticulturists often take advantage of this compensatory response by mechanically or chemically thinning young fruits so that the remaining ones will grow larger. *Topiary,* the art of training shrubs and trees into unnatural shapes by removal of certain buds to stimulate the growth of others, utilizes compensatory correlations.

Other growth correlations are of a more humoral nature and result in promoting or inhibiting a certain response. For example, growth factors such as auxins, cytokinins, and gibberellins interact with natural inhibitors or with themselves in such a way that the balance of these substances may cause either *stimulatory* or *inhibitory* responses. Young leaf primordia and immature leaves may exert a pronounced stimulatory effect on the elongating internodes beneath apparently through the growth-promoting activity of auxin and auxin precursors they produce. In other cases, leaves are known to exert inhibitory effects on axillary buds, or even the terminal bud of the main shoot (see Chapter I, Section 4c).

One of the best examples of a stimulatory effect of one structure on another is the effect of young, developing ovules on fruit set and size. Nitsch (1950) has clearly shown that the presence of young developing achenes promote the growth of the receptacle in strawberries, and the natural stimulatory effect can be replaced by the application of synthetic auxin to receptacles where the achenes are artificially removed.

Many growth relationships may be traced to inhibitory correlations, i.e., one part inhibits the growth of another by some means other than competition for food. A classical example is the phenomenon of apical dominance in which auxin produced by the actively growing apex or expanding terminal bud inhibits the growth of the lateral buds beneath. In other cases, natural inhibitors produced in one place may also exert their inhibitory effect in another (see Chapter I, Section 8b).

Our present concepts of growth correlations in woody plants are constantly changing by the discovery of additional naturally occurring growth promotors and inhibitors. A few years ago almost all humoral responses were explained solely on the action of naturally occurring auxin, i.e. indole-3-acetic acid; whereas, today workers are beginning to think in terms of growth hormone interactions and levels of different substances in controlling the biochemical machinery of cells and tissues. This should in no way be interpreted to mean that auxin is indirectly involved in correlation phenomena; rather, it points out that growth factors other than auxin are also important in determining what process(es) can proceed at any given time.

b. Relationship between extension growth and radial growth

Some of the early observations on the relationship of stem growth to diameter growth were made by Theodor Hartig (1862) who showed a causal relationship between shoot growth and cambial activity. Later, Jost (1891, 1893) revealed that an ample supply of nutrients did not cause diameter growth unless the cambium was first activated by some stimulus coming from the young growing shoot. Jost demonstrated this by debudding shoots of *Pinus* and *Rhododendron* and observed that even in the presence of leaves the stems did not grow. He also showed that the stimulus was not transmitted below a girdle and that it was always basipetal in nature, being transported through the bark. Coster (1927) confirmed the findings of Jost and interpreted them in terms of a hormonal stimulus. Since this time numerous workers have contributed to our knowledge of cambium activation, yet there are still many questions to be answered about the physiology of cambial activity (see Chapter II, Section 1g).

Münch (1938) extended some of the earlier work on debudding and girdling of young seedlings to older trees and added considerably to our knowledge of the relationships between stem and branch diameter growth at various points along the bole. When Münch began his work in the mid-thirties the general concepts of cambial growth at that time could be summarized as follows: (1) growth hormones were produced in expanding buds and young leaves which not only stimulated growth of the shoot, but also stimulated the cambium into activity in the stem beneath, (2) the movement of the growth hormone(s) occurred in the bark in a basipetal manner, and (3) assimilates moving in the bark could move equally well in both directions and normally to the places where growth was stimulated by the growth hormone itself (Chapter V, Section 2c).

In his early experiments, Münch completely debudded young white pine (*Pinus strobus* L.) trees before the initiation of spring growth and carefully followed the activity of the cambium in the branches and stem beneath. To his surprise, and in contrast to the experiments of earlier workers with angiosperms, the suppression of extension growth by debudding inhibited cambial activity in the young branches and stems but promoted it in the older portion of the tree. A decrease in cambial activity was found only near the shoot tips in the first- and second-year portion; the third-year portion of branches and the main stem was normal or above, and in older portions of the tree bole further down cambial growth was greatly increased over the controls. The effect of debudding caused a downward shift of diameter growth in both stem and branches (Fig. III-20).

In additional experiments, all twigs on another group of white pines were debudded except the weakest twig in the uppermost whorl which quickly became the dominant leader. The former debudded leader grew very little in diameter, whereas the main stem grew equally well and there was no downward shift of cambial activity as in the first experiment. Growth of the stem immediately adjacent to the new leader was quite eccentric however, but a short distance below the eccentricity completely disappeared.

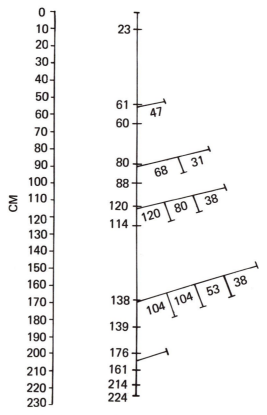

Fig. III–20. Diagram showing the effect of debudding young white pine (*P. strobus* L.) trees on the growth of the main axis and lateral branches. Figures to the left of the stem and beneath the branches indicate diameter increment during the year of debudding as percentage of the previous year's increment (after Münch, 1938).

In other experiments, Münch studied the effects of defoliation alone, as well as defoliation and debudding together, on cambial activity and distribution of growth along the stem. In the completely defoliated trees the buds grew out very slowly to form "brush shoots," and cambial activity was greatly reduced. Apparently the new needles and reserve materials were insufficient to supply the cambium with ample food in these young trees. In trees which were defoliated and debudded at the same time, the cambium failed to become active and no increment was added. This confirmed the observations of Th. Hartig (1862) that completely defoliated and debudded young white pines failed to grow in diameter, although Münch mentioned that Robert Hartig did obtain some diameter growth in older trees following the same treatment.

Because debudding without defoliation in the earlier experiments of Münch caused a downward shift in the amount of diameter growth, additional trees were debudded and girdled near the base to determine if some stimulus were moving upward from the roots through the bark. This treatment had no apparent effect, however, on the downward increase in diameter growth. If such a stimulus came from the roots, it was transported in the xylem.

Also, in the debudding experiments it was noted that the lower lateral branches possessed most of the tree's foliage. The question was raised if the abundance of foliage on the lateral branches directly contributed to the increased growth toward the base following debudding. Pruning of the lower branches of debudded trees did reduce diameter growth all along the bole, but the basal portion still added more increment than the upper part nearest the debudded shoots. In distinct contract, when the lower branches were debudded and the terminals left intact, there was an upward shift in the pattern of growth. The uppermost portion of the bole grew more than the lower, indicating the mobilizing effect of the upper growing shoots on diameter growth in the upper portion of the main stem.

In studying the time course of cambial activity in the control and treated trees, Münch found that the debudded trees stopped growing considerably earlier in the upper portion, but the lower part of the bole grew as late as the controls and even at a greater rate. Thus, not only was the pattern of growth shifted downward by debudding, but the debudded trees had a greater total volume than the controls.

Münch (1938) explained the results of these experiments in terms of both stimulatory and compensatory correlations. Debudding caused a pronounced decrease in the level of auxin in the upper portion of that shoot and a concomitant decrease in diameter growth at that point. The older needles apparently contributed enough auxin to stimulate the cambium into activity beneath. With the mobilizing effect of the uppermost debudded branches removed, the carbohydrate normally attracted to them was free to go elsewhere; hence, the cambium beneath was stimulated into greater activity because of increased nutrition. Some may object to Münch's conclusion that the older needles on debudded twigs of white pine stimulated diameter growth beneath on the assumption that the debudding created a wound response and therefore the formation of auxin; however, Münch pointed out that the cambium of white pine becomes active in early spring long before the buds show any growth. We now know this condition also occurs in ring-porous but not diffuse-porous hardwoods (see Chapter II, Section 1f).

Thus, in looking at growth correlations between extension and radial growth, there is ample evidence that growing shoots have a definite influence on the amount and distribution of growth in the stem beneath. This effect is more noticeable in young trees than in older ones because of problems relating to transport and competition among different branches of massive tree crowns. Although growth factors are produced in copious quantities in young extending shoots, they are also produced in older shoots and leaves and undoubtedly in the cambium itself. The pattern of cambial activity and distribution of growth differs, as we have seen in Chapter II, between ring- and diffuse-porous hardwoods and gymnosperms, the latter being more like the ring-porous hardwoods so that rapid extension growth has less effect on diameter growth in this group than others. Nevertheless extension growth and cambial activity interact to produce the final form of the tree. It is significant that shoot extension has such a direct pronounced effect on secondary activity whereas the cambium has virtually no effect on shoot elongation. This difference in response is only natural because the initiation of secondary activity evolved from, and under, control of the primary plant body.

5. EFFECT OF GRAVITY ON FORM

Gravity, because it is continuous, uniform in intensity, and constant in direction, is one of the most important formative factors in plants. Land plants must constantly regulate their growth with respect to gravity because they are restricted to the site in which they develop. The physiological mechanisms for adapting plants to respond to gravity are relatively simple in some instances but unusually subtle in others. For example, the well known opposite geotropic response of roots and shoots in the young developing plant is attributed to the unilateral displacement of auxin on the lower sides of these organs which causes a rapid differential growth response. Auxin accumulation on the underside of the young epicotyl stimulated the cells to elongate more rapidly in this region thereby causing the stem to turn upward; whereas, in the primary root the cells on the lower side are inhibited resulting in the downward curvature of the young root. This explanation of the geotropic response in young plants has not gone unchallenged by plant physiologists, and the question is often raised as to how auxin (indole-3-acetic acid), in such low physiological concentrations and even in adjacent tissues, can promote growth in one instance and inhibit it in another. The most plausible explanation is that the sensitivity of cells in different tissues differ markedly in respect to auxin action, and one can readily show in the laboratory that the level of auxin which inhibits root growth greatly enhances the growth of shoots. This principle, in fact, has been the basis for developing very sensitive auxin bioassays using excised roots of different species.

Rigid geotropic responses in early life usually become modified as trees become older and more massive in size. One should recognize that a wide range of differences exists in species response; for example, some trees such as the spruces and firs are more responsive to geotropic effects at maturity than many broadleaved trees at a much younger age. The shape or form of the tree crown as already shown is associated with inherent branching patterns which permit an optimal utilization of space and light. Branches do not grow randomly in various directions, but are regulated in their direction of growth by the interaction of gravity and light on internal hormonal mechanisms. Trees with excurrent form exert a high degree of apical control over the direction of growth of the lateral branches beneath. One would expect this condition because strong terminal leaders are more geotropically active or sensitive than first-order branches; and the latter, more responsive to gravity than third- or lower-order branches. In decurrent species with tree crowns consisting of myriads of separate shoots which occupy different angles with the vertical, strong apical control is lacking. In both forms, however, there is a constant regulation of branch angle with respect to gravity and the position of other branches. This regulation and positioning of lateral organs (shoots and roots) in space is termed *plagiotropism*.

a. Plagiotropism

Since the middle of the 19th century, many workers have attempted to answer the questions of why lateral branches grow in a certain direction or in a characteristic pattern in different species, and why branches displaced from their position in respect to gravity respond in a specific way to regain their original position. During the late 1800's numerous observations were made on the responses of lateral branches to decapitation of the terminal leader, and the subsequent growth of such branches when placed in different positions with respect to gravity. From such studies DeVries came to the conclusion that the inclined position of lateral branches was the result of two opposing forces: (1) negative geotropism which tends to erect a twig, and (2) epinasty which tends to depress it.

Following the isolation of the native hormone in plants in the early 1930's, interest was renewed on the mechanism of control of plagiotropic growth in woody plants. Münch (1938), in a series of experiments with several coniferous species (mostly spruces and firs), repeated and confirmed many of the earlier observations of DeVries and extended these observations to different-aged branches along the stem of young trees.

As pointed out by Münch, species differ in their plagiotropic responses. In spruce, fir and other conifers the new extension growth exerts a continuous epinastic effect; i.e., the geotropic response is counteracted from the very beginning of shoot elongation so that the new growth on lateral branches is outward. In the branches of pines the new extending twigs are vertically oriented indicating a strong negative geotropic response and the initial lack of counteracting epinastic response (Fig. III-21a, b). However, in pine, during the growing season, the new extension growth gradually moves downward to the normal position of the branch. This response is referred to by Münch as an example of "delayed epinasty" because the terminal leader or main stem still exerts control over this later movement.

Prior to Münch's published work in 1938, the majority of observations on plagiotropic growth were made on young extending twigs rather than older branches containing secondary xylem. It is important to make this distinction because plagiotropic movements in older branches are controlled by the unilateral formation of reaction wood rather than by the differential elongation of cells in the tropic responses of primary shoots.

From the many experiments conducted by Münch, consistent observations were made that girdling at the base of the leader, as well as debudding, or removal of the leader caused the erection of the lower branches one to two meters below, the degree of erection decreasing with distance from the apex

Fig. III–21a, b. Delayed and continuous epinastic responses in pine and cedar. (a) Strong negative geotropic response of lateral branches in slash pine (*P. elliottii* Engelm.) during extension growth in spring, and (b) continuous outward growth of lateral branches in deodar cedar (*Cedrus deodara* (Roxb.) Loud.).

(Fig. III-22). Following any of the above treatments, an auxillary leader soon forms which in turn epinastically depresses the branches beneath. Thus, Münch concludes that the terminal shoot not only prevents the lower branches from erection, but in effect pushes them down. The epinastic effect coming from the terminal shoot is still effective even when it is covered for an entire season with a black cloth. The girdling experiments performed at different places along the main stem further indicated that the hormonal stimulus controlling epinastic movements is transported downward through the bark, but never upward. This observation led Münch to suggest that the hormone is probably identical to that produced by the young leaves.

As pointed out by Münch, the terminal leader not only affects radial growth on the underside of the stem (i.e., inhibition of excessive compression wood formation), it can also actively depress the branch by promoting the formation of compression wood on the upper side of the branch. Hartmann (1942, 1943) and

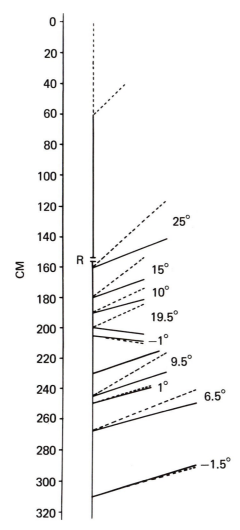

Fig. III–22. Diagram showing the effect of ringing (R) on the erection of lateral branches in young spruce trees. Changes in branch positions at the end of one growing season are indicated with dashed lines (after Münch, 1938).

Sinnott (1952) demonstrated this effect by bending and holding lateral branches out of their normal position. In every case, reaction wood formed on the upperside of the lateral branches bent upward, and on the lower side of those bent downward, thereby the branch is returned to its normal position (see Fig. II-19).

These epinastic responses, at least in conifers, have been either directly or indirectly attributed to the stimulatory effect of auxin which comes from the terminal leader and regulates in some way the amount of reaction wood needed to position the branch in its normal direction with respect to gravity. The manner in which the basipetally transported auxin of the main leader counteracts the endogenously and polarly transported auxin of the lateral branch to check the negative geotropic response of the latter is not easily explained.

Several important questions arise as to the actual pathway of auxin movement into and out of lateral branches. Because the phloem is continuous from the main stem with that of the branches in a manner comparable to the fitting of a glove over the hand and fingers, certain problems of polar auxin transport are encountered. Auxin produced by the young expanding leaves and rib meristems of the extending lateral twig is polarly transported in a proximal direction in primary tissues of the cortex, phloem parenchyma, and pith. In the secondary phloem, polar transport from cell to cell would have to be via the vertical phloem parenchyma, whereas non-polar transport could occur in the sieve elements along with other materials in mass transport. From a histogenic standpoint there seems to be no reason for a disruption of polar transport in the phloem parenchyma from the underside of the branch, but on the upper side two opposing polar systems appear to meet with respect to the phloem parenchyma, the polarity of each tissue being previously determined by their respective shoot axis. This obviously would not prevent the transport of exogenous auxin from the leader or main stem into the upper side of the lateral branch by mass flow in the phloem, but it could logically impede or block the transport of endogenous auxin out of the upper side of the branch. Perhaps only a slight difference in threshold levels of auxin between upper and lower sides is needed to inhibit or promote the formation of compression wood in conifers, and this difference could result from a lateral redistribution of auxin in the phloem parenchyma under the influence of gravity. The explanation of the formation of tension wood in the angiosperms in terms of an auxin-gravity response can also be explained by a similar mechanism (see Chapter II, Section 4b).

b. Gravimorphism

In the previous section we focused our discussion upon geotropic and epinastic responses. These are primarily curvature responses brought about by the unilateral or unequal growth of young twigs or older branches. Gravity, however, is known to have many other formative effects on vegetative growth, and the term *gravimorphism* has been used by Wareing and Nasr (1961) to describe these causal relationships.

Horticulturists have known for a long time that bending the upright shoots of fruit trees out of the vertical and training them in a horizontal or pendent position will promote earlier and heavier flowering and fruiting (Sax, 1962). Foresters and others have also observed for many years the release of buds from inhibition along the uppermost side of wind or ice-thrown trees in the forest. In more recent studies, Wareing and Nasr (1958, 1961) and Wareing and Longman (1958) explored in considerable detail the effects of gravity on extension growth, apical dominance, and flowering in several fruit trees and a conifer, Japanese larch (*Larix leptolepis,* Murr.). When young clonal varieties of apple, plum, and cherry trees were grown in pots in a horizontal position, the total amount of extension growth was considerably less than that of the vertically grown controls. The effect was even greater when the horizontally placed plants were rotated twice daily. Reduction in total length in some species was due to a reduction in both number and length of internodes; in other species it was mainly due to internode length. Flowering was also greatly increased in the clonal varieties of cherry, plum, and apple, and strobili production was much greater in the young Japanese larch trees when grown in a horizontal position.

In these same experiments, Wareing and his co-workers found that apical dominance (apical control) was exerted by the terminal leader only when it occupied its normal vertical position. Placing the terminal leader in an horizontal position had essentially the same effect as decapitation in that the uppermost lateral branch assumed dominance in the vertical position. In addition, there was a marked tendency for lateral buds to extend on the upperside of horizontally placed plants. One can observe the same naturally occurring phenomena in different species of "weeping" woody shrubs and trees. For example, the annual height increment of the weeping willow (*Salix babylonica* L.) is added in a "stair-step" fashion by the release of one or more lateral buds on the summit of the uppermost shoot as it bends over under the influence of gravity (Fig. III-23).

Some interesting observations were made by Wareing and Nasr (1961) on the pattern of bud release in horizontally placed cherry trees when the proximal and distal portions of the main stem were oriented in different positions with respect to gravity. In these experiments none of the current year's lateral buds were released from inhibition in any of the treated trees or controls; rather, two or more buds on the 2-year-old proximal portion of the horizontally placed stems normally extended. From these various treatments it appears that the outgrowth of lateral shoots at the proximal end of the stem is very little affected by the orientation of the distal portion of the main shoot, instead the outgrowth seems to be concentrated in any proximal portion of the shoot deviating from the normal vertical position.

To learn more about this pattern of bud release, Wareing and Nasr (1961) placed complete stem girdles on arched seedlings (i.e., stems of vertically growing seedlings bent over to form an arch) in the following ways: (1) below the summit of the arch, (2) above the summit, but only a few centimeters below the terminal bud, and (3) in both positions. In treatment 1, the laterals grew out below the girdle in about the same way as in non-girdled trees, but the uppermost branch was always the most vigorous, which was not always the case in the non-girdled trees. In treatment 2, the pattern was similar to the non-girdled controls, except a few weak lateral shoots did extend at the distal end just beneath the girdle. When the double girdle was applied in treatment 3, the pattern of bud release was essentially the same as in treatment 2, the upper distal branches being even weaker. It is seen, therefore, that girdling horizontally arched stems had little effect on the basic pattern of bud release.

We have observed similar patterns of bud release along the main bole of older sweetgum trees (*Liquidambar styraciflua* L.) i.e., trees from 10–20 inches in

Fig. III–23. Growth habit of weeping willow (*Salix babylonica* L.) showing release of lateral buds near the summit of the arch in the uppermost pendant branches.

Fig. III–24. Release of suppressed buds all along the bole of a horizontally displaced sweetgum (*Liquidambar styraciflua* L.). Note larger size of branches at the summit of the arch near the ground, the largest of which will remain dominant and develop into an upright tree.

diameter and 40–80 feet tall. Sweetgum trees inherently possess innumerable suppressed buds embedded in the periderm all along the main bole (see Chapter I, Section 7) which can readily be released just below a girdle in upright stems (Kormanik and Brown, 1967). In this species, however, girdling only releases the inhibited buds for a distance of 1–2 feet below the girdle and successive girdles spaced about two feet apart are required to release the majority of inhibited buds. In distinct contrast, similar sized trees when wind or ice-thrown to a near horizontal position release numerous buds and form epicormic branches for some distance along the uppermost side of the main bole (Fig. III-24).

Wareing, in interpreting the results of his experiments on gravimorphism, points out that none of the present day concepts of the mechanism of auxin action in correlative inhibition fully satisfy the patterns of bud release in horizontally placed stems. For example, the hypothesis that buds grow out on the upper side of horizontally placed shoots because of reduced auxin levels does not explain why bud release is primarily restricted to the proximal portion of the stem. Furthermore, the placing of a complete girdle near the distal end of the shoot has little effect on the release of proximal buds; i.e., whether or not basipetally transported auxin from the apex is blocked has little effect on the pattern of bud release on the basal portion of the stem. If the "direct" theory of auxin inhibition of buds (Thimann, 1937) is applied, those buds just beneath the girdle should show optimal vigorous growth. The "indirect" theory of auxin inhibition as proposed by Went (1939) suggests that the topmost bud, because of its higher auxin content, attracts or mobilizes nutrients and food factors to it. This hypothesis is also difficult to reconcile with the fact that there is initially *less* auxin in the buds on the upper side of horizontal shoots. Neither does the nutritional hypothesis proposed by Gregory and Veale (1957) adequately explain the pattern of bud release in these studies.

Wareing and Nasr (1961) were led to the conclusion that the outgrowth of buds in young trees occurs at the point nearest the roots at which the shoot is diverted from the vertical. This indicates, as he suggested, that position effect, itself, is involved in the release of lateral buds from inhibition. Nutrients seem to be diverted into the highest buds on arched stems, and proximity of these buds to the roots appears to be favorable to their release.

We agree with Wareing's conclusion that it is difficult to explain these correlative inhibitions solely in terms of basipetally transported auxin coming from the shoot apex. Perhaps some of the apparent discrepancies relating to apical dominance and bud inhibition in woody plants lie in the fact that we have always attempted to explain correlative growth promotion or inhibition in these plants in precisely the same manner as in herbaceous annuals, failing to realize, however, that the sites of auxin production, type of transport, age of tissues, presence of dormancy periods, and interaction of growth inhibitors are obviously quite different in secondary tissues. For example, in the past some physiologists have indiscriminately used the term apical dominance to include everything from currently inhibited lateral buds by actively growing apices in herbaceous annuals to lateral buds all along the bole of woody stems. Some of the latter have undergone several periods of dormancy and have long been free of the influence of apical dominance, i.e. auxin produced by an actively growing apex during shoot extension. It is surprising how many physiologists still think that all the auxin produced in massive tree trunks can be traced back to the shoot apex in young leaves and elongating twigs. One should realize that actively dividing cells in the cambial zone can produce auxin and other growth factors autonomously, and any metabolically active parenchyma cell may likewise function in this respect but at a much lower level of production. Münch (1938) came to this conclusion over 30 years ago.

In the experiments of Wareing and Nasr (1961) one could hypothesize that gravity caused a shift in the balance of growth factors at the point where the vertically oriented shoot meets the horizontally displaced portion (summit of the arch). As a result, the internal conditions are more favorable for the initial *in situ* production of cytokinins releasing these buds from their inhibition. Once such buds are released from inhibition, synthesis of other growth factors in the rib-meristem of the bud stimulates additional cell division and elongation resulting in rapid shoot extension.

c. Dorsiventral symmetry

In addition to the gravimorphic effects already discussed, gravity also has marked formative effects on the growth and development of radially symmetrical twigs and branches when these are displaced from the vertical in plagiotropic growth. Such twigs tend to assume a dorsiventral symmetry by the secondary twisting or alignment of buds and leaves into a two-ranked position. This condition is very pronounced in such broadleaved trees as beech (*Fagus grandifolia* Ehrh.) (Fig. III-25a,b), alder (*Alnus serrulata* (Ait.) Willd.) mimosa (*Albizia julibrissin*, Durazz.), and other species. The two-ranked habit of lateral branches becomes most pronounced in different genera of the *Coniferae*, viz. *Taxus, Cephalotaxus, Tsuga, Taxodium, Abies, Picea, Araucaria, Cunninghamia*, and *Cedrus* because of the compact arrangement of their twigs and foliage (Figure III-26).

Aside from the tendency of lateral branches to become flattened or two-ranked, the dorsiventrality of shoots may lead to a conspicuous dissimilarity of the leaves borne on the two sides. These differences to which Wiesner (1895) gave the term *anisophylly* are common in many plants and are discussed in length by Goebel (1928). In woody plants, anisophylly is induced by the interaction of gravity and light, and is especially noticeable in many opposite-leaved trees such

Fig. III–25a, b. Dorsiventrality of lateral branches in beech (*Fagus grandifolia* Ehrh.). (a) Horizontal view of lateral branch, (b) view of same branch from above.

Fig. III–26. The perfect dorsiventral symmetry of *Araucaria excelsa* L. branches.

as the maple (Fig.III-27.) In maple the upper leaf of a vertically oriented pair is small, and the lower portion of horizontally oriented leaves is large. Differences in petiole length are very noticeable, and usually attributed more to a light response than to gravity. In many trees with alternately arranged buds and leaves, anisophylly exists by the formation of asymmetric leaves in a regular and predictable pattern. For example, in horizontal branches of elms (Ulmus spp.) the

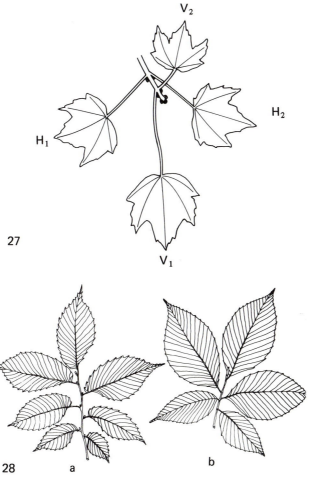

Fig. III-27. Diagram of lateral twig of red maple (*Acer rubrum* L.) showing anisophylly. The vertically oriented pair of leaves (V_1 and V_2) are symmetrical but differ greatly in size. The horizontally oriented pair of leaves (H_1 and H_2) are similar in size, but asymmetrical, the lower half of each leaf is larger than the upper.

Fig. III-28a, b. Differences in asymmetry of leaves in various species. (a) Asymmetric leaves in elm (*Ulmus* spp.) where the inner half of the leaf blade toward the shoot apex is larger and extends further down the midrib. (b) In beech (*Fagus grandifolia* Ehrh.) the outer portion of the blade away from the apex is often larger.

inner half of the leaf directed toward the apex of the branch is larger than the outer portion, and the blade extends further down the mid-rib. In beech, the reverse asymmetry occurs, with the outer part of the leaf being larger (Fig. III-28a, b).

Asymmetric patterns of branch development are also observed in many trees. Commonly, the second-order branches are larger on the outer side away from the apex of the lateral branch. Wiesner (1895) termed this condition *exotrophy* and explained it on the basis of better nutrition. These patterns of asymmetry seem to be induced by shifting a radial system to a dorsiventral one. The actual mechanism through which gravity works appears to involve both hormonal and nutritional growth responses.

The leaves of trees, with a few exceptions, are typically dorsiventral structures because they have evolved in the seed plants to become best adapted for the absorption of light and exchange of gases; i.e., they function best in the production of photosynthate as broad, thin structures oriented at right angles toward incident light. The dorsiventrality of angiosperm leaves is particularly evident in their internal structure, not only in the arrangement of the palisade cells and spongy parenchyma cells but also in the dorsiventral nature of the xylem and phloem. The vascular supply to each leaf passes outward from the primary vascular ring, and in this pattern of differentiation the phloem must necessarily occupy the lower portion of the veins while the xylem occupies the uppermost part in a typical dorsiventral pattern from the very beginning of leaf differentiation.

Roots of trees, even though they develop extensive lateral systems, fail to show distinct dorsiventrality in either external or internal structure. The primary root emerging from the seed, almost without exception, possesses a strong positive geotropic response; however, the lateral roots as they become older and further removed from the primary root system become much less reactive to the effects of gravity. In fact, the direction of growth of roots depends primarily upon the environment to which they are subjected; i.e., they grow into soil areas where water and nutrient availability are highest whenever temperatures are favorable. Hence, their direction of growth may be upward, downward, horizontally, or somewhere in between these extremes (see Chapter I, Section 11a).

6. ENVIRONMENTAL INFLUENCES AND FORM

a. Mechanical forces

During their life history trees are constantly subjected to stresses such as compression and tension brought about by differential rates of growth in the secondary plant body, annual increases in total mass, and the mechanical effects of bending and swaying under the influence of wind. Differential warming and cooling of various tissues and parts of the tree also have a pronounced mechanical effect on expansion and shrinking of tissues.

Numerous studies have been conducted in the past on the effects of longitudinal tension (pulling) and compression (weighting down) of stems in herbaceous plants and, to a lesser extent, in woody plants (Sinnott, 1960). Most of the effects of induced traction and compression are indecisive and contradictory, mainly because researchers used different species in various stages of growth and development where sensitivity to response was neglected. The effects of bending and swaying on the form of plants is more definitive than those of applied tension or compression. Various workers have subjected herbaceous and woody plants to continuous swaying by mechanical devices and found that, in general, the stem axis tends to be elliptical with its wider dimension in the plane of sway (Knight, 1811; Burns, 1920). In these instances, more mechanical tissue, especially secondary xylem, is developed in the treated plants than in the controls.

Jacobs (1954) used a different approach in studying the effects of bending and swaying on the growth of trees by guying the trunk of young Monterey pines (*Pinus radiata* Don.) with wires about 20 feet from the ground so that they could only sway above this point. The portion of the stem above the guy wires which was permitted to sway grew much more rapidly than the portion beneath. When the guy wires were removed, the lower portion of the bole again grew in a normal manner. Swaying, therefore, may in some way stimulate the cambium to divide more, and movement could have an appreciable effect on the bole form of open- versus densely-grown trees. The increased activity of the cambium at the base of the stem resulting in prominent butt swell of many trees is, in part, influenced by mechanical forces such as compression and swaying (see Chapter II, Section 6b).

b. Light

Light, together with gravity, is one of the most important constituents of the environment in determining the course of development in woody plants. The growth and form of trees from the time of seed germination to maturity is directly affected by light intensity, quality and duration. One of the most commonly described effects of high on the direction of growth is the general phenomenon of phototropism. Phototropic responses of individual twigs play an important role in the positioning of branches in the much-branched crowns of decurrent species. Light, gravity, and competition for growing space interact to determine the overall size and shape of tree crowns. That light has a direct formative effect on tree crowns is readily seen by the unilateral growth of branches into openings in the forest canopy created by partial cutting or natural causes.

The direct formative effects of light on leaf and stem structure are well known. Light intensity has much influence on the general structure and morphology of leaves, stems, and roots. Tree seedlings grown in weak light in contrast to full sunlight usually possesses longer internodes; thinner stems; broader, thinner leaves; and poorly developed root systems. Internally, such plants have longer and thinner-walled parenchyma cells, reduced vascular tissues, and weakly lignified tracheary elements.

Thomson's (1954) opinion is that increasing amounts of light accelerates whatever growth processes are taking place. Thus, if rapidly-growing stems are exposed to high light intensity, the light will effect a quicker cessation of cell division and/or cellular elongation, resulting in both a decrease in cell number and size and shorter internodes. Leaves, however, respond differently to stems in these respects and much significance has been attached to the physiological and structural qualities of shade versus sun leaves. The latter are more xerophytic in nature, possess thicker cuticles, more and longer palisade cells, and well-developed vascular tissues (Fig. III-29a, b).

Light quality, i.e. the various wave lengths of light, have been shown to effect these same morphogenetic processes quantitatively. In general, it seems that

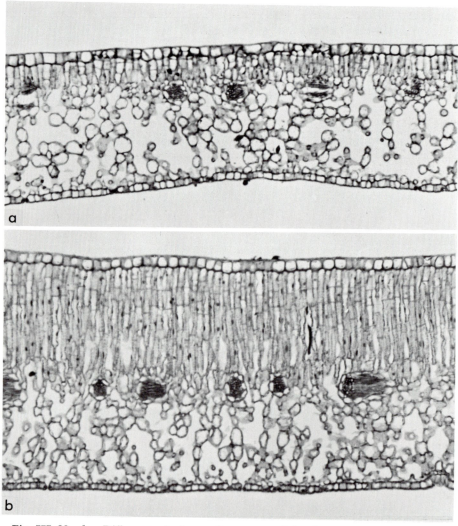

Fig. III–29a, b. Differences in internal structure of (a) shade and (b) sun leaves of cherry laurel (*Prunus caroliniana* (Mill.) Ait.) Note extensive development of palisade layer and vascular tissue in latter. Both 150 x.

blue light hastens the cessation of cell division and elongation to a greater degree than red light, and red light is more effective than far-red; whereas, the greatest cell numbers and lengths are obtained in complete darkness (Theodoresco, 1929; Vince, 1956; LeNoir, 1967). Hence, plants growing in blue light of sufficient energy tend to develop in essentially the same way as those grown in white light, while those grown under red or far-red light tend to develop etiolated characteristics. The morphogenetic effects of light quality have been reviewed by Parker and Borthwick (1950) and Wassink and Stolwijk (1956).

The effect of the daily duration of light, or *photoperiod,* on growth and development in woody plants has been studied extensively in recent years. Because the length of day varies considerably from the tropics to the higher latitudes, it has had a significant adaptive influence on the growth habit of plants. Although there are wide differences among woody plants in their reaction to photoperiod, even among species growing together at the same latitude, photoperiodism has been demonstrated to have a marked effect on many physiological processes involving growth and development. Among these are rate and duration of shoot and diameter growth, breaking of dormancy, cessation of growth, seed germination, leaf abscission, frost resistance, and the flowering response. Although an experimentally imposed photoperiod may have a distinct effect on one or more of the above processes, the same process(es) may not be controlled by photoperiod under natural conditions. Whereas, the cessation of growth of many species in the north temperate zones may be brought about by the shortening day lengths in late summer, the growth of numerous species in the south temperate zones stops long before day length becomes a limiting factor. Likewise, many tropical species respond favorably to long photoperiods even though they have evolved and thrive under a natural short day.

These differences in response to photoperiod may have much practical application to foresters, horticulturists, and others in moving species outside their geographic range. North temperate zoned species whose cessation of growth is controlled by photoperiod cease growth much earlier in the season when moved southward, resulting in an adverse affect on growth rates, vigor, and possible susceptibility to insects and disease (Pauley and Perry, 1954). Conversely, species from the south temperate zones moved northward may likely continue growth under the longer photoperiods of summer and fail to harden off in time to resist injury or death from winter cold.

From a morphogenetic viewpoint, photoperiod becomes important because it affects the total amount of growth through its effects on rates and duration of growth. In the initial epicotyl growth of one-year-old conifers and in those species of angiosperms which grow late into the season by the continued activity of the apical meristem, the increased total amount of extension growth under long photoperiods results from an increased number of nodes as well as greater elongation of internodes. In those species containing all of their preformed nodes in the winter bud, long photoperiods only influence the length of the internodes (Wareing, 1950a, 1950b, 1956). In this latter group, however, long days may bring about continued growth for extended periods in some species by promoting the formation of recurrent flushes of growth. Although this may occur, there is a gradual inhibition of growth in that each successive flush of activity is shorter than the previous one until growth finally ceases even under continuous light. For a more detailed account of these photoperiodic growth responses the reader is referred to the observations of Downs and Borthwick (1956) and Downs (1958, 1962).

In concluding this brief discussion on some of the effects of photoperiod on tree growth, we would like to point out that virtually nothing is known concerning the histogenetic effects of long and short photoperiods on the rates and duration of cell division and elongation in the various internodes of extending shoots.

c. Water stress

The availability of water is the most singly important environmental factor limiting growth and distribution of trees. Almost every physiological process occurring in trees is in some way affected or limited by the availability of water at some critical time during development. Because water relationships and tree growth encompass such a broad field of study, we will of necessity limit our discussion to some of the more important morphogenetic aspects of water on growth and form.

Anyone who has observed trees growing under moisture stress in semi-arid regions or on locally severe sites such as dry ridges, deep sands, or precipitous slopes, has noticed their unusual shrubby appearance due to reduced growth and early loss of apical control. In many cases the tree crowns become knarled and grotesque because of repeated dieback of terminal and lateral branches during recurrent years of severe moisture stress. Tree species that occupy such sites commonly possess structural characteristics collectively referred to as *xeromorphy*. For example, xeromorphic plants tend to have reduced leaf surfaces, heavy cuticles, small and thick-walled cells, increased mechanical tissues, high stomatal frequency, and large root systems. The question often arises as to the adaptive significance of xeromorphic traits because many plants possessing such traits transpire more water than do mesophytes when water is readily available. Likewise, most mesophytes will develop various xerophytic traits, not as an adaptation to drought, but because water is limiting during certain stages of development. Such structural changes occurring during ontogeny are obviously the result of the environment and not an adaptation to conserve moisture. Many studies have been conducted with both herbaceous and woody plants showing that the upper leaves in the crown are more xeromorphic than lower ones even under favorable water regimes, and that these differences become even greater under moisture stress (Zalenski, 1904; Maximov, 1931 and Shields, 1950).

Some of the morphological differences mentioned earlier between sun and shade leaves may also be enhanced by water stress. Leaves on the outside of tree crowns, especially those on the south side in the north temperate zone, are normally more xerophytic in that they are smaller, thicker, and transpire more per unit area than shade leaves from the interior of the crown (Hanson, 1917). Huber

(1926) is inclined to agree that the structure of sun leaves is due, at least in part, to water deficits as well as higher light intensity. Söding (1934) grew tree seedlings under conditions of physiological drought by adding salt to the soil and found that the plants produced leaves very similar to sun leaves.

Another interesting aspect of developmental effects of water on higher plants is the relationship between rate of transpiration and the development of vascular tissues. Because plants grown under high light intensity normally transpire much more and possess considerably more xylem than those grown in shade, the role of transpiration in stimulating xylem development is sometimes raised. Huber (1924), in comparing the amount of water transpired from oak branches growing in the sun with those growing in the shade on the basis of leaf area and cross-sectional area of the stems, found a correlation between the amount of water transpired and size of the vascular system. Huber points out, however, that the rate of water transported through stems is a function of physical forces established in the leaves and resistance to flow in the xylem elements themselves and not simply a function of size (see Chapter IV). It is a well known fact that one may drastically reduce the volume of conducting xylem elements by wounding and not seriously affect the growth and development of the crown. The fallacy of proposing a causal relationship between the amount of water transpired and the cross-sectional area of stems because the two are correlated is comparable to attributing the increased growth of trees on moist versus dry sites to increased rates of transpiration or the total amount of water transpired.

d. Temperature

Temperature, like light, is an important factor in tree growth and development because it influences many physiological activities through its affect on rates of metabolism. Although temperature does have a direct and pronounced effect on the form of trees in certain localities, e.g., on tree growth at the timber line, its formative effects are usually less direct than those of light and water. Our discussion, therefore, will be restricted to a few of the most obvious effects of temperature on development.

Numerous studies of tree growth have been conducted in the higher latitudes of the Scandinavian countries since the turn of the century, and a considerable amount of data is available correlating height and diameter growth of several conifers with mean temperatures during the four summer months (Mikola, 1962).

Hesselman (1904) in Sweden showed over 50 years ago that an excellent correlation existed between the length of the terminal shoot of Scots Pine (*Pinus silvestris* L.) and the mean July and August temperatures of the preceding year. This correlation exists because the total length of shoots in coniferous species is largely dependent upon the number of needles (nodes) it contains in the preformed terminal bud. Therefore, the temperatures during the time of bud formation, i.e. July and August of the previous year, become considerably important. Needle length, in contrast, depends on the climatic conditions existing during their growth, temperature being the most important or limiting factor at or near the timber line. Similar relationships have been found in other temperate zone forest trees that normally make only one rapid flush of terminal growth in spring and early summer (Büsgen and Münch, 1929).

Another aspect of temperature in relation to development in trees is the effect of different day and night temperatures on patterns of shoot growth. The term *thermoperiodism* was used by Went (1948) to describe the reaction of herbaceous plants to different combinations of day and night temperatures.

Kramer (1957, 1958), in studying the response of loblolly pine (*Pinus taeda* L.) and northern red oak (*Quercus rubra* L.) seedlings to different combinations of day and night temperatures, found both species grew best when night temperatures were 6° to 12° C lower than day temperatures. The least shoot growth was made when the seedlings were grown under the same day and night temperature (23°C).

In a similar study, Hellmers (1962) observed that the recurrent flushing of loblolly pine seedlings was closely related to temperature. Increased temperatures, either day or night, caused an increase in the number of flushes (Table III-1).

TABLE III-1

Height Growth of Loblolly Pine Seedlings Grown 64 Weeks from Cotyledon Stage Under Different Day and Night Temperature Combinations. (after Hellmers, 1962).

Day Temperature	Night Temperature		
	7°C.	17°C.	26°C.
	Height in Centimeters		
30°C.	——	52 (6.4)	29 (6.6)
23°C.	60 (4.2)[a]	50 (5.6)	35 (7.0)
17°C.	43 (3.0)	38 (4.1)	——

[a] Numbers in parentheses are the average numbers of flushes of growth produced.

As Hellmers pointed out, while there was a reduction in total height growth with increasing night temperatures, there was also a tendency to form more terminal buds. It has been suggested by Vegis (1956) that high temperatures may induce dormancy or rest in tree buds; but in Hellmer's studies, the highest day and night temperatures (30° and 26° respectively), although reducing total growth significantly, failed to induce dormancy in the buds of loblolly pine.

Hellmers (1962) also found that some forest species were less sensitive to differences in day and night temperatures than they were to a specific day or night temperature regime. For example, redwood seedlings (*Sequoia sempervirens* (D. Don) Endl.) responded significantly to increasing day temperatures up to 23° C, whereas the day-night temperature differential appeared to have little or no effect on top growth. In Digger pine (*Pinus sabiniana* Dougl.) a night temperature of 17° C was more effective on height growth than were increasing day temperatures. In still other species, Hellmers found that the daily heat sum (total daily temperatures) irrespective of application time was more important for total shoot growth.

Thus, it is seen that considerable variation exists in species response to thermoperiodism and considerably more research must be done before its role in nature can be clearly evaluated. Kramer (1958) suggests the possibility that thermoperiodism through its effect on growth, vigor, and competition could have an important influence on the range and distribution of certain species. Although the suggestion is quite plausible, one also must take into consideration the effect of temperature on daily and seasonal CO_2 fixation and rates of respiration in studying growth, reproduction, and distribution of forest trees. The problem is also complicated by interactions between temperature and photoperiodic effects on both vegetative and reproductive development.

LITERATURE CITED

Beissner, L. 1930. Handbuch der Nadelholzkunde, 3rd ed. Paul Parey, Berlin. 765 pp. —Braddick, J. 1822. Trans. Hort. Soc. London. 4: 410–411 (cited in Sax, 1962).— Brown, C. L., R. G. McAlpine, and P. P. Kormanik. 1967. Apical dominance and form in woody plants: A reappraisal. Amer. Jour. Bot. 54: 153–162.—Burns, G. P. 1920. Eccentric growth and formation of redwood in the main stem of conifers. Vermont. Agr. Exp. Sta. Publ. 219: 1–16.—Burtt, H. 1899. Ueber den Habitus der Coniferen. Inaug.-Dissert., Tübingen. Cited from Büsgen and Münch (1929, p. 26).—Büsgen, M. and E. Münch. 1929. *The structure and life of forest trees.* 3rd ed., transl. by T. Thomson. John Wiley and Sons, N.Y. 436 pp.

Coster, C. 1927. Zur Anatomie und Physiologie der Zuwachszonen und Jahresringbildung in den Tropen. Ann. Jard. Bot. Buitenzorg. 37: 49–160.

Downs, R. J. 1958. Photoperiodic control of growth and dormancy in woody plants. In: *Physiology of Forest Trees.* Ed. K. V. Thimann. Ronald Press, N.Y. pp. 529–537.— Downs, R. J. 1962. Photocontrol of growth and dormancy in woody plants. In: *Tree Growth.* Ed. T. T. Kozlowski. Ronald Press, N.Y. pp. 133–148.—Downs, R. J. and H. A. Borthwick. 1956. Effects of photoperiod on the growth of trees. Bot. Gaz. 117: 310–326.

Goebel, K. 1898. *Organography of Plants.* Oxford Press. Part I. 270 pp.—Goebel, K. 1928. *Organographie der Pflanzen.* 3rd ed. G. Fischer. Jena. 642 pp.—Gregory, F. G. and J. A. Veale. 1957. A reassessment of the problem of apical dominance. Soc. Exptl. Biol. Symp. 11: 2–20.

Hanson, H. C. 1917. Leaf structure as related to environment. Amer. Jour. Bot. 4: 533–560.—Hartig, T. 1862. Ueber die Bewegung des Saftes in den Holzpflanzen. Bot. Ztg. 20: 73–76.—Hartmann, F. 1942. Das statische Wuchsgesetz bei Nadel- und Laubbäumen. Neue Erkenntnis über Ursache, Gesetzmässigkeit und Sinn des Reaktionsholzes. Springer, Vienna. 111 pp.—Hartmann, F. 1943. Die Frage der Gleichgewichtsreaktion von Stamm und Wurzel heimischer Waldbaume. Biol. Gen. 17: 367–418.—Hellmers, H. 1962. Temperature effect on optimum tree growth. In: *Tree Growth.* Ed. T. T. Kozlowski. Ronald Press, N.Y. pp. 275–287.—Hesselman, H. 1904. Om tallens höjdtillväxt och skottbildning somrarne. 1900–1903. Meddel fran Statens Skogsförsoksanstalt. L. cited from Mikola (1962).—Huber, B. 1924. Die Beurteilung des Wasserhaushaltes der Pflanze. Ein Beitrag zur vergleichenden Physiologie. Jahrb. wiss. Bot. 64: 1–120.—Huber, B. 1926. Ökologische Probleme der Baumkrone. Planta 2: 476–488.

JACOBS, M. R. 1954. The effect of wind sway on the form and development of *Pinus radiata* Don. Australian Jour. Bot. 2: 35–51.—JOST, L. 1891. Über Dickenwachstum und Jahresringbildung. Bot. Zeit. 49: 485–630.—JOST, L. 1893. Über Beziehungen zwischen der Blattentwicklung und der Gefässbildung in der Pflanze. Bot. Zeit. 51: 89–138.

KNIGHT, T. A. 1795. Philosophical Transactions. 85: 290–295.—KNIGHT, T. A. 1811. On the causes which influence the direction of the growth of roots. Phil. Trans. Roy. Soc. London. 1811: 209–219.—KORMANIK, P. P. and C. L. BROWN. 1967. Epicormic branching: A real problem in plus tree selection. Proc. 9th Sou. Conf. Tree Improve. Public. #28. SFTIC. Macon, Georgia.—KORMANIK, P. P. and E. J. PORTERFIELD. 1966. Rooting yellow poplar cuttings. Forest Farmer 26 (2) : 41–42.—KRAMER, P. J. 1957. Some effect of various combinations of day and night temperatures and photoperiod on the height growth of loblolly pine seedlings. Forest Sci. 3: 45–55.—KRAMER, P. J. 1958. Thermoperiodism in trees. In: *The Physiology of Forest Trees*. Ed. K. V. Thimann. Ronald Press, N.Y. 573–580.

LENOIR, W. C. 1967. The effect of light on the cellular components of polarized growth in bean internodes. Amer. Jour. Bot. 54: 876–887.

MAXIMOV, N. A. 1931. The physiological significance of the xeromorphic structure of plants. Jour. Ecol. 19: 273–282.—MICHURIN, I. V. 1949. *Selected Works*. Foreign Languages Publishing House. Moscow, Russia.—MIKOLA, P. 1962. Temperature and tree growth near the northern timber line. In: *Tree Growth*. Ed. T. T. Kozlowski. Ronald Press, N.Y. pp. 265–274.—MOLISCH, H. 1930. Pflanzenphysiologie als Theorie der Gärtnerei. 6th ed. G. Fischer, Jena. 367 pp.—MOORBY, J. and P. F. WAREING. 1963. Aging in woody plants. Ann. Bot. 27: 291–308.—MÜNCH, E. 1938. Investigations on the harmony of tree shape. Jahrb. wiss. Bot. 86: 581–673. (English translation available on microfilm from: Translation Center, John Crerar Library, 35 West 33rd St., Chicago, Ill. 60616) .

NITSCH, J. P. 1950. Growth and morphogenesis of the strawberry as related to auxin. Amer. Jour. Bot. 37: 211–215.

PARKER, M. W. and H. A. BORTHWICK. 1950. Influence of light on plant growth. Ann. Rev. Plant Physiol. 1: 43–58.—PAULEY, S. S. and T. O. PERRY. 1954. Ecotypic variation of the photoperiodic response in *Populus*. J. Arnold Arbor. 35: 167–188.

SAX, K. 1962. Aspects of aging in plants. Ann. Rev. Plant Physiol. 13: 489–505.—SCHAFFALITSKY DE MUCKADELL, D. 1959. Investigations on aging of apical meristems in woody plants. Kandrup and Wunsch's Bogstrykkeri. Kobenhaven, Denmark.—SHIELDS, L. M. 1950. Leaf xeromorphy as related to physiological and structural influences. Bot. Rev. 16: 399–447.—SINNOTT, E. W. 1952. Reaction wood and the regulation of tree form. Amer. Jour. Bot. 39: 69–78.—SINNOTT, E. W. 1960. *Plant Morphogenesis*. McGraw-Hill, N.Y. 550 pp.—SÖDING, H. 1934. Über die Bendingungen für Entstehung der Sonnenblätter. Ber. Deutsch. Bot. Ges. 52:110–120.

THEODORESCO, E. C. 1929. Observations sur la croissance des plantes aux lumières de diverse longueurs d'onde. Ann Sci. Nat. Bot. X, 11: 201–336.—THIMANN, K. V. 1937. On the nature of inhibitions caused by auxin. Amer. Jour. Bot. 24: 407–412.—THIMANN, K. V. and A. L. DELISLE. 1939. The vegetative propagation of difficult plants. Jour. Arnold Arboretum. 20: 116–136.—THIMANN, K. V. and F. SKOOG. 1933. Studies on the growth hormone of plants. III. The inhibiting action of the growth substance of bud development. Proc. Nat. Acad. Sci. 19: 714–716.—THIMANN, K. V. and F. SKOOG. 1934. On the inhibition of bud development and other functions of growth substances in *Vicia faba*. Proc. Roy. Soc. London. B. 114: 317–339.—THOMSON, B. F. 1954. The effect of light on cell division and cell elongation in seedling oats and peas. Amer. Jour. Bot. 41: 326–332.

VEGIS, A. 1956. Formation of the resting condition in plants. Experientia 12: 94–99. —VINCE, D. 1956. Studies of the effects of light quality on the growth and development of plants. Jour. Hort. Sci. 31: 16–24.—VRIES, H. DE 1872. Ueber einige Ursachen der Richtung bilateral-symmetrischer Pflanzenteile. Arb. Bot. Inst. Würzburg 1. H,2, 223. (cited from Münch, 1938.—WAREING, P. F. 1950a. Growth studies in woody species. I. Photoperiodism in first-year seedlings of *Pinus silvestris*, Physiol. Plantarum. 3: 258–276.— WAREING, P. F. 1950b. Growth studies in woody species. II. Effect of day length on shoot growth in *Pinus silvestris* after the first year. Physiol. Plantarum. 3: 300–314.—WAREING, P. F. 1956. Photoperiodism in woody plants. Ann. Rev. Plant Physiol. 7: 191–214.— WAREING, P. F. and K. A. LONGMAN. 1958. Effect of gravity on flowering and shoot growth in Japanese larch (*Larix leptolepis*, Murray) Nature, 182: 380–381.—WAREING, P. F. and T. A. NASR. 1958. Effects of gravity on growth, apical dominance, and flowering in fruit trees. Nature 182: 379–380.—WAREING, P. F. and T. A. NASR. 1961. Gravimorphism in Trees. 1. Effects of gravity on growth and apical dominance in fruit trees. Ann. Bot. 25: 321–339.—WASSINK, E. C. and J. A. J. STOLWIJK. 1956. Effects of light quality on plant growth. Ann. Rev. Plant Physiol. 7: 373–400.—WENT, F. W. 1939. Some experiments on bud growth. Amer. J. Bot. 26: 109–117.—WENT, F. W. 1948. Thermoperiodicity. In: *Vernalization and Photoperiodism*—A Symposium. by: A. E. MURNEEK and R. O. WHYTE. pp. 145–157. Chronica Botanica Co. Waltham, Mass.—WIESNER, J. 1895. Über Trophieen nebst Bemerkungen über Anisophyllie. Ber. Deutsch. Bot. Ges. 13: 481–495.—WILSON, B. F. 1966. Development of the shoot system of *Acer rubrum* L. Harvard Forest Paper No. 14. 21 pp. Petersham, Mass.—WOYCIKI, S. 1954. On the origin of the *Retinospora* forms of *Thuja, Biota,* and *Chamaecyparis*. Acta. Soc. Bot. Poloniae. 23: 443–458.

ZALENSKI, V. 1904. Materials for the study of the quantitative anatomy of different leaves on the same plant. Mem. Polytech. Inst. Kiev. 4: 1–203. (In Russian. Cited from Maximov).

CHAPTER IV

TRANSPORT IN THE XYLEM

Martin H. Zimmermann

INTRODUCTION

There is no need for a water-conducting system nor for a self-supporting structure for plants that live entirely submerged. There is no xylem in algae. Even large kelp does not possess a rigid self-supporting structure. Most large brown algae simply lie on the bottom of the sea, others, like the giant *Macrocystis* or *Nereocystis,* acquire some sort of erect habit by means of gas-filled, buoyant vesicles. Numerous vascular plants have returned secondarily to a submerged habit and live either in the sea (like the turtle grass *Thalassia*) or in fresh water (like water lilies, *Nymphaea*). An examination of their vascular anatomy shows that the xylem is either very much reduced or completely absent.

Interestingly enough, mechanical support of the plant body and long-distance transport of water and minerals from roots to aerial parts have been achieved with the same development in the land plants, namely with the loss of the protoplast and incrustation of the cell walls with lignin. Living cells obtain a certain amount of rigidity, turgescence, through osmotic forces. However, the protoplast, the structure that makes turgor possible, is a severe barrier to any rapid water movement through the cell. Re-inforcement of the cell walls, i.e. the addition of a secondary wall, incrustation of the walls with lignin, and the loss of the protoplast gives xylem cells rigidity and at the same time makes the cell lumen available for water conduction. It is a very peculiar and remarkable fact that a vital function (i.e. rapid conduction of water over long distances) is fulfilled by cells which have to die before they become functional!

The sheer size of trees indicates that their translocation systems are developed to a very high degree. Long-distance transport problems are, therefore, among the most important problems in tree physiology. From the point of view of the plant physiologist, trees are ideal experimental plants for certain aspects of transport studies, although many questions can be studied more easily with small plants.

A discussion of the ascent of sap into the tops of tall trees is unthinkable without a discussion of certain structural aspects of the xylem. Reference to anatomical features will have to be made frequently; it is therefore not only desirable but essential that the reader have a basic knowledge of plant anatomy in general and xylem anatomy in particular. It is highly recommended that the chapter on xylem in Esau's plant anatomy text be read (Esau, 1965).

1. THE PATH OF WATER MOVEMENT IN STEMS

Forest botanists of the last century followed the path of water movement visually after the injection of a dye. In more recent years a variety of similar methods have been used, such as observation of fluorescence in the ultraviolet after injection of fluorescent dye (especially useful with small objects, i.e. the tracing of extrafascicular water movement, cf. Strugger, 1953). Radioactive isotopes have also been used as tracers as well as salt solutions in connection with subsequent electrical conductivity measurements of the sap. All these methods take advantage of the fact that during the time of intensive transpiration, during the summer months in temperate climates, the xylem is under less than atmospheric pressure, and liquids will be taken up when brought into contact with a fresh wound. Interpretation of such experiments has to be made with caution because injection of liquid usually alters the normal hydrostatic gradients drastically. When a liquid is brought into contact with a wound, a point of +1 atm. is introduced in a system of lower, perhaps much lower (i.e. negative), pressures. Movement is then along all newly established pressure gradients, downward as well as upward from the point of injection.

a. The extent of the conducting unit

Water movement, naturally, is along the path of least resistance in the wood. In conifers this is the axial direction of the tracheids. The axial arrangement of tracheids in the stem follows intricate and interesting patterns which will be discussed in the next section. Within an individual tracheid the flow pattern can only be postulated. Water enters near the lower tip through the bordered pits, flows axially through the lumen and leaves the tracheid near the upper end. One assumes that flow is paraboloid except near the tips and that the axial flow velocity, greatest in the center, decreases towards both tips.

In considering the extent of the conducting unit in dicotyledons one not only has to think of how long and how wide vessels are, but also where and how they are located within the wood tissue. Vessel diameter is immediately visible on transverse sections; vessel lengths, on the other hand, are far more difficult to determine. In fact, quantitative information on vessel length has only recently become available. When wood is fresh (i.e. wet) air can be blown through a piece of stem only if there are vessels which extend through the whole length and are cut open at both ends. With this and similar techniques minimum lengths of the longest vessels have been obtained. Handley (1936), for example, reported 60 cm for *Acer* and 3 m for *Fraxinus*. A different technique, one for finding an average length of shorter vessels, has been described by Scholander (1958) who measured the volume of sap discharged from a freshly cut piece of stem of a vine. When the piece is held in a vertical position and a section cut from the upper end, sap will run out of the lower end. The volume of discharged sap is approximately proportional to the length of section cut off up to a cut length of 60 cm in *Vitis*. Longer sections than 60 cm yield no greater volume. The basis of this phenomenon is the fact that water cannot be lost from a full vessel because air cannot enter through wet pits (cf. Section 7b). Previously closed and water-filled vessels which are opened at the upper end allow air to enter from above. Water then drains out of the severed vessel into the stem, and the displaced water drains out from the bottom end (Fig. IV-1).

A full quantitative analysis of vessel-length distribution has been attempted by Skene and Balodis (1968) who pushed an oil-base paint through pieces of stem. Oil paint, like air, will only go through vessels which are cut open at both ends. To understand Skene and Balodis' analysis, first consider a very much

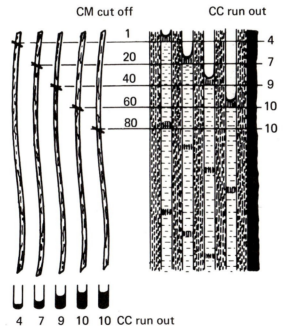

Fig. IV–1. Sap discharge from a fresh section of a vine stem when pieces of different length are cut off the upper end. A diagrammatic interpretation in terms of average vessel length on the right. Note: vessels longer than the initial stem section are ignored. That there are longer vessels is indicated by the fact that air can be blown through longer pieces of vine. From Scholander (1958).

simplified model, a stem piece with randomly distributed vessels of uniform length (Fig. IV-2) assuming a vessel length of 100 arbitrary length units. A piece of stem longer than 100 units will not be penetrated throughout its whole length. The first paint will appear in open vessels at the cut transverse surface as the stem is cut a bit shorter than 100. As the stem piece is still cut shorter, more and more vessels will show emerging paint, until on an infinitely short piece all of the vessels let the paint pass. The plot showing number of open vessels versus length of the stem is a straight line (Fig. IV-2, top). Visualize now two kinds of vessels, one of the unit length 100, the other of the unit length 50. If their individual distribution is plotted, lines a and b (Fig. IV-2, bottom) result. The actual vessel count per unit length yields the line c in Fig. IV-2. It is now easy to see that vessels of many different lengths, randomly distributed, will yield a curve from 0%–100% at maximum vessel length (Fig. IV-3, top). Such curves have been mathematically analyzed and the vessel distribution calculated (Fig. IV-3, insert) (Skene and Balodis, 1968). Although this analysis is based on a number of (quite reasonable) assumptions, such as random distribution of vessels, and has some limitations, it yields by far the most complete information on vessel length. It may be added here that this method measures all vessels, water-filled or embolized. It is clear that such analyses should be made with young sapwood. If vessels are obstructed by tyloses etc. shorter vessel lengths are simulated.

After this brief consideration of the extent of the individual conducting units, the arrangement of these units within the stem will be discussed. How the quantity of flow through a piece of wood differs from that of capillaries of equal diameter and infinite length will also be shown later.

b. Axial water movement in conifers and dicotyledonous trees

From a physical point of view it has been stated that the water is expected to follow the path of least resistance, i.e. the axial direction of xylem tissue which is often referred to as the "grain" of the wood, or, more precisely, the axial direction of tracheids and vessels. Axial water movement will now be analyzed step by step from the most simple to the more complex example.

The simplest example of axial water movement is represented by a ring-porous tree such as an oak (*Quercus*), chestnut (*Castanea*), elm (*Ulmus*) etc. of the north temperate regions. Here water conduction takes place primarily through the large earlywood vessels of the current year, larger vessels of older growth rings are mostly gas filled (Huber, 1935). Vessels in these trees are not only wide but also long and show relatively limited lateral contact. In large-porous *Quercus* species, for example, water ascends from one particular region of the root system along a strip of young xylem to one particular portion of the crown. This path may follow a line roughly parallel to the stem axis if the tree has straight grain, or it may follow a helical path around the stem if the tree trunk is twisted. The independence of the various sides of the tree have reached an extreme in the ring-porous species. The following observation may serve as an example. During the 1953 floods in Holland, salt water got into some drainage ditches along which trees were growing. Where these trees were elms, the parts of the crown facing

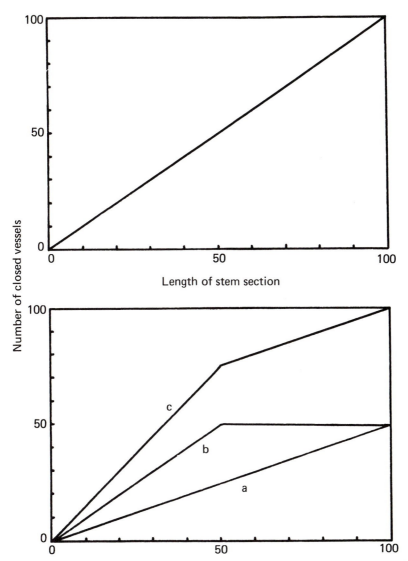

Fig. IV–2. Top: Number of vessels closed at either one or both ends in a piece of wood variable length. Vessels are assumed to be all of the uniform length 100, randomly distributed. Bottom: Equal number (per transverse section) of vessels of the length 50 and 100, closed at either one or at both ends in a piece of wood of a given length. See text for explanation.

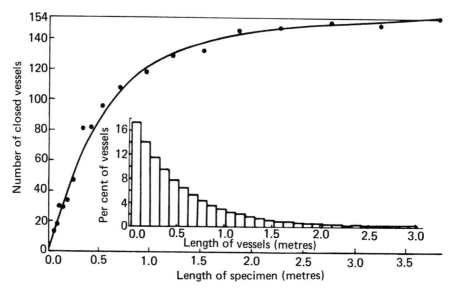

Fig. IV–3. Relationship between stem length and number of closed vessels in *Euca-lyptus obliqua*. The block diagram (insert) shows the percentage of vessels in all length classes. From Skene and Balodis (1968).

the ditch showed dieback, but the other side of the elms remained alive (Richardson, 1958).

The pattern of axial water movement is more complicated wherever more than one growth ring is functioning in conduction. This is the case in the conifers as well as in many dicotyledonous trees, particularly those in which vessel diameters are smaller (diffuse-porous trees). Most trees show spiral grain to a lesser or greater extent; moreover, the pitch of the spiral grain often changes year after year. The helical path of water movements is, therefore, different in different growth rings. Dyes introduced into a radial bore hole in the wood show the situation very clearly. The radial dye pattern on a transverse section of the stem at the height of dye injection becomes a spiral pattern higher up (Fig. IV-4). Vité (1958) and Vité and Rudinsky (1959) who investigated this matter in detail with numerous coniferous species, found that the change in pitch of the spiral grain is different in fast and slow growing trees and can be influenced by silvicultural treatment. In some cases left-turning spiral grain can change over the years into right-turning grain. In some species this change happens regularly and repeatedly, a pattern that is called interlocked grain. Many tropical dicotyledonous trees have interlocked grain and are for this reason of particular value in cabinet work. Not only does the varying tissue angle of the grain make a finished surface look attractive, but the wood derives from this structure an internal stability that is somewhat comparable to plywood.

The physiological significance of these complicated patterns of water movement is obvious. A specific root may be axially connected to a specific part of the crown in any given year. When the pitch of the spiral grain changes in the fol-

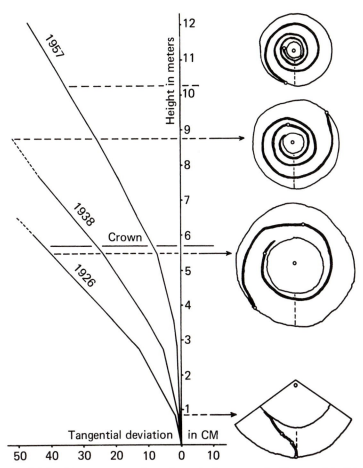

Fig. IV–4. Right: Transverse sections through the stem of a 97-year-old *Abies concolor* at 0.84, 5.49, 8.74 and 10.24 m height. Dye had been injected into the xylem through a radial bore hole at the base of the tree. This hole, vertically projected onto the sections, is shown as a dashed line. The dye marks in the sections are indicated by a bold line. Left: The course of dye movement, indicating the axial orientation of tracheids, is shown diagrammatically on the unfolded layers of growth rings. The changes of pitch of spiral grain are obvious from the comparison of the growth rings of 1926, 1938 and 1957. Redrawn from Vité (1958).

lowing year, axial contact is made to another part, and so on. Over a few years' growth axial connection from a single root is to many different branches via different growth rings, at the same time any branch is axially connected to a number of different roots (Vité, 1958; Vité and Rudinsky, 1959; Kozlowski and Winget, 1963).

It is not known precisely what makes the angle of the spiral grain change from one year to the next, though the angle of the pseudo-transverse division of the cambial initials must be causally involved (Bannan, 1966). Spiral grain is also correlated with the fibril angle of the central layer of the secondary wall of tracheids (Vité, 1958).

Beside the spiral and interlocked grain patterns of stems, Vité and Rudinsky (1959) described "sectorial straight" and "sectorial winding" patterns in some conifers. These patterns are essentially based on a tangential spreading of the water within the growth rings. Tangential spreading is common in dicotyledonous trees (Fig. IV-5). The anatomical basis for this has been described by Braun (1959). On a transverse section one can see vessels distributed among other tissue

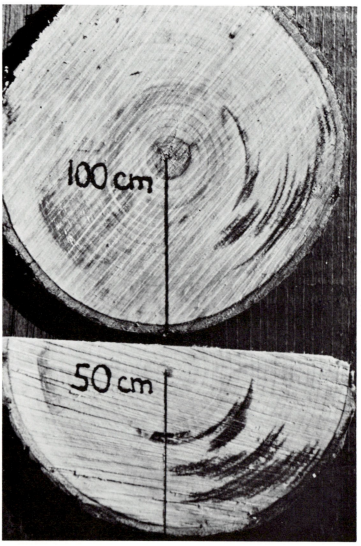

Fig. IV–5. Dye ascent from a radial hole in *Populus* sp. The dye distribution is shown in disks 50 and 100 cm above the point of injection.

(fibers, parenchyma, etc.), either in small clusters, or more or less singly. The three-dimensional distribution of vessels in wood is very poorly known and has been investigated only in recent years. A certain amount of "inter-weaving" seems to be quite common, i.e. individual vessels run obliquely from cluster to cluster (Fig. IV-6). In *Fraxinus americana* L., a ring-porous tree, it has been found that younger earlywood vessels may run at a slightly different angle than older early-wood vessels of an individual growth ring. Whenever two vessels cross, they run parallel in intimate contact for a certain distance where water exchange via pit pairs can take place (Zimmermann and Tomlinson, 1967). Thus, there are even ring-porous trees in which water conduction is not as strictly linear as previously described.

All this interweaving of vessels is primarily in a tangential direction. From a functional point of view this means that the axial path of conduction fans out within the individual growth ring and dye ascent patterns such as the one in Fig. IV-5 result.

c. Water movement around interruptions of the axial path

So far only the axial path of water has been discussed. However, water can move in other ways through the stem if circumstances require. The classical example of such movement is the so-called "double-sawcut experiment" which

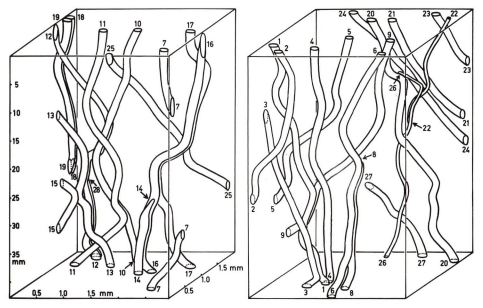

Fig. IV–6. Course of vessels in a piece of wood of *Cedrela fissilis* Vell. Individual vessels are arbitrarily separated into two blocks so that they can be seen more clearly. Vessels are numbered at the point where they leave the block. Numbers with arrows indicate vessels terminating within the block. Vessel-to-vessel movement of water must be visualized through pits in areas where vessels run in pairs (or groups). Note that the drawing is axially foreshortened about 10 times.

was well known to the early botanists and has been reported at least as early as 1806 (Cotta, 1806, cited in Hartig, 1878). The phenomenon has been rediscovered relatively recently and caused a great deal of puzzlement among plant physiologists for reasons to be explained later. If two sawcuts are made into a tree stem from opposite sides, each a little beyond the stem center (some distance apart so that the tree does not break), all direct axial paths appear to be interrupted. A tree which is treated in such a way does not necessarily wilt, the leaves may continue to receive sufficient water (Greenidge, 1958; Preston, 1952). If a dye solution or any other tracer is introduced into the stem below the sawcuts, it can be seen that the water moves around the cuts. Movement does not have to be so drastically different from axial movement, but this point will be discussed in a later section (Section 7b).

Trees which are treated with a double sawcut are, of course, mechanically very weak and have to be supported so that they do not break. If the tree does survive, the axial path of conduction is partially or completely recovered during the fol-

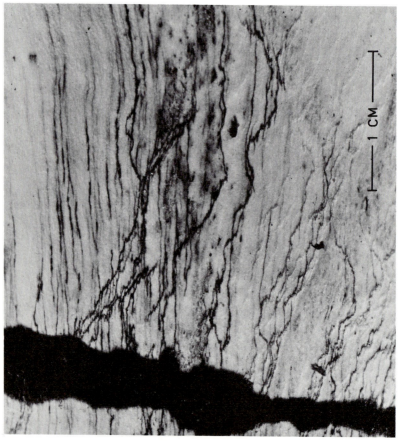

Fig. IV–7. Dye ascent from a cut into superficial xylem layers of a stump of *Acer rubrum* L. showing reorientation of vessels from stump sprouts. From Wilson (1968).

lowing growing period by a reorientation of vascular tissue (Wilson and Wilson, 1961). Vessels also reorient after any other injury to the vascular system whereby vascular continuity is re-established. Figure IV-7 shows the reorientation of vessels from sprouts to the stump and roots of a recently cut tree.

d. Path of water movement in stems of arborescent monocotyldeons

It has been known for some time that arborescent monocotyledons such as palms have a very efficient transport system which cannot easily be disturbed. Unilateral injuries to the stem or the root mass seldom result in the development of an asymmetric crown. Occasionally one can find a palm with the stem almost completely broken, yet it still survives. If a dye solution is introduced in a radial bore hole of a palm stem, one can find the dye distributed over a good percentage of transverse section even a short distance above the point of injection (Fig. IV-8).

The pattern of vasculation upon which this water distribution is based is shown in Fig. IV-9. Axially running stem bundles gradually approach the stem center in distal direction, then turn sharply towards the periphery where they are leaf traces. Continuity of vasculation is based upon branching of the leaf trace. One of these branches is usually the continuation of the stem bundle, the others, "bridges" connect to neighboring axial bundles. If one visualizes this same pattern of branching for every bundle (a single transverse section of a coconut palm stem includes around 20,000 bundles!), one realizes that the whole vascular system of the monocotyledonous stem forms an extremely complex and dense network.

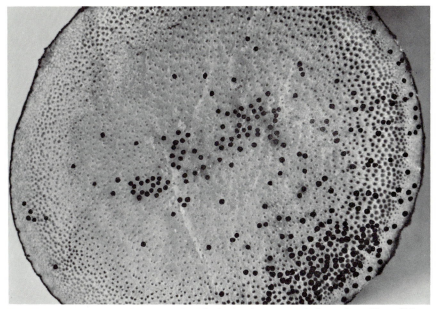

Fig. IV–8. Dye ascent from a radial hole in the stem of the palm *Chrysalidocarpus lutescens.* The disk shown was taken 25 cm above the point of injection. Stained vascular bundles are marked with a black spot.

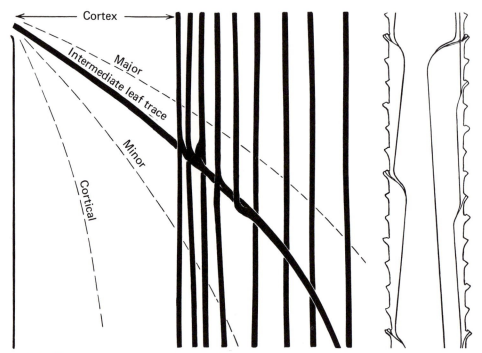

Fig. IV–9. Course of vascular bundles in the stem of an arborescent monocotyledon. Overall view right and nodal area left. From Zimmermann and Tomlinson (1965, 1968).

Further complexity of the vascular pattern arises from the fact that the bundles of the central, uncrowded stem area follow a helical path. The different sides of the stem are thus in direct vascular ("axial") contact. This complex pattern, therefore, indicates that any point of the vascular system can be reached via innumerable alternate pathways, and makes dye-ascent experiments like the one shown in Fig. IV-8 understandable.

It is, perhaps, necessary at this point to stress that the densely knit system of vascular bundles in the monocotyledonous stem does not mean that *vessels* are continuous throughout this whole system. Bundle continuity has nothing to do with vessel continuity; vessels are of limited length within bundles (Zimmermann, 1966).

e. Quantitative aspects of xylem channels

It is quite interesting to look at the transverse-sectional area of the xylem channels from a quantitative point of view and compare different plants with each other. Plants of the north temperate zones possess a water conducting system with a transverse-sectional area of about 0.5 mm² per gram (fresh weight) of leaves that they supply. Humid and shady sites produce lower, sunny and dry sites produce higher values. This is true for different plant species (e.g. forest plants versus desert plants) as well as for a single plant (sun leaves versus shade leaves). Certain desert plants have a transverse-sectional area about ten times as great as plants of northern temperate forests. It is interesting to note, on the other hand, that with the succulent habit the problem of water supply has been solved in an entirely different manner, namely the storage of water. Succulents can, therefore, afford a much reduced xylem. Table IV-1 illustrates the situation.

TABLE IV–1

Transverse-sectional area of the water conducting system in various plants (in mm^2 per gram fresh wt. of leaves). Figures from Huber (1928), value for Nymphaeaceae from Gessner (1951).

Nymphaeaceae (water lily family)	0.02
Deciduous trees	0.50 (0.26–0.79)
Conifers	0.48 (0.3 –0.61)
Herbs of the forest floor	0.19 (0.01–0.80)
Desert succulents	0.10 (0.04–0.16)
Other desert plants	3.40 (1.42–7.68)

Everybody who has carefully looked at trees realizes that branches become ever thinner as they branch. One could, therefore, suspect that the transverse-sectional area per weight of leaves is constant throughout a single tree. For example, in a Y-shaped branch, the transverse-sectional xylem area of the two outer portions of the branch combined are approximately equal to that of the common bottom part. In other words, one would expect the transverse-sectional area of the trunk of a tree to be equal to the combined transverse-sectional areas of all the branches. This is not quite the case. Huber (1928) studied this problem in young spruce trees and found xylem transverse-sectional areas to range from 0.45 to over 4.2 mm^2 per gram fresh weight of leaves. The leader is very greatly favored (Fig. IV-10). The implication of this is obvious: in case of drought, the leader suffers last. This is one of the expressions of apical dominance.

Comparative measurements of xylem area within a single tree can only be made in relatively young parts. Older parts of xylem gradually lose their water-conducting function (cf. Sec. 8). This loss of water-conducting ability has reached an extreme in ring-porous trees in which the large earlywood vessels conduct essentially only during a single season. One can, therefore, not just measure transverse-sectional area, if one does not know how much of the xylem is actually conducting. Comparative measurements of sap velocities are much more reliable indicators of the distribution of relative xylem transverse-sectional areas within a tree. In birch, for example, the transverse-sectional area of xylem seems to decrease acropetally because the sap-flow velocity increases from the base of the stem towards the twig tips. In oak the situation is the reverse (cf. Fig. IV-13 and Sec. 5b).

f. Path of water movement in primary tissues

Before presenting the quantitative aspects of water movement, the path of the water into primary tissues will be explored. Like uptake of water by roots, or like transpiration from leaves, this topic could easily be omitted as a topic of

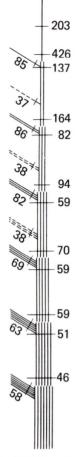

Fig. IV–10. Transverse-sectional area of xylem in stem and branches of a young *Abies concolor.* Numbers indicate square millimeters per gram fresh weight of supplied needles. From Huber (1928).

general plant physiology. However, it is much less frequently covered by general texts than transpiration or the entry of water into roots. A very brief description is, therefore, given here.

Xylem elements that are formed while tissue is still elongating are structurally very distinct. In contrast to other xylem cells their primary walls and the middle lamella between cells remain unlignified. Secondary walls are deposited in the form of rings or helices. These protoxylem elements become functional as conductors of water; presently they die and lose their protoplast. The helical or annular reinforcement prevents the elements from collapse when pressure drops below atmospheric; yet the still-flexible primary wall permits appreciable stretching of the cell (Fig. IV-11). In other words, growing tissues have unique water conductors that are both radially rigid and longitudinally stretchable.

When the xylem water, after its ascent into the leaves, has reached the xylem ends, it has to move towards the stomata from where most of the transpiration of water (though not all) takes place. Many textbooks still describe this as an osmotic movement of water through the cells, though osmotic movement evidently plays a minor role. Extrafascicular water movement through cell walls was shown many years ago by Strugger and coworkers. From a structural point of view this is obviously the path of least resistance; in many careful studies with fluorescent dyes (Strugger, 1953) and metal suspensions (Strugger and Peveling, 1961) this path has been demonstrated (Fig. IV-12). Theoretical considerations make this path also the most likely one (Tyree, 1969). The concept is that water moves from xylem ends through the cell walls of leaf parenchyma to stomatal cavities from whence water vapor escapes into the atmosphere. Parenchyma cells are, of course, in osmotic equilibrium with the hydrostatic pressure of the water around them.

It is well known that transpiration is regulated by the opening and closing of stomata, but it is less well known that there is also a nonstomatal regulation of water movement, presumably based on the decrease of porosity of cell walls under stress conditions (Klemm, 1956). Other forces, such as electrical ones, may also affect water movement within the leaf.

Fig. IV–11. Two generations of protoxylem in the elongation zone of the shoot of *Syringa* sp.

2. EVIDENCE INDICATING THAT WATER IS NORMALLY LIFTED INTO THE LEAVES

If water is pushed up into the top of trees by the roots, pressures are positive in the xylem and decreasing from bottom to the top of the tree. These conditions are relatively rarely met. In some species they prevail at our latitudes in late winter and early spring at a time when roots are actively absorbing water but transpiration is minimal, i.e. before the leaves expand. From the time when the leaves have unfolded until they are shed in autumn, pressures in the xylem are less than atmospheric; in fact, one can often hear, upon injury of the xylem with a knife or an axe, the hissing sound of air being drawn into the injured xylem vessels. Dye solutions will be taken up by a wound in the xylem whenever pressures are below, but, of course, not when they are above atmospheric pressure.

It has been found that absorption of water by roots lags considerably behind transpiration of water by leaves (Kramer, 1937); this in itself would indicate that

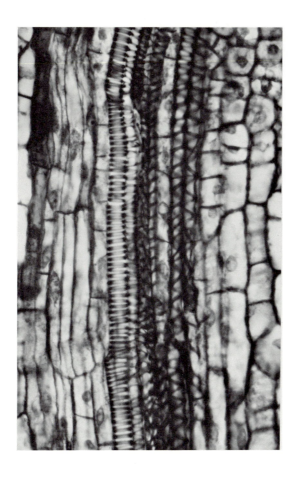

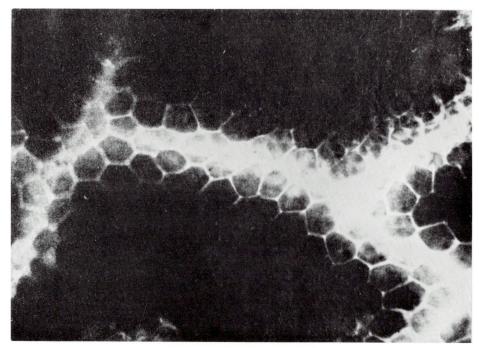

Fig. IV–12. Surface view of the leaf blade of *Episcia,* taken with the fluorescence microscope, showing extrafascicular movement of a fluorescent dye solution from xylem ends through cell walls of the epidermis. The microscope is focused on the epidermal cells, veins underneath are out of focus. From Strugger (1953).

water is pulled rather than pushed into the leaves. But even more interesting is the discovery by Huber and Schmidt (1936) that movement of water begins in the outermost parts of the stem near the leaves after sunrise, movement further down in the stem begins later. In the late afternoon when transpiration declines the velocity of water movement again decreases first in the upper, later in the lower part of the stem. If velocities in stem are plotted against velocities in branches, the diurnal course of the curve follows a loop (Fig. IV-13), indicating a descending tension wave in the tree. The method with which these measurements were made is described in Section 5b.

When water begins to move in the top of the tree and is lost by transpiration without instantaneous replenishment from the soil, the stem must actually suffer a net loss. Since it is hardly possible that water is replaced by gas (or "vacuum") to account for this loss, one must assume that the tree trunk shrinks when transpiration begins in the morning and expands when transpiration declines in late afternoon and water replenishment exceeds loss. This is indeed the case. Diurnal shrinkage of tree stems was discovered by Friedrich (1897) who designed a device for the accurate recording of diameter growth. Instruments of this type, called dendrometers or dendrographs, have subsequently been used by numerous in-

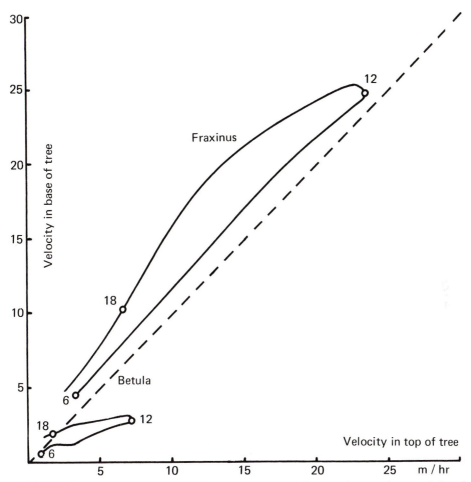

Fig. IV–13. Velocities in upper and lower part of the tree in *Fraxinus* and *Betula* throughout the course of the day. The points marked on the curves are 6 a.m. (6), noon (12) and 6 p.m. (18). Note the following three points: (1) the absolute velocities are quite different in the large- and the small-porous species. (2) In birch, velocities are greater in distal than in proximal parts, the reverse is true in ash. (3) In both species velocities increase in the morning and decrease in the afternoon always first in the upper, later in the lower part of the tree. Redrawn from Huber and Schmidt (1936).

vestigators (e.g. MacDougal *et al.*, 1929). The concept of a shrinking stem as a result of an inertia of the water-conducting system has been further substantiated by Huber and Schmidt (1936) who made dendrometer recordings simultaneously at two different heights. These showed that stems shrink first in the upper, later in the lower part of the stem.

Another very clear indication that water is pulled into the leaves is the fact that a cut-off twig, put into a container of water, takes up water from this reservoir and survives. It can still pull water and continue transpiration even when the water container is sealed and the air space above the water surface is evacuated. In other words, a transpiring twig can successfully compete with a vacuum pump. Later it will be shown that a transpiring twig can not only compete with a vacuum pump but can actually pull with a very much greater force than a pump (Sec. 6). Many woody species have been used successfully for such experiments, indicating a general phenomenon. *Robinia Pseudo-Acacia* L. is one of the few species known to fail this experiment (Ursprung, 1913). It is a ring-porous tree which seems to depend very heavily upon the large earlywood vessels. If these are embolized by the application of vacuum at the cut end, the few smaller latewood vessels are insufficient to maintain the leaves turgescent.

3. THE MECHANISM OF SAP ASCENT

One of the crucial early findings was that the ascent of water into the leaves proceeds in dead tissue passively without any direct involvement of living cells. Strasburger (1891) showed that poisonous liquids such as copper sulfate and picric acid, which rapidly kill living cells in the wood with which they come in contact, would nevertheless ascend all the way up into the transpiring foliage of trunks of trees up to 20 meters tall which had been cut and put into buckets containing such liquids. Strasburger also rolled up long woody vines and dipped their stems into boiling water to kill all living cells in the stem. When stretched again to their full height, transpiration and the rise of sap continued unimpaired for days.

The view that long-distance transport of water in the xylem is a passive movement through dead tissue did not remain unchallenged. It was mainly Ursprung (1906 and others papers) who reported experimental results which seemed to contradict those of Strasburger. In some cases, for example, when a portion of a branch of a standing tree was killed with boiling water, the leaves of this branch soon withered and died. Ursprung's explanation of this was that the living cells are somehow involved in water transport. However, the solubility of gas in water decreases with increasing temperatures. When the xylem water is heated bubbles form, because xylem water always contains dissolved gases (Scholander, 1958); if the xylem is under very low pressure, these bubbles expand and interrupt the passage.

Killed portions of a stem allow water movement through them only for a few days. Failure is brought about by drying out of the xylem. Even minute drying cracks represent air leaks that can cause embolism and thus interruption of the water-conducting channels (Sec. 7b). One can, therefore, say that living cells are indeed necessary for the ascent of sap, not for conduction *per se*, but rather for an effective seal of the conducting cells toward the outside. Many trees possess a type of wood in which vessels are surrounded by living parenchyma cells (vasicentric parenchyma); surely this type of wood must have a good survival value.

Another reason why living cells were thought to be directly involved in sap ascent was the finding that low but nonfreezing stem temperatures caused wilting of the leaves above (Handley, 1939). However, when such experiments were repeated with modern instrumentation, it was found that wilting did not take place unless freezing temperatures had been reached (Johnston, 1959; Zimmermann, 1964; cf. also Webb and Gorham, 1965).

Many different theories to explain the ascent of sap have been put forward over the past hundred years or so. They ranged from a pulsating pumping of living cells to that of pumping action of wind sway. Only one theory, however, has survived the tests of repeated critical evaluation: the so-called cohesion theory. The concept of the cohesion theory is described herein, and various aspects of sap ascent will be discussed in the remaining sections of this chapter.

a. The cohesion theory

It is well known that mercury normally cannot be pulled up higher than 760 mm, or more precisely, the height of ambient barometric pressure. It is the atmospheric pressure that *pushes* the mercury to this height whenever this pressure is removed with a pump at the upper end of the mercury column. This principle is, of course, the basis of mercury barometers. The height of a water column equivalent to 760 mm mercury is about 10 m. In other words, it is ordinarily not possible to pull water to a height of more than 10 m. This statement seems to contradict what has just been said in the previous section, namely that water is pulled to the top of the trees. The height of a great many trees exceeds 10 m considerably, some of the giants reaching about 100 m in height. How do they pull the water into their crowns?

Imagine that water is pulled up directly rather than via vacuum. Transpiration causes a loss of imbibition water from leaf cell walls. Since the water in cell walls is continuous with the water columns of the xylem tracheids and vessels, lost imbibition water is replaced from the xylem. This ultimately causes an upward movement of water through the xylem towards the leaves. Energetically this is easily possible because imbibition deficits can produce suction forces of many atmospheres. Now, it is obvious that such a system can only exist if adhesive forces between water and cell walls and cohesive forces within the water itself are sufficient to prevent breakage of water continuity under stress. Adhesion does not seem to be a problem, but the cohesive strength of water appears to be the critical factor. This is what gave the theory its name.

Josef Böhm was the first one to demonstrate tension in the xylem of a transpiring shoot. He fitted a leafy twig to a glass tubing which was filled with water and from which all air had been carefully expelled. When this tube was immersed with its lower end into mercury and the twig at the upper end was allowed to transpire, mercury could be lifted above barometric height (Böhm, 1893). This finding was later confirmed by Dixon and Joly (1896) as well as Askenasy (1895) and extended by experiments with models in which a clay cup replaced the transpiring leaves. Gradually, these and similar experiments led to the concept of the cohesion theory (Dixon, 1914). In summary it states that water flows along gradients of decreasing pressures through the xylem. The gravitational force requires that the gradient in the stem of a standing tree must be at least 0.1 atmospheres per meter of the tree's height under conditions of minimal flow, greater if transpiration goes on and resistance to flow becomes significant. Such gradients will be discussed in more detail later on (Section 5d). The crucial point is that in such a system pressures would very often have to be below zero; i.e., the water columns would have to be under liquid tension. This requirement raises many extremely interesting questions, some of which will have to be discussed in more detail.

Liquid water columns under tensile stress cannot be very stable; moreover, once broken they are very difficult to repair. It is for this reason that the cohesion theory was not immediately accepted by plant physiologists. Many objections were raised and a great deal of experimentation was done as a result of the excitement which had been caused by the provoking proposal. But one by one the objections were removed and the weight of all evidence today is heavily in favor of the cohesion theory, although many fascinating detail questions have not yet been answered.

4. THE TENSILE STRENGTH OF WATER

One of the most important and immediate questions that arose was whether the cohesive strength of the water itself is great enough to withstand tensions as they might develop in the tops of the tallest trees. There are many ways to approach this problem. Tensile strength can be calculated from physical formulas such as surface tension relationships, Laplace's theory of capillarity, heats of vaporization, etc. All these calculations yield values of the order of 15,000 atm., enormous figures. These are theoretical values, to be sure, but many investigators have tried to answer the question experimentally.

The question can be formulated as follows. In a tree all water in the stem *hangs* (at times at least) on the water in the top. The taller the tree the greater the stress on the water in the top. Just how much of a pull can develop before the water columns break?

The classical method of measuring the tensile strength of water is a very interesting one, because it uses an experiment that nature itself provides (Fig. IV-14). Certain fern sporangia possess an annulus which goes halfway around their back. The cell walls of this annulus are thinner on the outside than on the inside. By the time the spores are ripe, the structure is ready to function (Fig. IV-14, I). Evaporation of water from the annulus cells decreases their volume. This opens the annulus (Fig. IV-14, II). The tension within the water of the annulus cells increases (holding the sporangium open against the springy force of the annulus) until a point is reached where the tensile strength of the water is overcome. A vapor bubble appears in each of the cells, the sporangium snaps closed and the spores are thrown out (Fig. IV-14, III). Renner (1915) arranged a set-up with which he could observe this sequence of events with the microscope while the sporangia were enclosed in a container in which the relative humidity could be controlled with solutions. The tension in the annulus cells could thus be stabilized. By doing this with series of solutions he found that the sporangia would not snap closed unless the solution had an osmotic value of 300–500 atm. This value range then was the first measurement of the tensile strength of water.

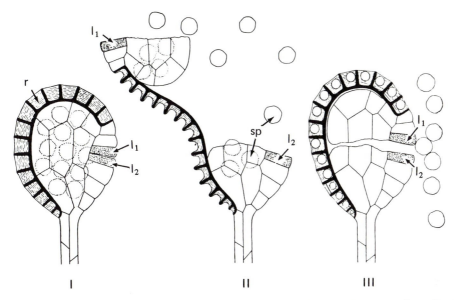

Fig. IV–14. Cohesion mechanism in the sporangium of a fern. (I) Sporangium closed. (II) Sporangium opens because transpirational loss of water from annulus cells produces tensions. (III) Increasing tension overcomes the cohesive strength of water, gas bubbles appear in annulus cells, the sporangium snaps closed, spores are thereby ejected. From Stocker (1952).

Many other procedures have been used to measure the tensile strength of water experimentally. For example, one can spin water-containing capillaries in a centrifuge at various velocities and thus determine at what internal tension the water in the capillary breaks. These methods yield values of the order of 200 atm., sometimes lower (cf. citations in Greenidge, 1957).

Other methods have yielded lower values. Loomis *et al.* (1960), for example, sealed water into glass capillaries and gradually warmed them up until the remaining small vapor bubble disappeared (heat expanding the water, increasing the pressure in the bubble until it finally dissolved completely). The capillary was then cooled slowly until the bubble reappeared with a click. The tensile strength of the water was then calculated from the temperature difference, values of 25–30 atm. were obtained.

Another method may be mentioned, one which gives an excellent demonstration of the function of the tensile strength of water. Budgett (1912, cited in Greenidge, 1957) wrung two steel plates together with water between them, then pulled them apart. His measurements were of the order of 30 atm.

Many other experiments have been made during the years; not only botanists, but also physicists are interested in the phenomenon. Readers interested in more theoretical aspects of this question are referred to the papers of Wakeshima (1961) and Briggs (several papers cited in Greenidge, 1957, and Wakeshima, 1961).

Last, but not least, what tensile strength is required to lift water into the tallest trees. To merely hang it from the top of a 100-m-tall *Sequoia,* 9 atm.

would be required if one assumes atmospheric pressure at ground level. But since the resistance to flow has to be overcome, and the resistance to uptake by the roots, greater stresses undoubtedly develop.

5. RESISTANCE TO FLOW IN THE XYLEM

The hydrostatic pressure gradient in a standing vertical water column is approximately 0.1 atm. per meter. If one assumes ambient pressure (i.e. +1 atm.) at ground level in the xylem of a tree stem in which water movement is infinitely slow, one has to expect zero pressure (equivalent to vacuum) at a height of 10 m, −1 atm. (i.e. 1 atm. tension) at a height of 20 m, and −9 atm. at a height of 100 m. in the top of a giant *Sequoia* or *Eucalyptus*. Such a condition could, for example, exist in the early morning hours before sunrise. Now, assume that the sun rises, stomata open and transpiration, which was minimal during the night, increases drastically. Water begins to flow through the stem of the tree. This requires steepening of the pressure gradient. Water has now not only to be lifted against the forces of gravity, it must also be moved against the resistance to flow. What are these additional requirements?

a. Pressure gradients in flow through ideal capillaries

Assume that the tree stem is just a bundle of capillaries, ideally smooth and of infinite length. Of course, this is not the case but let us begin with the simplest model and look at the more complex situation later. The volume of water flowing through ideal capillaries is, according to Hagen-Poiseuille,

$$\text{Volume} = \frac{\pi}{8\eta} \times \frac{\Delta p}{l} \times t \times \Sigma r^4 \qquad \text{(Eq. IV-1)}$$

in which η = viscosity of the fluid [1 centipoise = 0.01 poise (g cm^{-1} sec.$^{-1}$) for water at 20°C]; $\Delta p/l$ = pressure gradient along the capillary; t indicates time, and r = radius of the capillary. This relationship was found by Poiseuille empirically with tubes varying between 0.01 and 0.3 mm of the length (l) of 0.5 to 10 m (Reiner, 1960).

Equation IV-1 includes the required pressure gradient. In order to calculate this the radius of the capillaries must be known; this is easy to measure on a wood section in the microscope. It is much more difficult to find the quantity of water flowing through a tree stem within a certain time. Such a figure for a laboratory model experiment could be obtained by forcing water through a piece of wood, but how does one know what volume is flowing through a living, transpiring tree?

The Hagen-Poiseuille equation indicates the fact that water moves through capillaries at graded velocities. Water molecules immediately adjacent to the capillary wall are stationary, molecules in the center of the tube move fastest. If one could tag all the water molecules on a single transverse-sectional area at zero time and look at them a little later, at time t, one could see them all spread over the surface of a paraboloid. In other words, there is a paraboloid grading of water velocities between wall and center. The volume of water flowing through the capillary within time t must, of course, fit this paraboloid. The volume of the paraboloid is exactly one half that of the cylinder with the same height h, i.e.,

$$\text{Volume of the paraboloid} = \frac{1}{2} r^2 \pi h \qquad \text{(Eq. IV-2)}$$

If this is set equal to the volume flow in a single capillary in Eq. IV-1, one obtains,

$$\frac{\Delta p}{l} \times t \times \frac{r^2}{4\eta} = h \qquad \text{(Eq. IV-3)}$$

This relationship is independent of flow volume and the term h/t represents peak velocity,

$$\frac{h}{t} = \frac{\Delta p}{l} \times \frac{r^2}{4\eta} \qquad \text{(Eq. IV-4)}$$

The peak velocity of water movement through stems of intact trees can be measured much more easily than the moving water volume. Moreover, by measuring flow velocity, one does not have to worry about how much of the wood is actually serving as a conducting channel and how much might be inactive, a factor of crucial importance if one were dealing with volumes. It is now merely a matter of routine arithmetic to calculate the pressure gradients that are necessary to push or pull water through capillaries of a given diameter at certain peak velocities. If this is done one gets a series of curves as shown in Fig. IV-15, from which we can read the required pressure gradients for pulling water through capillaries of a given diameter at a given peak velocity. For example, 0.09 atm./m are required to pull water through a tube of a diameter of 250 μ at a velocity of 128 m/hr, or 0.07 atm./m for a velocity of 4 m/hr in a tube of the diameter of 50 μ, etc.

It has been suggested that the Hagen-Poiseuille equation might not be applicable if water is under tension. Fortunately this complication does not arise, at least not if tensions remain small (Johnson and Dixon, 1965). A more serious difficulty is the fact that wood does not contain ideal capillaries. Neither are the walls smooth, nor are vessels of infinite length. In conifers, there are only tracheids a few millimeters long!

b. Velocities of water movements in tree stems

There are a number of different ways to measure, more or less accurately, the velocity of sap ascent (cf. Crafts *et al.*, 1949). One can, for example, inject a dye into the stem, cut the tree down after a certain time, and by cutting the stem into segments, see how far up the dye has moved. Such a procedure cannot be reliable for a number of reasons. The most important of these has already been mentioned; a dye injection alters the existent pressure gradient drastically.

A very ingenious method of velocity measurement was developed by Huber and his coworkers in the 1930's; it is called the thermo-electric measurement of

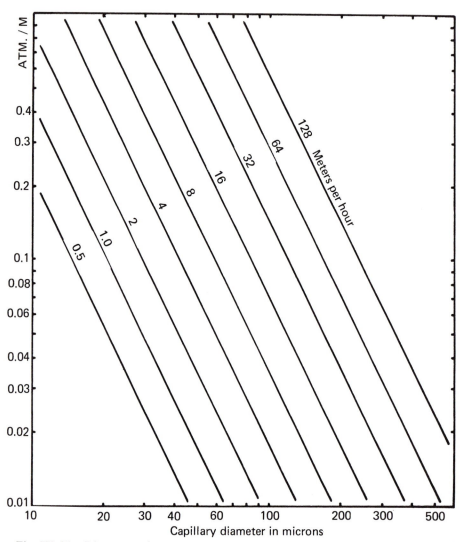

Fig. IV–15. Diagrammatic representation of the Poiseuille equation. Peak velocities are given.

sap velocities. A little wire loop which can be heated by the application of a voltage is embedded under the bark in the surface of the wood. A short heat pulse is applied with a switch, and the arrival of the heat wave is recorded with a thermo-couple which is embedded 4 cm above the wire loop. Figure IV-16 is a diagrammatic representation of the setup and the recorded galvanometer deflection. For practical purposes not the peak of the heat wave is measured, but rather the very first indication of its arrival (Huber and Schmidt, 1936). The method becomes unreliable at sap velocities much below 1 m/hr. A different technique was developed for slow sap movements, the so-called compensation method (Huber and Schmidt, 1937). In this case the thermo-couple is placed

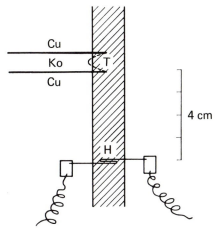

Fig. IV–16. Experimental setup for the thermo-electric measurement of sap-flow velocities above 60 cm/hr. H = heating element; T = thermo-couple. From Huber and Schmidt (1936).

asymmetrically above and below the loop (Fig. IV-17). A method measuring the volume flow of water in intact trees, based on Huber's thermo-electric method, was described by Ladefoged (1960). Vieweg and Ziegler (1960) described a method for continuous registration of flow velocities with thermistors.

Marshall (1958) did further work on conifers with the heat-pulse method, and particularly gave the method a theoretical consideration. He found that the actual sap velocity in conifers could be up to nearly four times as great as the measured heat-pulse velocity. The error is estimated to be much less in dicotyledonous

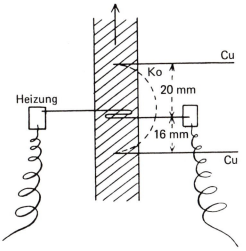

Fig. IV–17. Experimental setup for the thermo-electric measurement of slow sap movements (compensation method). From Huber and Schmidt (1937).

trees. Fortunately, Huber and Schmidt (1937) compared the compensation method
on cut twigs under laboratory conditions with the standard method; the error in
their measurements, therefore, seems to be proportional to that of the standard
method. However, the order of magnitude of Huber's values is certainly the right
one, and some of the most important findings concern comparative measurements
where the absolute values are of little significance.

Thermo-electric measurements of sap velocities have yielded valuable information. The main advantage of the method is the fact that measurements can be
taken repeatedly at any number of given points in a tree. Thus, diurnal as well
as annual changes in the velocity of sap movements were measured (Fig. IV-18).
One of the most important findings has already been discussed, namely the delayed onset of water movement in the lower part of the tree (cf. Fig. IV-13).
Another interesting discovery was that the velocity distribution is not the same
in the different tree species. In oaks and ashes, for example, greatest velocities are
found in the basal part of the stem; higher up they are smaller, smallest in the
twigs. In birches the situation is reversed; velocities increase from the base of the
tree towards the twigs. The two different types can be recognized clearly in Fig.
IV-13. The differences are ascribed to differences in the transverse-sectional area
of conducting tissue. Birch has less conducting area (per unit leaf weight supplied) in the twigs than in the stem; in oak it is the reverse. This can actually be
seen from the general appearance of the trees; birches have very slender and thin
twigs, oaks have stubby twigs.

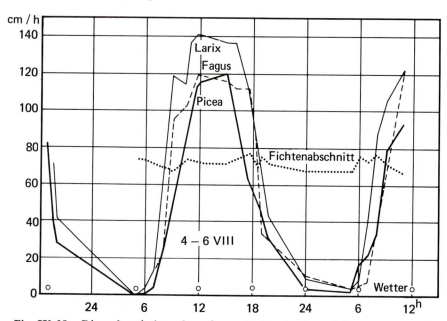

Fig. IV–18. Diurnal variation of sap-flow velocities in three different tree species, as
measured with the compensation method, August 4 to 6. The dotted line indicates measurements taken on a detached spruce twig which served as a control. From Schubert
(1939).

From the point of view of resistance to flow one needs to know peak velocities in various tree species. Such a survey was made by Huber and Schmidt (1936, 1937); it is given in Table IV-2. It is good to remember that, according to Marshall (1958), these may be minimum values. Table IV-2 gives part of the information that is needed to estimate pressure gradients which are required to move water against resistance to flow. But two further pieces of information are still required, namely (1) diameters of conducting channels, and (2) an estimate of the efficiency of xylem as a water conductor.

TABLE IV–2
Mid-day peak velocities in some trees, measured at breast height (from Huber and Schmidt, 1936).

	Velocity, in meters per hour	Vessel diameter, in microns
Ring-porous		
Quercus pedunculata	43.6	200–300 [a]
Robinia pseudacacia	28.8	160–400
Quercus rubra	27.7	250
Fraxinus excelsior	25.7	120–350
Castanea vesca	24.0	300–350
Ailanthus glandulosa	22.2	170–250
Carya alba	19.2	180–300
Rhus glabra	16.0	—
Ulmus effusa	6.0	130–340
Cytisus laburnum	3.9	60–250
Diffuse porous		
Populus balsamifera	6.25	80–120
Juglans regia	4.12	120–160
Juglans cinerea	3.79	—
Tilia tomentosa	3.43	25– 90
Salix viridis	3.00	80–120
Liriodendron tulipifera	2.62	50–120
Acer pseudoplatanus	2.40	30–110
Magnolia acuminata	2.06	—
Alnus glutinosa	2.00	20– 90
Betula verrucosa	1.60	30–130
Carpinus betulus	1.25	16– 80
Pirus communis	1.11	50– 80
Fagus silvatica	1.07	16– 80
Aesculus hippocastanum	0.96	30– 60
Conifers		
Larix decidua	2.1	up to 55
Pinus strobus	1.7 [b]	up to 45
Picea excelsa	1.2 [b]	up to 45
Tsuga canadensis	1.0	up to 45

[a] Size of the large earlywood vessels.
[b] Data from Huber and Schmidt, 1937.

c. The hydraulic conductivity of xylem

The structure of the xylem, this time from the point of view of efficiency of conduction is now presented. Wood does not contain ideal capillaries. In conifers the conducting elements are the tracheids, 0.5–3 mm long slender elements (up to 11 mm in certain species). The diameters in most North American and European species are around 30μ and reach a maximum of about 80μ in *Sequoia*. The transverse-sectional area is usually not exactly circular, but more similar to a rectangular form. Water flows through these elements, but has to pass from one to the next every few millimeters. The pathways for passage from one tracheid to the next are the bordered pits which are located mostly on the radial walls (Fig. IV-19).

The construction of dicotyledonous wood is more complicated, vessel elements are lined up to form vessels, the transverse walls between individual cells are reduced to some remnants, or, in some species, disappear completely during differentiation. It must be realized that these vessels are of limited and indeed very variable length, even within a single tree, as seen in Section 1a. It may suffice here to say that limited vessel length is probably the most important factor reducing hydraulic conductivity to below the theoretical (i.e. Poiseuille) value. In those diffuse-porous trees and monocotyledons where the vessel perforations are incomplete (for example, scalariform perforations) the cross-wall remnants may

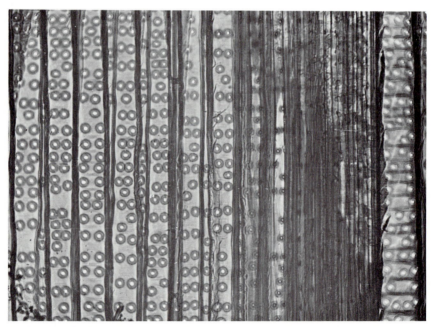

Fig. IV–19. Radial section through the wood of *Taxodium* sp. showing bordered pits, the paths of water movement from tracheid to tracheid. Photomicrograph courtesy of H. H. Bosshard.

also interfere with flow. However, it is rather unlikely that the roughness of the walls has any appreciable effect, because lianas, which have quite long vessels and no cross-wall remnants, show in experimental tests an hydraulic conductivity which is equal to the theoretical one.

Conductivity of xylem can be obtained experimentally by measuring either quantities of flowing water or peak velocities. This may seem a fairly straightforward procedure, but unfortunately the matter is complicated by the fact that the conductivity may decrease drastically during the time of the experiment, especially if unphysiologically high pressure gradients are used. This was investigated in some detail in coniferous wood by Huber and Merz (1958). The interesting point is that, while the conductivity decreases over time, it is partially restored when the direction of flow is reversed (Fig. IV-20). This was ascribed to the well-known valve action of the bordered pits; at excessive pressures the torus is displaced and pushed against the pit border, thus closing the passage. Evidence for this explanation was as follows. The effect increased if the experimental pressure gradient was increased; it was not detectable, however, when the pressure gradient was maintained low, at about 0.1 atm./m. Such a gradient may be considered a

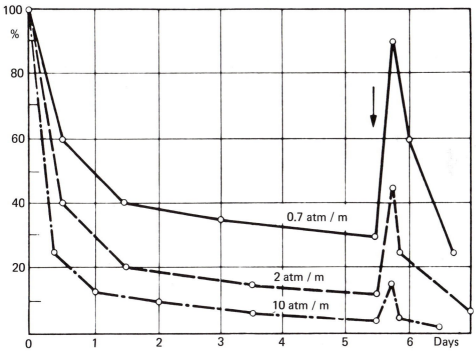

Fig. IV–20. Quantities of water, given in percentage of the initial value, flowing through a piece of coniferous wood at pressure gradients of 0.7, 2 and 10 atm./m. Hydraulic conductivity decreased drastically over time at such pressure gradients. This is probably due to closure of bordered pits. When the direction of flow was reversed (arrow), hydraulic conductivity was partially and temporarily restored. From Huber and Merz (1958).

normal one. Furthermore, if water contained $HgCl_2$ at a concentration of 100 ppm. the effect did not appear. It was assumed that tori were then fixed in their positions. It may be true that the decreasing conductivity is partly or entirely due to the valve function of the bordered pits, but the difficulty with this explanation is that dicotyledonous woods display a very similar effect, which is also reversible upon reversal of the flow direction. Dicotyledonous woods have no tori, their bordered pits should not show a valve action. It has been suggested that the phenomenon is due to air embolism (Kelso *et al.*, 1963). One can well imagine that the cutting of the wood introduces small bubbles at the cut surface, even if the cut is made under water. These bubbles may gradually be pushed toward the vessel ends and there partially block the passage to the next vessel. With the reversal of the pressure gradient the bubbles would move away from the pits, thus increasing conductivity again. Increasing resistance to water flow through a piece of wood at high pressures is not universal. It is also possible that the resistance to flow decreases at high pressures. Tyree (personal communication) made this observation with small pieces of *Acer rubrum* L. in his electro-osmometer (cf. Fig. VI-1). It is assumed, in this case, that high positive pressures dissolve any occasional bubbles and thus increase hydraulic conductivity until embolism is completely eliminated. Hydraulic conductivity can be increased (up to a constant value) particularly if boiled (i.e. gas free) water is pushed through.

In spite of these complications one can probably rely fairly well on the values of hydraulic conductivity that are given in the literature. Riedl (1937) and Münch (1943) used the following experimental setup. A solution of 0.1% (w/v) potassium thiocyanate was pushed downwards through a vertically mounted piece of wood at 0.3 atm./m. Emerging water was collected in a beaker containing an $FeCl_3$ solution which had been slightly acidified with HCl. The length of the piece of wood, divided by the time it took the indicator to traverse the piece of wood was taken as the peak velocity of flow through the largest vessels (or tracheids in the case of coniferous wood). The result was then expressed as a percent of the value calculated with the Poiseuille equation (Eq. IV-4). Results of such experiments for various wood types are given in Table IV-3.

The values in this table are very interesting indeed. Vines have vessels that behave just like ideal capillaries. Of course, vessel length is limited even in vines, but they are long enough so that the resistance to flow through them is not noticeably different from capillaries. Next on the list with 53–84% is rootwood of oak, a ring- (i.e. large-) porous tree. Stem wood is probably a bit lower. Flow through diffuse- (i.e. small-) porous wood is about one third as fast as through ideal capillaries of the same diameter as their vessels. The most surprising figure is that of fir (*Abies pectinata* DC.) which yielded values between 26 and 43%. This is really remarkable because water has to pass from cell to cell every 2 mm or so, around the pit border through the extremely fine pores in the pit membrane. The combined paths through the numerous pits on the radial walls seem to permit this incredibly low resistance to flow. Tyree (personal communication) has recently made many measurements of hydraulic conductivity on small pieces of sapwood of *Acer rubrum* L. in his electro-osmometer (cf. Fig. VI-1). He mea-

TABLE IV–3

Hydraulic conductivity of xylem of various species in percent of the
theoretical value of ideal capillaries of the same diameter.

Plant species	Hydraulic conductivity as a percentage of the calculated Poiseuille value	Author [a]
Atragene alpina, 5 and 1 years old, both	100	B
Vitis vinifera (grapevine), 3 years old	100	B
Aristolochia sipho (Dutchman's pipe), 2 years old	100	B
Quercus (oak) root wood	53–84	R
Abies pectinata (fir)	26–43	M
Fagus (beech) root wood	37.5	R
Betula (birch) root wood	34.8	R
Salix (willow) root wood	34.8	R
Corylus avellana (hazelnut)	33.3	M
Crataegus coccinea (hawthorn)	21.7	M
Populus robusta (poplar)	21.7	B
Rhododendron ferrugineum, 3 years old	20	B
Rhododendron hirsutum, 6 years old	13	B
Various other herbs and shrubs	12–22	B

[a] Authors: (B) Berger (1931), (M) Münch (1943), (R) Riedl (1937)

sured volume flow and therefore averaged the fourth power of measured vessel
diameters. The results nevertheless came out quite scattered (depending on the
age of trees etc.) and ranged from 15% to about 80% of the calculated values.
This finding indicates that the values in Table IV-3 should be regarded as
approximate.

d. Estimated pressure gradients in transpiring trees

Putting all the information gathered together thus far a rough estimate can
be made of the pressure gradients that are required to pull water into the tops
of transpiring trees. The fact that 0.1 atm./m is needed to overcome gravity has
already been discussed. To this gradient must be added whatever is necessary to
overcome resistance to flow. Tables IV-2 and IV-3 give the necessary information
with which to take readings from Fig. IV-15.

Quercus has a maximum vessel diameter of 300 μ, a peak velocity of 43.6 m/hr.
This corresponds to a pressure gradient of about 0.022 atm./m for ideal capillaries. This value must be roughly tripled to make it match the experimental
value and thus arrive at a gradient of 0.066 atm./m. Unfortunately one cannot
look up any specific single species of a diffuse porous and a coniferous tree, because species present in Table IV-2 are absent in Table IV-3 and vice versa.
However, one still can make a fair estimate. *Populus balsamifera* L., with a
maximum vessel diameter of 120 μ has a peak velocity of 6.25 m/hr. This would
require approximately 0.02 atm./m for ideal capillaries; if one multiplies this
value by five (*Populus robusta* Table IV-3), one obtains 0.10 atm./m. Using a

correction factor of five for some other diffuse porous trees, one obtains values of around 0.05 atm./m. For conifers, values are quite of the same order of magnitude.

In summary, one can say that the total pressure gradient, expected to be sufficient to lift water into the tops of trees at peak transpiration, is between 0.15 and 0.2 atm./m. It is quite interesting and perhaps important to note that this value is independent of the pore diameters; large-porous trees simply show much greater flow velocities than small-porous trees. It should be emphasized that these calculations are only approximate. It would be highly desirable to obtain all these measurements from a few single individual trees. It is all the more remarkable that these predictions were made before pressure gradients could be measured in trees. They proved to be quite accurate, as shall be seen in the next section.

6. EXPERIMENTAL EVIDENCE OF NEGATIVE PRESSURES AND OF PRESSURE GRADIENTS

a. Negative pressures in xylem

The cohesion theory assumes, as its name indicates, that tensions are frequently present in the xylem, although pressures can be positive at times. Flow is supposed to be along a hydrostatic pressure gradient, whether part or all of it consists of negative pressures. One can easily detect below-atmospheric pressure in the xylem when a tree is transpiring, but it is less easy to detect pressures below zero.

The first indication of tensions in the xylem was obtained by Böhm (1893) when his transpiring *Thuja* twig pulled mercury beyond atmospheric height. This was repeated many times by other workers, and greater heights were often achieved than those of Böhm. But this experiment works only if water and containers (glass tubing etc.) are carefully made gas-free. An ingeniously simple and effective experiment was described later by Renner (1912). A transpiring twig can not only draw water from a container in competition with a vacuum pump, it can pull very much more water through a clamped stem section than a vacuum pump. Renner's experiment is ideal for teaching purposes, it can easily be performed by students in the laboratory. A branch is fitted to a potometer, and its water consumption is measured until it becomes stabilized. When the top of the branch is cut at this time and replaced by a vacuum pump, the pump draws a great deal more water than the branch. Under these conditions the branch has pulled with a gradient throughout its length of much less than one atmosphere. The course of the experiment can be changed if a point of high resistance is introduced in the branch (Fig. IV-21). When transpiration has stablized after the experiment has been set up (at 1½ hours in Fig. IV-21), the resistance to flow somewhere along the branch is increased either by squeezing it with a pair of vice grips or by making sawcuts into the branch from opposite sides (some distance apart, of course, so that the branch is not cut completely through). Water may be pushed back into the potometer initially, but the leaves continue to transpire,

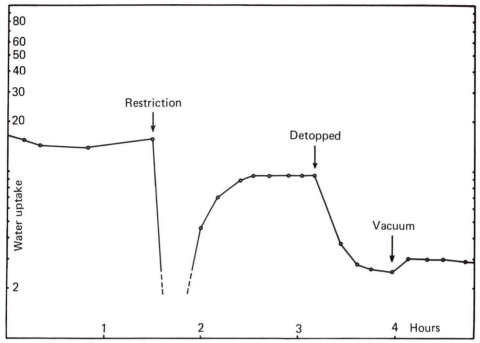

Fig. IV–21. The "Renner Experiment." Uptake of water by a branch from a potometer. When transpiration is stabilized a restriction is introduced in the branch axis (at 1½ hours). This results in an initial reversal of water flow at the basal end of the branch. As transpiration continues, however, water uptake is resumed and eventually reaches a level only slightly lower than before (at 3 hours). The leafy top is now severed from the branch axis and a vacuum pump is allowed to pull in its place. Water consumption, in this particular experiment, drops to about one third.

and when the conditions have stabilized again the branch may draw almost as much water as it has done before (at 3 hours in Fig. IV-21). At this time the branch is detopped and the vacuum pump is allowed to suck in place of the leafy top. The amount of water now pulled from the potometer falls far short of what has transpired from the leaves (at 4½ hours in Fig. IV-21), provided the restriction has been made severe enough. From the difference in water uptake one can calculate the tension that had developed at the upper end of the branch axis during transpiration. A vacuum pump can pull with a pressure of approximately one atmosphere (+ 1 atm. at the potometer and slightly above zero at the pump end). If the water flow caused by the pump was one third of that caused by the transpiring leaves as shown in Fig. IV-21, then one can assume that the leaves had pulled with a gradient of about three times that of the pump, i.e. 3 atm., or from +1 atm. at the potometer end to −2 atm. at the leaf end of the axis. In this calculation proportionality is assumed, an assumption which is not necessarily justified. However, the exact absolute magnitude of the tension is really immaterial; important at this point is the clear-cut demonstration of tensions in the xylem.

Renner (1912) used various woody plant species in his experiments and found, assuming proportionality, tensions of up to 10 atm. The objection could be made that the pump has to pull under unfavorable conditions once the branch is cut. To remove this objection, Nordhausen (1917, 1921) used a similar setup, but worked with an artificial clay resistance between branch axis and pump or transpiring leafy twig.

Jost (1916) showed that transpiring *Sanchezia* shoots could pull a great deal more water out of their root system than a vacuum pump. In more recent times these experiments were successfully repeated by other authors.

Scholander *et al.* (1961) demonstrated tensions in the xylem of the rattan vine (*Calamus*, a member of the palm family). Their experiment was based on the fact that only an extremely small amount of air is soluble in ice. When water freezes, air bubbles form almost invariably because the air dissolved in water is being forced out of solution. If air bubbles appear in water columns which are under tension, the columns break. In Scholander's experiment, a short section of a long vine was briefly frozen, and then thawed again. Thus the vessels were embolized. Water uptake from the potometer to which the bottom end of the vine was fitted continued as long as the embolized section remained on the ground. However, when the upper end of the vine was raised to a height of 11 m, water uptake stopped, water even drained out at the cut bottom end of the vine. This clearly demonstrated embolism in the frozen section, i.e. the presence of tensions in the xylem portion which was raised above a height of 10 m.

b. Pressure gradients

As long as pressures in the xylem are positive, hydrostatic gradients are not too difficult to measure. It is sufficient to puncture the xylem and measure the pressure with a manometer. Ideal objects for such measurements are grapevines in early spring before the leaves are out. Grapevines develop positive pressures at this time of the year; when their stem is cut they will "bleed". Scholander *et al.* (1955) measured pressures in such stems with an especially designed manometer and obtained points on a plot of height versus pressure which line up beautifully along a 0.1 atm./m line (Fig. IV-22).

Difficulties are encountered in pressure measurements as soon as pressures drop below atmospheric. Negative liquid pressures cannot be measured with a manometer, in fact one must assume that columns under tension break as soon as any instrument is brought into contact with them. Measurements of gradients of negative pressures in the xylem of tall plants were the greatest single missing piece of evidence in support of the cohesion theory. It came as a pleasant surprise when Scholander *et al.* (1965) published gradients in the xylem of tall trees with their new pressure bomb technique. The principle of the method is extremely simple (as in all ingenious devices) and consists of enclosing a small shoot in a thick-walled container (a "pressure bomb") that can be pressurized. The cut end of the shoot protrudes from the bomb and can be observed with a magnifier. The twig axis is, of course, tightly sealed against the bomb (Fig. IV-23). The pressure inside the bomb is then slowly raised from a tank of compressed nitrogen, thus

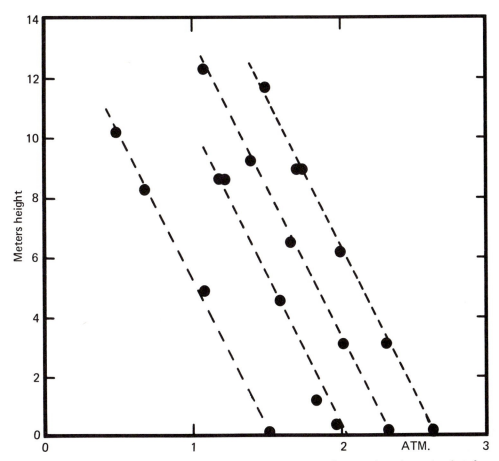

Fig. IV–22.   Gradients of positive pressures in stems of grapevines in springtime before the leaves are out. From Scholander *et al.* (1955).

the tension in xylem and leaf-cell walls is counterbalanced. At the moment equilibrium is reached, water is pushed back through the xylem toward the cut end. This point can be clearly recognized when one observes the cut twig end, and the pressure can then be read from the dial of the regulator.

This method enabled Scholander *et al.* (1965) to measure tension gradients throughout the stems of tall Douglas firs (*Pseudotsuga taxifolia* (Poir.) Britt. and redwood trees (*Sequoia sempervirens* (Lamb.) Endl. (Fig. IV-24). The magnitude of these gradients is of the expected order, a bit more than 0.1 atm./m. Two points may perhaps appear surprising. One concerns the absolute values, the other the values in relation to each other. The absolute pressure values are surprisingly large and show appreciable drift throughout the course of the day. Drift must be expected, because while the slope of the pressure curve, i.e. the pressure gradient, is determined by gravity and the resistance to flow, the absolute pressure values must be subject to fluctuation if water uptake cannot keep pace with water loss. But the drift in Fig. IV-24 seems somewhat exaggerated, and one

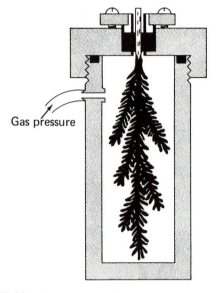

Fig. IV–23. Pressure bomb for measuring negative sap pressures in the xylem of twigs. From Scholander *et al.* (1965), slightly modified.

wonders if part of it might not be seated in leaf-cell walls rather than the stem xylem. This difficulty could be overcome if twigs to be measured are bagged (or double bagged) a day or so before measurements are taken. The second surprise is the fact that gradients are nearer to 0.1 atm./m than 0.2 atm./m. The large drifting shows that transpiration was going on and resistance to flow surely must have been noticeable. It is possible that on the basis of different structure, twigs from the top of the tree are not strictly comparable to twigs from the bottom of the tree. If this were the case, then the apparent gradients in the trees shown in Fig. IV-24 would have to drop somewhat below 0.1 atm./m during the night, and the apparent gradient in a felled tree of horizontal position should be slightly negative.

There is, indeed, some indication that these considerations are right. During a brief visit at Fairbanks, Alaska in 1965, Professor Scholander lent the author his pressure bomb, and some hydrostatic gradients were measured in collaboration with Robert A. Gregory of the U.S. Forest Service on white spruce [*Picea glauca* (Moench.) Voss.]. Measurements were taken on twigs which had been bagged the day before at heights between 0.8 and 15.5 m. The gradient in the standing tree was indeed a bit steeper than the hydrostatic slope, but when the tree was cut and carefully lowered to the ground on a rope (to avoid tearing of the bags), the gradient turned slightly negative.

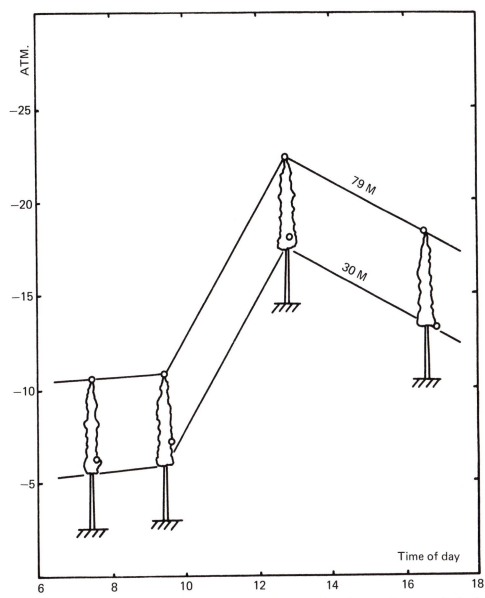

Fig. IV–24. Gradients of xylem pressure in a Douglas fir. The samples were obtained by shooting down twigs with a rifle. Redrawn from Scholander *et al.* (1965).

The pressure bomb method was also used by Scholander *et al.* (1965) to measure tensions in various plants, whereby desert shrubs showed the maximum values (up to 80 atm.). Absolute values of tensions thus measured have to be accepted with caution, of course. The real value of the method lies in comparative results, notably the results concerning gradients in trees. The method will certainly be a very useful tool for future research.

In summary then, the following statement about hydrostatic gradients in the xylem can be made. Under conditions of no flow or very little flow, the slope of the pressure gradient is 0.1 atm./m. The slope is greater, perhaps about 0.15 atm./m under conditions of high transpiration, i.e. maximum flow. If the stem contains a restriction such as a sawcut, the gradient is expected to be very steep across the restriction. Regardless of the gradient's slope one must consider the position of the gradient on the pressure scale. Under conditions of root pressure, the gradient is located on the positive side, at least in the basal part of the stem. Under conditions of transpiration, it is below +1 atm., reaching into the negative side of the scale. Under conditions of increasing drought, it moves deeper into the negative side. Mangroves, growing in sea water, must also be expected to have their gradients on the negative side.

It is obvious that the top of the tree is the place under greatest stress, and it is well possible that a height growth limitation is, at least in some species, imposed by water stress. Some species can be expected to be able to suffer higher tensions than others, but there is no question that the tallest trees can only grow in reasonably humid areas.

7. THE PROBLEM OF BUBBLES

a. Are vessels the main channels of water conduction?

The consideration of the problem of bubbles in the xylem can begin with the question: what evidence indicates that xylem vessels are filled with continuous columns of water? Injury results in the immediate breakage of water under tension. It is, therefore, not surprising that botanists of the last century found chains of bubbles in xylem vessels (so-called Jamin's chains) when they looked at them with the microscope. Even during recent years the function of xylem vessels as water conductors was questioned because, according to certain experimental results, vessels had appeared gas-filled. Alternate explanations of these experiments are easily possible (Zimmermann, 1965), and it is beyond the scope of this outline to go into further detail here.

In all the cases where plants or plant parts are transparent enough for direct observation, one can see that vessels are water-filled, and can follow the movement with dyes (e.g. Strugger, 1953). When such vessels are cut under the microscope, the retreating menisci of the entering air can be observed (Bode, 1923). Milburn and Johnson (1966) recorded the clicks of snapping water columns in xylem vessels of *Ricinus* under conditions of increasing water stress. In woody plants evidence for water-filled vessels is more indirect, but also available. In the experiment of Scholander *et al.* (1961) in which a section of previously frozen vine was raised, water ran back out at the bottom end of the vine, because ice formation, through bubble formation, had broken the continuity of the water columns. This is, of course, clear-cut evidence that the vessels were water-filled and conducting prior to freezing.

No matter how firmly one believes in water-filled vessels, it is obvious that sooner or later water columns which are continuously under tension must be broken by accident. The accident may be winter freezing, mechanical injury, or merely the random break-down of a metastable condition, maybe triggered by cosmic radiation. The larger the unit volume of the vessel and the longer the given time, the more likely is this to happen. It is interesting to see that palms, whose vascular system in the stem is never renewed throughout their life, often show considerable root pressure (Davis, 1961). Plants that do not renew their vascular system might not be able to afford continuous high tensions.

b. Confinement of air embolism

When a bubble appears in a water-filled space which is under tension, one must assume that it will expand until the liquid-vapor interface is stopped. The pressure required to push an air-water interface through a pore can be calculated from the rise of water in a vertical capillary. It must be equal to the pressure exerted by the water column of the height to which it would rise in a capillary of a diameter equal to that of the pore. The height is equal to $2T/rgs$, whereby T = the surface tension of water (against air at room temperature about 73 dynes/cm); r = the capillary radius; s = the specific gravity of water; and g = the acceleration of gravity.

According to this, the pore diameter times pressure necessary to drive an air-water interface through the pore should be a constant, roughly 3 if the pressure is given in atmospheres and pore diameter in microns (Frenzel, 1929).*

The passage from vessel to vessel or from tracheid to tracheid is via pits. Thus, if the tiny perforations in the pit membranes had a diameter of 3 μ, embolism could be confined under tensions up to 1 atm., if diameters were 0.3 μ, tensions up to 10 atm. could be resisted, etc. The membranes of coniferous, bordered pits possess numerous minute perforations; this was first found by Bailey (1913) in perfusion experiments with emulsions. Frenzel (1929) who investigated the matter quantitatively found that colloidal gold with a particle diameter of 144 mμ would just barely pass through bordered pits of *Ginkgo*. Liese and Bauch (1964), investigating other species, found similar sizes. Such pores could hold a pressure of about 20 atm. The order of magnitude of Frenzel's findings was confirmed by electron microscopy, although the pores of pit membranes seem to be variable depending on the species (Fig. IV-25). It is probable that in conifers the valve action of the torus represents an additional protection against entry of air into tracheids. Pit perforations in vessel elements are much smaller (Fig. IV-26) (Côté, 1963). It is probably fairly safe to assume that, under normal circumstances, embolism remains confined to the tracheid or vessel in which it has occurred.

In conifers accidental embolism, if a saw cut is made for example, will remain confined to the injured tracheids, i.e. to a few millimeters within the cut. Subsequent drying of the exposed wood can, of course, produce cracks in previously uninjured tracheids, embolism may thus spread a bit. In dicotyledonous woods

---

* The same relationship shows that capillarity cannot provide the driving force for the ascent of sap. In order to raise water to a height of 10 m, the capillary diameter would have to be 3μ or less. Vessel diameters are greater than that, hence capillary rise would be much less.

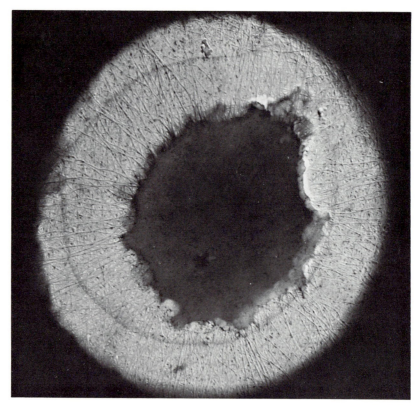

Fig. IV–25. Surface view of pit membrane and torus of a bordered pit in a tracheid of *Picea* sp. From Frey-Wyssling *et al.* (1956). Electron micrograph courtesy of H. H. Bosshard.

the situation is somewhat different; if the larger diameter and length of vessels is an advantage to the tree in respect to resistance to flow, it is at the same time a greater risk.

From the point of view of confinement of embolism, vessel length in angiosperm wood is of considerable importance. The wide and long vessels of vines and ring-porous trees are excellent water conductors, but the short and narrow vessels of diffuse-porous trees are much safer.

It is perhaps desirable to discuss once more the so-called double sawcut experiment which was mentioned in connection with the path of water movement in injured trees. Botanists are often quite puzzled to see that trees which receive such treatment often survive, particularly if the treated species is a ring-porous one. The large earlywood vessels of ring-porous trees are long, and conduction takes place primarily through the latest growth ring, a fact that has been well known to the early botanists (cf. Huber, 1935). A double sawcut should, therefore, interrupt all water channels. If one carefully analyzes the situation, however, one sees that some direct axial (i.e. vessel–) continuity still might exist across

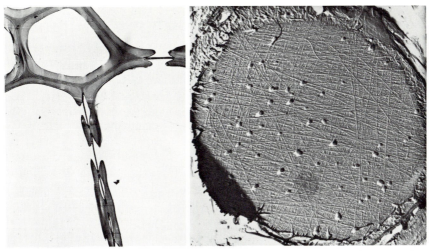

Fig. IV-26. Left: Transverse section through wood of *Tilia americana* L. showing bordered pits (without torus) between vessels. Magnification × 2,100. Right: Surface of pit membrane from an intervessel bordered pit pair in *Tilia americana* L. Pseudoreplica shadowed with uranium. Magnification × 11,500. Electron micrographs courtesy of W. A. Côté.

double-cut stem portions. First of all, two sawcuts from opposite sides can only be made at a certain distance (say, 50 cm) from each other; otherwise the tree will break. Now, referring back to Section 1a of this chapter, one remembers that there is usually a wide range of vessel lengths to be found in wood. In Fig. IV-3, in the case of *Eucalyptus obliqua* L. Hérit. about 60% of the vessels are shorter than 50 cm. Even of the vessels longer than 50 cm, many must reach uninterrupted into the area between the sawcuts. Furthermore considering that vessel-to-vessel movement of water takes place laterally over a certain length, rather than end-to-end, it becomes obvious that axial water movement is still possible in the area between the two sawcuts, in spite of the fact that many of the vessels are embolized. Even ring-porous species have short latewood vessels and may survive the double-sawcut treatment especially if the earlywood vessels are slightly crossed as has been described in Section 1b of this chapter for *Fraxinus*. If the tree survives the growing season during which the experiment has been performed, reorientation of newly-formed vascular tissue will eventually repair the damage (cf. Wilson and Wilson, 1961).

In summary then, xylem is constructed in such a way that if the water is at pressures greater than +1 atm., the xylem sap will leak through any injury; if pressures are below +1 atm., the smallness of the pores of the pit membranes will not permit air to enter beyond the injured tracheid or vessel. This is, in fact, a valve action which seems to be of significance in the mechanism of maple sap flow (cf. Chap. VII, Sec. 4b). In the case of conifers, where pit perforations are relatively large, valve action of tori in bordered pits may represent an additional protective device.

c. The problem of winter freezing

It was Scholander (1958) who pointed out the danger to which tall perennial plants are exposed if they grow in regions with cold winters. When water freezes, bubbles appear almost invariably in the ice, because the solubility of air in ice is extremely low. Water in the xylem of trees does contain dissolved gases; freezing must, therefore, produce bubbles (Scholander, 1958). Thus, the continuity of water columns is broken when the ice thaws in the spring. How can tall trees exist in regions with cold winters?

Older literature suggests that xylem water freezes only at temperatures considerably below 0°C. This idea probably arose from the fact that it is difficult to freeze moving water if low temperature is applied locally, because the chilled xylem water continuously "escapes." Scholander et al. (1961), for example, were unable to freeze xylem water in *Calamus* with pieces of dry ice unless water movement was stopped artificially. The freezing of moving xylem water is easily possible, however, if the chilled length is increased.

The freezing point of extracted xylem sap is only a few hundredths of a degree below the freezing point of pure water, because the solute content of xylem sap is very small (this is why one often refers to xylem water rather than xylem sap). Freezing-point measurements show beyond any doubt that xylem water freezes without much supercooling (Lybeck, 1959; Zimmermann, 1964). This concerns water in vessels and tracheids. It must be noted that 30–40% of the total water (based upon the dry weight of wood) remains unfrozen and is probably bound to cell walls (Lybeck, 1959) (cf. also Fig. IV-27).

Considering all these findings it can be taken as quite certain that winter freezing represents a serious danger to the water-conducting system of trees. It can be taken as equally certain that embolism resulting from freezing exerts a controlling influence upon the distribution of tall plants on earth. The question then arises: how do tolerant species cope with this situation? There could be at least three different mechanisms as follows.

1. Trees with very small conducting units, conifers with only tracheids, and certain diffuse-porous trees with very small vessels can easily survive low temperatures. Bubbles confined in small spaces must be very small and might redissolve before the need for tensions arises, especially because the freezing process itself represents a considerable volume and thus pressure increase (Hammel, 1967). If one freezes a transpiring oak tree for a brief period, subsequent dye-injection experiments indicate that small latewood vessels remain functioning while the large earlywood vessels are, and remain, embolized.

2. Some diffuse-porous species, such as birches (*Betula* sp.), as well as certain vines (*Vitis* sp.) produce considerable root pressure in early spring. It is very likely that root pressure can refill empty vessels.

3. The vegetation of north-temperate regions with low winter temperatures contains many ring-porous species with large earlywood vessels.

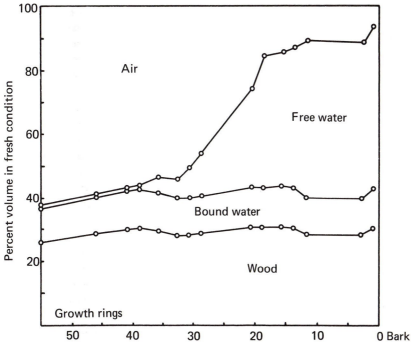

Fig. IV–27. Distribution of wall substance and water in growth rings of a 55-year-old spruce. Tracheids are gradually embolized over a period of 40 years following their formation. Note that in this representation distances *between* curves (not from abscissa to curve) show amounts. From Trendelenburg (1939).

These vessels are produced in the spring before leaves expand. Moreover, ring-porous species conduct water mostly in the youngest growth ring (Huber, 1935). In this interesting case trees produce a very efficient water-conducting system within the short time before it is needed; therefore they can afford the loss of it every winter. This fabulous efficiency takes place at the expense of safety. The slightest injury to the latest growth ring can cause the collapse of the whole water-conducting system. The chestnut blight which wiped out literally all the native chestnut trees (*Castanea dentata* (Marsh.) Borkh.) in North America, and the Dutch elm disease which threatens European and American elms (*Ulmus* sp.) are two most dramatic examples.

In summary there are, at least, three essential features responsible for the survival after air embolism caused by winter freezing: the smallness of the conducting units, root pressure in the spring, and renewal of vessels before leaf expansion. But one must not forget that conducting tissues eventually do go out of function permanently (Fig. IV-27). Tissue renewal may, thus, be the most important of the three factors; no arborescent monocotyledons, no tree ferns, no tall cycads and no large-porous evergreens can survive where temperatures drop low enough to allow the freezing of xylem water.

8. PERMANENT EMBOLISM
AND HEARTWOOD FORMATION

In his discussion of vascular movement of water, Huber (1956) writes: "We are virtually certain that the water columns in the xylem are under tension and that these tensions play a role in the movement of water. It is equally certain that, sooner or later, water columns under tension must break and the vessels embolize, probably irreversibly. This loss of water from conducting elements is but the beginning of a chain of events which we call heartwood formation." (Free translation from the German). The loss of water from a single conducting unit is a much more serious matter in dicotyledons than in conifers, because the volume of a single vessel may be many thousand times greater than the volume of a tracheid. One must, therefore, expect that the irreversible loss of water from xylem is more rapid in large- than in small-porous tree species. Large-porous trees, however, are much more efficient water conductors and can afford the greater loss. Some of these problems have been discussed in the preceding section.

Measurement of the water content of coniferous wood is a relatively simple matter even though the water content might come out a little bit low if the sample is collected under conditions of high transpiration when the xylem is in a contracted condition. Figure IV-27 shows rather nicely how water is gradually lost from spruce tracheids as they get older. Irreversible embolism seems to have occurred in all tracheids of a given growth ring by the time it has reached the age of 40 years.

Measurement of the water content of dicotyledonous wood is much more difficult if samples are to be collected under conditions of transpiration, because water immediately withdraws from cut vessels (cf. Section 7b). Measurements as the ones shown in Fig. IV-27 would best be made on samples collected during a rainy night. The fluctuations in water content of wood samples taken throughout the year (Gibbs, 1958) may be partly a reflection of the collection technique, but they undoubtedly also show water-content changes of the living tree. Most of Gibbs' curves show a low water content during late summer and a "refilling" of xylem after leaf fall in autumn. This refilling must not be visualized as a refilling of gas-filled spaces with water, but rather a refilling due to expansion of wood tissues caused by relaxation of tensions in the xylem.

Gas embolism is gradually followed by histological changes in the wood. In many large-porous species embolized vessels are filled with tyloses, an outgrowth of ray or axial parenchyma cells through pits into the vessel lumen. Tyloses may be few or many crowded together, thin- or thick-walled, pitted or unpitted, with or without starch, crystals, resins, gums, etc. (Committee on Nomenclature, IAWA, 1964). It is important to realize that tyloses are the *result* of gas embolism. Klein (1923) demonstrated with a simple experiment in which water and air respectively were pulled through a forked twig, tyloses appeared only in the branch through which air had been drawn.

One often reads in accounts of tree pathology that failure of water conduction in a tree was caused by plugging of vessels with fungal hyphae. This is indeed very unlikely. One must assume that initial failure of water conduction is due to embolism caused by the first puncture of a vessel wall by a fungal hypha, and that plugging of the vessel lumen by hyphae is only a secondary effect.

Aging of the living wood of a tree finally ends with the formation of heartwood, the central core of a tree stem which may or may not be macroscopically recognizable as a darkly-colored zone. Cells of this zone are dead and have ceased to function as storage places of assimilates. Pigmentation, if present, is the result of biochemical changes during heartwood formation in the so-called transition zone. Many of these changes have recently been described (Bosshard, 1968; Stewart, 1966; Ziegler, 1967). Physiologically speaking, they can be regarded as mechanisms of internal excretion of biochemical "waste" products. The toxic nature of many of these substances protects the dead central part of the tree (at least some species) from internal decay. Structurally sound heartwood continues to serve the living tree as mechanical support tissue.

9. SOLUTE MOVEMENT IN THE XYLEM

In the case of phloem transport an interesting way to find the essential phloem-mobile substances is to grow roots in sterile culture and to compare their requirements with those of roots of intact plants growing in a nutrition solution. The only additional requirements of isolated roots in culture is that of sugars and a few vitamins of the B complex (depending on the species) (cf. Chap. V, Sec. 3c). A great many different substances can "ride" the transport stream in the sieve tubes, but only a few seem to be absolutely required for the growth of roots. For the xylem, one could ask the same kind of question: what are the absolutely essential solutes, supplied by roots to shoots via xylem? This question has not yet been systematically investigated, but is nevertheless of fundamental importance. The classical concept is that the xylem supplies the shoot with "water and mineral nutrients." This concept of "inorganic transport" refers today only to the nutrients' origin; for during the course of more recent years it has become increasingly clear that the roots are very important centers of synthesis of more or less complex organic substances. In fact, xylem sap contains primarily organic, not inorganic solutes, and it is very likely that the requirements of xylem nutrients by shoot tips is much more complex than the phloem-nutrient requirement of root tips.

a. Extraction of xylem sap

In a few species, bleeding xylem sap can be obtained for analysis from the stump of a cut tree. This is usually only possible in late winter or early spring before leaves have emerged. Some authors collected xylem exudate from the distal ends of roots which had been severed from the tree but remained *in situ* in the soil. It is possible in certain (e.g. coniferous) species to obtain exudation from root ends even if the stump of a cut tree ordinarily does not yield exudation (Reuter and Wolffgang, 1954). If exudate cannot be obtained, xylem sap has to be extracted from a sample of wood.

The extraction of xylem sap requires any of a few tricks for reasons which should be clear to the reader after he has read the preceding Sections 1a and 7b. The problem is to get the liquid out of the closed conducting units, be they one cell (tracheids) or several cells (vessels) in extent. Mere vacuum is not sufficient to extract sap, and positive gas pressures would have to be unreasonably high. Several simple methods have been used in the past. One can, for example, mount one end of a branch to a suction flask, and, while applying vacuum, successively cut small disks off the other end of the branch. Vessels are, thus, opened at one end and can run out at the other (Bennett *et al.*, 1927). This method works quite successfully with angiosperm wood where the conducting units are relatively large. In the case of conifers the disks would have to be made extremely thin. Simpler perhaps is to displace the xylem content with distilled water. If distilled water is added at the upper end, xylem sap emerges at the lower (vacuum) end. In fact, vacuum pull is then not even essential, though it speeds up the procedure considerably. If the sap is to be used for quantitative analysis, its electrical conductivity could be monitored and extraction could be stopped at the first indication of a conductivity decrease so that a dilution of sap with distilled water is avoided. A dye dissolved in the distilled water might serve the same purpose. A first run with fractionated collection might serve as a guide in finding the quantity of water needed for extraction of a certain volume of wood.

b. Solutes in xylem sap

The total solute content of xylem sap is ordinarily very low (about of the order of 0.1% (w/v), of which ⅓ is ash), the freezing-point depression seldom amounts to more than a few hundreds of a degree C. If one considers, however, that the velocity of transport is quite appreciable (Sec. 5b), one realizes that leaves are amply supplied with nutrients from roots. The pH of extracted xylem sap is generally around 5 throughout the year (Bollard, 1958). All minerals, essential to the growth of the plant have to ascend via xylem, older reports of upward transport from roots via phloem are quite certainly misinterpretations (cf. Chap. VII, Sec. 4a).

It is difficult to give reasonable sample figures of the mineral content of xylem sap, because individual mineral contents change quite drastically throughout the course of the year. The levels of four elements in xylem sap of apple trees are given in Fig. IV-28. Mineral content is low in the winter, perhaps because xylem sap is hardly moving and solutes are taken up by living cells along the way. At time of blooming there is a dramatic increase in all minerals, N, P and Mg reach their peak concentration then. Whether this is due to the onset of significant transpiration (leaves emerge about the same time as flowers) is unknown. Simple dependence of mineral content upon transpiration intensity is ruled out because the peak concentration of K is not reached until 11 weeks later.

Nitrogen almost invariably moves in organic form; Bollard (1958) reported that in numerous rosaceous fruit trees amino acid and amide fractions represented total nitrogen. Within a wide range of trees nitrate could only be found in xylem sap of about a third of the species, and even there it never amounted to more

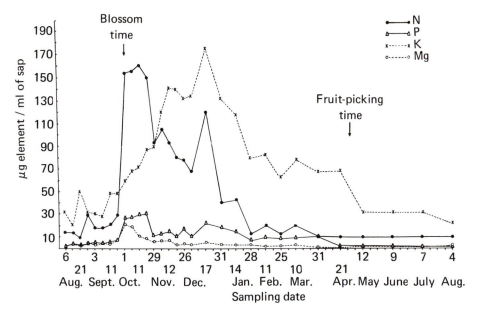

Fig. IV–28. Variation in the content of four elements (nitrogen, phosphorus, potassium and magnesium) in xylem sap of apple trees throughout one season. Note that these data are from the southern hemisphere. From Bollard (1958).

than 1–2% of the total nitrogen. It, therefore, seems that incorporation of inorganic nitrogen into organic compounds is largely accomplished in the roots before translocation in the xylem. This point will have to be discussed again elsewhere (Chap. VII, Sec. 4a).

Nitrogen was found by Bollard (1958) primarily in the form of aspartic acid and asparagine, glutamic acid and glutamine, but many other amino acids as well as small amounts of peptides were also frequently present. Though many different compounds were generally present, occasionally including citrulline, allantoin or allantoic acid (earlier reported by Reuter and Wolffgang, 1954), one or two of these were predominant, accounting for 70% or more of the total nitrogen. In most species, either asparagine or glutamine (or both) were the dominating compounds; in others it was citrulline, allantoin or allantoic acid.

The recognition of the root as the seat of assimilation of mineral nitrogen into organic form is not a very new one (cf. Thomas, 1927); a voluminous literature about this topic has accumulated. An interesting case is nicotine synthesis in tobacco roots. In reciprocal grafts of tobacco and tomato, nicotine-free tobacco leaves and nicotine-containing tomato leaves have been produced (Dawson, 1942).

During recent years the array of solutes known to occur in xylem sap has increased. Gibberellin activity (Jones and Lacey, 1968), auxin activity (in certain plants) as well as numerous enzymes have been detected (Sheldrake and Northcote, 1968). Sheldrake and Northcote consider the possibility that some of these substances are products of autolyzing, differentiating xylem cells in the growing roots. Vascular elements do lose their protoplasmic content at the point of maturity, and it is very likely that the cell content, or perhaps parts of it, then gets swept upwards in the transpiration stream.

The physiological significance of assimilation of inorganic nutrients into organic form by roots may be manifold. The organic form of a substance in the xylem may be the result of the mechanism of nutrient uptake. Possibly as a result of this, the shoot may have developed partial heterotrophy in respect to certain organic substances which are regularly supplied by the roots via xylem. Furthermore, the organic form may have an important function in translocation. Iron, for example, seems to be poorly mobile in xylem if it is not chelated, i.e. bound in organic form. Readers who are interested in further details about these matters are referred to the reviews of Bollard (1960) and Stewart (1963) (for newer literature see also Tiffin, 1967).

c. Distribution of nutrients by the xylem

Some minerals, when applied to roots, accumulate to a different degree in different leaves. The fact that some of them (e.g. phosphorus) may accumulate more in young than in old leaves has given rise to the idea that some minerals follow a mysterious distribution mechanism different from that of the transpiration stream. It is very peculiar that some workers, when studying xylem transport, forget the phloem, or when studying the phloem transport, ignore the xylem (cf. Chap. V, Sec. 2d). There is nothing mysterious about the varying distribution of minerals among different leaves. The case of phosphorus is very simply explained by re-export of phosphorus from old leaves via phloem. In experiments of a duration of hours or even days one cannot study xylem distribution alone, for such long periods of time are ample to allow repeated circulation within the plant. Further discussion of distribution of nutrients will be taken up in Chapter VII, Section 4.

LITERATURE CITED

ASKENASY, E. 1895. Ueber das Saftsteigen. *Verh. naturwiss.-med. Ver.* Vol. 5 Heidelberg (Ref. in: Bot. Cbl. 62: 237–238. 1895).

BAILEY, I. W. 1913. The preservative treatment of wood. II. The structure of the pit membranes in the tracheids of conifers and their relation to the penetration of gases, liquids and finely divided solids into green and seasoned wood. *For. Quart.* 11: 12–20.—
BANNAN, M. W. 1966. Spiral grain and anticlinal divisions in the cambium of conifers. *Can. Jour. Bot.* 44: 1515–1538.—BENNETT, J. P., F. G. ANDERSSEN and Y. MILAD. 1927. Methods of obtaining tracheal sap from woody plants. *New Phytol.* 26: 316–323.—
BERGER, W. 1931. Das Wasserleitungssystem von krautigen Pflanzen, Zwergsträuchern und Lianen in quantitativer Betrachtung. *Beih. bot. Cbl.* 48 (I): 363–390.—BODE, H. R. 1923. Beiträge zur Dynamik der Wasserbewegung in den Gefässpflanzen. *Jahrb. wiss. Bot.* 62: 91–127.—BÖHM, J. 1893. Capillarität und Saftsteigen. *Ber. dtsch. bot. Ges.* 11: 203–212. —BOLLARD, E. G. 1958. Nitrogenous compounds in tree xylem sap. p. 83–93 In *The Physiology of Forest Trees.* Ed. K. V. Thimann. New York: Ronald Press.—BOLLARD, E. G. 1960. Transport in the xylem. *Ann. Rev. Plant Physiol.* 11: 141–166.—BOSSHARD,

H. H. 1968. On the formation of facultatively colored heartwood in *Beilschmiedia tawa*. *Wood Sci. and Tech.* 2: 1–12.—BRAUN, H. J. 1959. Die Vernetzung der Gefässe bei *Populus. Z. Botanik* 45: 421–434.

COMMITTEE ON NOMENCLATURE, INTERNAT. ASSOC. WOOD ANATOMISTS. 1964. *Multilingual glossary of terms used in wood anatomy.* Winterthur, Switzerland: Verlagsanstalt Konkordia.—CÔTÉ, W. A. 1963. Structural factors affecting the permeability of wood. *Jour. Polymer Sci.:* Part C, No. 2, 231–242.—CRAFTS, A. S., H. B. CURRIER and C. R. STOCKING. 1949. *Water in the Physiology of Plants.* Waltham, Massachusetts: Chronica Botanica Co.

DAVIS, T. A. 1961. High root pressure in palms. *Nat.* 192: 277–278.—DAWSON, R. F. 1942. Accumulation of nicotine in reciprocal grafts of tomato and tobacco. *Amer. Jour. Bot.* 29: 66–71.—DIXON, H. H. 1914. *Transpiration and the Ascent of Sap in Plants.* London: Macmillan & Co. Ltd.—DIXON, H. H. and J. JOLY. 1896. On the ascent of sap. *Roy. Soc. (London) Phil. Trans.,* B186: 563–576.

ESAU, K. 1965. *Plant Anatomy.* 2nd ed. New York: John Wiley & Sons.

FRENZEL, P. 1929. Ueber die Porengrössen einiger pflanzlicher Zellmembranen. *Planta* 8: 642–665.—FREY-WYSSLING, A., H. H. BOSSHARD and K. MÜHLETHALER. 1956. Die submikroskopische Entwicklung der Hoftüpfel. *Planta* 47: 115–126.—FRIEDRICH, J. 1897. Ueber den Einfluss der Witterung auf den Baumzuwachs. *Zbl. ges. Forstw.* 23: 471–495.

GESSNER, F. 1951. Untersuchungen über den Wasserhaushalt der Nymphaeaceen. *Biol. Generalis* (Wien) 19: 247–280.—GIBBS, R. D. 1958. Patterns in the seasonal water content of trees. In *The physiology of forest trees,* ed. K. V. Thimann, pp.43–69. New York: Ronald Press.—GREENIDGE, K. N. H. 1957. Ascent of sap. *Ann. Rev. Plant Physiol.* 8: 237–256.—GREENIDGE, K. N. H. 1958. Rates and patterns of moisture movement in trees. In *The physiology of forest trees.* Ed. K. V. Thimann, pp. 19–41. New York: Ronald Press.

HAMMEL, H. T. 1967. Freezing of xylem sap without cavitation. *Plant Physiol.* 42: 55–66.—HANDLEY, W. R. C. 1936. Some observations on the problem of vessel length determination in woody dicotyledons. *New Phytol.* 35: 456–471.—HANDLEY, W. R. C. 1939. The effect of prolonged chilling on water movement and radial growth in trees. *Ann. Bot.* 3: 803–813.—HARTIG, Th. 1878. *Anatomie und Physiologie der Holzpflanzen.* Berlin: Springer.—HUBER, B. 1928. Weitere quantitative Untersuchungen über das Wasserleitungssystem der Pflanzen. *Jb. wiss. Bot.* 67: 877–959.—*HUBER, B. 1935. Die physiologische Bedeutung der Ring- und Zerstreutporigkeit. *Ber. dtsch. bot. Ges.* 53: 711–719.— HUBER, B. 1956. Die Gefässleitung. In *Encyclopedia of plant physiology.* Vol. 3. Ed. W. Ruhland, pp. 541–582. Berlin-Göttingen-Heidelberg: Springer-Verlag.—HUBER, B. and W. MERZ. 1958. Ueber die Bedeutung des Hoftüpfelverschlusses für die axiale Wasserleitfähigkeit von Nadelhölzern. I. and II. *Planta* 51: 645–672.—*HUBER, B. and E. SCHMIDT. 1936. Weitere thermo-elektrische Untersuchungen über den Transpirationsstrom der Bäume. *Tharandt. forstl. Jb.* 87: 369–412.—*HUBER, B. and E. SCHMIDT. 1937. Eine Kompensationsmethode zur thermo-elektrischen Messung langsamer Saftströme. *Ber. dtsch. bot. Ges.* 55: 514–529.

JOHNSON, B. and J. R. DIXON. 1965. Ascent of sap in trees: effect of negative absolute pressure on flow resistance. *Nature* 208: 1347–1348.—JOHNSTON, R. D. 1959. Control of

* English translations of these papers are available on microfilm from: Translation Center, John Crerar Library, 35 West 33rd St., Chicago, Ill. 60616.

water movement by stem chilling. *Austral. Jour. Bot.* 97–108.—Jones, O. P. and H. J. Lacey. 1968. Gibberellin-like substances in the transpiration stream of apple and pear trees. *Jour. Exptl. Bot.* 19: 526–531.—Jost, L. 1916. Versuche über die Wasserleitung in der Pflanze. *Z. Botanik* 8: 1–55.

Kelso, W. C., C. O. Gertjejansen and R. L. Hossfeld. 1963. The effect of air blockage upon the permeability of wood to liquids. Univ. Minnesota Agric. Res. Station *Tech. Bull.* 242.—Klein, G. 1923. Zur Aetiologie der Thyllen. *Z. Bot.* 15: 417–439.—Klemm, G. 1956. Untersuchungen über den Transpirationswiderstand der Mesophyllmembranen und seine Bedeutung als Regulator für die stomatäre Transpiration. *Planta* 47: 547–587. —Koslowski, T. T. and C. H. Winget. 1963. Patterns of water movement in forest trees. Bot. Gaz. 124: 301–311.—Kramer, P. J. 1937. The relation between rate of transpiration and rate of absorption of water in plants. *Amer. Jour. Bot.* 24: 10–15.

Ladefoged, K. 1960. A method for measuring the water consumption of larger intact trees. *Physiol. Plantarum* 13: 648–658.—Liese, W. and J. Bauch. 1964. Ueber die Wegsamkeit der Hoftüpfel von Coniferen. *Naturwiss.* 51: 516.—Loomis, W. E., R. Santamaria-P and R. S. Gage. 1960. Cohesion of water in plants. *Plant Physiol.* 35: 300–306.— Lybeck, B. R. 1959. Winter freezing in relation to the rise of sap in tall trees. *Plant Physiol.* 34: 482–486.

MacDougal, D. T. and J. B. Overton and G. M. Smith. 1929. *The hydrostatic-pneumatic system of certain trees: movements of liquids and gases.* Carnegie Inst. of Washington, Publ. No. 397.—Marshall, D. C. 1958. Measurement of sap flow in conifers by heat transport. *Plant Physiol.* 33: 385–396.—Milburn, J. A. and R. P. C. Johnson. 1966. The conduction of sap II. Detection of vibrations produced by sap cavitation in *Ricinus* xylem. *Planta* 69: 43–52.—Münch, E. 1943. Durchlässigkeit der Siebröhren für Druckströmungen. *Flora* 136: 223–262.

Nordhausen, M. 1917. Zur Kenntnis der Saugkraft und der Wasserversorgung transpirierender Sprossen. *Jb. wiss. Bot.* 58: 295–335.

Preston, R. D. 1952. Movement of water in higher plants. In *Deformation and flow in biological systems,* ed. A. Frey-Wyssling, pp. 257–321. Amsterdam: North Holland Publ. Co.

Reiner, M. 1960. *Deformation, strain and flow: An elementary introduction to rheology.* London: H. K. Lewis & Co. Ltd.—Renner, O. 1912. Versuche zur Mechanik der Wasserversorgung. I. Der Druck in den Leitungsbahnen von Freilandpflanzen. *Ber. dtsch. bot. Ges.* 30: 576–580.—Renner, O. 1915. Theoretisches und Experimentelles zur Kohäsionstheorie der Wasserbewegung. *Jb. wiss. Bot.* 56: 617–667.—Reuter, G. and H. Wolffgang. 1954. Vergleichende Untersuchungen über den Charakter der Stickstoffverbindungen von Baumblutungssäften bei Betulaceen und andern Holzarten. *Flora* 142: 146–155.—Richardson, S. D. 1958. Discussion. In: *The physiology of forest trees,* ed. K. V. Thimann, p. 38. New York: Ronald Press.—Riedl, H. 1937. Bau und Leistungen des Wurzelholzes. *Jb. wiss. Bot.* 85: 1–72.

Scholander, P. F. 1958. The rise of sap in lianas. In *The physiology of forest trees,* ed. K. V. Thimann, pp. 3–17. New York: Ronald Press.—Scholander, P. F., H. T. Hammel, E. D. Bradstreet and E. A. Hemmingsen. 1965. Sap pressure in vascular plants. *Sci.* 148: 339–346.—Scholander, P. F., E. Hemmingsen and W. Garey. 1961. Cohesive lift of sap in the rattan vine. *Sci.* 134: 1835–1838.—Scholander, P. F., W. E. Love and J. W.

KANWISHER. 1955. The rise of sap in tall grapevines. *Plant Physiol.* 30: 93–104.—SCHUBERT, A. 1939. Untersuchungen über den Transpirationsstrom der Nadelhölzer und den Wasserbedarf von Fichte und Lärche. *Tharandt. forstl. Jb.* 90: 821–883.—SHELDRAKE, A. R. and D. H. NORTHCOTE. 1968. Some constituents of xylem sap and their possible relationship to xylem differentiation. *Jour. Exptl. Bot.* 19: 681–689.—SKENE, D. S. and V. BALODIS. 1968. A study of vessel length in *Eucalyptus obliqua* L'Hérit. *Jour. Exptl. Bot.* 19: 825–830.—STEWART, C. M. 1966. The chemistry of secondary growth in trees. Div. of Forest Products Technol. *Paper No. 43,* C.S.I.R.O., Australia.—STEWART, L. 1963. Chelation in the absorption and translocation of mineral elements. *Ann. Rev. Plant Physiol.* 14: 295–310.—STOCKER, O. 1952. *Grundriss der Botanik.* Berlin: Springer.—STRASBURGER, E. 1891. *Ueber den Bau und die Verrichtungen der Leitungsbahnen in den Pflanzen.* Jena: G. Fischer.—*STRUGGER, S. 1953. Die Erforschung des Wasser- und Nährsalztransportes im Pflanzenkörper mit Hilfe der fluoreszenzmikroskopischen Kinematographie. *Arbeitsgemeinsch. f. Forschung d. Landes Nordrhein-Westfahlen.* Heft 21a. Westdeutscher Verlag Köln und Opladen.—STRUGGER, S. and E. PEVELING. 1961. Die elektronenmikroskopische Analyse der extrafasciculären Komponente des Transpirationsstroms mit Hilfe von Edelmetallsuspensoiden adäquater Dispersität. *Ber. dtsch. bot. Ges.* 74: 300–304.

THOMAS, W. 1927. The seat of formation of amino acids in *Pyrus Malus* L. *Sci.* 66: 115–117.—TIFFIN, L. O. 1967. Translocation of manganese, iron, cobalt and zinc in tomato. *Plant Physiol.* 42: 1427–1432.—TRENDELENBURG, R. 1939. *Das Holz als Rohstoff.* Munich-Berlin: Lehmann.—TYREE, M. T. 1969. The thermodynamics of short-distance translocation in plants. *Jour. Exptl. Bot.* 20: 341–349.

URSPRUNG, A. 1906. Die Beteiligung lebender Zellen am Saftsteigen. *Jb wiss. Bot.* 42: 503–544.—URSPRUNG, A. 1913. Ueber die Bedeutung der Kohäsion für das Saftsteigen. *Ber. dtsch. bot. Ges.* 31: 401–412.

VIEWEG, G. H. and H. ZIEGLER. 1960. Thermoelektrische Registrierung der Geschwindigkeit des Transpirationsstromes I. *Ber. dtsch. bot. Ges.* 73: 221–226.—VITÉ, J. P. 1958. Ueber die transpirationsphysiologische Bedeutung des Drehwuchses bei Nadelhölzern. *Forstwiss. Cbl.* 77: 193–256.—VITÉ, J. P. and J. A. RUDINSKY. 1959. The water-conducting systems in conifers and their importance to the distribution of trunk-injected chemicals. *Contrib. Boyce Thompson Inst.* 20: 27–38.

WAKESHIMA, H. 1961. On the theory of the fracture of liquids. *Jour. Physical Soc.* Japan 16: 6–14.—WEBB, J. A. and P. R. GORHAM. 1965. The effect of node temperature on assimilation and translocation of ^{14}C in the squash. *Can. Jour. Bot.* 43: 1009–1020.—WILSON, B. F. 1968. Red maple stump sprouts: development the first year. *Harvard Forest Paper No. 18:* 1–10.—WILSON, J. and P. M. W. WILSON. 1961. The position of regenerating cambia—a new hypothesis. *New Phytol.* 60: 63–73.

ZIEGLER, H. 1967. Biologische Aspekte der Kernholzbildung. In *Proc. 14th Congress Internat. Union of Forestry Res. Organ.* (IUFRO). Vol. 9. pp. 93–116. Munich.—ZIMMERMANN, M. H. 1964. Effect of low temperature on ascent of sap in trees. *Plant Physiol.* 39: 568–572.—ZIMMERMANN, M. H. 1965. Water movement in stems of tall plants. In *The state and movement of water in living organisms,* 19th Symposium of the Soc. for Exptl. Biol. pp. 151–155. England: Cambridge, Univ. Press—ZIMMERMANN, M. H. 1966. Translocation of water and nutrients in palms. *Principes (Jour. Palm Soc.)* 10: 105–114.

* English translations of these papers are available on microfilm from: Translation Center, John Crerar Library, 35 West 33rd St., Chicago, Ill. 60616.

—ZIMMERMANN, M. H. and P. B. TOMLINSON. 1965. Anatomy of the palm *Rhapis excelsa* I. Mature vegetative axis. *Jour. Arnold Arb.* 46: 160–178.—ZIMMERMANN, M. H. and P. B. TOMLINSON. 1967. A method for the analysis of the course of vessels in wood. *Bull. Internat. Assoc. Wood Anatomists* 1: 2–6.—ZIMMERMANN, M. H. and P. B. TOMLINSON. 1968. Vascular construction and development in the aerial stem of *Prionium* (Juncaceae). *Amer. Jour. Bot.* 55: 1100–1109.

CHAPTER V

TRANSPORT IN THE PHLOEM

Martin H. Zimmermann

INTRODUCTION

A great number of publications on phloem transport have appeared during the past few years. It is, therefore, impossible to write a comprehensive account without filling it with innumerable "facts." Such a review is not only hard to read, but it quickly goes out of date as well. As in the case of Chapter IV, and indeed the whole book, the authors are not trying to impress the reader by swamping him with myriads of bits of information, but prefer to discuss some important aspects systematically. In this way we hope to show how a problem is approached, thought out, and how individual publications are critically judged.

The following specific example may illustrate this intention, perhaps, better than many words in a general statement. There are dozens of reports of translocation velocities. One could recite or tabulate these and perhaps compare figures obtained from various species. Such a procedure would be a waste of time and paper. The concept of velocity has been so confused in the literature that mere citation of figures would be meaningless. The problem of graded velocities in sieve tubes is very similar to that of flow velocities in the xylem, even though it is likely that this is the case for entirely different reasons. It is, therefore, far more useful to introduce the reader to the various aspects of what is indiscriminately called "velocity" and let him find and properly judge individual literature reports for himself.

Points of view of various translocation workers differ quite sharply; some of the disagreements are caused by hasty publication of papers, for example, before consideration of all the factors (such as the returning transpiration stream). Others may result from preconception, i.e. the investigator may try to prove his point of view rather than to try to find out how nature does the trick. The situation is probably no worse than in other fields of scientific endeavor; it is merely the reflection of human nature.

To an "outsider," phloem transport might be a very confusing field, and one often hears the complaint that "no progress has been made since 1930," and that "the same miserable old models are used as 40 years ago," a remark directed at Münch's pressure-flow model, of course. Münch's model is still used, not because investigators of phloem are more stupid than those of other fields, but because of the brilliant simplicity of Münch's proposal. Let us not forget that progress *has* been made; it is hoped that the following chapter will make this clear.

1. GENERAL ORGANIZATION OF PHLOEM IN TREES

For a general description of phloem anatomy, the reader is referred to the existing excellent plant anatomy text books (e.g. Esau, 1965; Fahn, 1967; Huber, 1961). If the reader desires to get an idea of the variety of bark structures in different tree species, he may want to look at Holdheide's (1951) photomicrographic atlas of European barks. Some information about the organization and formation of phloem is also given elsewhere in this book. In this chapter only aspects of structure and organization which concern the translocation process more or less directly will be discussed.

One of the characteristics of phloem in conifers and dicotyledons is its regular renewal, i.e. in respect to translocation, its short functional life. Phloem renewal in monocotyledons such as palms, is absent. In some members of the Liliflorae, secondary vascular tissue is produced, but nothing is known about the functional life of sieve tubes in these plants. A variety of structures have arisen in the plant kingdom to serve the same function. Three of these groups will now be discussed very briefly.

a. Conifers

The secondary phloem of conifers is produced centrifugally by the vascular cambium. This means that older layers of phloem must increase in circumference, a feat which is accomplished by divisions within the outer phloem parenchyma. Certain cell types are produced by the cambium at certain intervals, etc. The formation of phloem is quite homologous to that of xylem. This is particularly obvious if one compares the formation of sieve cells with that of tracheids. Both these cell types are the major products of the cambium, as derivatives both are similar in shape to the fusiform initials of the cambium. Sieve areas, like the bordered pits of tracheids, are primarily located on radial walls. A very thorough histological investigation of Gymnosperm phloem has been published by Den Outer (1967).

Formation of coniferous phloem varies with the season in the temperate zones of the earth, the result is that annual growth rings can often be recognized in the phloem (cf. e.g. Holdheide, 1958). Naturally, the function of the phloem varies also with the seasons. Translocation as well as other activities must come to a complete or nearly complete halt during the deep winter when the tissue is frozen. This state of dormancy is reached gradually. The anatomically most obvious expression of this is the closure of sieve areas by dormancy callose. Reactivation during late winter and early spring occurs also gradually. Kollmann and Schumacher (1961–1964) described the changes which take place in the phloem of *Metasequoia* throughout the year. Since the majority of conifers grow in temperate and cold climates, seasonal changes are of relative importance in this group.

The functional life of sieve cells in coniferous phloem is quite limited. Sieve cells may serve as translocation channels for one or more years after which time they collapse (Fig. V-1). There may be a functional relationship between the life-span of needles and axial sieve cells of the same age, so that, for example, as three-year-old needles abscise from twigs, the three-year-old sieve cells in the stem beneath collapse. Not too much is known about this relationship, however, but the problem would certainly be worthy of investigation.

Little is known about the overall axial extension of conducting elements in a tree as a whole, i.e. the axial path of phloem transport from any one point in the crown to any one point in the roots. We may with quite reasonable justification speculate that the newly differentiated sieve cells in the phloem are arranged in the same way as the newly differentiated tracheids in the xylem. This means that the axial arrangement of sieve cells is the mirror image of the arrangement of tracheids in the xylem. In other words, the path of translocation in young phloem would be very similar to the path of sap movement in the youngest xylem, except that their respective movement directions are usually opposite. The path of movement in xylem has been discussed at some length in Chapter IV, Section 1b. The situation in the phloem is simpler than in the xylem, because sieve cells function only for one year. The changing pitch of the spiral grain can, therefore, not be of as much significance in the phloem as it is in the xylem. A given portion of the crown would presumably be connected with a different portion of the root system every year as the spiral grain changes; because old sieve cells collapse, a given crown portion would not be axially connected with many different roots, as it is via xylem.

b. Dicotyledons

Much of what has been said about the phloem of conifers applies also to the phloem of most dicotyledons. Phloem is formed centrifugally and proliferation of ray or vertical parenchyma in older tissues has to keep pace with the circumference increase. Conducting elements in both the phloem and the xylem are more highly specialized in dicotyledons than in conifers, and the homology of phloem and xylem is also obvious here. End walls of sieve-tube as well as vessel elements are more highly specialized than those of the lateral walls; the evolutionary trend seems to be from the spindle-shaped cells with lateral connection (sieve areas and bordered pits respectively), to more highly specialized end walls, oriented from oblique to transverse (sieve plates and vessel perforations respectively). However, end walls of even the most highly specialized sieve-tube elements have not disappeared during evolution as they have in xylem vessel elements. The reason for this is not known, of course, but one can make some speculations. One possibility is that the sieve plate is an essential structure for

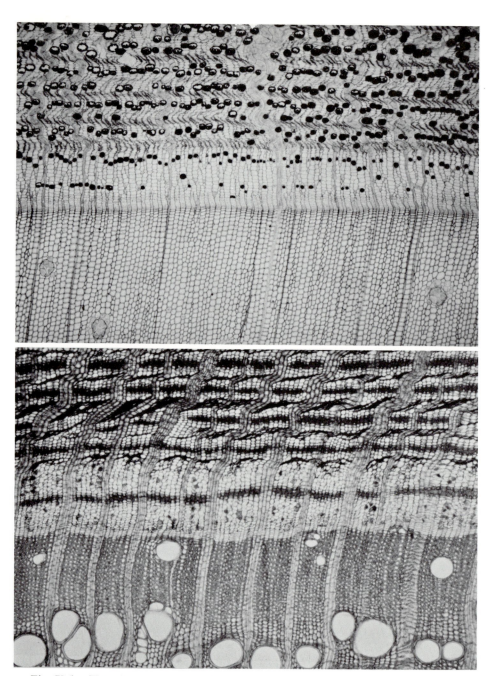

Fig. V–1. Top: Transverse section through the cambial region of *Pinus strobus* L. showing youngest xylem and phloem. Only the most recently formed sieve cells are functioning, older ones are collapsed. Magnification × 50.

Fig. V–2. Bottom: Transverse section through the cambial region of teak (*Tectona grandis* L.) showing the collapse of older sieve tubes. Note that the layer of conducting phloem here as well as in the conifer (Fig. V–1) is less than 0.5 mm thick. Magnification × 50.

the mechanism of translocation, for example the seat of the driving power. The other, more likely explanation for the sieve plates' persistence during evolution is that they serve another vital function, namely the function of valves which can be closed when the sieve tube is injured. This point will be discussed in Sections 6 and 8 of this chapter.

The functional life of sieve tubes is quite limited. In most trees of the temperate regions, sieve tubes may function for one year. The functional life may begin with differentiation of new sieve tubes in the early summer, continue with a rest period during the winter, during which the sieve plates are closed with dormancy callose, and it may end with a brief period of reactivation during the early summer of the next year. After the differentiation of the new sieve tubes, the old ones often collapse. Even in tropical trees, which live under conditions of little or no seasonality, longevity of sieve tubes appears to be limited to a few months (Fig. V-2).

As in the case of the conifers, the axial course of conducting tissue in the stem must be the mirror image of the course of xylem tissue. Since the functional life of sieve tubes is very short, the pattern of axial translocation cannot be very complex. For a discussion of the axial path of translocation, the reader is again referred to the preceding section (1a).

c. Monocotyledons

A great number of monocotyledonous species acquire the arborescent habit with the primary stem structure alone. The palms may serve as an example. Vascular bundles (with a few exceptions which do not concern us in this context) consist of both xylem and phloem. Distribution of vascular tissue throughout the stem as well as the functional life span of the two tissues are, therefore, very similar. Arborescent monoctyledons are continuously growing, their phloem does not go through a dormant stage as does that of many conifers and dicotyledons.

The most remarkable single aspect of the phloem of arborescent monocotyledons is the longevity of their phloem in general and sieve tubes in particular. Sieve tubes which have been formed in the basal part of the stem during the early life of the plant, must remain functional throughout the whole lifetime of the plant. This is in sharp contrast to conifers and dicotyledons where sieve elements are very short lived. Only the sieve tubes of leaf traces, from the leaf scar to somewhat beyond the bundle branches (see Fig. IV-9) cease to function after abscision of the leaves (Parthasarathy and Tomlinson, 1967).

The axial course of vascular bundles in arborescent monocotyledons is very complex. A description has been given in connection with the ascent of sap (Chap. IV, Sec. 1d). Since, within the central cylinder of the stem, xylem and phloem run parallel, the paths of the two translocation systems are largely identical.

Interesting, but very poorly known are the monocotyledons which produce vascular bundles by secondary growth in their stem (Tomlinson and Zimmermann, 1969). Their primary structure is in principle the same as that of palms, but a cambium outside the central cylinder produces additional vascular bundles centripetally. As long as leaves are functional, leaf traces keep growing within the expanding secondary tissue, and anastomoses keep vascular contact between leaf traces and secondary vascular bundles. The secondary vascular tissue is fairly simple in construction, bundles are merely added to the central cylinder. They are anastomosing frequently, more tangentially than radially, in a fashion somewhat reminiscent of the vessel network in dicotyledonous wood (cf. Fig. IV-6). The secondary vascular tissue may not be continuous from the base of the plant up into the crown, the axial tissue of the crown area is often entirely primary. How long phloem remains functional in monocotyledonous trees with secondary growth is not known.

2. PATH AND DIRECTIONS OF TRANSPORT

a. Evidence for transport in the sieve tubes

So far it has been merely stated that translocation of photosynthetic products takes place through the sieve tubes, but this statement has yet to be supported with evidence. The reaction of the tree to girdling, the removal of a ring of bark, follows a well-known pattern. Water transport from roots to leaves is not directly affected, but the flow of photosynthetic products from leaves downward is stopped at the girdle. Numerous variations of this experiment have been made by botanists for over 200 years and the conclusion has always been essentially the same, namely that water ascends through the wood and photosynthetic products descend in the bark.

Theodor Hartig described the sieve tubes in 1837 (Fig. V-3) and sieve-tube exudation in 1860. Channels of translocation and the translocated material were thus recognized, but it took another 70 years before further progress was made. Interestingly enough, the next significant contribution was made by an entomologist.

It had been learned during the past century that the rate of photosynthesis of leaves during the day is greater than the rate of transport of carbohydrates out of the leaves. Considerable quantities of starch accumulate in the leaf during the daytime even though translocation exports sugars. Photosynthesis ceases as the daylight vanishes, but translocation continues, and the starch which has accumulated in the leaf during the day is mobilized and translocated out of the leaf during the night. Iodine reactions, carried out with cleared leaves collected throughout the 24-hour period, demonstrate this quite readily (cf. also Chap. VII, Sec. 1). Schneider-Orelli (1909) was interested in the moth *Lyonetia clercella* L. which has a leaf-mining larval stage of development. The insect lays its eggs into the tissue of apple leaves. The larvae eat their way through the leaf tissue and finally, after metamorphosis, emerge through the epidermis. Studying starch deposition and mobilization in apple leaves invaded by *Lyonetia*, Schneider-Orelli found that sugar export was blocked in areas where phloem was injured by the mining larvae. Starch remained in those areas of a leaf which had the outgoing phloem channels severed (Fig. V-4a-d). An interesting detail is the fact that movement from leaf parenchyma to vascular bundle sheath still took place

(Fig. V-4f). During photosynthesis starch was deposited in leaf parenchyma, but it was mobilized there during the night, moved to the vascular bundles (presumably in the form of sugars) and deposited again in the form of starch in the parenchymatous bundle sheath. In a recent study, Leonard and King (1968) reported on this vein-loading process in detached leaves. Their results confirm those of Schneider-Orelli; in addition they illustrated the absence of vein loading in very young, growing leaves (Fig. V-5).

Mason and Maskell (1928) made various types of girdling experiments with cotton, studying translocation by sugar analysis. They found that diurnal fluctuations of sugar concentrations in the leaf were reproduced a few hours later in the inner bark. The fluctuating sugar was sucrose; it was also sucrose which accumulated above a girdle. This indicated sucrose transport in the innermost portion of the bark where living (i.e. functional) sieve tubes are located. Schumacher (1930, 1937) separated by surgical means the phloem of the central petiolar vascular bundle of *Pelargonium* and showed that translocation out of leaves was localized in the phloem tissue. Negative evidence, i.e. lack of transport in the presence of sieve tubes closed by callose, supported the concept of sieve-tube transport.

More recent evidence for transport in the phloem has come from two experimental procedures. One of these is autoradiography of tissue sections through which translocation of a radioactively labeled photosynthetic product has taken place; the other makes use of phloem-feeding insects, aphids. Autoradiographic studies have largely been done with herbaceous plants, it shall not, therefore, be discussed at any length in this text which deals primarily with trees. Suffice it to say that transport of radioactively labeled photosynthates has been shown to take place in the phloem (e.g. Mortimer, 1965). Further refinement of autoradiographic procedures has shown that sieve tubes are the pathways of translocation (Trip and Gorham, 1967).

Fig. V-3. The first illustration of a sieve element. From Hartig, 1837.

Transport in woody plants can be studied with the aid of phloem-feeding insects (Fig. V-6). Mittler (1957, 1958) developed this technique whereby aphids, while feeding, are severed from their mouth parts under anaesthesia. Sieve-tube pressure then maintains flow through the stylet bundle and the liquid can be collected from the cut stump with a pipet (Fig. V-7). When the phloem with such an exuding aphid stylet bundle is sectioned, the stylet-bundle tip can be found in a single sieve element (Fig. V-8). Investigations by Weatherley *et al.* (1959) indicate that the exudate is supplied to the stylet bundle in an axial direction

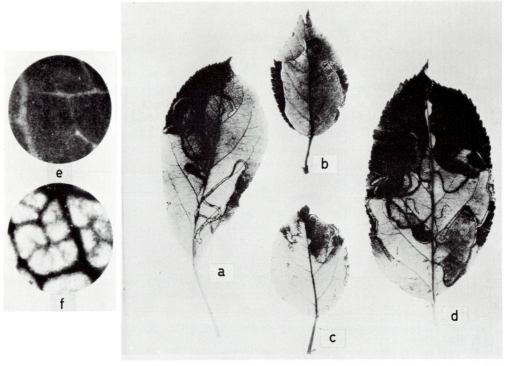

Fig. V-4. Iodine reaction with cleared leaves normally shows the blade full of starch at the end of the day, empty at the end of the night. Such transistory "afternoon" starch is located in the leaf parenchyma, not the veins (e). In apple leaves invaded by the mining moth *Lyonetia clercella* L. export is prevented from those parts of the leaves whose phloem channel to the petiole is interrupted (a-d). At this time, all starch is concentrated in the bundle sheath (f). From Schneider-Orelli, 1909.

(Sec. 2b). Structural implications and the fact that the stylet bundle tips are located in a single sieve element show that this longitudinal movement is via a single sieve tube. Furthermore, aphids feeding on the phloem of a stem release radioactive honeydew soon after radioactive carbon dioxide is supplied to leaves for photosynthesis (Canny, 1962a). In conclusion then, all available evidence indicates that transport of photosynthetic products from leaves takes place through the sieve tubes of the phloem. In dicotyledonous trees these sieve tubes are conspicuously functioning only for a limited period of time after which they collapse (Fig. V-2).

Translocation in coniferous trees as well as in arborescent monocotyledons is visualized as being analogous to that in dicotyledons. Exudation from cut aphid stylet bundles has been obtained from a few coniferous species (*Picea abies* (L) Karst, Ziegler and Mittler, 1959; *Pinus strobus* L. and *P. resinosa* Ait., unpublished results by G. P. Hill, 1960). In the case of *Metasequoia* (Kollmann, 1965) and *Juniperus* (Kollmann and Dörr, 1966) the tips of exuding aphid stylet

Fig. V–5. Left: Autoradiographs showing distribution of label in detached bean leaves directly following their exposure to $^{14}CO_2$. Right: Distribution of label following a transport period of 24 hours. Label has moved to the veins in old, but not in young leaves. From Leonard and King, 1968.

bundles have been located in young sieve cells in the phloem which, in autoradiographic studies, had proved to be conducting.

b. Axial and tangential transport

As pointed out in the preceding Section of this chapter, translocation in the axial direction of sieve tubes throughout the stem can be inferred from the direction of xylem elements, which had been discussed in Chapter IV, Section 1b. This is justified, because the cambial initials (or, in arborescent monocotyledons, procambial initials) are known to produce derivatives which are oriented the same way in xylem and phloem.

The discussion of arborescent monocotyledons can be very brief here. Extremely few transport studies have been made with them and almost all information comes from anatomical data and from circumstantial evidence. The intricate paths of axial translocation have been discussed in Chapter IV, Section 1d. The primary structure consists of a network of vascular bundles which, presumably, are all available for translocation. In the case of injury of the stem, innumerable alternate axial paths are available which lead around the injury.

Fig. V–6. The aphid *Longistigma caryae* Harris feeding on a branch of linden (*Tilia americana* L.). The insect is just releasing a droplet of honeydew. It does so about once every 30 minutes. From Zimmermann, 1961.

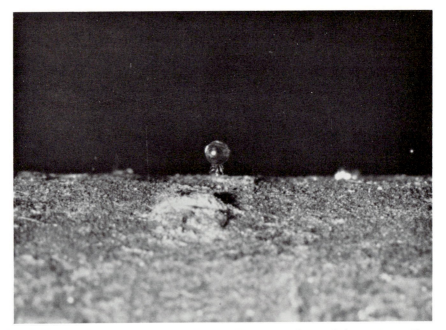

Fig. V–7. Exudation from a cut stylet-bundle stump of *Longistigma*. From Zimmermann, 1961.

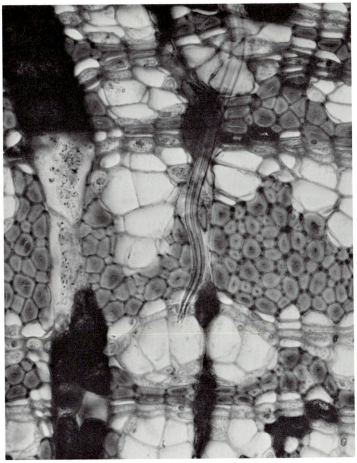

Fig. V–8. Transverse section through the bark of *Tilia americana* L. showing the tip of an aphid stylet bundle which had been exuding (as shown in Fig. V–7) prior to sectioning of the bark on the microtome. Note that the tips of the stylets are inside the sieve element; the saliva canal, however, ends outside. Magnification × 425. From Zimmermann, 1961.

Wound tissue, i.e. new vascular bundles leading around the wound, are unknown in the primary stem of monocotyledons (Tomlinson, pers. comm.). The possibility of extrafascicular transport (from bundle to bundle via parenchyma) has not been investigated. It is theoretically possible because in many palms great quantities of starch are deposited in parenchyma and remobilized. However, this process is probably slower than vascular transport and under all but the most drastic disturbances, axial paths would be available anyhow. Extremely little is known about the translocation path in monocotyledons with secondary vascular tissue. It is hoped that future work will shed some light on these problems.

In conifers and dicotyledons, which are far better known than monocotyledons, an almost continuous cylinder of sieve cells or sieve tubes surrounds the

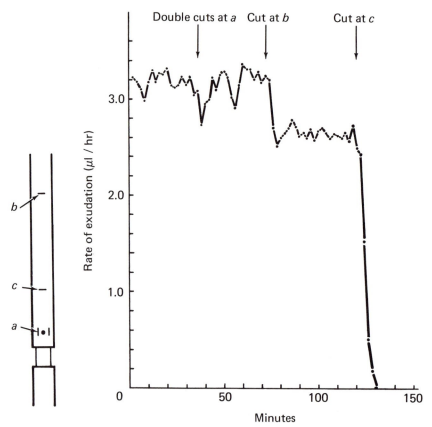

Fig. V–9. Left: A ringed stem of *Salix viminalis* L. with an exuding stylet bundle (indicated by a dot). Incisions were made into the bark at a, b and c. The effect of these incisions upon the exudation rate is shown on the right. From Weatherley, Peel and Hill, 1959.

stem. The evidence of axial transport will now be analyzed. Exudation studies by Weatherley *et al.* (1959) are relevant here. Longitudinal incisions into the bark tangentially adjacent to the exuding stylet bundle had no effect upon the rate of exudation, even if placed as near as 3 mm from the stylet bundle (Fig. V-9, at *a*). But when the bark was transversely cut, even 6.5 cm away, the exudation rate dropped noticeably (Fig. V-9, at *b*). Full exudation rate was obtained when a total axial length of 16 cm of phloem was available, regardless of the position of the stylet bundle within this length of tissue. These 16 cm of axial supply tissue were called the "contributory length." The experiment indicates axial movement through sieve tubes, it also indicates mobilization of storage materials, an aspect to be discussed later. Axial sieve-tube movement was also shown in dilution studies with the incision method with *Fraxinus* (Zimmermann, 1960). This will be discussed in Section 4c.

Once axial transport is demonstrated, the interesting question arises: how sharply defined is this axial direction? Are sieve tubes branched? In other words, is there a certain degree of tangential spreading of the axial transport direction in the tree stem? Such a study has been made with *Fraxinus americana* L. (Zimmermann, 1960). Defoliation of a tree interrupts the sugar supply in the phloem, consequently the sugar concentration in the phloem drops, and in *Fraxinus* the sugar composition changes significantly after defoliation. This will be discussed in some detail in a later section. At this point the effect of partial defoliation is of interest. One half of the crown of a Y-shaped tree was defoliated and the sieve-tube exudate was quantitatively analyzed 17 days after defoliation, a time long enough to make a sharp distinction between the foliated and defoliated sides. Figure V-10 shows the result: the tangential spreading of the foliated side axially down along the trunk is slight, less than 1°, though it is very distinct.

Now comes the question of extrafascicular phloem transport. Can nutrients be moved laterally out of the phloem from cell to cell, and feed a point removed from the direct axial path? Such experiments have been carried out by Peel (1964, 1966) with willow cuttings in which the sink was on a different side of the stem

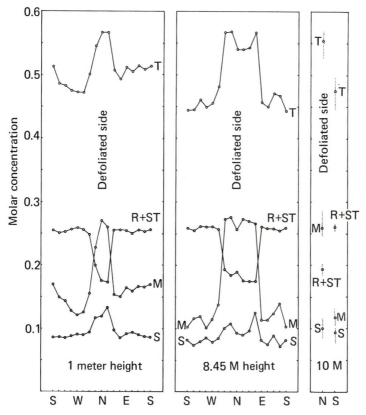

Fig. V–10. An experiment in which one half of the crown of a Y-shaped tree was defoliated. Seventeen days later sieve-tube exudate samples were taken on each of the two branches at 10 m height, and around the trunk both at 8.45 m (20 cm below the fork) and at 1 m. Molar concentrations are shown: S (sucrose), R+ST (raffinose and stachyose), M (D-mannitol), T (total molar concentration). Note the spreading of the sieve tubes of the foliated side of the tree into the defoliated side in the downward direction of the stem. From Zimmermann, 1960.

than the source. Movement of sucrose from one side of the stem to the other did occur under these circumstances.

Finally it must be pointed out that conditions under which extensive lateral extrafascicular movement takes place do not normally occur in the plant and are almost invariably the result of injuries. The vascular cambium repairs such injuries with reorientation of new vascular derivatives. Examples are the bridging of girdled stems, the invasion of vascular tissue below a dying or broken-off branch, the reorientation of vascular tissue on a stump of a cut tree when new stump sprouts appear, etc. In all these cases the wound reaction is that of a reorientation of vascular tissue to re-establish continuity. As long as a branch is alive, vascular tissue on the stem below the branch "belongs" to the branch. When the branch dies, the now unconnected and thus "useless" area on the stem below is regained by the production of vascular tissue from reorienting cambial initials. This has been described many times (e.g. Münch, 1937). If the injury is a very drastic one, reorientation may take many years. Robert Hartig (1889) described this for a Y-shaped 100 year-old *Pinus silvestris* L. one half of which had been girdled by his father, Theodor Hartig, in 1871. Reorientation of vascular tissue from a sprout on the stump of a cut tree is shown in Fig. IV-7. The illustration concerns xylem, but one must assume that sieve tubes differentiate parallel to the vessels.

c. The question of polar transport

Sax (1954) and Dickson and Samuels (1956) studied the effect of inverted rings of bark in fruit trees. The phloem remained blocked even after the wound had healed, at least superficially. This raises the interesting question of polar movement in sieve tubes. Is the phloem blocked because transport can only take place in one direction through the sieve tubes? The answer is no, because there are numerous examples in which the reversal of flow is directly evident. In the experiments of Weatherley *et al.* (1959) flow toward the aphid stylet bundle could take place from either side with equal ease. Furthermore, in every growing shoot, transport is initially into a growing leaf and at a certain stage of maturity; when the leaf can produce more than it requires for growth, it begins to export. In the leaf petiole, then, the direction of flow becomes reversed. In the case of inverted bark rings, the phloem is damaged and tissue polarity seems to prevent the renewal of sieve tubes. This is probably why inverted bark rings block phloem transport until new vascular tissues are regenerated at the vertical seam.

The most illustrative example of the nonpolar nature of phloem transport has been given by Münch (1930). He girdled twigs of apple trees in such a way that the growing apples were supplied by phloem transport in either direction. Continued growth of the apples in both cases indicate that phloem transport *per se* is not polar (Fig. V-11).

The only evidence favoring polar transport has come from translocation studies with cut sugar-cane leaves (Hartt and Kortschak, 1964). It is possible, however, to explain their results in terms of transport regulation (cf. Sec. 8).

At any one time, translocation appears to be unidirectional from source to

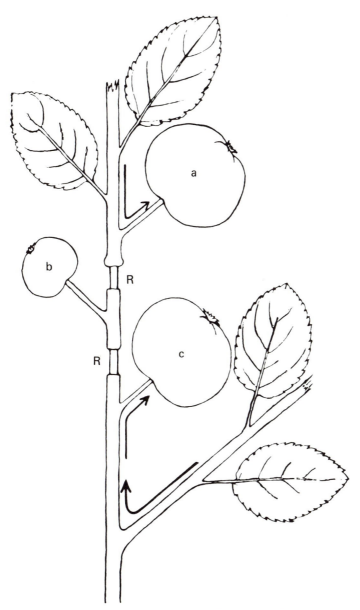

Fig. V–11. The growth of apples on a twig girdled at two different places (*R*). Apple *b*, isolated from the foliage by the two girdles, does not grow. Apples *a* and *c* grow equally well; *a* is supplied through twig phloem in basipetal, *c* in acropetal direction. This experiment shows that assimilates are not transported in a polar direction as far as the transport tissue is concerned. From Münch, 1930.

sink. This, however, has nothing to do with a structurally based transport polarity but rather is the result of the respective locations of source and sink. If these locations are naturally or experimentally altered, as has been described in the previous paragraphs, a reversal of translocation readily takes place.

d. Bidirectional phloem transport

The question of whether or not transport can take place through a single section of sieve tube simultaneously in opposite directions is of crucial importance in respect to the translocation mechanism. If transport is a flow of solution, it can obviously only flow in one direction at any one time through any given channel. Furthermore, all solutes as well as the solvent water must move simultaneously in the same direction. Superficially seen, the question of bidirectional transport appears to be a very simple one. It is not surprising, therefore, that many efforts have been made during the past 40 years or so, to see if bidirectional transport can take place. But the problem is far from simple and most investigators who had attempted such experiments and claimed success, had stumbled over the same difficulty, xylem transport. The intimate spatial relationship of the two long-distance transport systems, xylem and phloem, makes it extremely difficult to study phloem transport in the absence of xylem transport. When two different tracers are applied at two different points, they both are readily moved upwards in the xylem and downwards in the phloem and can thus reach almost any point in the plant. If one considers the transport velocities (several meters per hour in the xylem and about one meter per hour in the phloem) it becomes obvious that circulation in a small plant takes only a few minutes. With this in mind, the reader may now himself dispose of most claims of bidirectional phloem transport in the older literature.

Another phenomenon, easily misinterpreted as bidirectional transport, is transport toward a sink from opposite directions. Recall a willow branch with an exuding aphid stylet bundle, and Weatherley's incision to study the contributory length (Sec. 2b and 2c). The stylet bundle exudes at full rate if it is located anywhere within the extent of the contributory length. In other words, considering only the single sieve tube in which the stylet bundle is located, a solution can flow towards the stylet tips within the same sieve tube from either or both axial directions simultaneously. This is bidirectional transport through a single sieve tube, but not through a single section of it, i.e. it is not incompatible with the concept of mass flow (Eschrich, 1967) (see also Fig. V-21 e).

Growing leaves of an expanding shoot or seedling import photosynthates (for example, the leaf a in Fig. V-12). As such a leaf reaches a certain stage of maturity (about 30–50% of its final size), it becomes self-sufficient and then begins to export (leaf b in Fig. V-12). The direction of transport from exporting leaves near a growing shoot tip is almost invariably both acropetal and basipetal from the point of petiole insertion, because the growing shoot tip as well as the proximal parts of the plant are strong sinks. Therefore, bidirectional phloem transport is found in the internodes between newly matured leaves (between b and older leaves in Fig. V-12). It is under these conditions where bidirectional transport is best studied. The question is, of course, whether or not bidirectional

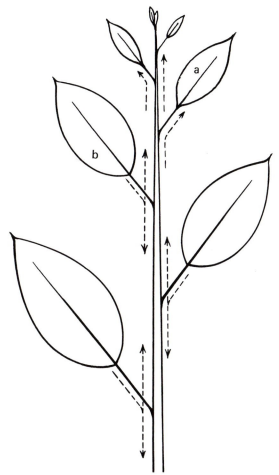

Fig. V–12. Diagrammatic representation of transport directions in a growing shoot tip. Leaves *a* and younger ones import assimilates for the support of their growth. When a leaf has reached about 30 to 50% of its final size, it becomes self-sufficient and begins to export sugars (leaf *b* and older ones). Transport directions in a young shoot are usually both up and down from the point of petiole insertion. Hence there is bidirectional transport between two recently matured leaves of a growing shoot.

transport in such internodes takes place within a single conducting bundle, or more specifically, within a single sieve tube. Great efforts to decide this question have been made by Biddulph and Cory (1960), but their results have not yet been conclusive.

The latest and most refined demonstration of bidirectional transport is that of Trip and Gorham (1968a) with *Cucurbita*. These authors fed tritiated glucose to a fully grown leaf and $^{14}CO_2$ to a half-grown one and could demonstrate, by autoradiography, both tracers in the same sieve tube of the petiole of the half-grown leaf. Even though this might appear to be the ultimate demonstration of bidirectional movement, the procedure had a weakness. The experiment was only successful during a critically short period of time, while transport reversal in the half-grown leaf took place, i.e., during the transition period of the half-grown leaf from developmental stage *a* to *b* in Fig. V-12. Furthermore, one of the tracers was offered to the fully grown leaf 160 minutes before the other tracer was offered to the half-grown leaf. During this critical period of flow, one must expect movement first from leaf *b* to leaf *a,* and as *a* reaches maturity, movement of both tracers out of the half-grown leaf. The experiment would be far more weighty (and would probably fail to succeed) if the half-grown leaf were fed with the tracer first. Another point is that one must expect the transport direction to reverse repeatedly in a maturing leaf. Export probably takes place initially only during periods of peak photosynthesis. One should not forget, in spite of this difference in interpretation, the beautifully refined technique which has been achieved with these experiments.

e. Differential translocation

Solutes flowing in a solution cannot be translocated selectively in different directions. There are indications that this might happen under certain circumstances, though alternate interpretations of the experiments in question are possible. The question has been approached in two different manners.

The first of the two approaches is exemplified by the work of Penot (1965) who studied the specificity of demand at different sinks. He found, for example, that phosphorus was translocated preferentially downward from a fed leaf. However, Penot's experiment were of a duration of several days and it is not unlikely that he was dealing with combined circulation via phloem *and* xylem (see Sec. 8 and Chap. VII, Sec. 4).

In the second type of experiment, sucrose export from a newly matured sunflower leaf to shoot tip and to roots (cf. Fig. V-12) was studied. The source leaf was treated with ATP and DNP respectively, and export from it was compared with a control plant. ATP treatment appeared to promote downward translocation but left upward translocation unaffected, while DNP treatment had a larger inhibitory effect upon downward than upon upward transport (Shiroya, 1968). If there are two translocation mechanisms operating, one predominantly to the shoot tip, the other predominantly to the roots, then one could assume that the two mechanisms had been differentially affected by the experimental treatments. ATP and DNP were administered 30 minutes before the leaf was exposed to $^{14}CO_2$. It is, therefore, possible that these substances were translocated to the two respective sinks during this time. The difference in sucrose translocation could, therefore, have been due to altered sink activities.

3. NATURE OF TRANSLOCATED SUBSTANCES

a. Methods

There are a number of different ways in which the nature of the translocated substances can be investigated. Radioactive isotopes have been used to great advantage during recent years. The plant is made to carry out photosynthesis with $^{14}CO_2$, and the radioactive substances some distance away from the point of photosynthesis are then extracted. This method has the disadvantage that one does not know whether a substance has been translocated to the extraction site in its detected form, or if it has been produced at the site from another substance which had been translocated to the site from the area of photosynthesis. This danger can be greatly reduced if (a) the experimental time is kept as short as possible, and (b) if a time study is carried out in an attempt to differentiate between translocate and local product. Such studies have indicated, for example, that sucrose is an important translocation sugar, and the hexoses, glucose, and fructose are secondary local break-down products (Swanson and El-Shishiny, 1958). Kursanov *et al.* (1958) double grafted sunflower (*Helianthus annuus* L.) and Jerusalem artichoke (*H. tuberosus* L.) and found sucrose to move through the grafts from species to species even though the storage sugars are different in the two plants.

Another method of identification of the translocation substances is the analysis of sieve-tube exudate. When the innermost layer of the phloem, containing the functioning sieve tubes, are severed, exudation takes place. This exudation may be more or less intense, depending on the species. The exudate is a clear liquid of a highly concentrated sugar solution (10 to 30 % w/v). There is good evidence indicating that this liquid is actually the transported solution. The phenomenon has been known to man for a long time, for in some places of southern Europe the method has been used for obtaining sugar before sugar was produced commercially from sugar cane and sugar beets (Huber, 1953). The botanical discovery of sieve-tube exudation was made in 1859 and recognized as a general phenomenon (Hartig, 1860). The method is ideally suited for studies with large trees, because it enables the investigator to sample the sieve-tube content at many places along the tree stem within a short time. It must be realized, of course, that each incision respresents an interruption of the phloem (for the rest of the summer); incisions must, therefore, be kept very small in comparison with the total stem circumference. Experimental work with exudates is, therefore, only possible with tree species which have ample exudation. The number of species having this property is relatively small. In most species exudation is quite limited by the internal responses to phloem injury (cf. Sec. 6). Thus, many species are available for collection of exudate for analysis of a sample. But not many species are suitable for experimentation where a minimum of disturbance is a requirement.

Sieve-tube exudate can also be obtained from the mouth parts of aphids as has been briefly mentioned. This method has been developed by Mittler (1957, 1958). Any reasonably large aphid species which feeds on twigs or branches can probably be used for the purpose; small green leaf-feeding species are less suitable because their mouth parts get more easily disturbed when the insect is cut. Figure V-6 shows an individual of the large species *Longistigma caryae* Harris feeding on a *Tilia* branch. While aphids are feeding they release honeydew at more or less regular intervals (this particular species about once every 30 minutes). If the insect is anaesthetized while feeding, and one carefully cuts off its mouth parts, exudation from the cut stylet stump continues (Fig. V-7). Exudation may continue for several days at a rate of, in some cases, exceeding 5 mm³ per hour, and the exudate may be collected with pipets. When phloem containing exuding and nonexuding stylet bundles were sectioned, it was found that whenever stylet bundles were exuding, their tips were located inside a sieve element (Fig. V-8). The aphid-stylet method of collecting sieve-tube exudate (often called stylet exudate to distinguish it from exudate collected from an incision) is very useful for certain purposes. It yields, for example, exudate uncontaminated by trace substances eluted from a cut bark surface. If one, for example, would want to analyze exudate for moving trace substances, the aphid stylet method would be ideal. Its drawbacks are the technical delicacy of handling; it is, for example, practically impossible to take many samples within a short time at various points of a large tree. The second disadvantage is the fact that it takes a relatively long time for a single sample of analyzable quantity to accumulate. In order to collect 5 mm³, a good sample size, one has to wait not only about an hour, but at least half an hour before the aphid can be cut, because one has to make certain that the insect is feeding. This means that the sieve tube is being drained for a long time before the sample is collected. The implications of this are quite obvious: if turgor drop causes a dilution of the exudate, surely stylet exudate is diluted. Dilution results in mobilization of reserve materials. Stylet exudate is, therefore, not only diluted, but it must contain a certain amount of mobilized, near-by reserve materials. These questions will be discussed in more detail in Sections 4c and 8.

EVIDENCE SHOWING THAT SIEVE-TUBE EXUDATE IS TRANSLOCATED MATERIAL. The phenomenon of exudation itself is the strongest evidence to show that the exudate is translocated. The tips of aphid stylets are inserted in a single sieve element (Fig. V-8); exudation is maintained at about 5 mm³ per hour in *Longistigma*, a rate necessitating the refilling of the sieve element 3 to 10 times per second. This phenomenon is entirely unconceivable in any other way than a flow of solution. The fact that transport towards the stylet bundle is axial has already been discussed before (Sections 2a and b). Further evidence showing that sieve-tube exudate is phloem-mobile material is the fact that radioactive sugars appear in honeydew from stem-feeding aphids soon after $^{14}CO_2$ is supplied to the foliage above (Canny, 1962b). In *Yucca* sieve-tube exudate contains radioactive sugars soon after $^{14}CO_2$ is supplied to leaves (Van Die and Tammes, 1964). Hill (1963) found a radioactivity peak moving from one to another (farther) aphid colony after a radioactivity "pulse" had been given to the leaves above.

In addition to all this weighty evidence, there are all kinds of additional pieces of circumstantial evidence supporting the concept that sieve-tube exudate is the translocated material. The types of carbohydrates found in sieve-tube exudates, for example in *Fraxinus* (Zimmermann, 1957b), are the same as those found moving in experiments with radioactive isotopes (Trip *et al.*, 1965). The ratio-wave experiments, discussed in Section 4a, are very pertinent here. Nitrogenous substances are known to be exported from naturally or experimentally senescing leaves (e.g. Schumacher, 1930). These substances, which are normally present in

sieve-tube exudates only in extremely low concentrations, appear conspicuously
in exudates collected during senescence (Mittler, 1958; Ziegler, 1956). Further
evidence in support of the idea that sieve-tube exudate is a moving solution will
be discussed in Sections 4a and 7b.

b. Carbohydrates

Quantitatively, carbohydrates are the most important products of photosynthesis, and, therefore, the bulk of exported material from leaves are carbohydrates. In most cases, carbohydrates are transported as sugars; exceptions of this
rule are relatively rare. *Sucrose* is by far the most common of the translocation
sugars; in a great many cases it represents over 95% of the dry weight of translocated material. In many plant families, sucrose is the exclusive form in which
carbohydrates move over long distances. This has been found with all methods
of investigation. For example, in exudates of more than 50 tree species of the
family Leguminosae, sucrose was the only sugar that could be detected chromato-
graphically (Zimmermann, unpublished results). Sugars other than sucrose are of
variable importance as translocates. They are the oligosaccharides of the raffinose
family, *raffinose, stachyose* and *verbascose*. They are all related and consist of
sucrose with one, two and three alpha-galactose units attached in 6 position (Fig.
V-13). These sugars are always transported in addition to sucrose. In many plant
families they play a minor role when compared with sucrose, but in some families
(Bignoniaceae, Celastraceae, Combretaceae, Myrtaceae, Oleaceae, Verbenaceae
and others), the higher oligosaccharides are of considerable quantitative importance (Zimmermann, 1957a, and unpublished results).

Sugars are not the only form in which carbohydrates move through plants,

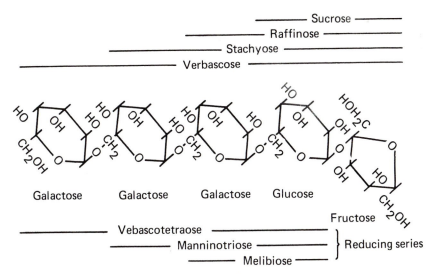

Fig. V-13.   The raffinose family of oligosaccharides. These sugars consist of sucrose
with one or more alpha-galactose units attached at the 6 position of glucose (or galactose).
Sugars of the reducing series are not found in sieve-tube exudate.

sugar alcohols are of a certain importance, at least in some taxonomic groups. D-*mannitol* is a translocation carbohydrate in the Oleaceae and a few other families. Typical molar concentrations of carbohydrates in sieve-tube exudate of *Fraxinus americana* L. are, for example, sucrose 0.08, raffinose 0.07, stachyose 0.2, verbascose (trace), D-mannitol 0.18 (Zimmermann, 1957b). These concentrations are quite variable with height, season, and a number of other factors. The fact that there are so many different carbohydrates translocated in *Fraxinus* makes it a particularly interesting species for experimental work. Some of this will be discussed in the following sections of this chapter. From the point of view of the plant physiologist, Parker's (1966) recent report of the nature of sieve-tube exudate of *Macrocystis* is of particular interest. In this very large species of marine alga carbohydrate transport is as pronounced as in higher plants; the bulk of translocated material is in the form of D-mannitol (no sugars).

Sorbitol is another translocation sugar alcohol. It has been found, so far, in some members of the Rosaceae, like apple trees (*Pyrus malus* L.) (Webb and Burley, 1962) and cherry trees (*Prunus* sp.) (Zimmermann, 1961). In these trees, sucrose and sorbitol are transported in about equal amounts.

In summary then, it is rather noteworthy that carbohydrates are translocated through the phloem in a nonreducing form. There is no physiological explanation for this fact, though one could speculate about the physiological significance of oligosaccharide transport (conservation of bond energy). The reasons why transport carbohydrates are nonreducing may become apparent as more is learned about the mechanism of transport.

c. Other substances

So far we have discussed the quantitatively most important translocation substances, the carbohydrates. They represent almost invariably the bulk of moving solutes. Rare exceptions have been reported in the case of seedlings where the prominent substances may be serine and malic acid under certain conditions (Nelson *et al.*, 1961). Normally, however, substances other than carbohydrates are very low in concentration, but they are very varied. Indeed, one gains the impression that just about any water-soluble nutrient can move in the phloem. Readers who are interested in what has been found in sieve-tube exudates are referred to Ziegler's recent review (Ziegler, 1968). Of interest is the presence of ATP, it has been detected in exudate from incisions (Kluge & Ziegler, 1964) and from aphid stylets (Gardner & Peel, 1969), in concentrations of 0.1% (w/v) and less. One could, of course, attach all sorts of speculations to this finding, but at the present we do not know its significance. ATP could be utilized as an energy source for the driving mechanism of long-distance transport directly, or indirectly for lateral transport across membranes.

Interesting is also the presence of various enzymes in aphid stylet exudate. For example ATPase and acid phosphatase (with a pH optimum of about 5.5) have been found (P. Matile, pers. comm.). The significance of this lies, at the present at least, less in the nature of the enzymes themselves, but rather in the fact that enzymes (i.e. proteins) are secreted into sieve tubes and are movable.

Methods of investigation of the nature of minor translocation substances have to be selected rather critically. The incision technique has to be used with caution, because minor solutes in the exudate may have been washed from the cut surface of the bark. Ziegler's criterium for a translocate in sieve-tube exudate is its fluctuation in concentration with time and height of the tree (Ziegler, 1956). If the concentration of a substance in sieve-tube exudate does not fluctuate during the course of a day or a year, nor vary with the height of collection, it must be regarded as non-mobile. The aphid-stylet method may be an ideal tool provided the investigator is fully aware of the fact that much of what he analyzes is material which has been mobilized due to induced turgor drop (see Section 8). The enzymes mentioned in the previous paragraph have probably been secreted into the sieve tubes during collection of exudate, but there is no reason to doubt that they do not normally occur in sieve tubes and are normally moving. Nevertheless, caution is necessary when one deals with *quantities* of substances in stylet exudate.

Break-down products of proteins are exported from the leaves during leaf senescence, whether senescence is naturally occurring in autumn or is induced artificially by placing the plant in the dark (Schumacher, 1930). Under these circumstances one finds amino acids, amides, and phosphorus-containing substances in the exudate (from incisions or stylet bundles) (Mittler, 1958; Ziegler, 1956; and others).

Inorganic ions were found to be translocated in the phloem. Stylet-exudate analyses, for example, indicated sodium and potassium (but no calcium) ions, as well as anions of a few organic acids (Peel and Weatherley, 1959). The absence of calcium is rather significant; calcium is well known for its poor phloem mobility. It seems to be easily and irreversibly deposited along the translocation path, for many barks have conspicuous Ca-oxalate crystals in the phloem, sometimes in special cells.

It is very interesting that even virus particles have been found to be translocated in the phloem. Early evidence for this has been described by Bennett (numerous citations in Crafts, 1961). From this early work it is not clear in what form the virus is transported. More recent evidence, however, leaves little doubt that virus particles move as such (e.g. Kluge, 1967). Esau, Cronshaw and Hoefert (1967) showed presumably transported virus particles in sieve pores on electron micrographs.

An interesting indication of translocation comes from a very different kind of evidence. Isolated roots can be cultured on a nutrient solution. They require an array of inorganic nutrients just about like roots of an intact plant. In addition, an energy source such as sucrose is needed, because roots are nonphotosynthetic and normally (on the intact plant) receive sugars via phloem. An additional requirement is that of certain vitamins, especially vitamin B_6, depending on the species (cf. Torrey, 1967; p. 4). Evidently, these substances are translocated to the roots via phloem together with the sugars; indeed vitamins have been found in sieve-tube exudates of many species (Ziegler and Ziegler, 1962).

Many papers have appeared reporting translocation of applied substances. This is of a certain practical importance for foliar application of mineral nutrients to cultural plants. It is also of significance in respect to the effectiveness of sprayed herbicides for weed control (cf. Crafts and Yamagouchi, 1964).

4. QUANTITATIVE ASPECTS OF PHLOEM TRANSPORT

a. Velocity of movement

Hardly any other aspect of phloem transport is more confusing to the general reader than that of velocity. There are minimum velocities, average velocities, or merely rates. It often seems that even investigators working in the field of phloem transport do not have a very clear concept of the relationship of velocity figures which are obtained with different methods of investigation. The word "velocity" means a distance traveled per unit time. It has nothing to do with quantity of material moved. The term "rate," on the other hand, implies either velocity and/or quantity of material moved. "Rate" should only be used in a very general way, because its meaning is not sharply defined.

Although the term "velocity of movement" has a very precise meaning which can be expressed in, say, centimeters per hour, its use can create confusion. The reason is the fact that many different velocities can and probably do exist simultaneously within a sieve tube. In order to appreciate this, let us return to the relatively simple case of capillary flow in xylem vessels of vines (cf. Chap. IV, Sec. 5b). There one has become acquainted with the paraboloid nature of capillary flow. In other words, velocities are graded from zero at the capillary wall to a peak in the center. In sieve tubes, presence of sieve plates between elements complicates the flow pattern; indeed, there are numerous investigators who do not believe in liquid flow at all. However, it can be taken as virtually certain that velocities of movement in the phloem are not uniform, but somehow graded. In other words, some molecules move faster than others. While in the case of flow through ideal capillaries, it is known that the peak velocity is twice as great as the average velocity, the velocity distribution in the sieve tubes is unknown.

There are a number of ways in which a figure can be obtained for the velocity of transport. The important thing is that the figure is properly interpreted (cf. also Canny, 1960, 1961). For example, a radioactive tracer may be applied to a leaf, and the arrival of radioactivity at any point in the stem may be timed. The distance traveled within the measured time yields a velocity value. In considering such an experiment, one must realize that by detecting the advancing radioactivity front, one measures a velocity front, or peak velocity, comparable to the tip of the paraboloid of capillary flow. Since detection sensitivity is limited, one is really not measuring the very front of the velocity, but a slightly lower value. Therefore the measured value should be called a "minimum peak velocity." But in doing this experiment, one has assumed that the radioactivity enters the sieve tubes instantaneously. This does not have to be the case. In order to make the measurement more realistic it is better to have two detectors downstream, one a short distance and the other a longer distance below the point of application. Distance between the two checkpoints divided by the time interval between the two arrivals is, therefore, the proper "minimum peak velocity." In other words, the fastest molecules have moved at least that fast. Reports of such velocities are usually 100 cm/hr or more.

Another concept, that of "average velocity," is useful in mass transfer calculations. It is the velocity of a hypothetical moving liquid cylinder. Assuming translocation from point A to point B in a stem, different molecules get from A to B at different velocities. Within a given time t, x grams have arrived at B. The uniform velocity at which x grams would have moved from A to B within the time t, is the average velocity. The velocity of about the midpoint of an advancing radioactivity front in tracer experiments is an average velocity (cf. Sec. 4d).

The experimenter who works with radioactive substances faces the difficulty of radioactivity loss by removal of substances from the sieve tubes along the way. For example, in a rapidly growing bean seedling, leaves export sugars; sugars move towards the roots, but since the stem is growing, much of the sugar is removed from sieve tubes and used in growth along the path of transport. This distorts the measurement of velocity, making it appear smaller. It is obvious that the greater the removal rate of a substance along the way, the lower its apparent velocity. Thus, if two simultaneously moving substances have a different removal rate along the path of transport, their *apparent* velocities differ even if they are in reality identical. Some of these aspects have been mathematically treated by Spanner and Prebble (1962).

The experimental difficulty caused by lateral loss can be minimized if the plant material is carefully chosen. Lateral loss occurs in places where growth or storage goes on along the way. Lateral loss is the penalty one has to pay for using an applied tracer, no matter whether the tracer is a radioactive isotope, a fluorescent dye, or anything else. In the case of a nonnaturally occurring substance (like a fluorescent dye) one has to anticipate the phenomenon in any plant or plant part. Indeed, fluorescent dyes are known to be absorbed along the way, for they can be seen all along after termination of the experiment (Schumacher, 1930, 1937). Their measured transport velocity, therefore, must be lower than the actual one. In the case of labeled natural substances such as a radioactive sugar, the phenomenon can be minimized by choice of a plant and plant part which neither grows nor stores material along the path of translocation. Mature petioles of sugar-beet leaves, for example, should give fairly good values even though a small lateral loss by random (enzymatic) exchange of sugar with the surrounding tissues might still have to be expected, as well as a small loss for respiration along the way.

Returning now to trees, one finds opportunities for measuring average velocity with very different methods. The first attempt was made by Huber *et al.* (1937) who measured the velocity of a concentration wave advancing in the downward direction of a tree trunk. The velocity thus obtained was 3.6 m/hr. An advancing concentration wave should not represent a peak, but rather an average velocity. From the point of view of mass transfer, this velocity is some 5 to 10 times too great, as shall be seen later. It is suspected that the absolute concentration in the sieve tubes was influenced by the pressure in the xylem. A descending concentration wave in the sieve tubes could be simulated by a descending tension wave in the xylem. Huber was actually aware of this danger but dismissed it, because the highest concentrations occurred during the night when the tension in the xylem should be low. But one knows that there are tension waves in the xylem, this has been first demonstrated by Huber himself (cf. Chap. IV, Sec. 2), and also xylem tensions affect the concentration in sieve tubes. One, therefore, assumes that the concentration wave is real but distorted. A distorted wave will not give a realistic velocity figure.

The problem can be overcome with a very simple trick. Instead of measuring the *absolute* sugar concentration, one measures a sugar *ratio*. A ratio is independent of absolute concentrations and thus independent of xylem pressure. Such experiments were done with *Fraxinus americana* L. where several sugars are transported simultaneously. By collecting samples of sieve-tube exudate at various heights in the tree and at various times of the day, it was possible to detect the presence and advance of a "ratio wave." Production of sugars in the leaves changes

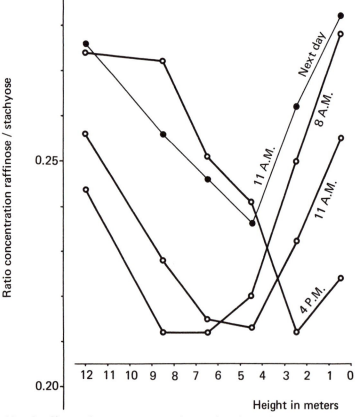

Fig. V–14. Gradients of sugar-concentration ratios along the stem of *Fraxinus*, Sept. 7 (open circles) and 8 (filled circles), 1966. The ratio wave advances in the downward direction of the trunk. Note that the 11 a.m. curves of the two subsequent days are approximately parallel. From Zimmermann, 1969.

sometimes enough diurnally so that a natural ratio wave can be followed on its way down along the stem. Such measurements gave values of average velocities of the order of 0.5 m/hr, values which are of the right order of magnitude to account for mass transfer (Fig. V-14).

Another way of obtaining an average velocity also utilizes the fact that several sugars are simultaneously translocated in white ash. In a normally functioning tree, the concentration decrease of a sugar, say stachyose, can be measured over a given length of translocation path, Δ conc./length. Immediately following defoliation, one can measure the concentration drop of this same sugar over time, Δ conc./time. If one divides the second by the first, the concentration difference drops out of the equation and a velocity, again presumably an average velocity because concentrations are dealt with, is obtained. The figures reported for three experiments were 73, 62 and 54 cm/hr (Zimmermann, 1958). When this was reported, the possibility of the effect of xylem pressure on sieve-tube exudate concentration was not considered. The author, therefore, went back to the old data and made the same calculations, but with *relative* stachyose concentrations (stachyose/sucrose). Thus, velocities came out to be 32, 30 and 23 cm/hr. These values again exclude the disturbing xylem effect.

Now compare these average velocity values, obtained with large trees, with values obtained with herbaceous plants. Mortimer (1965), working with sugar-beet petioles, experimental material in which one would have to worry little about lateral loss, found the velocity of the advancing radioactivity front to be 50 to 135 cm/hr. These values are somewhat higher than those obtained for *Fraxinus,* but are still quite comparable. The significance of these measurements of average velocities will be discussed in connection with mass transfer.

b. Mass transfer

Translocation can be quantitatively described by the dry weight of material moved per unit time. This is usually expressed as grams per hour. In the simplest case of translocation, diffusion, mass transfer is inversely proportional to the translocation distance:

$$\frac{dm}{dt} = \text{const.} \times TS \times \frac{\Delta \text{ conc.}}{\text{distance}} \quad \text{(Fick's diffusion equation)}$$

whereby TS = transverse-sectional area through which transport takes place; and Δ conc./distance = concentration gradient. When Mason and Maskell (1928) did their work with cotton, they measured mass transfer and calculated that the constant of the diffusion equation (the diffusion coefficient) would have to be many thousand times as great as that of diffusion of sugar in water. Certain transport characteristics still resembled diffusion; therefore they coined the terms "activated" and "accelerated diffusion". With this they suggested that translocation is similar to the diffusion process, but that metabolism somehow increases the coefficient. Canny (1962b) described a hypothesis which is based upon diffusion principles; it will be discussed briefly in a later section (7a).

Mass transfer has been measured with a wide variety of plants, mostly with growing fruits or tubers, but also with the growth of tree trunks. Canny (1960) reviewed the literature about this topic and made the results of the various investigators comparable by introducing the concept of specific mass transfer (SMT), which is mass transfer per unit time, per unit transverse-sectional area. He expressed it in grams transported material per square centimeter transverse-sectional area of phloem SMT_{ph}, or sieve tubes SMT_{st}, per hour. Canny's literature review revealed the interesting fact that the capacity of dicotyledonous phloem is a well-defined unit. In other words, no matter whether mass transfer measurements were made with a growing potato, a squash, a "sausage" of the African sausage tree *Kigelia,* or the growth of tree stems (Münch, 1930), specific mass transfer per phloem area is approximately the same:

$$SMT_{ph} = 2 \text{ to } 5 \text{ } g \text{ } cm^{-2} \text{ } h^{-1}$$

(for dicotyledonous stem phloem)

The capacity of petiole phloem is somewhat lower, namely,

$$SMT_{ph} = 0.56 \text{ to } 0.7 \text{ } g \text{ } cm^{-2} \text{ } h^{-1}$$

(dicotyledonous petioles)

Sieve tubes are generally considered to occupy approximately 20% of the transverse-sectional area of phloem, SMT_{st} values are, therefore, about 5 times greater than SMT_{ph} values, hence:

for dicotyledonous stems, $SMT_{st} = 10 \text{ to } 25 \text{ } g \text{ } cm^{-2} \text{ } h^{-1}$,
for dicotyledonous petioles, $SMT_{st} = 2.2 \text{ to } 3.5 \text{ } g \text{ } cm^{-2} \text{ } h^{-1}$,
and for coniferous stems, $SMT_{sc} = 2.2 \text{ to } 2.5 \text{ } g \text{ } cm^{-2} \text{ } h^{-1}$ (Münch, 1930).

These values include estimates for respirational loss of dry material from the growing region. Münch (1930) made estimates of mass transfer with forest trees. For dicotyledonous trees, these fit nicely into the first category; the third category is taken from Münch's book.

Many investigators were particularly interested in expressing the mass transfer value as a moving column of a sugar solution. If the velocity of such a moving liquid were uniform, specific mass transfer should be equal to the product of the solution's concentration and its velocity:

$$SMT \text{ } [g \text{ } cm^{-2} \text{ } h^{-1}] = \text{conc. } [g \text{ } cm^{-3}] \times \text{velocity } [cm \text{ } h^{-1}]$$

(Mass transfer equation)

The velocity in this equation is that of a moving rigid liquid cylinder. Such a thing does not exist in nature. Even in ideal capillaries, velocities are graded across the capillary diameter, a phenomenon which has been described in some detail in Chapter IV, Section 5. Therefore, the above velocity is called an "average" or a "cylindrical" one. If velocities of movement in the phloem are graded, and they most certainly are, then the velocity peaks may be considered greater than the average velocity in the preceding equation. Under conditions of Poiseuille flow in capillaries, velocities are distributed over the surface of a paraboloid;

the peak velocity, in that case, is exactly twice as great as the average velocity (see Chap. IV, Sec. 5). Assuming an average sieve-tube exudate concentration of 15% w/v, which in the dimensions of the mass transfer equation is 0.15 g cm^{-3}, if such a solution is allowed to move, it would have to move at an average velocity of 100 cm/hr to accomplish a specific mass transfer of 15 g/hr, considering sieve tubes alone. If one deals with ideal capillaries, the peak velocity would have to be 200 cm/hr under the same conditions. It should be stressed that this statement is by no means meant to imply that sieve tubes are comparable to ideal capillaries. It merely means that if there are graded velocities in the sieve tubes, some sugar molecules would move faster, others slower than 100 cm/hr. Clearly, from what is known about velocities of phloem transport (Sec. 4a), this is a very reasonable figure.

Trees are ideal, and at present the only, plants in which the right side of the mass transfer equation can be investigated. Münch's (1930) mass transfer measurements are of particular interest, because he gives values per sieve tubes (or sieve cells in *Pinus*) and at the same time gives the concentrations of the sieve-tube exudate for the same individual tree. Average velocities can be calculated from these data; they are 40 to 70 cm/hr for the dicotyledonous trees and 18 to 20 cm/hr for pine. In the authors' own experiments with *Fraxinus* a sieve-tube exudate concentration of 0.2 to 0.25 g cm^{-3} has been found and an average velocity of 30–70 cm/h (Zimmermann, 1969) which yields a specific mass transfer value $SMT_{st} = 6$ to 18 g cm^{-2} h^{-1}, a value very close to that found by other authors who measured mass transfer directly (Münch, 1930; Canny's review, 1960). Certainly the statement can be made that if the solution which can be tapped as exudate moves through the sieve tubes in the measured concentration and at the measured average velocity, a mass transfer of the observed magnitude will result. In other words, as far as the quantity of translocated material is concerned, mass flow is a very reasonable concept.

An interesting calculation with SMT values has been published by Canny *et al.* (1968). From specific mass transfer and the transverse-sectional area of conducting phloem, these authors estimated absolute mass transfer (g h^{-1}) down a tree stem and calculated how much leaf-surface area would be required at a known rate of photosynthesis, to provide for this flow. The result was extraordinarily high, partly because the calculation was based upon the apparent translocation velocity of Huber's concentration wave (cf. Sec. 4a), partly because of unreasonable assumptions of transverse-sectional area of conducting phloem. The following is a recalculation, carried out with the author's own SMT values (Zimmermann, 1969) and unpublished additional information about the same individual trees. The diameters of our trees were about 25 cm at midpoint of the stem, the thickness of the conducting phloem layer about 0.2 mm. This gives a total phloem area in the stem of around 1.5 cm², or about 0.3 cm² sieve tubes. Mass transfer in the stem $(SMT_{st} \times$ transverse-sectional area of sieve tubes) therefore is about 3.5 g/hr. According to Canny *et al.* (1968) leaves produce about 0.7 g dry matter per hour, per m². About 5 m² of leaf area could, therefore, produce the measured mass transfer. Since leaves photosynthesize only during daylight

hours but translocate day and night, twice the leaf area is necessary to account for
the mass transfer, i.e. about 10 m². This result is quite reasonable indeed.

c. Sieve tubes as an osmotic system

When sieve tubes are severed, exudation takes place provided sieve plates are
not immediately plugged by slime bodies or sealed by callose. Exudation releases
the turgor, this, in turn, causes water to enter from the surrounding apoplast.
Exudation from *Fraxinus americana* L. phloem is sufficiently ample that the
phenomenon can be studied in detail. When an incision is made into the functioning sieve tubes, and exudate samples are continually collected and analyzed,
entry of water into the sieve tubes is indicated by a drop of concentration with
time (Zimmermann, 1960, 1962). The concentration of the exudate drops rapidly
within a few minutes and levels off about 30 minutes after the incision has been
made at a concentration of about 70% of the initial one (Curves with open circles
in Fig. V-15).

Dilution curves are an excellent means of studying longitudinal permeability
of sieve tubes. When a second incision is made 30 minutes after the first one,
either to the right or to the left of the first one and at the same height, a similar
dilution curve is obtained, with the concentration of the samples again starting at
100% and gradually falling to 70% (Fig. V-15, top, curve with filled circles). If,
however, the second incision is made either above or below the first one, the first
exudate sample from the second incision will yield immediately the same concentration as a sample obtained at the same time from the first incision, i.e. 70%,
not 100% (filled circles, Fig. V-15, bottom). In other words, two incisions, placed
side by side tap different exudate "pools", so to speak; two incisions, one above
the other, tap the same "pool". This finding indicates that the exudate flows
axially towards the incision from both above and below, it also suggests that sieve
tubes are permeable in a longitudinal direction.

Dilution curves show that the sieve tubes behave like very long osmotic cells.
In other words, sieve tubes must be semipermeable laterally, but permeable to
the flow of sugar solution longitudinally, through the sieve plates. Experiments
of Weatherley *et al.* (1959) in which xylem (or apoplast neighborhood) was per-
fused with a mannitol solution of various concentrations provide further evidence
of the sieve tubes' osmotic behavior. When the osmotic concentration in the
apoplast was raised, the concentration in the sieve tubes increased and the turgor
dropped (Fig. V-16).

Of particular interest is the observation that sieve-tube turgor may be maintained by the plant even while other tissues (leaf parenchyma) have reached the
wilting point. Turgor is also maintained after the tree is defoliated (Zimmermann, 1958). This is another indication of metabolic pumping of osmotically
active molecules into sieve tubes. Translocation of sugars in wilting plants is,
therefore, by no means evidence against the pressure-flow hypothesis of transport;
it merely means that wilting is not prevented by turgescence of the sieve-tube
system alone.

Last, but perhaps not least, plasmolytic studies should be recalled. Many
workers have tried, quite unsuccessfully, to plasmolyze sieve tubes. It can be done,

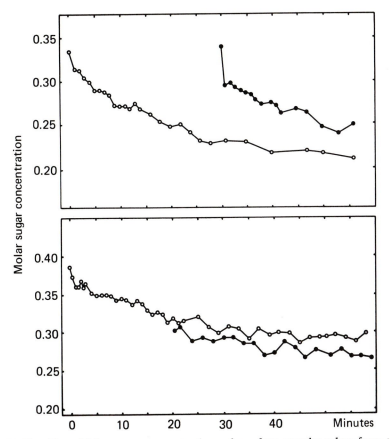

Fig. V-15. Top: Molar sugar concentrations of exudate samples taken from two bark incisions made side by side, each covering 3 cm width of phloem tissue. One of the cuts (open circles) was made at zero time, the second 30 minutes later. Note that the two incisions tap two different sugar pools. Bottom: A different tree from the one of the illustration above. Molar sugar concentrations of exudate samples, taken from two bark incisions made one above the other. The first incision was made at zero time (open circles), the second one was made a few millimeters below the first one, twenty minutes later. Note that in this case the same sugar pool is tapped by the two incisions. Redrawn from Zimmermann, 1960 and 1962.

but it is not an easy operation (Currier *et al.*, 1955). Sieve tubes are semipermeable laterally, as shown, but they are highly permeable in a longitudinal direction. Whenever an external solution of high concentration is applied, longitudinal displacement of sieve-tube content can largely prevent plasmolysis. This is indicated by the surging flow within sieve tubes, as reported by Currier *et al.* (1955).

d. Gradients

There are essentially two kinds of concentration gradients reported in the literature. They are two entirely different pieces of information. One of them is the concentration of radioactivity along the path of translocation; the other is the concentration gradients of solutes in sieve-tube exudates. The former gives infor-

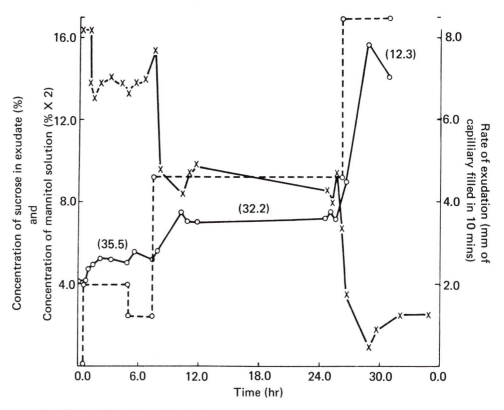

Fig. V–16. The effect of irrigating the inner surface of a bark of *Salix* with mannitol solutions of various concentrations. Concentration of mannitol solution (o - - - - o). Rate of exudation from stylets (x———x). Concentration of sucrose in stylet exudate (o———o). Figures for sucrose secretion given in brackets. From Weatherley, Peel and Hill, 1959.

mation on the translocation velocity (cf. Section 4a); the latter is useful for osmotic and other considerations.

RADIOACTIVITY GRADIENTS. Essentially similar information is obtained whether radioactivity is measured externally with a counter, or tissue segments are extracted along the way, and the counting is done after extraction. The main difference between the two methods is the greater sensitivity of the latter. Radioactivity can be measured with great precision, but the investigator has to cope with a whole array of difficulties. First, and perhaps most important, moving material cannot be distinguished from non-moving material. Indeed, one must anticipate that much of the moving material is removed from sieve tubes along the way, more, the more actively the stem is using assimilates by growth or by deposition of storage products. Even if one were sure that none of the transported material were stored or utilized along the way, one still would have to expect the moving radioactive material to be somewhat randomized enzymatically with non-radioactive stationary material. It has been reported many times that the advancing radioactivity front is concave when plotted on a linear scale, and approximately a straight line when plotted on a logarithmic scale. Advancing volumes of a liquid transported through an ideal capillary, on the other hand, have a linear front on a linear scale and a convex front on a logarithmic scale. Concave radioactivity fronts seem to be consistently obtained with large lateral loss (cf. Spanner and Prebble, 1962). In the case of low lateral loss (i.e. mature conductive tissue with little growth and/or storage), such as sugarbeet petioles, the advancing front is more linear in shape, i.e. somewhat more like that of capillary flow. An added difficulty in the case of tracer experiments is the uncertainty of what happens at the point of sieve-tube loading. Can radioactivity be fed into the sieve tubes evenly and with an instantaneous start? The even loading is probably more reliable than the instantaneous start. This means that tracer experiments are very difficult to interpret.

GRADIENTS OF EXUDATE CONCENTRATIONS.   Two methods of collection are available: the incision method and the aphid-stylet technique. The latter, unfortunately, has to be dismissed for gradient studies for a very obvious reason. An initial concentration (100% as described in the previous section) cannot be obtained with the aphid-stylet technique, because it takes at least an hour from the time the aphid punctures the sieve tube until the sampling is complete (about 30 minutes until evidence of feeding is obtained, and at least another 30 minutes for the collection of the sample). Thus one must assume that stylet exudate is diluted because of the pressure reduction caused by tapping. It is not known to what extent the exudate is diluted, because comparative data on the concentrations of stylet exudate and incision exudate has not yet been published. The dilution may be very small, because the sieve tube is not opened directly to atmospheric pressure, but via a resistance (the stylet bundle canal). Another difficulty with the stylet method is the fact that sampling would have to be done at two points along the same channel, i.e. on a branch of a tree and at the same time at the base of the tree. It may be difficult to have aphids feeding on large tree stems. Obviously a lower lateral branch cannot substitute for the base of the stem, because the lateral branch represents a separate channel.

Concentration gradients in sieve tubes, therefore, are only known from measurements taken with the incision method of obtaining sieve-tube exudate. The order of magnitude of the concentration gradient is 0.01 mole per meter, i.e. approximately 0.2 atm./m, for both *Quercus rubra* L. (Huber et al., 1937) and *Fraxinus americana* L. (Zimmermann, 1957b), with the concentration decreasing in the downward direction of the stem. An older report, covering a number of different tree species, gives a range of 0.1 to 1.04 atm./m; i.e. it includes values both lower and higher than those of oak and ash (Pfeiffer, 1937).

If gradients in herbaceous plants are of the same order of magnitude as those of trees, they would be difficult to detect in small plants. Dealing with a 20-cm long distance of a translocation path, the investigator would have to anticipate a concentration difference of only 0.002 mole between the end points. It is clear, therefore, that trees are better objects to study gradients than small plants.

The effect of defoliation on the concentration gradient of sieve-tube exudate is of particular interest. Natural leaf abscission in autumn as well as experimental defoliation lowers the concentration of the exudate in the whole tree. This is to be expected for two reasons. First, the sugar source, the leaves, are eliminated, but sugar removal from the sieve tubes goes on; the concentration of the sieve tubes, therefore, drops. Second, the tension in the xylem is drastically reduced, water enters the sieve tubes and the water-entering tendency of the osmotic equation is lowered. The effect of defoliation on the concentration gradient is even more interesting. The total molar gradient tends to disappear, while individual gradients remain positive or turn negative (Fig. V-17). In other words, the concentration gradient in the sieve tubes is positive in the direction of flow, and disappears when flow stops (one must expect cessation of flow when the sugar source is removed). A concentration gradient in the direction of transport is required by most translocation theories, as shall be seen in a later section.

The pressure-flow theory assumes that a turgor gradient is the driving force of flow. In other words, it requires that the previously-mentioned osmotic gradients reflect turgor gradients. To what extent this is the case is not known. One certainly has to assume that tension gradients in the xylem affect the concentration gradient. During times of minimal transpiration (at night) the estimated turgor gradient in the sieve tubes is probably identical with the osmotic gradient (i.e. ca. 0.2 atm./m), because the hydrostatic gradients of phloem and xylem are identical. During times of intensive transpiration, however, one has to expect the turgor gradient of the sieve tubes to be reduced by that part of the tension gradient in the xylem which is caused by the resistance to flow. This latter value is, according to Chapter IV, Section 5d, around 0.05 atm./m. The estimated value for a turgor gradient in the sieve tubes of a transpiring tree is, therefore, 0.2 less 0.05, around 0.15 atm./m. Direct measurements of sieve-tube turgor in standing trees are extremely rare. Hammel (1968) measured sieve-tube turgors in red oak with a syringe-type manometer. He found in most of his measurements a pressure drop of 1–2 atm. over a 5-m length of stem from about 6.5 to about 1.5 m height. In other words the pressure gradient was 0.2–0.4 atm./m, amazingly close to the estimate given previously. The question remains as to how reliable Hammel's measurements are; e.g. how good is the seal between sieve tubes and syringe? Individual values show an uncomfortably large scatter. But so far, at least, they are the only sieve-tube turgor measurements available.

5. METABOLISM AND TRANSPORT

There is one point on which all translocation workers agree: phloem transport is dependent upon the plant's metabolism. Metabolism supplies the driving force of translocation; it may also be required all along the path in order to keep the sieve tubes functioning, at least to maintain their semipermeability. The role of metabolism in transport has been studied in essentially two ways: (1) by studying the effect of metabolic inhibitors and (2) the effect of temperature. Efforts have been made to study direct effects on translocation, and avoid indirect effects. One

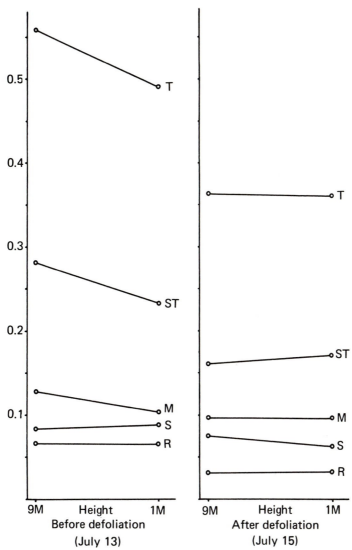

Fig. V-17. Gradients of molar sugar and mannitol concentrations in the sieve-tube exudate of *Fraxinus americana* L., before and after defoliation of the tree. The gradient of total molar concentration is positive in the downward direction of the trunk before defoliation, and disappears after defoliation when transport (presumably) has stopped. S (sucrose), R (raffinose), ST (stachyose), M (D-mannitol), T (total molar concentration). From Zimmermann, 1958.

cannot merely enclose a whole leaf in a chamber to subject it to low temperature or a metabolic inhibitor. Decreased export from this leaf would in this case not necessarily indicate an effect upon the translocation process, but it might as well indicate a depressed rate of photosynthesis, i.e. a decreased supply of carbohydrates to the translocation tissue.

Superficially viewed, the problem of separating indirect from direct effects on translocation seems very simple. One can build a small chamber around a section of stem or petiole and thus subject the phloem to various factors in a very localized area. This is, indeed, the proper approach to the problem, but it does not, by any means, solve it entirely, because of the transpiration stream which moves in the opposite direction. For example, if a low temperature is applied to a point of the petiole locally, the water of the transpiration stream is cooled down as well as the phloem. The chilled water moves up into the blade and there may lower the rate of photosynthesis or rate of secretion of sugars into the sieve tubes. Similarly, any applied metabolic inhibitor might be dissolved in xylem water, carried up and affect translocation in an indirect way. Even if there is little transpiration, in a humid growth chamber, for example, the transpiration stream is kept going by the plant with root pressure.

Various attempts have been made to avoid or minimize this difficulty. In the case of temperature application (chilling), the section distal to the point of chilling could be warmed up again with a small, carefully controlled heating jacket. Another possibility is to monitor photosynthesis and other processes in the leaf blade to assure that these are not affected by the treatment (Webb and Gorham, 1965). In some cases it is possible to isolate phloem from xylem surgically for a certain distance of otherwise attached phloem. This has been done by Ziegler (1958). When a section of phloem is isolated from the otherwise intact plant, one has to realize that the osmotic conditions of the sieve-tube system are quite disturbed. The sieve tubes of the intact plant part are in a sharply defined osmotic environment (possibly negative apoplast pressure). The phloem has to be kept moist in the isolated section, be it with water or a sugar solution. It is quite impossible to determine the xylem pressure in the intact plant part and precisely match the conditions in the isolated part of the phloem with the correct sugar concentration. In addition to this difficulty, Ziegler (1958) has found that the respiration rate of isolated phloem bundles in *Heracleum* is drastically raised upon isolation, probably because of increased access of oxygen. These considerations call for extreme caution in interpretation of experiments with isolated phloem bundles.

a. Effect of metabolic inhibitors

A number of workers reported experiments involving local application of metabolic inhibitors. Willenbrink (1957, 1966), for example, enclosed *Pelargonium* petioles in a small chamber, after he had surgically removed all tissue but the central vascular bundle. Thus, he found cyanide to have a reversible inhibitory effect on translocation, various other poisons stopped translocation irreversibly. The xylem was still there, an effect upon uptake into sieve tubes in the leaf blade could, therefore, not be ruled out. Uptake did occur, but at a very much reduced rate. Thus, the question whether metabolic inhibitors affect translocation locally has not definitely been answered with these studies. Nor would they mean much if it were found that they do stop translocation. If, for example, semipermeability of sieve tubes is lost, sieve-tube content would leak out into the xylem and be returned to the leaf blade via transpiration stream.

b. Effect of temperature

Three kinds of information have become available during recent years. In Webb and Gorham's (1965) experiments (*Cucurbita* node) maximum translocation was found at 25°C; 0°C stopped it almost completely. This seems to have been a direct effect on translocation, for photosynthesis was unaffected by the experimental procedure. Inhibition was not correlated with protoplasmic streaming, nor could the decrease at low temperature have been due to a simple viscosity increase, because there was an appreciable recovery lag. This lag seems to indicate some effect upon the plant's metabolic machinery, but it is unknown how this machinery is linked up with translocation.

Swanson and Geiger (1967) studied the time-course response to low-temperature inhibition of sucrose translocation in sugar-beet petioles (*Beta vulgaris* L.). A 50% inhibition of transport was reached within 4 to 15 minutes when the temperature was lowered from 25°C to 1°C in a 2-cm long section of petiole. When the duration of the experiment was long enough, translocation recovered to essentially the precooling level. The half time of this recovery varied from 30 to 100 minutes. Rewarming of the petiole at this time had no further effect. The authors' curves of the time course of translocation rate look very similar to those of the "Renner experiment" illustrated in Fig. IV-21. In this latter case we are dealing with a pressure drop in the xylem of the demand end of the axis. In the case of Swanson and Geiger's phloem experiment, the phenomenon could have been an analogous one, namely an adjustment in the source and/or sink end resulting in a steepened gradient. If, however, the driving force of translocation is located at the sieve plates, cold adaptation of this metabolic machinery would be the explanation. The authors discuss all these possibilities in detail.

The third type of experiment is that of Ford and Peel (1966) in which aphids were used. An aphid-stylet stump will exude at full rate even in an isolated piece of a willow stem, provided its length is at least 16 cm, the contributory length (Weatherley *et al.*, 1959). (With different methods, Ford and Peel showed the contributory length to be greater, but this fact is immaterial in this context.) What apparently happens in willow in that upon cutting the bark, slime plugging or callose seals the sieve tubes at their cut ends (cf. Sec. 6), and the drain of an aphid-stylet in the sieve tube causes mobilization of reserve material (cf. also Sec. 8). The contributory length, then, is the minimum length necessary to allow sufficient mobilization to go on so that full exudation is maintained. Ford and Peel (1966) found that in chilling experiments they had to increase the contributory length beyond the chilled area in order to eliminate the chilling effect. In other words, not translocation *per se,* but mobilization, or secretion of sugars into sieve tubes was decreaseed by chilling.

The fact that translocation depends upon proper functioning of living and metabolizing tissue provides a very useful tool to distinguish transport in xylem and phloem. Woody plants can be girdled if xylem and phloem transport are to be distinguished. This is not possible with herbaceous plants or monocotyledons. However, a section of such a plant can be killed with a small jet of steam ("steam girdling"). Phloem transport will not take place through dead tissue, and the residual transport can be assumed to pass via xylem.

6. THE PLANT'S PROTECTION AGAINST INJURIES OF THE PHLOEM

a. Slime plugging

Sieve tubes are highly turgescent, as seen, and at the same time longitudinally permeable. It is, therefore, not surprising that they are extremely sensitive to injury. When the phloem is cut, exudate moves with an initial rush towards the incision from both sides. As this happens, the sieve plates near the point of injury are sealed off. It is generally recognized that there are two mechanisms responsible for that, slime plugging and callose formation. Slime plugging is instantaneous, and it is of variable effectiveness in different species. When the sieve tubes suffer turgor loss at any point along their length, the slime contracts, is displaced toward the downstream sieve plate, and plugs it.

Slime arises in the sieve element during cell differentiation as "degradation" (or perhaps better "specialization") product of the protoplast, it is a proteinaceous material. It is easily visible in the light microscope, particularly in the form of plugs (Esau, 1965; cf. also citations therein). In the electron microscope, slime appears to be filamentous in nature (e.g. Esau and Cheadle, 1965; Evert and Murmanis, 1965; Parthasarathy and Mühlethaler, 1969) and is usually referred to as P-protein. Crafts (1968), reviewing the literature on slime, even considers two different mechanisms, slime plugging and filament plugging.

Slime is important in many respects. When an incision is made into the phloem to collect exudate, the success varies considerably with different species. If no exudate emerges it may be because slime plugging has been quite instantaneously effective. Any small amount of initial exudate could be sucked into the apoplast, particularly if the incision has reached the xylem. In many tree species, an initial amount of exudate appears, can be collected, but exudation then stops. Cessation in that case is undoubtedly due to slime plugging. Recutting, i.e. elimination of the small amount of plugged tissue, often results in resumption of exudation (for example in palm inflorescences, cf. Tammes, 1933; *Cucurbita* stems, cf. Crafts, 1961). Few species, among them *Fraxinus americana* L., exude copiously and for a long time (say, half an hour or so). This indicates minimal slime plugging and makes the tree a very suitable species for experimental work involving the collection of many sieve-tube exudate samples. But what does it

mean to the tree? It is not known, of course, whether the tree enjoys any beneficial effect (increased conductivity perhaps?), but it is known that it suffers sugar
loss in the case of injury.

Slime plugging must have been an important survival factor during the
course of evolution as a protective device. In fact, it may have proved so useful
that it prevented the plant from losing its sieve plates. This will be discussed
again briefly in connection with resistance to flow.

The sieve tubes' high turgescence, slime plugging, and callose formation have
caused a great deal of grief when phloem was fixed for anatomical investigation.
When a piece of phloem is collected for anatomical study, sieve tubes suffer slime
plugging while the piece is removed from the plant and before it is put in the
fixing solution. The solution thus fixes slime-plugged sieve tubes and not tissue
as it exists under normal functioning conditions. There are ways of avoiding this
difficulty, at least partially. One may bathe a long piece of vascular tissue in a
concentrated sugar solution in order to gently release turgor prior to cutting.
But one has to be aware of the fact that turgor is propagated over long distances
in sieve tubes, in trees over many meters (Münch, 1930; Zimmermann, 1960). This
method may, therefore, not be entirely effective. Some petioles are hollow. Investigators, therefore, often inject the fixing fluid directly into this petiolar
cavity so that the tissue is fixed while still on the intact plant (e.g. Esau and
Cheadle, 1965). Still another possibility is to freeze the tissue on the intact
plant prior to collection. The success of anatomical investigation, especially at
the level of the electron microscope, thus depends to a very great extent upon
fixation and prefixation treatment of tissue.

b. Callose

Even though callose formation is slower than slime plugging, it can still take
place within minutes. It is triggered not only by turgor release but in addition
also by other stimuli. Callose is a β-1–3, glucose polysaccharide (Kessler, 1958)
which is deposited around the sieve pores, and, if much is deposited, closes pores
entirely. In deciduous tree species of temperate zones, at least those which have
been looked at, masses of callose accumulate in sieve pores in autumn after
cessation of sieve tube function. This is called definitive callose (Fig. V-18). This
callose may be redissolved in spring if sieve tubes are reactivated (cf. e.g. Evert
and Murmanis, 1965; Kollmann and Schumacher, 1962).

Massive callose formation takes place in some species after turgor release. For
example, when *Carya* or *Castanea* branches are removed from the tree and placed
in water, branches may look healthy in spite of the fact that the cutting of the
branch has triggered callose formation and completely closed all active tubes in
the branch (cf. the discussion in Zimmermann, 1964). Callose formation can also
be induced in many other ways; for example when a piece of tissue is placed in
a chemical fixing solution, callose formation may occur before the cells in the
interior of the piece die. For a more detailed description of staining reactions,
physiology, etc., the reader is referred to the papers of Currier (1957), Currier
and Webster (1964) and Eschrich (1965).

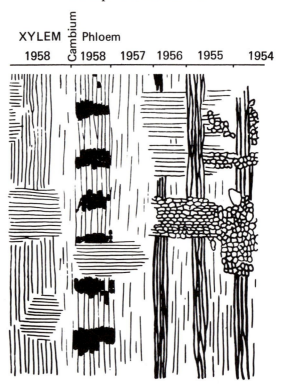

Fig. V–18. Diagrammatic representation of a radial section through the bark of *Fraxinus americana* L., two weeks after leaf abscission showing five annual growth rings in the phloem. All sieve plates of the 1958 conducting phloem are closed by callose (marked black on this drawing). From Zimmermann, 1964.

7. PROPOSED MECHANISMS OF TRANSPORT

If one considers observed specific mass transfer (grams of translocated dry material per unit time and transverse-sectional area; cf. Sec. 4b), and sets this equal to movement by diffusion, one finds that the process of diffusion is entirely inadequate. A few calculations illustrate this. One can, for example, take the known diffusion coefficient of sugar in water, a gradient of 1 molar sugar solution to pure water and calculate the distance over which the observed mass transfer could take place. The result is quite striking: diffusion can move such vast quantities over a distance of only a small fraction of a millimeter! While in the past century notable plant physiologists still assumed diffusion to be able to take care of sugar distribution in the plant, Mason and Maskell (1928) and others clearly demonstrated that this was impossible. Alternate mechanisms of translocation were therefore sought. Many proposals have been made throughout the years; most of them are merely vague descriptions like "activated diffusion", "metabolic transport", etc., rather than clearly defined theories. There are probably about as many concepts as there are investigators.

Concepts of mechanisms of translocation can be divided into essentially two groups, depending on whether it is assumed that solute molecules move with the solvent water as a flowing solution, or whether solute molecules are transported independently from the water by some metabolic process.

a. Movement of solutes independent from solvent water

Concepts of independent movement of solute molecules vary, most of them are mere descriptive statements of one form or another, making the plant's metabolism directly responsible for translocation. The main argument in favor of independent "metabolic movement" of solutes is the assumption that different types of substances are translocated simultaneously at different velocities and even in opposite directions. That this may only be a matter of interpretation has been discussed in Sections 2d and 4a. There is no really convincing evidence for independent movement; quite to the contrary, it is amazing how uniform distribution patterns and velocities are for the wide variety of translocated substances: sugars, inorganic ions, herbicides, virus particles, etc. Evidence, indeed, speaks more against, than for independent movement.

MOVEMENT ALONG INTERFACES. Oleate introduced at the interface between water and ether spreads rapidly. This gave rise to the speculation that phloem transport might be a comparable phenomenon (Van den Honert, 1932). Obviously, the model of oleate spreading is a very specialized case which could not explain the movement of as widely differing molecules as are known to be transported; such passive spreading along interfaces has to be dismissed as an unreasonable speculation. On the other hand, there are investigators who combine the two previously-mentioned concepts into a speculation of "metabolic movement along interfaces", whereby the plant's metabolism is supposed to be the driving force. Such a concept is again a mere speculation and, because of lack of any clear definition, can be neither dismissed nor is it very useful.

PROTOPLASMIC STREAMING HYPOTHESIS. The phenomenon of protoplasmic streaming is well known, even though it is not yet fully understood (Kamiya, 1965). As early as 1885 it was suggested that protoplasmic streaming might provide the driving force for translocation (De Vries, 1885). This idea found a strong supporter in Curtis (1935), fell into disrepute, but has been revived again by Thaine (1962) and Canny (1962b). Curtis' concept was that streaming actuated mass movement within living cells, as well as within sieve elements. Movement from sieve element to sieve element was then supposed to take place with a different mechanism. It is possible that transport by protoplasmic streaming is important in the slower cell to cell movement in parenchymatous tissues. For rapid long-distance transport via sieve tubes such a mechanism would be inadequate from a quantitative point of view. Thaine's (1962) revival of the protoplasmic streaming concept is based upon the claim of transcellular streaming within sieve tubes. The validity of this claim is highly questionable (Esau *et al.*, 1963). Thaine, in his later papers, modified his views, but meanwhile the concept seems to have found a number of supporters. Apparent support comes from electron microscopic work which has demonstrated transcellular fibrillar or tubular material in sieve tubes (e.g. Evert and Murmanis, 1965). It must be emphasized, however, that Thaine's original "transcellular strands" and the electron microscopically visible fibrils are entirely different things.

It was Canny (1962b) who gave the protoplasmic streaming theory a precise definition. His theory is based upon the assumption of transcellular protoplasmic streaming in the sense of Thaine. The strands are supposed to move both ways (i.e. half of them one way, the other half the other way), carrying dissolved substances. The sieve-element lumen contains the vacuolar solution (to be identical with the sieve-tube exudate) which at any one point remains in equilibrium with the solutes of the strands. Sugar produced at one end of the sieve tubes raises the concentration in the vacuole; this equilibrates with that of the strands; the strands with the higher concentration move to places where the concentration is lower, where net diffusion out of the strands discharges sugar into the vacuoles. Such a mechanism is clearly definable, once certain quantitative assumptions are made (Canny and Phillips, 1963). It would evenly distribute any substance entering the sieve tubes to all plant parts. It should basically show the characteristics of diffusion, although accelerated by protoplasmic streaming.

Three arguments speak against this theory. First, transcellular streaming in sieve tubes is not confirmed. In fact, careful investigators have stated many times that protoplasmic streaming cannot be observed in sieve tubes. What Thaine (1962) observed seems to have been streaming in parenchyma cells either above or below sieve elements. Second, the theory is quantitatively inadequate from the point of view of mass transfer as well as velocity. If a radioactive front advances with a velocity of 60 cm per hour, then it simply cannot have been moved by protoplasmic streaming which is known in higher plants to go not faster than 5 to 10 cm per hour. Proponents assume that some component of the protoplasm moves faster than the visible, included particles. Another argument against the theory is its mode of action. Any applied substance which is not already present in the sieve tube should be distributed more or less evenly throughout the plant; i.e. it should move both ways from the point of application, even into old leaves. This is not the case. It is important to point out that aphids should not be used for such experiments, for aphids create strong local sinks.

In summary, one can say that protoplasmic streaming is a very unlikely explanation for phloem transport, though it may be occasionally a significant factor in the slower cell-to-cell transport through parenchymatous tissues.

b. Transport as a flowing solution

The question of whether solutes are translocated in a flowing solution seems, at first glance, an easy one to answer. When ^{14}C-labeled sugar and tritiated water are simultaneously applied to the phloem, the two tracers should move together if there is solution flow. This experiment has been done repeatedly (though not with trees), but the results were not quite as clear as one might have hoped. In Biddulph and Cory's (1957) experiments THO did move with the solutes; Gage and Aronoff (1960), however, were unable to detect THO movement. Trip and Gorham (1968b) were again successful in finding that two tracers move in the same direction; moreover, both of them were stopped by a steam girdle, an indication that they both moved in living tissue, probably the phloem. The principle difficulty with this experiment is that in applying water one has to compete with the natural source of water, the xylem, which is always very intimately associated with the phloem. Even if water has been successfully introduced into the phloem, it can, in contrast to the sugar, quite easily be lost again by diffusional exchange with the surrounding tissue. This is particularly true if one experiments with a single sieve tube (Peel *et al.,* 1969; Peel, 1970). Diffusional exchange of water with the surrounding tissue is so rapid that sieve tubes always contain quite "local" water.

The phenomenon of exudation, from incisions as well as from severed aphid stylet bundles, is the most direct evidence of solution flow. Exudation from incisions is limited by the plant's reaction to injury (cf. Sec. 6). Therefore, consider stylet-bundle exudation. The stylet bundle represents a sink at its point of insertion in the sieve tube, draining the content of the sieve element. It is interesting to compare the volume of exudation (2 to 5 mm^3 per hour, i.e. of the order of 0.001 mm^3 per second) with the volume of a single sieve element (diameter about 0.025 mm, length about 0.35 mm, i.e. about 0.0002 mm^3), in *Tilia.* This means that a single sieve element delivers exudate at a rate of some five times its own volume per second. In other words, the sieve element has to be refilled (from an axial direction as seen in Sec. 2b) about five times per second. It is entirely inconceivable that such a rate of exudation could be maintained in any way other than by a flowing solution, though it is augmented by osmotically entering water.

It is an interesting consideration that if phloem transport is a solution flow, water must be lost from sieve tubes for osmotic reasons wherever sugars are removed. In the tree trunk, where sugar is deposited at places of storage, this liberated water is thought to return to the leaves via xylem, contributing according to Münch (1930) about 5% to the transpiration stream. If a downward-pointing bark flap is enclosed in a container such as a polyethylene bag, osmotically released water can be collected, provided, of course, that transport continues after the bark flap has been pried loose. Continuation of phloem transport into the bark flap can be recognized by the continuation of cambial activity, that is, the formation of wood on the cambium-side of the flap (Münch, 1930; Brown, 1964).

In summary then, there is overwhelming evidence suggesting that phloem transport, at least in those plants from which the evidence has been obtained, takes place in the form of a flowing solution. This, it must be emphasized, does not indicate what the driving force of the flow is. Mass flow could be pressure flow, electro-osmotic flow, or flow activated in still another way.

PRESSURE-FLOW HYPOTHESIS.   There are many possible ways in which a solution could be "pumped" through a plant. Münch's (1930) mass-flow hypothesis, more precisely called "pressure-flow hypothesis", is the best-known proposal. In its original form it envisaged the plant's whole symplast (all living cell parts) to behave like one giant osmotic cell. Plasmodesmata were thought to be permeable passages between cells, the connecting strands of sieve plates more highly specialized plasmodesmata (Münch, 1930). Thus, a flow of vacuolar solution could take place within this system along any hydrostatic gradient. Hydrostatic gradients, i.e. turgor gradients are thought to exist between "source" and "sink" (cf. Sec. 4d). In translocation work a source is called any point from which export takes place; a sink is any point into which import takes place. Münch's concept is very simple. In a source area, solutes are introduced into solution (by photosynthesis or mobilization of reserve material), the concentration is raised, water is drawn osmotically from the surrounding apoplast (cell walls and xylem) and thus the turgor is raised. In the sink area, on the other hand, turgor is lowered either by expansion of growing tissue (increased plasticity of cell walls in meristematic tissue) or by removal of solutes from the vacuole, for example by polymerization of sugars into starch. In the latter case, osmotic concentration is lowered, water is lost to the surrounding apoplast, and the turgor drops. Thus, a gradient of decreasing turgor is maintained from source to sink. Models of this mechanism can easily be built in the laboratory (Fig. V-19). The great advantage of such a mechanism is the simplicity with which transport regulation could be explained. This aspect will be discussed in a later section (8).

Münch's pressure-flow hypothesis had a very stimulating effect on translocation research, an effect which is still lasting. It soon became obvious that in its original form the hypothesis was too generalized; it had to be restricted to the

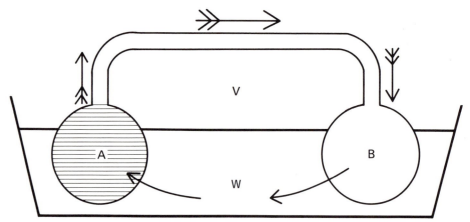

Fig. V–19. A model of Münch's pressure-flow mechanism. Two osmotic cells, one with a higher (A) the other with a lower (B) solute concentration are connected with a tube (V). The cells are immersed in water (W). Net water diffusion is out of the cell B and into the cell A. Flow of solution continues from A to B through the tube V until the concentrations in the two cells are equal. From Münch, 1930.

sieve tubes. Uptake into sieve tubes (often also referred as as "loading"; Barrier and Loomis, 1957) may take place against a concentration gradient. This is indicated by the observation that leaf parenchyma cells can be plasmolyzed with sieve-tube exudate of the same plant (Curtis and Asai, 1939; Röckl, 1949).

Münch's (modified) mechanism must work in the plant, whether it is sufficient to provide the full driving force for transport or not, if the following three conditions are met. (1) The sieve-tube system as a whole must be semipermeable toward the apoplast. In other words, the side walls of sieve tubes must be lined with a semipermeable membrane (possibly the plasmalemma, for it is uncertain whether the tonoplast still exists in mature sieve tubes) which prevents osmotically active substances (such as sugars) from leaking out. At the same time, entry of solutes into and removal from sieve tubes must be caused by metabolic "pumping". (2) The sieve tubes must be permeable in a longitudinal direction, from element to element through the sieve pores. (3) A turgor gradient must be maintained from source to sink. According to previous discussion, three points can be commented upon as follows. Condition (1) is unquestionably met in sieve tubes. Exudation from aphid stylet bundles indicates a high turgescence which could not exist without semipermeability of the system. Further evidence has been presented in Section 4c. Condition (2) is also met, according to evidence discussed in Sections 4c and 7b. The last point (3), the question whether a turgor gradient exists from source to sink, cannot yet be fully answered. Reasons to believe that it does have been discussed in Section 4d.

In summary then, two questions still have to be answered before deciding whether a pressure-flow mechanism is important. (1) One has to obtain more precise evidence for a *turgor* gradient in the sieve tubes in the direction of transport. (2) One has to know the resistance to flow in the sieve tubes. This second question will determine how effective a pressure-flow mechanism could be. If the turgor gradient is real (and all evidence agrees so far), then turgor is a driving force of flow, no matter whether it is the only one or not.

ELECTRO-OSMOTIC FLOW THEORY. Not only pressures, but also electric potentials could be the driving force of liquid flow provided the solution includes ions (which are practically always present). The idea of electrically driven flow is particularly attractive if the pores, through which flow takes place, are small, because the flowing liquid has to be close to the seat of the electrical potential. The theoretical background of this is discussed in Chapter VI.

Fensom (1957) and Spanner (1958) independently proposed electro-osmotic theories of transport. Fensom has since withdrawn his hypothesis. He still believes that transport is a flowing solution, but neither driven by turgor gradient, nor by electro-osmosis, rather by some other, as yet unknown driving force (Fensom *et al.*, 1968). Spanner's theory involves a metabolically driven circulation of ions such as potassium in the area of the sieve plates. Potassium ions are thought to be introduced into the sieve-tube lumen on the upstream side of a sieve plate and removed on the downstream side. The sieve plate, thus electrically polarized, would cause electro-osmotic flow of solution through the plate. The

electric potential is thought to be metabolically maintained by ion return outside the sieve-tube lumen, for example in the companion cells (Fig. V-20). Evidence in support of this theory has recently been produced by Bowling (1968)
who inserted microelectrodes into sieve tubes and measured potentials across
sieve plates.

OTHER POSSIBILITIES.   There are workers who consider neither turgor nor
electro-osmotic forces sufficient to maintain transport, even though they are con-
vinced that transport is a mass flow of a solution. One could think of many other
possibilities. To mention just one example, it is conceivable that the filaments
seen by electron microscopists in the sieve pores maintain a flagella-type of action
to drive the solution. These are interesting speculations awaiting further exploration.

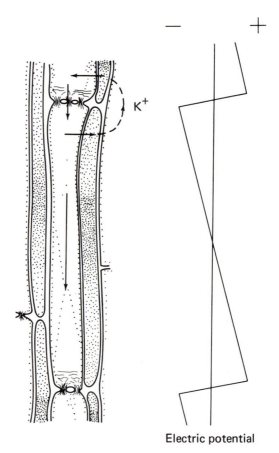

Electric potential

Fig. V–20.   Representation of Spanner's electro-osmotic theory. The diagram shows the variation of electric potential down
a sieve tube associated with the circulation of potassium ions
across sieve plates. llustration courtesy D. C. Spanner.

RESISTANCE TO FLOW IN SIEVE TUBES. This question is of crucial importance in regard to the mechanism of flow. If the driving force is turgor pressure, the resistance to flow must be sufficiently small so that a reasonable turgor gradient can overcome it. Resistance calculations were made when the ascent of sap in the xylem was discussed in Chap. IV, Sec. 5. In the case of the xylem we were fortunate enough to be able to measure resistance to flow experimentally. Then we compared these experimentally obtained values with a theoretical model. The situation is far less simple in the case of phloem. In Section 4c it was pointed out that sieve tubes are highly turgescent, and in Section 6 that they are very sensitive to injury. For these reasons, one cannot, unfortunately, merely cut a sample block of phloem from the tree and measure resistance to flow. Although it is conceivable that eventually, with the proper instrumentation (perhaps at a time when one is able to counterbalance pressure on a cut aphid stylet bundle), and with a suitable plant species, one might be able to measure resistance to flow in sieve tubes.

Until recently the question of resistance to flow in sieve tubes has been subject to wild speculations and calculations. As a model for these calculations, the Poiseuille equation is generally used, a description of the steady state of laminar flow through ideal capillaries. The difficulty is that sieve tubes are not ideal capillaries. Resistance calculations are, therefore, nothing more than educated guesses. However, it is useful to go through the mental exercise of such a calculation and find the points where uncertainties are introduced. To facilitate the procedure one may refer to Fig. IV-15. In sieve tubes a rather concentrated sugar solution is dealt with; pressure gradients to drive capillary flow do, therefore, have to be larger. The viscosity of a 20% sucrose solution is roughly 2 centipoise at room temperature. Since the pressure gradient required to drive a solution at a certain flow rate through a given diameter is directly proportional to the viscosity, one must double pressure-gradient values of Fig. IV-15 when using them for sieve tubes. Now assume that ideal capillaries are being dealt with. A pressure gradient of 0.1 atm. per meter will drive a 20% sucrose solution through a tube of 30 μ diameter at a peak velocity of 100 cm per hour. As the diameter is increased to 50 μ, a gradient of 0.07 atm. per meter would suffice to achieve a peak velocity of 200 cm per hour. So far the situation is quite easy to comprehend. As one (mentally) introduces the sieve plates in this theoretical system one complicates the flow to such an extent as to make mathematical treatment impossible. One cannot merely apply the Poiseuille equation to sieve pores, because it is based upon paraboloid flow which can only develop if the length of the tube is about 50 times its diameter. Clearly, this requirement is not met in sieve pores. However, nature has provided us with a model which is ideally suited to test the situation: coniferous wood. Resistance to flow in wood was discussed in Chapter IV, Section 5; the reader is referred to Table IV-3. We have seen there that the hydraulic conductivity of *Abies* tracheids is 26–43% of ideal capillaries of the same diameter. It is necessary to visualize the complex structure of bordered pits in order to appreciate the significance of this finding. This has been presented in Chapter IV and does not need further elucidation. It means that if the pressure gradients which have been calculated for "plate-less" sieve tubes are multiplied by three, pores of extremely small diameter (small fractions of a micron in the tracheid model) have been accommodated in the flow path sieve. Such pressure gradients are still reasonable.

One must go still a step further toward complication. Electron microscopists present pictures of sieve pores which seem to be "filled" with some sort of electron-dense material. Considering the sieve tubes' high turgescence and their extreme sensitivity towards injury, many of the early electron micrographs must be considered pretty crude artifacts. As preparation techniques were refined, however, the quality of the pictures improved. Just how well recent electron micrographs illustrate the natural state of the sieve tubes is difficult to say. In some electron micrographs sieve pores look quite "empty" (Esau and Cheadle, 1965), in others sieve pores appear to be traversed by filamentous or even tubular material (e.g. Evert and Murmanis, 1965; Kollmann and Schumacher, 1963; Parthasarathy and Mühlethaler, 1969). Which is the real situation, and which is the artifact? Do some fixation procedures dissolve the filamentous structures? Or do some fixatives polymerize with the cell content to form these structures? At the present, it is safe to say that the rheological significance of connecting strands is not known. The following possibilities should be considered: (1) The filamentous structures in sieve pores are polymerization products due to fixation; (2) the filamentous material is stationary and represents a considerable resistance to flow; (3) the filamentous material is stationary and has some rheological "lubrication" effect (slippage through pores, superfluidity in the sense of Crafts [1961, p. 149]); (4) the filamentous material is part of the flowing solution, thus movement of the solution would not be paraboloid, but more like a pencil being pushed through a pore. Chain molecules are known to decrease resistance to flow of a solution (e.g. Gadd, 1968); or (5) the filamentous material could be the seat of the driving force of flow. It is hoped that these questions will eventually be resolved.

c. Conclusions

The quest for the mechanism of transport in general, and Münch's pressure-flow hypothesis in particular, has had a very stimulating effect upon research. This is the justification for having presented in somewhat more detail the proposed mechanisms. The present state of knowledge may now be briefly summarized as follows. There is good evidence indicating that transport is taking place in the form of a flowing solution. Evidence contradicting this is very shaky, even though the mass-flow concept has many opponents. The question of the driving force is still unsettled, however. Mass flow does not have to be pressure flow; there are numerous other possibilities. In principle, the question is whether the driving force is seated along the side walls of the sieve tubes, or at the sieve plates. If the driving force acts along the side walls, and Ford and Peel's (1966) findings indicate that this is the case, then the sieve plates would be mere resistances to flow. If the driving force is located at the sieve plates, solution would be forced across pores in a more direct way, such as Spanner's (1958) electro-osmotic theory. There is not as yet a final answer to these questions.

If the sieve plates are mere resistances, why have they not disappeared during the course of evolution as have the cross walls of the vessels in the xylem? Even in the xylem, large and long vessels are not only a rheological advantage, but also, at the same time, an increased risk. Once injured, the vessels embolize and the damage remains confined within that one vessel. In sieve tubes, the situation is somewhat different. Once injured, not only would the whole sieve tube drain and go out of function, but even all reserves along its way would be mobilized and leak out from the injury, were it not for the protective device seated at the sieve plates. Therefore, during the course of evolution the protective advantage of the sieve plate seems to have proven more valuable to the plant than the advantage of decreased flow resistance by the loss of the sieve plate. This would be so particularly if the plant had found a trick for decreasing flow resistance at the plate by some structural means.

The driving force of long-distance translocation in sieve tubes is the plant's metabolism. The question of whether this driving force acts via osmotic pressure or in some other way may not have to be answered clearly one way or the other. They are all structural intermediates between plasmodesmata and the sieve plates with very large pores (up to 15 μ in *Fraxinus excelsior* L). In the case of plasmodesmata one can be reasonably certain that transfer from cell to cell is a secretion type of process. In ash trees, on the other hand, there is quite good evidence for a pressure-flow mechanism. It is, therefore, entirely conceivable that both mechanisms are functioning, i.e. that in the more highly specialized sieve tubes of the large trees, pressure flow has become more efficient as flow resistance decreased during the course of evolution. Differing effects of temperature on mass transfer in young and old willow stems may be taken as supporting evidence for this notion (Ford and Peel, 1967).

8. REGULATION OF PHLOEM TRANSPORT

Regulation is one of the most fascinating aspects of translocation. It also often happens that as one studies the regulation of a physiological process, one learns a good deal about its mechanism. In the case of transport in the phloem, it is clear from all experimental evidence, which has been gathered throughout the years from many different plants and with many different methods, that the demand at the sink and the supply at the source regulate translocation. Translocation is always from source to sink. A source can be a photosynthesizing leaf, a mature leaf at night mobilizing starch accumulated during the day; it can even be a mature leaf in the dark depleted of its reserve material provided the experimenter dips the blade into a sugar solution (Hay and Thimann, 1956). Any storage tissue where mobilization goes on can be a source. A sink is any growing tissue or any storing tissue where material is deposited. On the other hand, a mature leaf placed in the dark and depleted of its reserves is not a sink. Why is it not a sink? It is not a sink because its metabolic machinery is not geared to consumption. Interestingly enough, it can be experimentally induced to become a sink if kinetin is applied (Mothes, 1961). Occasional reports mention transport of very small amounts of radioactivity into mature leaves. This comment is usually made in connection with bidirectional transport. However, in each of these cases it is most likely that these traces have been imported into mature leaves via xylem. Furthermore, aphids on a mature leaf represent strong sinks which draw assimilates into the leaf through the tapped sieve tubes even while export via other, untapped ones goes on.

What makes a storage tissue at certain times an importing and at other times an exporting tissue? It is, again, the question of whether the metabolic machinery has received the signal to demand or to supply. In the case of cotyledons the signal may be triggered by the photoperiod (Hock and Mohr, 1965).

Storage along a woody axis (in wood and bark parenchyma) appears to be in a very delicate intermediate balance, and may act as a sink or as a source, depending upon the concentration of the translocation carbohydrate in the sieve tubes. When leaves export during the summer, storage in the woody axis usually goes on. If, however, a piece of this axis is removed from the tree and a sieve tube drained with an aphid stylet bundle, reserve material is again mobilized. This has, at least, been found in the case of *Salix* (Weatherley *et al.*, 1959).

Now look at regulation in terms of the various proposed translocation theories. A translocation theory must not only explain the process of translocation itself, but also how the process is regulated. Consider, for example, an isolated branch of willow with an exuding aphid stylet bundle sticking in about the middle of it. The branch is, say, 50 cm long, i.e. much longer than the contributory length. The stylet bundle exudes at full rate, say, 3 mm^3 per hour. Under these conditions one must assume that flow towards the stylet bundle is equally from both sides, because the stylet bundle is a strong sink and the whole channel (the contributory length) is the source. If an incision is now made on either side to interrupt the supplying sieve tube, exudation does not diminish, provided the uncut side of the sieve tube is still as long as the contributory length (Weatherley *et al.*, 1959). This means that twice as much translocation takes place towards the stylet bundle from the intact side than before. In other words, regulation is practically instantaneous as the demand is changed. How does the sink "tell" the intact side, "supply twice as much sugar, the supply from the other side has been interrupted"?

Canny's (1962b) theory predicts an even and equal distribution of all mobile substances throughout all plant parts (cf. Sec. 7a). This is, in fact, one of the theory's attractive aspects as well as the point in which it disagrees with nature. Any tracer, be it a radioactive isotope or a fluorescent dye, would have to move both ways from the point of application, but it fails to do so.

Change in turgor is the signal of regulation in other translocation theories. In Spanner's (1958) theory, turgor differences cause a minute pressure flow, which, in turn, triggers the electro-osmotic mechanism (cf. Sec. 7b). If the driving mechanism is neither a turgor gradient nor electro-osmosis, but still mass flow, then regulation could be electrically triggered. Turgor change could then, as in Spanner's mechanism, cause a minute pressure flow, which in turn might produce the signal through a streaming potential (Fensom, personal communication).

By far the simplest and most elegant regulation mechanism is pressure flow. The steps are as follows. Removal of carbohydrate molecules from sieve tubes in the sink region is metabolic (enzymatic). The result is a lowered concentration, which must be followed, for osmotic reasons, by a loss of water. In other words, the turgor drops at the sink and a turgor gradient is established. Assume that the sink ceases to require sugar. Flow towards the sink will continue as long as there is a turgor difference, then it will stop. The situation is shown diagrammatically in Fig. V-21a. Two sets of arrows indicate the setting of the metabolic balance, i.e. the demand or supply tendency (the setting of the "concentrationstat" as it were, arrow pairs) and solution flow respectively (single arrow). Assume now a section of a willow branch (Fig. V-21b), self-contained by plugged ends. All balance settings are presumably the same along the whole length. It does not really matter how long one draws the individual arrows as long as one draws two respective lengths within each pair the same everywhere (Fig. V-21b or 21c). There is no flow. Suppose one could change the balance setting on the left by application of kinetin; sugar would then be removed at this point; water lost; the turgor would drop, and flow would take place from right to left along the turgor gradient (Fig. V-21d). Still another example is shown in Fig. V-21e. An aphid stylet bundle sticks in the central part of the stem piece. The drain of the stylet bundle physically lowers the turgor; water enters osmotically where the turgor drops. The resulting concentration drop causes sugars to enter the sieve tube; this in turn mobilizes sugar. It is perfectly clear that the mobilizing effect is diminished with increasing distance from the stylet bundle and reaches an unmeasurably small value at the limits of the contributory length.

The last example of regulation is given in Fig. V-21f which represents the hypothetical situation in a monocotyledonous leaf. These leaves grow at their base, i.e. leaf parts are progressively older in a distal direction. Therefore, if one takes a piece from a grass leaf, the respective settings of the "concentrationstats" may be as shown in the illustration. Note that for our purposes absolute lengths of arrows within a pair does not matter. What matters is only the respective lengths when different positions are compared with each other. If sugar is applied to such a leaf section in one experiment distally, in the other proximally, one would find more translocation from top to base than vice versa. This has been reported by Hartt and Kortschak (1964) and interpreted as polar transport. Viewed in the light of transport regulation, these experiments may have nothing to do with polar transport *per se,* but may indicate slight differences in "concentrationstat" settings in a monocotyledonous leaf. If one would apply sugar evenly throughout the whole length of the isolated blade, one would probably get a slight net movement in basipetal direction.

In summary then, consider the seat of translocation regulation to be the secretion of sugars into and out of sieve tubes, the "concentrationstat" (Fig. V-22). Once such a secretion balance has been set, the regulation of flow becomes entirely automatic. The really interesting question then is, what sets the "concentrationstat"? We have seen that kinetin can reset the device to "out-of-the-sieve-tubes" (Mothes, 1961); photoperiod can set it either way in certain cotyle-

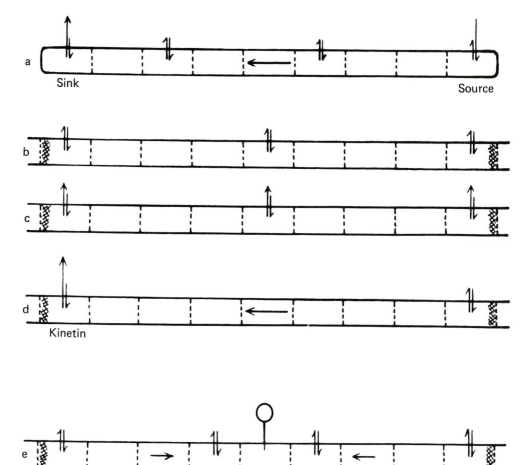

Fig. V–21. Model of transport regulation in sieve tubes according to the pressure-flow hypothesis. The driving force is thought to be identical with the secretion mechanism into and out of the sieve tubes, here marked with arrow pairs. (a) A sieve tube leads from a source (e.g. a leaf) to a sink (e.g. a storage organ). Secretion into the sieve tube in the source region raises, secretion out of the sieve tube in the sink region lowers the turgor. Flow through the sieve tube (single arrow) takes place along a turgor gradient. (b) A piece of willow stem, self-contained by plugged sieve plates at the cut ends, there is no transport in longitudinal direction. It is immaterial whether one draws arrows of identical lengths in each pair as in (b) or of different lengths as in (c), as long as one draws them the same everywhere along the stem. (Of course the concentration in the sieve tube b would be

(continued on bottom of facing page)

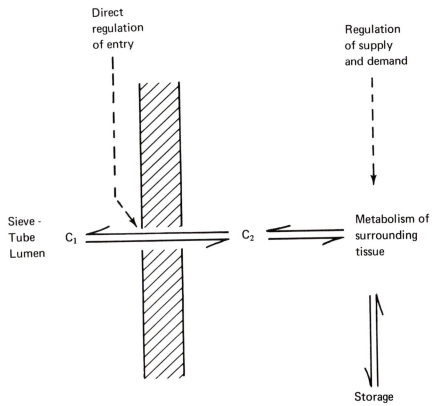

Fig. V-22. Model of transport regulation in sieve tubes. The last step of secretion into the sieve tube is indicated by the arrow pair between C_1 and C_2, which crosses the semipermeable membrane (M) (the plasmalemma?). The permease is linked to a whole array of enzymatic steps to the surrounding tissues' metabolism and to storage. Regulation of secretion into sieve tubes could conceivably take place at a number of points.

dons (Hock and Mohr, 1965). One could now go on and speculate a step further. How, for example, could leaves of a tree regulate removal of sugars from phloem by hormonal messengers (Zimmermann, 1958). Removal of substances from sieve tubes and secretion into sieve tubes is, undoubtedly, a complex matter involving a number of enzymatic steps. One should, therefore, not be too narrow-minded and visualize the "concentrationstat" as being seated in a single en-

---

higher than that in c.) (d) The hypothetical case of kinetin application at one end of the willow stem. The secretion mechanism is re-set at that point to remove sugars from sieve tubes. Translocation (single arrow) is toward this point. (e) An exuding aphid stylet bundle in an isolated willow stem section. The stylet bundle drains the sieve tube, lowered turgor results in water entry, this in turn lowers the concentration which causes secretion into sieve tube without changing the secretion mechanism's setting. (f) The presumed situation in a monocotyledonous leaf whose distal parts are older than proximal parts. This difference in age may go parallel with a difference in the secretion mechanism's setting, an apparent polarity of transport may thus result.

zymatic step. There are many steps between the removal of substances from sieve tubes and the actual consumption of these substances (such as the deposition of cellulose in a cell wall); any of these steps could be the seat of regulation. Thus, kinetin may not have anything to do with the removal of sugars from sieve tubes, but may merely stimulate growth, which then in turn draws sugars from the sieve tubes.

It is clear that the substance(s) of the highest molar concentration in the sieve tubes will pretty much determine the direction of flow. In most cases this is sugar. Every movable molecule in the sieve tubes, thus, will have to go where sugar goes, even if it is against its own concentration gradient. This is the point in which the protoplasmic streaming theory differs fundamentally from the mass-flow theories. The protoplasmic streaming theory predicts diffusion type distribution, i.e. every molecule type moves down its own gradient. In mass flow, every movable molecule moves with the same stream, even if it is against its own concentration gradient. In the case of *Fraxinus* one finds, occasionally, the sucrose gradient negative in the downward direction of the stem while all other gradients are positive. This does not mean that sucrose moves up while all other sugars move down; it merely means that sucrose is moved against its gradient, because its removal is relatively slow, or its production along the way from the higher oligosaccharides is greater than its removal (Zimmermann, 1959).

A substance may be moved against its concentration gradient within the sieve tubes when its removal from sieve tubes is relatively slow or absent. This does not have to be a problem to the plant, because whenever an "unusable" substance is accumulated in the sieve tubes to a certain concentration, it can be transferred to the xylem where it will be moved in the opposite direction. Therefore, foreign introduced substances may circulate and recirculate repeatedly in the plant (cf. Chap. VII, Sec. 4).

CONCLUDING REMARKS

This chapter represents an attempt to give the reader a survey of phloem transport in plants in general and trees, in particular. It is not a comprehensive review; many important papers remain to be cited. However, anyone who wishes to go further into the details will easily find his way into the literature via the citations given at the end of this chapter.

A survey like this, especially if it is written by someone working in the field himself, is almost necessarily somewhat biased, and the present chapter is certainly no exception. On the other hand, nothing makes duller reading than a review in which the writer tries to be impartial to the extent of having no opinion. The question thus arises as to where to draw the line between a colorless and a prejudiced representation. One of the reviewers (D. S. Fensom) of this chapter called it "a clear statement of 'party line' " and, in order to balance it, asked me to add his own (different) postulates. I am doing this with pleasure.

D. S. Fensom's Phloem Postulates (August 1969)

Structure.

1. Sieve tubes contain a network of *microfibrillar* material made up of units 60, 130 to 280 Å in diameter, in the form of microhelices or microtubules or banded microfilaments.

2. The microfibrillar material is interlinked, but mainly runs *from plate to plate* and through the sieve-plate pores. The amount may vary in plants with age, species, and location in stem. This material is *very easily* damaged.

3. *Particles,* bound by membranes, are attached to the reticulum through the lumen of the sieve tubes. Since the reticulum is elastic in appearance, the particles appear to move as the liquid flows past them.

Function.

4. The sieve plates act as pumps, not barriers.

5. Flow has two modes: (1) mass flow which is unidirectional, and (2) micro-tubular (or microfibrillar flow) which may be unidirectional, but can also appear to be bidirectional.

6. The apparent mass flow is a down-hill pressure flow, and probably has a (small) electro-osmotic component. It is mainly activated by the micro-fibrillar flow.

7. The microtubular (or fibrillar) flow is from source to sink, loading sucrose at a high concentration or high pressure place with K as coenzyme. Movement is by contractile protein (p-protein) involving ATP and K ions, and *may* be microperistaltic in nature. It will be modified by the state of the microfibrils in each direction and by the surrounding mass flow portion. Excellent reviews with alternate conclusions have appeared elsewhere (e.g. Eschrich, 1970; Kursanov, 1963; Weatherley and Johnson, 1968).

The careful reader will see that one still depends heavily upon interpretation. As new evidence becomes available, one must be prepared to change his opinion. Even though everyone will tend to interpret new evidence in his own way, one should never become rigid to the extent of merely defending his point of view.

LITERATURE CITED

Barrier, G. E. and W. E. Loomis. 1957. Absorption and translocation of 2,4-dichloro-phenoxyacetic acid and P^{32} by leaves. *Plant Physiol.* 32: 225–231.—Biddulph, O. and R. Cory. 1957. An analysis of translocation in the phloem of the bean plant using THO, P^{32}, and C^{14}. *Plant Physiol.* 32: 608–619.—Biddulph, O. and R. Cory. 1960. Demonstration of two translocation mechanisms in studies of bidirectional movement. *Plant Physiol.* 35: 689–695.—Bowling, D. J. F. 1968. Measurement of the potential across the sieve plates in *Vitis vinifera. Planta* 80: 21–26.—Brown, C. L. 1964. The influence of external pressure on the differentiation of cells and tissues cultured *in vitro.* Ed. M. H. Zimmermann, pp. 389–404. In *The formation of wood in forest trees.* New York: Academic Press.

CANNY, M. J. 1960. The rate of translocation. *Biol. Reviews* 35: 507–532.—CANNY, M. J. 1961. Measurements of the velocity of translocation. *Ann. Bot.* 25: 152–167.—CANNY, M. J. 1962a. The translocation profile: sucrose and carbon dioxide. *Ann. Bot.* 26: 181–196.—CANNY, M. J. 1962b. The mechanism of translocation. *Ann. Bot.* 26: 603–617.—CANNY, M. J., B. NAIRN and M. HARVEY. 1968. The velocity of translocation in trees. *Aust. Jour. Bot.* 16: 479–485.—CANNY, M. J. and O. M. PHILLIPS. 1963. Quantitative aspects of a theory of translocation. *Ann. Bot.* 27: 379–402.—CRAFTS, A. S. 1961. *Translocation in plants.* New York: Holt, Rinehart and Winston.—CRAFTS, A. S. 1968. Problem of sieve-tube slime. *Sci.* 160: 325–327.—CRAFTS, A. S. and S. YAMAGUCHI. 1964. *The autoradiography of plant materials.* Div. of Agricult. Sciences, Univ. of Calif. Manual 35.—CURRIER, H. B. 1957. Callus substances in plant cells. *Amer. Jour. Bot.* 44: 49–53.—CURRIER, H. B., K. ESAU and V. I. CHEADLE. 1955. Plasmolytic studies of phloem. *Amer. Jour. Bot.* 42: 68–81.—CURRIER, H. B. and D. H. WEBSTER. 1964. Callose formation and subsequent disappearance: studies in ultrasound stimulation. *Plant Physiol.* 39: 843–847.—CURTIS, O. F. 1935. *The translocation of solutes in plants. A critical consideration of evidence bearing upon solute movement.* 273 p. New York: McGraw-Hill Book Co.—CURTIS, O. F. and G. N. ASAI. 1939. Evidence relative to the supposed permeability of sieve-tube cytoplasm. *Amer. Jour. Bot.* 26: 165–175.

DEN OUTER, R. W. 1967. Histological investigations of the secondary phloem of gymnosperms. Meded. Landbouwhogeschool Wageningen, Holland 67 (7): 1–119.—DICKSON, A. G. and E. W. SAMUELS. 1956. The mechanism of controlled growth of dwarf apple trees. *Jour. Arnold Arb.* 37: 307–313.

ESAU, K. 1965. *Plant anatomy.* 2nd ed. New York: John Wiley & Sons.—ESAU, K. and V. I. CHEADLE. 1965. Cytologic studies on phloem. *Univ. of Calif. Publications in Botany* 36: 253–344.—ESAU, K., J. CRONSHAW and L. L. HOEFERT. 1967. Relation of beet yellows virus to the phloem and to movement in the sieve tube. *Jour. Cell Biol.* 32: 71–87.—ESAU, K., E. M. ENGLEMAN and T. BISALPUTRA. 1963. What are transcellular strands? *Planta* 59: 617–623.—ESCHRICH, W. 1965. Physiologie der Siebröhrencallose. *Planta* 65: 280–300.—ESCHRICH, W. 1967. Bidirektionelle Translokation in Siebröhren. *Planta* 73: 37–49.—ESCHRICH, W. 1970. Biochemistry and fine structure of phloem in relation to transport. Ann. Rev. Plant Physiol. 21: 193–214.—EVERT, R. F. and L. MURMANIS. 1965. Ultrastructure of the secondary phloem of *Tilia americana. Amer. Jour. Bot.* 52: 95–106.

FAHN, A. 1967. *Plant anatomy.* Oxford: Pergamon Press.—FENSOM, D. S. 1957. An electrokinetic theory of transport. *Can. Jour. Bot.* 35: 573–582.—FENSOM, D. S., R. CLATTENBURG, T. CHUNG, D. R. LEE and D. C. ARNOLD. 1968. Moving particles in intact sieve tubes of *Heracleum mantegazzianum. Nat.* 219: 531–532.—FORD, J. and A. J. PEEL. 1966. The contributory length of sieve tubes in isolated segments of willow, and the effect on it of low temperatures. *Jour. Exptl. Bot.* 17: 522–533.—FORD, J. and A. J. PEEL. 1967. Preliminary experiments on the effect of temperature on the movement of ^{14}C-labelled assimilates through the phloem of willow. *Jour. Exptl. Bot.* 18: 406–415.

GADD, G. E. 1968. Effects of drag-reducing additives on vortex stretching. *Nat.* 217: 1040–1042.—GAGE, R. S. and S. ARONOFF. 1960. Translocation III. Experiments with carbon 14, chlorine 36, and hydrogen 3. *Plant Physiol.* 35: 53–64.—GARDNER, D. C. J. and A. J. PEEL. 1969. ATP in sieve tube sap from willow. *Nat.* 222: 774.

HAMMEL, H. T. 1968. Measurement of turgor pressure and its gradient in the phloem of oak. *Plant Physiol.* 43: 1042–1048.—HARTIG, R. 1889. Ein Ringelungsversuch. *Allg.*

Forst- und Jagdztg. 65: 365–373, 401–410.—HARTIG, Th. 1837. Vergleichende Untersuchungen über die Organisation des Stammes der einheimischen Waldbäume. *Jahresber. Fortschr. Forstwiss. u. forstl. Naturk.* 1: 125–168.—HARTIG, Th. 1860. Beiträge zur physiologischen Forstbotanik. *Allg. Forst- und Jagdztg.* 36: 257–261.—HARTT, C. E. and H. P. KORTSCHAK. 1964. Sugar gradients and translocation of sucrose in detached blades of sugarcane. *Plant Physiol.* 39: 460–474.—HAY, J. R. and K. V. THIMANN. 1956. The fate of 2,4-dichlorophenoxyacetic acid in bean seedlings. II. Translocation. *Plant Physiol.* 31: 446–451.—HILL, G. P. 1963. The sources of sugar in sieve-tube sap. *Ann. Bot.* 27: 79–87. —HOCK, B. and H. MOHR. 1965. Eine quantitative Analyse von Wachstumsvorgängen im Zusammenhang mit der Photomorphogenese von Senfkeimlingen (*Sinapis alba* L.). *Planta* 65: 1–16.—HOLDHEIDE, W. 1951. Anatomie mitteleuropäischer Gehölzrinden. In *Mikrosk. i.d. Technik V/1.* H. Freund, ed. Frankfurt: Umschau-Verlag.—HUBER, B. 1953. Die Gewinnung des Eschenmanna—eine Nutzung von Siebröhrensaft. *Ber. deutsch. bot. Ges.* 66: 341–346.—HUBER, B. 1961. *Grundzüge der Pflanzenanatomie.* Berlin: Springer-Verlag.—HUBER, B., E. SCHMIDT and H. JAHNEL. 1937. Untersuchungen über den Assimilatstrom I. *Tharandter forstl. Jahrb.* 88: 1017–1049.

KAMIYA, N. 1965. Rheology of cytoplasmic streaming. In *Proc. 4th Int. Congr. Rheology.* E. H. Lee and A. L. Copley, eds. Part 1. New York: Interscience Publishers (John Wiley & Sons).—KESSLER, G. 1958. Zur Charakterisierung der Siebröhrenkallose. *Ber. schweiz. bot. Ges.* 68: 5–43.—KLUGE, M. 1967. Viruspartikel im Siebröhrensaft von *Cucumis sativus* L. nach Infektion durch das Cucumisvirus 2A. *Planta* 73: 50–61.— KLUGE, M. and H. ZIEGLER. 1964. Der ATP-Gehalt der Siebröhrensäfte von Laubbäumen. *Planta* 61: 167–177.—KOLLMANN, R. 1965. Zur Lokalisierung der funktionstüchtigen Siebzellen im sekundären Phloem von *Metasequoia glyptostroboides. Planta* 65: 173–179. —KOLLMANN, R. and I. DÖRR. 1966. Lokalisierung funktionstüchtiger Siebzellen bei *Juniperus communis* mit Hilfe von Aphiden. *Z. Pflanzenphysiol.* 55: 131–141.—KOLLMANN, R. and W. SCHUMACHER. 1961–1964. Ueber die Feinstruktur des Phloems von *Metasequoia glyptostroboides* und seine jahreszeitlichen Veränderungen I–V. *Planta* 57: 583–607 (1961), 58: 366–386 (1962), 59: 195–221 (1962), 60: 360–389 (1963), 63: 155–190 (1964).—KURSANOV, A. L. 1963. Metabolism and the transport of organic substances in the phloem. *Advances in Bot. Res.* 1: 209–278.—KURSANOV, A. L., *et al.* 1958. Translocation of sugars in grafted plants. *Soviet Plant Physiol.* 5: 3–15 (translation).

LEONARD, O. A. and D. L. KING. 1968. Vein loading and transport in detached leaves. *Plant Physiol.* 43: 460–463.

MASON, T. G. and E. J. MASKELL. 1928a. Studies on the transport of carbohydrates in the cotton plant. I. A study of diurnal variation in the carbohydrates of leaf, bark and wood, and the effect of ringing. *Ann. Bot.* 42: 189–253.—MASON, T. G. and E. J. MASKELL. 1928b. Studies on the transport of carbohydrates in the cotton plant. II. The factors determining the rate and the direction of movement of sugars. *Ann. Bot.* 42: 571–636. —MITTLER, T. E. 1957. Studies on the feeding and nutrition of *Tuberolachnus salignus* (Gmelin) (Homoptera, Aphididae). I. The uptake of phloem sap. *Jour. Explt. Biol.* 34: 334–341.—MITTLER, T. E. 1958. Studies on the feeding and nutrition of *Tuberolachnus salignus* (Gmelin) (Homoptera, Aphididae). II. The nitrogen and sugar composition of ingested phloem sap and excreted honeydew. *Jour. Explt. Biol.* 35: 74–84.—MORTIMER, D. C. 1965. Translocation of the products of photosynthesis in sugar beet petioles. *Can. Jour. Bot.* 43: 269–280.—MOTHES, K. 1961. Aktiver Transport als regulatives Prinzip für gerichtete Stoffverteilung in höheren Pflanzen. In *Biochemie des aktiven Transportes.*

12. Colloquium der Ges. für physiol. Chemie. Berlin: Springer-Verlag.—MÜNCH, E. 1930. *Die Stoffbewegungen in der Pflanze.* Jena: Verlag Gustav Fischer, 234 p., 30 ill.—MÜNCH, E. 1937. Versuche über Wege und Richtungen der Stoffbewegungen im Baum. *Forstwiss. Zentralbl.* 59: 305–324, 337–351.

NELSON, C. D. *et al.* 1961. Selective translocation of products of photosynthesis in soybean. *Plant Physiol.* 36: 581–588.

PARKER, B. C. 1966. Translocation in *Macrocystis*. III. Composition of sieve tube exudate and identification of the major C^{14}-labeled products. *Jour. Physiol.* 2: 38–41.—PARTHASARATHY, M. V. and K. MÜHLETHALER. 1969. Ultrastructure of protein tubules in differentiating sieve elements. *Cytobiologie.* 1: 17–36.—PARTHASARATHY, M. V. and P. B. TOMLINSON. 1967. Anatomical features of metaphloem in stems of *Sabal, Cocos* and two other palms. *Amer. Jour. Bot.* 54: 1143–1151.—PEEL, A. J. 1964. Tangential movement of ^{14}C-labelled assimilates in stems of willow. *Jour. Exptl. Bot.* 15: 104–113. —PEEL, A. J. 1965. The effect of changes in the diffusion potential of xylem water on sieve-tube exudation from isolated stem segments. *Jour. Exptl. Bot.* 16: 249–260.—PEEL, A. J. 1966. The sugars concerned in the tangential movement of ^{14}C-labelled assimilates in willow. *Jour. Exptl. Bot.* 17: 156–164.—PEEL, A. J. 1970. Further evidence for the relative immobility of water in sieve tubes of willow. Physiology Plantarum 23: 667–672.—PEEL, A. J., R. J. FIELD, C. L. COULSON and D. C. J. GARDNER. 1969. Movement of water and solutes in sieve tubes of willow in response to puncture by aphid stylets. Evidence against a mass flow of solution. Physiology Plantarum 22: 768–775.—PEEL, A. J. and P. E. WEATHERLEY. 1959. Composition of sieve-tube sap. *Nat.* 184: 1955–1956.—PENOT. M. 1965. Etude du rôle des appels moléculaires dans la circulation libérienne. *Physiol. Vég.* 3: 41–89.—PFEIFFER, M. 1937. Die Verteilung der osmotischen Werte im Baum im Hinblick auf die Münch'sche Druckstromtheorie. *Flora* 132: 1–47.

RÖCKL, B. 1949. Nachweis eines Konzentrationshubs zwischen Palisadenzellen und Siebröhren. *Planta* 36: 530–550.

SAX, K. 1954. The control of tree growth by phloem blocks. *Jour. Arnold Arb.* 35: 251–258.—SCHNEIDER-ORELLI, O. 1909. Die Miniergänge von *Lyonetia clercella* L. und die Stoffwanderung in Apfelblättern. *Zbl. f. Bact.* 24 II: 158–181.—SCHUMACHER, W. 1930. Untersuchungen über die Lokalisation der Stoffwanderung in den Leitbündeln höherer Pflanzen. *Jahrb. wiss. Bot.* 73: 770–823.—SCHUMACHER, W. 1937. Weitere Untersuchungen über die Wanderung von Farbstoffen in den Siebröhren. *Jahrb. wiss. Bot.* 85: 422–449.—SHIROYA, M. 1968. Comparison of upward and downward translocation of ^{14}C from a single leaf of sunflower. *Plant Physiol.* 43: 1605–1610.—SPANNER, D. C. 1958. The translocation of sugar in sieve tubes. *Jour. Exptl. Bot.* 9: 332–342.—SPANNER, D. C. and J. N. PREBBLE. 1962. The movement of tracer along the petiole of *Nymphoides peltatum*. I. A preliminary study with ^{137}Cs. *Jour. Exptl. Bot.* 13: 294–306.—SWANSON, C. A. and E. D. H. EL-SHISHINY. 1958. Translocation of sugars in the Concord grape. *Plant Physiol.* 33: 33–37.—SWANSON, C. A. and D. R. GEIGER. 1967. Time course of low temperature inhibition of sucrose translocation in sugar beets. *Plant Physiol.* 42: 751–756.

TAMMES, P. M. L. 1933. Observations on the bleeding of palm trees. *Rec. Trav. bot. neerl.* 30: 514–536.—THAINE, R. 1962. A translocation hypothesis based on the structure of plant cytoplasm. *Jour. Exptl. Bot.* 13: 152–160.—TOMLINSON, P. B. and M. H. ZIMMERMANN. 1969. Vascular anatomy of monocotyledons with secondary growth—an introduction. *Jour. Arnold Arb.* 50: 159–179.—TORREY, J. G. 1967. *Development in flowering plants*. New York: Macmillan Co.—Trip, P. and P. R. Gorham. 1967. Autoradiographic study of the pathway of translocation. *Can. Jour. Bot.* 45: 1567–1573.—Trip, P. and P. R. Gorham. 1968a. Bidirectional translocation of sugars in sieve tubes of squash plants. *Plant Physiol.* 43: 877–882.—Trip, P. and P. R. Gorham. 1968b. Translocation of sugar and tritiated water in squash plants. *Plant Physiol.* 43: 1845–1849.—Trip, P., C. D. Nelson and G. Krotkov. 1965. Selective and preferential translocation of C^{14}-labeled sugars in white ash and lilac. *Plant Physiol.* 40: 740–747.

Van den Honert, T. H. 1932. On the mechanism of transport of organic materials in plants. *K. Akad. Wetensch. Amsterdam Proc.* 35: 1104–1112.—Van Die, J. and P. M. L. Tammes. 1964. Studies in phloem exudation from *Yucca flaccida* Haw. II. The translocation of assimilates. *Acta Bot. Neerl.* 13: 84–90.—De Vries, H. 1885. Ueber die Bedeutung der Circulation und der Rotation des Protoplasmas für den Stofftransport in der Pflanze. *Bot. Z.* 43: 1–6, 18–26.

Weatherley, P. E. and R. P. C. Johnson. 1968. The form and function of the sieve tube: a problem in reconciliation. *Internat. Rev. Cyt.* 24: 149–192.—Weatherley, P. E., A. J. Peel and G. P. Hill. 1959. The physiology of the sieve tube. *Jour. Exptl. Bot.* 10: 1–16.—Webb, J. A. and P. R. Gorham. 1965. The effect of node temperature on assimilation and translocation of ^{14}C in the squash. *Can. Jour. Bot.* 43: 1009–1020.—Webb, K. L. and J. W. A. Burley. 1962. Sorbitol translocation in apple. *Sci.* 137: 766.—Willenbrink, J. 1957. Ueber die Hemmung des Stofftransports in den Siebröhren durch lokale Inaktivierung verschiedener Atmungsenzyme. *Planta* 48: 269–342.—Willenbrink, J. 1966. Zur lokalen Hemmung des Assimilattransports durch Blausäure. *Z. Pflanzenphysiol.* 55: 119–130.

Ziegler, H. 1956. Untersuchungen über die Leitung und Sekretion der Assimilate. *Planta* 47: 447–500.—Ziegler, H. 1958. Ueber die Atmung und den Stofftransport in den isolierten Leitbündeln der Blattstiele von *Heracleum mantegazzianum* Somm. et Lev. *Planta* 51: 186–200.—Ziegler, H. 1968. La sève des tubes criblés. p. 205–217, In *Traité de biologie de l'abeille*. Vol. 3. R. Chauvin, ed., Paris: Masson.—Ziegler, H. and T. E. Mittler. 1959. Ueber den Zuckergehalt der Siebröhren bzw. Siebzellensäfte von *Heracleum Mantegazzianum* L. und *Picea abies* (L.) Karst. *Z. Naturforsch.* 14b: 278–281.—Ziegler, H. and I. Ziegler. 1962. Die wasserlöslichen Vitamine in den Siebröhrensäften einiger Bäume. *Flora* 152: 257–278.—Zimmermann, M. H. 1957a. Translocation of organic substances in trees. I. The nature of the sugars in the sieve-tube exudate of trees. *Plant Physiol.* 32: 288–291.—Zimmermann, M. H. 1957b. Translocation of organic substances in trees. II. On the translocation mechanism in the phloem of white ash (*Fraxinus americana* L.). *Plant Physiol.* 32: 399–404.—Zimmermann, M. H. 1958. Translocation of organic substances in trees. III. The removal of sugars from the sieve tubes in white ash (*Fraxinus americana* L.). *Plant Physiol.* 33: 213–217.—Zimmermann, M. H. 1960. Longitudinal and tangential movement within the sieve-tube system of white ash (*Fraxinus americana* L.). *Beih. Z. schweiz. Forstv.* 30: 289–300.—Zimmermann, M. H. 1961. Movement of organic substances in trees. *Sci.* 133: 73–79.—Zimmermann, M. H. 1962. Translocation of organic substances in trees V. Experimental double interruption of the phloem in the white ash (*Fraxinus americana* L.). *Plant Physiol.* 37: 527–530.—Zimmermann, M. H. 1964. The relation of transport to growth in dicotyledonous trees. p. 289–301. In *The formation of wood in forest trees*. M. H. Zimmermann, ed. New York: Academic Press.—Zimmermann, M. H. 1969. Translocation velocity and specific mass transfer in the sieve tubes of *Fraxinus americana* L. *Planta* 84: 272–278.

CHAPTER VI

THE STEADY STATE THERMODYNAMICS OF TRANSLOCATION IN PLANTS

Melvin T. Tyree

INTRODUCTION

In this text, as in most botanical ones, only the dominating "forces" have been represented in the transport equations in the quantitative treatment of translocation presented so far. For example, in Chapter IV, Poiseuille's Law was introduced because it is felt, with a high degree of confidence, that the dominating driving "force" in the flow of xylem sap is a pressure gradient. On the other hand, if one were treating the diffusional flow of a specific molecular species m, over a short distance in nonvascular tissue, one might deem it best to write down an equation which expresses the flow as a function of a different dominating "force," namely the concentration gradient of m.

As a matter of fact, a quick survey of the biological literature will yield a small family of transport equations that have been used to describe the flow of materials in plants over long distances and short distances and across membranes. All these equations, despite their varied uses, have one generic characteristic in common; i.e. they represent a flow of a substance a as being equal to a transport coefficient (or collection of constants and a transport coefficient) times a *single* driving "force." It should be carefully noted that the word flow is used here in the generic sense to mean either velocity of movement, or volume rate of flow, or mass rate of flow (specific mass transfer), or flux (flow per unit area). Similarly, the word "force" is used in the generic sense to mean, for example, a concentration gradient, a hydraulic pressure gradient, or an osmotic pressure gradient, etc. Some of the most commonly used transport equations in biology are shown in Table VI-1.

In recent years it has been demonstrated that the classical transport equations shown in Table VI-1 are not completely adequate. Indeed, a few striking deviations from the classical transport equations have been observed from time to

TABLE VI–1
Most commonly used transport equations

Name of equation	Flow	=	Con-stant(s)	×	"Forces"	Use and description of equation
Poiseuille's Law	$\dfrac{dV_s}{dt}$	=	$\dfrac{\pi r^4}{8\eta}$	×	$\dfrac{dP}{dl}$	Gives the rate of volume flow, dV_s/dt, of solution, s, of viscosity, η, through a right cylindrical tube of radius, r, under a pressure gradient, dP/dl
Jacob's Equation	$\dfrac{dV_w}{dt}$	=	$k_w A$	×	$RT\Delta C$	Gives the rate of volume flow, dV_w/dt, of water across a semipermeable membrane of water permeability, k_w, of area, A, under an osmotic pressure difference $\Delta \pi = RT\ \Delta C$, where R is the gas constant; T is the absolute temperature; and ΔC is the difference in solute concentration across the membrane
Fick's First Law	$\dfrac{dM_a}{dt}$	=	D_a	×	$\dfrac{dC_a}{dl}$	Gives the rate of passage per unit area dM_a/dt, of molecular species a, with a diffusion coefficient D_a, under a concentration gradient dC_a/dl
Solute Flow Equation	$\dfrac{dN_a}{dt}$	=	$k_a A$	×	ΔC_a	Gives the rate of movement of solute, a, across a membrane of area A under a solute concentration difference ΔC_a. The coefficient k_a is referred to as the permeability (of the membrane to a)

time. Part of the inadequacy can be understood intuitively simply by suggesting that whenever there is a multitude of different flows going on inside a confined area (like a plant), there will inevitably be a certain degree of mutual interference between these flows. Despite all the good intentions one might have in using the classical transport equations, one tacitly ignores these interferences and transport phenomena of secondary importance.

The purpose of this chapter herein is to introduce a more general set of transport equations. With these general equations a clearer insight will be obtained of the overall translocation process, and some new laboratory techniques for studying translocation will present themselves.

In order to accomplish these ends, one must refer to an entirely new discipline in the physical sciences called the thermodynamics of irreversible processes or, alternately, the thermodynamics of the steady state. This new science has the advantage over all other sciences in that it is the only discipline which correctly treats the energy considerations of a system undergoing uniform change. Some biologists have tried to approach this same problem by the use of classical thermodynamics, but classical thermodynamics can be applied strictly only to systems in a state of static equilibrium. However, it is a well-known fact that plants are dynamic and rarely in a state of static equilibrium.

The thermodynamics of the steady state originated from the pioneer work of Onsager (1931ab, 1932), a physical scientist, and was first applied to biology by Staverman (1951, 1952) who treated translocation across biological membranes. Since the early 1950's a sizable literature on the biological aspects of the subject has arisen treating primarily theoretical considerations, although a number of experimental works are in the literature too.

It should be emphasized, however, that to say that the classical transport equations are inadequate is *not* to say that the classical equations are not of great heuristic value. Indeed, the classical transport equations are very useful in the sense that they are simpler to handle than the more general equations to be presented and also in the sense that they describe many of the most important aspects of translocation with reasonable accuracy.

1. THE ONSAGER EQUATIONS

Philosophically speaking, thermodynamics rests on the securest foundation of any of the theoretical sciences. This is due to the fact that thermodynamics need not be other than a purely phenomenological science. That is, all the concepts and relations can be derived exclusively from *macroscopically* observable quantities, e.g. temperature, pressure, volume and mass. While in the past certain thermodynamic relationships have been derived in terms of *microscopic* or statistical models (e.g. atomic models), in the final analysis the same thermodynamic relations are in no way dependent upon postulated microscopic relations. Thus, the validity of thermodynamics does not depend upon the correctness of the *microscopic* models which may be invoked from time to time.* If a certain atomic model should prove wrong, the macroscopic relationship that was explained by the use of the atomic model is, nevertheless, correct.

The transport equations to be presented shortly are similarly derivable from purely macroscopic concepts. Indeed, these equations—called the Onsager equations—are thought to be truly independent of the specific molecular details of any one system (provided the system does not change state too rapidly). Thus, to be perfectly rigorous, the Onsager equations should be derived without reference to atomic models. While this can and has been done, the derivation requires a very firm background in classical thermodynamics and is beyond the scope of this chapter. Several rigorous monographs and articles are available on this subject. The physical chemical aspects can be found described in DeGroot (1966), Denbigh (1965) and Van Rysselberghe (1963). Some biologically important relations are derived rigorously by Stavermann (1951, 1952), Kedem and Katchalsky (1958) and Spanner (1964). Slightly less rigorous derivations based on mechanical models

---

* The "third law" of thermodynamics is dependent to some extent upon a microscopic model; however, since the third law is not as general and useful as the first and second laws, some authors do not give this law the same status as the other two.

have been carried out by Spiegler (1958) and Dainty and Ginzburg (1963). Nevertheless, an intuitively useful grasp can be had of the equations by reference to a few simple microscopic models. In the following this will be treated briefly.

a. Intuitive justification of the Onsager equations

The Onsager equations are phenomenological equations. Examples of phenomenological equations are easy to find; Ohm's Law from electrical theory is an example, and in fact all the equations in Table VI-1 are phenomenological. The phenomenological equations of steady state thermodynamics are very like these but more general.

The necessity for being more general is not difficult to appreciate. For example, Fick's Law of diffusion

$$\frac{dm_a}{dt} = D_a \frac{dc_a}{dl} \qquad \text{(Eq. VI-1)}$$

may be adequate in a simple system; but suppose that while one solute, a, is diffusing under its concentration gradient dc_a/dl, another solute, b, is simultaneously moving under *its* gradient, dc_b/dl. Can it be assumed that the movement of b is independent of the movement of a? Or, suppose substance a is diffusing through a finely porous plate, while at the same time the solution is being slowly pushed through the plate by a small pressure drop; would the flow of a be independent of the pressure? The answer to both questions is no. This is a consequence of the fact that in both examples two different flows are going on in the same region of space. The separately flowing molecules can not avoid interfering with each other through molecular collisions.

Thus, when two or more substances are diffusing, Eq. VI-1 often ceases to be adequate, and something more general is needed. Of the various possible approaches, it is found convenient and adequate to generalize Eq. VI-1 (confining ourselves to the simple one-dimensional case) to

$$\frac{dm_a}{dt} = D_a \frac{dc_a}{dl} + D_{ab} \frac{dc_b}{dl} \qquad \text{(Eq. VI-2)}$$

Note that Eq. VI-2 has incorporated a new coefficient D_{ab} which gives the possible effect of the gradient of a second solute on the rate of movement of the first. Since by Newton's Third Law the force of interaction of a and b has an "equal and opposite" character one must allow a similar equation for the flow of b:

$$\frac{dm_b}{dt} = D_{ba} \frac{dc_a}{dl} + D_b \frac{dc_b}{dl} \qquad \text{(Eq. VI-3)}$$

Should there be still further solutes, or other "forces" like electrical and pressure differences, extra terms are needed to account for them in a similar way. If one follows this simple formula of allowing an extra term for every additional flow occurring in the same place, one will be in a position to write down the Onsager equations.

Write the Onsager equations for the flows in a very complex system of n components where n can be any desired number. The choice of mathematical symbols is arbitrary, of course, but the conventional symbols will be used here. By convention, the flows are represented by J's; subscripts are used to represent the flows of the different components, e.g. J_1, J_2, J_3, $\ldots$, J_n. If any one unspecified flow is referred to, one speaks of the ith flow, J_i. J's are usually fluxes which can, by choice, have units of moles per second per square centimeter [moles sec^{-1} cm^{-2}] or cubic centimeters of volume per second per square centimeter [cm^3 sec^{-1} cm^{-2}], etc. The "forces" are represented by X's, and, as before, subscripts are used to represent which component these "forces" are acting on, X_1, X_2, X_3, $\ldots$, X_n. The ith "force," X_i, is the sum of all the possible "forces" (excluding frictional forces) acting on the ith component.

For example, if the ith component is a charged molecular species such as a potassium ion, then the "force" X_i acting on this ion would be the sum of the pressure gradient, concentration gradient, and the electrical gradient. One could also include temperature gradients along with this list of forces. The temperature gradient would produce a flow of heat, and one might guess that the flows of heat and matter will interact too. Indeed this phenomenon has been observed in many instances and is called thermo-osmosis. The introduction of temperature gradients, however, greatly complicates the transport equations; *for simplicity,* therefore, *discussion will be confined to isothermal systems.*

Using L's as the transport coefficients and allowing that every flow J_i may interfere with all the other flows, the Onsager transport equations can be written in a manner analogous to Eqs. VI-2 and 3:

$$J_1 = L_{11}X_1 + L_{12}X_2 + L_{13}X_3 + \ldots + L_{1n}X_n \qquad \text{(Eq. VI-4a)}$$
$$J_2 = L_{21}X_1 + L_{22}X_2 + L_{23}X_3 + \ldots + L_{2n}X_n \qquad \text{(Eq. VI-4b)}$$
$$J_3 = L_{31}X_1 + L_{32}X_2 + L_{33}X_3 + \ldots + L_{3n}X_n \qquad \text{(Eq. VI-4c)}$$
$$\vdots \qquad\qquad \vdots$$
$$J_n = L_{n1}X_1 + L_{n2}X_2 + L_{n3}X_3 + \ldots + L_{nn}X_n \qquad \text{(Eq. VI-4n)}$$

As can be seen, the coefficients L are distinguished from each other by two subscripts, L_{ij}. The first number tells the flow to which it is connected; the second number indicates the "force" to which it is connected. The coefficients that have repeated subscripts, L_{ii} (e.g. L_{11}, L_{22}, $\ldots$,L_{nn}) are called *conjugate* coefficients. They give the proportionality between the "force" of the ith component on the flow of the ith component. The coefficients that have unequal subscripts, L_{ij} (e.g. L_{12}, L_{32}, L_{47}, etc.) are called *cross* coefficients; they give the interference between the flows and tell how much the force on the jth component interferes with the flow of the ith component.

With some thought it can be seen that the two equations (VI-2 and 3) which give the diffusion of substances a and b are the special case of Eqs. VI-4 where

$n = 2$; $X_1 = dc_a/dl$; $X_2 = dc_b/dl$; $J_1 = dm_a/dt$; $J_2 = dm_b/dt$; $L_{11} = D_a$; $L_{22} = D_b$; $L_{12} = D_{ab}$; and $L_{21} = D_{ba}$.

There is one very important relation, called the Onsager reciprocity relation, which can be proven to hold between the L's. But the proof (DeGroot, 1966) is both lengthy and beyond the scope of this chapter. The reciprocity relation states that

$$L_{ij} = L_{ji}, i \neq j$$

This means, for example, that $L_{12} = L_{21}$ and $L_{32} = L_{23}$, etc. The reciprocity relation is useful, because it reduces the number of coefficients that are needed to describe a system of n components from n^2 to $n(n + 1)/2$. Intuitively, the Onsager reciprocity relation can be thought of as fulfilling Newton's Third Law, i.e. as saying that the influence (e.g. frictional drag) of J_i on J_k is equal and opposite to the influence (frictional drag) of J_k on J_i. (Indeed, equations of the form of Eq. VI-4 displaying the reciprocity relation have been worked out using an atomic model invoking only the concepts of friction and Newton's Third Law [Spiegler, 1958]).

It should be emphasized that the above should be taken as a discussion of rather than a derivation of the Onsager equations. For if the derivation were properly carried out it would become apparent that one cannot arbitrarily pick his "forces" and flows. In an isothermal system the "forces" and flows must be chosen in such a way that the sum of the products of the "forces" and flows, $\Phi = J_1 X_1 + J_2 X_2 + \ldots J_n X_n$, must give the total rate of irreversible energy dissipation in the system. It happens that Eqs. VI-4 fulfill this criteria.

b. The n-component plant

It was pointed out earlier that the Onsager equations (VI-4a, 4b, . . .) are derived without specific reference to any one system. For this reason it is possible to apply Eqs. VI-4 to plant tissues (xylem, phloem, parenchyma) without specific knowledge of the system, i.e. without a knowledge of how many molecular species (e.g. water, sucrose, KCl, etc.) are present.

However, before the Onsager equations in the form of Eqs. VI-4 can be put to any research use, it is necessary to specify *all* the n components by name, to measure all of the L coefficients, and to verify linearity between all the flows and "forces." This is indeed a difficult order! For to measure all the L coefficients, it is necessary not only to specify n, but also to measure the flow (flux) of each of the n components independently. Such a task might well prove experimentally too difficult.

In order to make Eqs. VI-4 useful for biological purposes, the equations are manipulated so as to give fluxes and "forces" that are easily measurable. To see how this is done, first examine the "forces" and fluxes found in Eqs. VI-4. The flow J_i is the flux of the ith molecular species given in moles sec^{-1} cm^{-2}; whereas the "forces" are the sum of the pressure, electrical and concentration differences. In symbols:

$$X_i = RT\Delta ln\gamma_i + \bar{v}_i\Delta p + z_i\mathcal{F}\Delta E \qquad \text{(Eq. VI-5)}$$

where $R = $ the universal gas constant; $T = $ the absolute temperature, $\gamma_i = $ the mole fraction of the ith component (the number of moles of the ith species divided by the total number of moles of all the species added together); $\bar{v}_1 = $ the molar volume of the ith species; p = the pressure; z_i = the electrical charge present on the ith species (zero for nonionic species); $\mathfrak{F}$ = the Faraday (which is Avogadro's number of elementary charges = 9.65×10^4 coulombs); E = the electrical potential, and ln = the natural logarithm.

The first term in Eq. VI-5, $RT\Delta ln\gamma_i$, accounts for concentration differences; if the ith species is dilute, then

$$RT\Delta ln\gamma_i = \frac{RT\Delta c_i}{\bar{C}_i} \qquad \text{(Eq. VI-6)}$$

where $\bar{C}_i$ = the mean concentration between the two sides. The concentration dependence is more easily seen here. It is often more convenient to express Eq. VI-5 in terms of gradients of "forces" rather than differences. In this case Eq. VI-5 becomes

$$X_i = RT\frac{d\,ln\gamma_i}{dl} + \bar{v}_i\frac{dP}{dl} + z_i\mathfrak{F}\frac{dE}{dl} \qquad \text{(Eq. VI-7)}$$

or, for dilute species

$$X_i = RT\frac{dc_i}{dl} + \bar{v}_i\frac{dP}{dl} + z_i\mathfrak{F}\frac{dE}{dl} \qquad \text{(Eq. VI-8)}$$

Now then, one should search for some easily measurable fluxes. Two fluxes which come into mind are volume flux (the flux of the bulk volume of the solution) and electrical current flux. This is the key to manipulating Eqs. VI-4. One can obtain total volume flux J by multiplying each mole flux in *each* equation of Eqs. VI-4 *by its own* molar volume, $\bar{v}_i$, and then by adding all of the resulting equations together. Similarly one can obtain total current flux I, by again multiplying each mole flux by $z_i\mathfrak{F}$ and then by adding all of these resulting equations together.

If this is done, one obtains two enormous equations, one for J and one for I. In order to make the equations a little more intelligible and useful, Eq. VI-8, which gives the "forces" in explicit terms, is substituted for each X_i. Then all the terms containing dP/dl are added together and all the terms containing dE/dl are added together and so on. This is a lengthy procedure, though only a matter of algebra. The result written in longhand would fill more than a page of type; however, for those familiar with the shorthand notation of summation signs the result is presented below:

$$J = \left(\sum_{k=1}^{n}\ \sum_{i=1}^{n} L_{ki}\bar{v}_k\bar{v}_i\right)\frac{dP}{dl} + \left(\sum_{k=1}^{n}\ \sum_{i=1}^{n} L_{ki}\bar{v}_k z_i\mathfrak{F}\right)\frac{dE}{dl} +$$
$$\left[\sum_{i=1}^{n}\left(\sum_{k=1}^{n} L_{ki}\bar{v}_k RT\right)\frac{d\,ln\gamma_i}{dl}\right] \qquad \text{(Eq. VI-9)}$$

$$I = \left(\sum_{k=1}^{n}\ \sum_{i=1}^{n} L_{ki}\bar{v}_i z_k\mathfrak{F}\right)\frac{dP}{dl} + \left(\sum_{k=1}^{n}\ \sum_{i=1}^{n} L_{ki}z_k z_i\mathfrak{F}^2\right)\frac{dE}{dl} +$$
$$\left[\sum_{i=1}^{n}\left(\sum_{k=1}^{n} L_{ki}z_k\mathfrak{F}RT\right)\frac{d\,ln\gamma_i}{dl}\right] \qquad \text{(Eq. VI-10)}$$

For those unfamiliar with summation notation, all that one has to realize is that the volume flux, J, is expressed as the linear sum of a series of coefficients and constants times the pressure gradient dP/dl, plus another series of coefficients and constants times the electrical gradient dE/dl, etc. The same holds for the electrical current flux.

In many cases it could be expected that the contribution of concentration gradients to J and I are negligible, e.g. in xylem where the sap is so dilute that no sizable gradient would form. When it is possible to ignore concentration gradients (i.e. when diffusion makes no contribution to energy dissipation), it is convenient to write Eq. VI-9 and 10 in an abbreviated form replacing L's with the double summations of Eqs. VI-9 and 10:

$$J = L_{PP}\frac{dP}{dl} + L_{PE}\frac{dE}{dl} \qquad \text{(Eq. VI-11)}$$

$$I = L_{EP}\frac{dP}{dl} + L_{EE}\frac{dE}{dl} \qquad \text{(Eq. VI-12)}$$

The last and greatest advantage of manipulating the Onsager Eq. VI-4 as described above is that the Onsager reciprocity relation is preserved. It can be shown by invoking reciprocity in the double summation before dE/dl in Eq. VI-9 and the double summation before dP/dl in Eq. VI-10 that

$$L_{PE} = L_{EP} \qquad \text{(Eq. VI-13)}$$

c. Units and interpretation of the Onsager equations

Before proceeding further, it will prove beneficial to review the interpretation of and the units used in the Onsager equations. The units used in the Onsager equations can, at first, be quite confusing. The confusion arises from the fact that electrical terms are included in the Onsager equations, and from the fact that the same units must be used throughout in order to preserve numerical equality in the reciprocity relation. The electrical gradient dE/dl, is measured in volts per centimeter. A volt is a measure of the energy imparted on a unit of charge (the coulomb) when said charges pass from one potential to another. The volt, therefore, has units of Joule coulomb^{-1}. Since there are no other commonly used units for potentials other than volts and since it is convenient to use the same units throughout, the pressures must be measured in terms of Joules and centimeters. The unit for pressure used is (Joule cm^{-3}). It happens that one (Joule cm^{-3}) equals (about) 10 atm. [Actually one (Joule cm^{-3}) equals 9.8692 atmospheres]. Thus the pressure gradient dP/dl, has units (Joule cm^{-3})cm^{-1}. The units for volume flux have been given before as cm^3 sec^{-1} cm^{-2}, and the units for current flux are ampere cm^{-2} where an ampere is the current resulting from the flow of one coulomb per second.

The units for the L coefficients are fixed by those selected for the fluxes and forces. The easiest way to remember (or figure out) what the proper units for the L's are, is to ask oneself what units when multiplied by units of "forces" will yield units of flow? The answer, of course, is that the units for the L's are equal

TABLE VI–2
Onsager Units

Terms	Units
Volume flux, J	$cm^3\ sec^{-1}\ cm^{-2}$
Current flux, I	Amp cm^{-2} (or coul $sec^{-1}\ cm^{-2}$)
Pressure gradient, $\dfrac{dP}{dl}$	(Joule cm^{-3}) cm^{-1}
Electrical gradient, $\dfrac{dE}{dl}$	volt cm^{-1} (or Joule coul $^{-1}\ cm^{-1}$)
Hydraulic conductivity, L_{PP}	$cm^3\ sec^{-1}\ cm^{-2}$ (Joule cm^{-3})$^{-1}$ cm
Electrical conductivity, L_{EE}	ohm$^{-1}\ cm^{-1}$ (or mho cm^{-1})
Electrokinetic coefficient, L_{EP}	Amp cm^{-2} (Joule cm^{-3})$^{-1}$ cm
Electrokinetic coefficient, L_{PE}	$cm^3\ sec^{-1}\ cm^{-2}$ volt^{-1} cm

to the units for the relevant flow divided by the units for "force." All the units, including the L's, are summarized in Table VI-2.

A closer examination of the Onsager equations is useful because in some respects Eqs. VI-11 and 12 are similar to the classical transport equations. For example, if the term containing dE/dl in Eq. VI-11 is ignored, a definite similarity between it and Poiseuille's Law can be seen:

$$\frac{dV_s}{dt} = \frac{\pi r^4}{8\eta}\ \frac{dP}{dl}\ \text{(Poiseuille's Law)}$$

$$J = L_{PP}\frac{dP}{dl}$$

In both cases the constants refer to the hydraulic conductivity. For this reason L_{PP} is called the hydraulic conductivity. Similarly, if the term containing dP/dl in Eq. VI-12 is ignored, the remainder assumes the form of Ohm's law; i.e.

$$I = \lambda E\ \ \ \ \text{(Ohm's Law)}$$

$$I = L_{EE}\frac{dE}{dl}$$

where $\lambda =$ the electrical conductivity (the inverse of the resistance) in ohm^{-1} (mho). In view of the similarities, L_{EE} is called the electrical conductivity.

If one now examines the terms ignored in both equations, one sees that they give the cross effects which are ignored in the classical equations, Poiseuille's and Ohm's Laws. That is, $L_{PE}(dE/dl)$ gives the influence of electrical gradients on volume flow and $L_{EP}(dP/dl)$ gives the influence of pressure gradients on current flow. L_{PE} and L_{EP} are both called electro-kinetic cross coefficients.

d. The nonclassical phenomena

Having discussed the Onsager equations it is now possible to discuss the non-classical phenomena which are not envisaged in the classical transport equations (cf. Table VI-1). Each phenomenon will be described both in terms of the Onsager equations and in terms of microscopic (molecular) models.

ELECTRO-OSMOSIS. It has been observed generally that the solid framework of plant tissues (e.g. membranes and cellulose) have a net negative bound surface charge. The tissue is, nevertheless, electrically neutral because of an excess of mobile cations (positive charges) in solution in the vicinity of the charged surfaces. Because there are more cations than anions in solution, there is a net flow of (charged) particles in the tissue when a voltage is applied and current passed. Cations and anions move in opposite directions under an eletrical gradient, and they both drag water along with them by frictional drag in their respective directions. But since more mobile cations are available than mobile anions, a net water flow results in the direction of the positive current flow. This phenomenon of water flow in the direction of the positive current (towards the negative battery terminal) is called electro-osmosis.

It is easy to see how this phenomenon is expressed in terms of the Onsager equations once the experimental conditions are understood. Electro-osmosis is usually detected in a so-called electro-osmometer (Fig. VI-1), a potometer especially fitted with electrodes so that a current can be passed through the tissue. Electro-osmosis through a piece of tissue is measured while the difference in pressure across the piece of tissue is held at zero ($dP/dl = 0$). When an electrical gradient dE/dl is applied, the observed water flow is given by Eq. VI-11 with dP/dl held at zero:

$$J = L_{PE} \frac{dE}{dl}, \quad \frac{dP}{dl} = 0 \qquad \text{(Eq. VI-14)}$$

and the current is given by Eq. VI-12

$$I = L_{EE} \frac{dE}{dl}, \quad \frac{dP}{dl} = 0 \qquad \text{(Eq. VI-15)}$$

In an electro-osmometer it is difficult to know exactly what the electrical gradient is through the tissue. For this reason a quantity independent of dE/dl has been defined; it is the electro-osmotic efficiency, the volume flow divided by the current flow. Dividing Eq. VI-14 by Eq. VI-15 one gets

$$\text{Electro-osmotic efficiency} = \frac{J}{I} = \frac{L_{PE}}{L_{EE}}, \quad \frac{dP}{dl} = 0 \qquad \text{(Eq. VI-16)}$$

STREAMING POTENTIALS. Suppose that no voltage is applied externally across the tissue but that a pressure is applied. What will happen to the ions? The pressure will, of course, cause a water flow through the tissue (however slight it may be); the flow of water will carry the dissolved ions along with it. But since the bound wall charges are not free to move, there will be a net charge separation whenever the cations are flushed downstream. As the water flows, this charge separation will continue until the electrostatic forces between the charges just balance the tendency of the water stream to flush the mobile ions along. At this point there will be no current flowing and the resulting electrostatic potential is

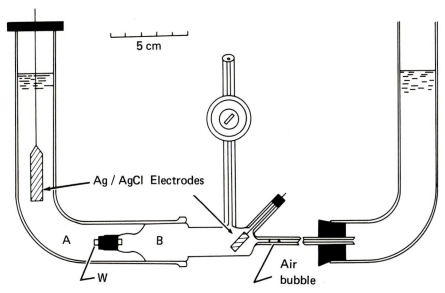

Fig. VI–1. Electro-osmometer design of D. S. Fensom. *A* and *B* are the two chambers separated by the sample *W* mounted in a rubber bung. Chamber B is connected to a capillary (typically 0.2 mm in diameter) with an air bubble for the determination of volume changes. From Tyree, 1968.

called a streaming potential. In terms of the Onsager equations the streaming potential is given by Eq. VI-12 when I is set to zero, i.e.

$$I = 0 = L_{EP}\frac{dP}{dl} + L_{EE}\frac{dE}{dl}$$

therefore

$$\frac{dE}{dl} = -\left(\frac{L_{EP}}{L_{EE}}\right)\frac{dP}{dl}, I = 0 \qquad \text{(Eq. VI-17a)}$$

or

$$\frac{\dfrac{dE}{dl}}{\dfrac{dP}{dl}} = -\left(\frac{L_{EP}}{L_{EE}}\right), I = 0 \qquad \text{(Eq. VI-17b)}$$

Streaming potentials have been observed in the cellulose cell walls of Nitella (Tyree, 1968) and in the excized phloem tissue of *Heracleum mantegazzianum* (Tyree and Fensom, 1970). The Onsager equations predict a linearity between the applied pressure and the observed potential as is apparent from Eq. VI-17a. A typical response for xylem is shown in Fig. VI-2.

STREAMING CURRENTS.   Suppose that the electrodes in the electro-osmometer (Fig. VI-1) are connected (short-circuited) during a streaming potential experiment; what will then happen to the ions? In this case the current has a return

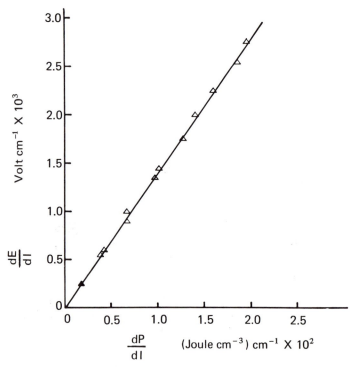

Fig. VI–2. Streaming potentials in *Acer rubrum*. Streaming potential gradients, dE/dl, are plotted versus the pressure gradient applied to sapwood samples 0.3 cm in diameter by 2 cm long in 4 mN KCl.

path of effectively zero resistance through the electrodes. Thus, a streaming potential ceases, and there is a continuous circulation of charges in place of the streaming potential. First, the charges are swept through the tissue by the water stream; then they are returned to the upstream side by the wires and electrodes. (Actually the streaming potential does not fall completely to zero. The electrodes and wire do have a slight resistance and a very small fraction of the streaming potential remains to drive the current through the wires). The returning current can be measured; its magnitude is given by Eq. VI-12 as

$$I = L_{EP} \frac{dP}{dl}, \quad \left(\frac{dE}{dl} = 0, \text{ no streaming potential} \right) \qquad \text{(Eq. VI-18)}$$

e. The measurement of the Onsager coefficients

Before the generalized transport equations can be applied to any tissue, it is necessary to establish the linearities between "forces" and flows, and the reciprocity relation predicted by the Onsager equations.

The L coefficients are measured in the following way: L_{EE} can be most easily measured using a standard d.c. or low frequency a.c. conductivity bridge. L_{PP} is measured in an electro-osmometer by short circuiting the two electrodes and

$$\textbf{TABLE VI-3a}$$

Materials	$\dfrac{J}{I}$ moles/faraday	L_{EE} mho cm⁻¹	L_{PE} cm³sec⁻¹cm⁻² volt⁻¹cm	L_{PP} cm³sec⁻¹cm⁻² (Joule cm⁻³)⁻¹ cm	Conditions	Ref.
Lens culinaris roots	53	—	—	—	in 10^{-4} N KCl	1
Heracleum mantegazzianum petiole phloem	94	5.2×10^{-4}	9.0×10^{-6}	0.16	in 0.3 M sucrose + 10^{-3} N KCl	2
petiole xylem	340	3.6×10^{-3}	2.3×10^{-4}	1.8×10^{2}	2 mN KCl	2
Nitella flexilis cell walls	104	1.3×10^{-3}	2.4×10^{-5}	—	in 10^{-4} KCl	3
cell walls	103	1.7×10^{-3}	3.2×10^{-5}	1.37×10^{-6}	in 10^{-3} KCl	3
cell walls	63	4.4×10^{-3}	5.1×10^{-5}	—	in 10^{-2} KCl	3
cell walls	15	1.9×10^{-2}	5.3×10^{-5}	1.37×10^{-6}	in 10^{-1} KCl	3
cell walls	2.5	1.1×10^{-1}	5.1×10^{-5}	—	in 1 N KCl	3
Acer rubrum Sapwood xylem from 30-yr.-old stem	700	3.0×10^{-4}	3.9×10^{-5}	65	in 2 mN KCl and 4 mN KCl	4

1. Fensom, Meylan and Pilet (1965)
2. Tyree and Fensom (1968)
3. Tyree (1968) and Tyree and Spanner (1969)
4. Tyree and Zimmermann (1971)

TABLE VI-3b

Material	$\dfrac{J}{I}$ moles/faraday	L_{EE} mho cm^{-2}	L_{PE} cm sec^{-1} volt^{-1}	L_{PP} cm sec^{-1} atm^{-1}	Conditions	Ref.
Nitella translucens						
membrane	—	—	1.9×10^{-6}	—	in 10^{-4} N KCl	1
membrane	160	2×10^{-5}	—	1.5×10^{-5}	in 10^{-4} N KCl	2
Nitella flexilis						
membrane	164	—	—	—	in 10^{-3} N KCl	3
membrane	185	—	—	—	in 10^{-3} N NaCl	3
Artificial membrane (crosslinked phenosulphonate)	51	—	—	—	in 0.01 N NaCl	4
"	37	—	—	—	in 0.1 N NaCl	4
"	11	—	—	—	in 1 N NaCl	4
Chara australis						
membrane	—	6.7×10^{-5}	—	—	in 10^{-3} N NaCl	5
Nitella flexilis						
membrane	—	1×10^{-5}	—	—	Upsala tap water	5

1. Tyree (1969)
2. Fensom and Dainty (1963)
3. Fensom and Wanless (1967)
4. Lakshminarayanaiah (1967)
5. Williams, Johnston, and Dainty (1964)

measuring the flow as a function of the applied pressure. L_{PE} and L_{EP} are determined by first measuring the electro-osmotic efficiency (Eq. VI-16) and the streaming potential (Eq. VI-17b) respectively, and then multiplying the result by L_{EE}. It can be seen from Eqs. VI-16 and 17a that if the reciprocity relationship is to hold, the value of the electro-osmotic efficiency in cm^3 $coul^{-1}$ should equal the value of the streaming potential in volt (Joule cm^{-3})$^{-1}$.

Various values of L_{PP}, L_{EE}, L_{PE}, and J/I (expressed in terms of the moles of water transported per Faraday of current) for tissues and cell walls are given in Table VI-3a.

Table VI-3b gives analogous values for membranes; however, in the case of membranes, the Onsager equations are written in terms of pressure and electrical differences (ΔP and ΔE) rather than gradients (dP/dl and dE/dl). This convention is adopted because it is not experimentally meaningful to speak of gradients inside very thin structures like membranes. Due to the convention for membranes, the L coefficients differ in units to accommodate the fact that the forces are expressed in different units. The L coefficients for membranes are distinguished from those in tissues by primes.

2. ENERGY DISSIPATION AND PHYSIOLOGICAL IMPORTANCE OF GRADIENTS

Now that the Onsager equations have been introduced, it is possible to move on to the application of these equations to topics of physiological importance. Two physiological questions which come to mind can be answered with the use of the Onsager equations: (a) What are the components and the magnitudes of energy exchanges with the biosphere during the process of translocation in trees? (b) What is the relative importance of pressure, electrical and concentration gradients in translocation in trees?

a. Energy exchanges in translocation

One of the most interesting subjects in tree physiology concerns the total transpiration process. Water must be lifted to great heights in the taller trees; in this process the energy exchanges with the biosphere can be broken up into a number of different contributions. What are the various components of this energy consumption? There are two major components.

(1). The energy exchanges that are invariant with regard to the rate of the transpiration process, i.e. the energy exchanges which are the same value whether the transpiration process goes on reversibly (at an infinitesimal rate) or irreversibly (at a finite rate). Examples of this are: (a). The binding energy of the water to the soil, i.e. the energy required to free the water that is bound to the soil. The lower the water content becomes in the soil, the higher the binding energy of the remaining water is. (b). The energy required to lift water against the gravitational forces of the earth. This is given simply by the mass of the water (m) times the acceleration due to gravity (g) times the height lifted (h), mgh. (c). The latent heat of vaporization, i.e. the heat energy absorbed by the water in the process of vaporization.

(2). The second is the dissipative energy exchange, i.e. the energy dissipation resulting from the frictional drag exerted on fluids transported at a finite rate. It should be appreciated that energy dissipation is associated with irreversible process and thus can be treated by irreversible thermodynamics. One could arbitrarily break this dissipative process up in plant-biosphere regions, i.e. energy dissipation resulting from movement of water (a) from the soil to the xylem stream in the roots, (b) from the base to the apex of the xylem stream, (c) from the apex of the xylem stream to the gaseous phase within the spongy mesophyll region, and (d) from the mesophyll air spaces to the outside air. There might also be energy expenditure resulting from metabolic water uptake. But this component cannot be treated by simple thermodynamic consideration and will be ignored here.

THE DISSIPATION FUNCTION. The energy dissipated when water is driven through a porous medium can be calculated from the Onsager equations. The first step is to calculate the power, the energy dissipated per second. The power or dissipation function Φ, was anticipated as early as 1873 by Lord Rayleigh and is currently defined for an *isothermal* system as the product of the absolute temperature and the rate of internal entropy production, d_iS/dt. In Onsager notation this is the sum of the products of the "forces" and the flows:

$$\Phi = T\frac{d_iS}{dt} = J_1X_1 + J_2X_2 + \ldots J_nX_n \qquad \text{(Eq. VI-19)}$$

Thus for fluxes and "forces" in terms of Eqs. VI-11 and 12 one has

$$\Phi = J\frac{dP}{dl} + I\frac{dE}{dl} \qquad \text{(Eq. VI-20)}$$

where Φ has units of Joules sec^{-1} per cm^3 of tissue.

If one wants the dissipation in a piece of tissue A cm^2 in cross section and 1 cm long one obtains

$$\phi = Al\,\Phi = Al\left(J\frac{dP}{dl} + I\frac{dE}{dl}\right) \qquad \text{(Eq. VI-21)}$$

As an illustration of the implications of Eq. VI-21, ϕ will be calculated for the simplest case where I is set to zero, i.e. where there is no return current path in the transpiration stream (see section on streaming potentials). Then, substituting in Eq. VI-11 the term dE/dl from Eq. VI-17a and considering that $L_{EP} = L_{PE}$, J is obtained in terms of L's and dP/dl:

$$J = \left(L_{PP} - \frac{L^2{}_{EP}}{L_{EE}}\right)\frac{dP}{dl} \qquad \text{(Eq. VI-22)}$$

Eq. VI-22 can then be used to solve for ϕ in terms of L's and dP/dl or L's and J by substituting for J in the first case or dP/dl in the second. The result in each case is (when $I = 0$):

$$\phi = Al\left(L_{PP} - \frac{L^2_{EP}}{L_{EE}}\right)\left(\frac{dP}{dl}\right)^2 \qquad \text{(Eq. VI-23a)}$$

or

$$\phi = Al\left(L_{PP} - \frac{L^2_{EP}}{L_{EE}}\right)^{-1} J^2 \qquad \text{(Eq. VI-23b)}$$

The last equation reveals that the energy dissipated in moving water through sapwood increases as the *square* of the volume flow. That is, if the tree doubles its transpiration it quadruples its energy dissipation!

For comparison's sake it is useful to use Eq. VI-23a to calculate the energy required to move one cubic centimeter of water through a length of l at a given pressure gradient. To do this one must multiply Eq. VI-23a by the time required to lift one cubic centimeter water, t_0. The time t_0 is simply given by $t_0 = l/AJ$. When the product is taken and simplified, one gets

$$\phi\, t_0 = \frac{l}{J}\left(L_{PP} - \frac{L^2_{EP}}{L_{EE}}\right)\left(\frac{dP}{dl}\right)^2 = l\,\frac{dP}{dl}, \qquad \text{(Eq. VI-24)}$$

i.e. the energy dissipated per cubic centimeter of water is equal to the length over which the water is transported times the operative pressure gradient.

ENERGY REQUIRED TO LIFT WATER.   It will now be instructive to compare the energy exchanges involved in lifting one cubic centimeter of water through a tree to the height of 10 m.

The invariant components of energy exchange with the biosphere (examples 1a, b, and c) are easily calculated from tables of physical constants. To calculate the dissipative energy exchanges, path lengths l and pressure gradients dP/dl (as can be seen from Eq. VI-24) must be known. This information requires a good deal of experimental knowledge of the anatomy and physiology of trees. In Chapter IV, dP/dl was calculated for the xylem stream from a knowledge of the vessel diameters, Poiseuille's law, and sap velocity fronts; the value is 0.1 atm. meter^{-1} ($= 10^{-4}$ [Joule cm^{-3}] cm^{-1}).

Although there is increasing evidence (Strugger, 1938/39; Levitt, 1956; Weatherley, 1965; and Tyree, 1969) that the pathway of the transpiration stream from the minor veins in the leaves to the mesophyll cell surfaces is exclusively via the cell wall, there has been some difficulty in estimating the pressure drop across the cell wall. From Eq. VI-22 it can be seen that in order to calculate dP/dl one needs to know L_{PP}, L^2_{EP}/L_{EE}, and J (the volume flux through the cell wall). It should be realized that transpiration rates are reported in cubic centimeters per second per square centimeter of *leaf surface*; therefore, to calculate J the cross-sectional area of the cell wall pathway per cm^2 of leaf surface must be known. In the past when calculation of dP/dl were attempted the significant term L^2_{EP}/L_{EE} was ignored; L_{PP} was estimated from Poiseuille's Law, and the cross section of the cell wall was guessed at. Today, values of L_{PP}, L_{EP}, and L_{EE} for cellulose cell walls are available (cf. Table VI-3a); furthermore, the area of the cell wall pathway can be calculated from the careful anatomical work carried out by Drs.

Geiger and Cataldo from the University of Dayton, Ohio. From the photomicrographs supplied by Dr. Geiger, I have estimated the area of the cell wall pathway in sugar beet leaves as about 2.6×10^{-2} cm²/cm² leaf surface; the mean path length, l is about 4.0×10^{-3} cm. From this it can be shown that at the maximum transpiration rate in sugar beet leaves (2.5×10^{-7} cm³ sec⁻¹ cm⁻²) the pressure drop from the minor vein to the mesophyll cell surface is about 0.5 atmospheres.

Table VI-4 gives an estimate of the components of energy exchange with the biosphere during the process of transpiration. It can be seen from this table that the largest energy exchange with the biosphere is associated with the heat of vaporization; the next largest is the dissipation in gaseous phase diffusion. The energy dissipation in the cell wall and the xylem and the energy required to lift the water 10 m are all of comparable magnitude, and all are much smaller than the heat of vaporization of water. The energy required to free water from the soil (at 15% moisture content) is about ten times the dissipative energy (and increases very rapidly as the soil moisture-content decreases). Table VI-4 suggests that, energetically speaking, the sapwood is a reasonably efficient conduit.

ENERGY REQUIRED TO MOVE SAP IN PHLOEM.   It is rather difficult to estimate Φ for phloem tissue for two reasons: (1) Eqs. VI-20 through VI-24 assume pressure flow, but it is not yet firmly established that the mass flow of phloem sap is a pressure-flow mechanism. (2) Values of L's are not adequately known for phloem tissue.

Table VI-3a gives the values of L_{PP}, L_{EE}, and L_{PE} for excised pieces of *Heracleum mantegazzianum* phloem in 0.3 M sucrose plus 1 mN KCl. The value of L_{PP} (0.16 cm³ sec⁻¹ cm⁻²(Joule cm⁻³)⁻¹ cm) is most likely an underestimate

TABLE VI–4
Sources of Energy Exchange with Biosphere in Transpiration

Source	Energy per cm³ H₂O Joules	Calories
Binding energy of water [a]	1.2*	0.29*
Energy required to lift water 10 meters (mgh) at $\frac{dP}{dl} = 0.1$ atm./meter	0.098	0.023
Dissipation in porous medium (ϕt_o) of xylem	0.1	0.024
Dissipation in porous medium of cell wall of leaf for path length of 40 μ [b]	0.05	0.012
Heat of vaporization	4.43×10^3	585
Dissipation in the gaseous phase from mesophyll (taken at 99% relative humidity) to the outside air (taken at 50% RH) [c]	100	24

[a] Calculated from soil moisture tension curves for Aiken soil at 15% soil moisture content from Griffin (1967)

[b] Calculated for sugar beet at maximum transpiration (2.5×10^{-7} gm sec⁻¹ cm⁻²) from data supplied by Dr. R. Geiger, Department of Biology, University of Dayton, Dayton, Ohio.

[c] Calculated from water potentials quoted in Slatyer (1967)

since it is probable that slime plugging had occurred when the phloem was excised.

Nevertheless one can obtain an upper bounded estimate of for *Heracleum* phloem assuming a pressure-flow mechanism. The details of the calculation will not be shown here, but by using Eqs. VI-22 and 24, and by taking the percentage of cross-sectional area occupied by sieve tubes as 20%, it can be shown that the energy dissipation per meter of phloem per cubic centimeter of 0.3 M sucrose transported at a mean velocity of 50 cm/hr will be about 1.7 Joules per cm^3 sap per meter of phloem tissue, ($= 0.4$ cal/cm^3 sap per meter phloem tissue). It can be calculated from data given by Canny (1960) and Beevers (1961) that the energy available for translocation will be 6.7×10^2 cal/cm^3 of 0.3 M sucrose. The value of Φ is not very large despite the fact that it is possibly overestimated by as much as two orders of magnitude because of slime plugs.

b. The relative importance of electrical gradients

Much has been said so far of the nonclassical phenomena such as electro-osmosis and streaming currents. Also, calculations have been presented which give the energy dissipation involved in pressure-flow translocation. However, as yet no mention has been made of the physiological significance of the nonclassical phenomena. That is, it has not been ascertained whether or not the electrical cross effects are ever anything more than minor side effects.

What criteria should one use to determine the relative importance of electrical effects? One might think of comparing thermodynamic efficiencies of electro-kinetic and hydrokinetic translocation. This, in fact, has been done (Dainty, Croghan and Fensom, 1963), and it has been shown from the principles of steady state thermodynamics that translocation via electro-osmosis is always less efficient than translocation via pressure flow.

While estimates about relative thermodynamic efficiencies are interesting, these statements do not indicate the relative importance of electrical as opposed to pressure driving "forces." A useful way to make the comparison is to ask what electrical gradient is required to produce a volume flow equivalent to that of a biologically reasonable pressure gradient?

For example in the xylem of a tree a reasonable pressure gradient might be 0.1 atm./meter (Chap. IV, Sec. 5d), and the volume flux associated with it is given by

$$J_p = L_{PP} \frac{dP}{dl}, \; \frac{dE}{dl} = 0 \qquad \text{(Eq. VI-25)}$$

What electrical gradient acting alone would one need to produce the same volume flux, J_p when $dP/dl = 0$? The electrical gradient is given by

$$J_P = L_{PE} \frac{dE}{dl} \text{ or } \frac{dE}{dl} = \frac{J_P}{L_{PE}}, \; \frac{dP}{dl} = 0 \qquad \text{(Eq. VI-26)}$$

Table VI-5 gives the electrical and concentration gradients required to produce the volume fluxes of given pressure gradients in various tissues. As can be seen from Table VI-5, the electrical gradients required to produce volume fluxes

TABLE VI-5

"Equivalent" gradients required to give volume fluxes J_p

Tissue	Biologically reasonable pressure gradients producing, J_p	Electrical gradient required to match flux, J_p	Concentration gradient required to match J_p
XYLEM			
(a) *Heracleum mantegazzianum* petiole xylem	0.1 atm/meter (10^{-4} (Joule cm^{-3})cm^{-1})	7.8×10^3 volt/meter [1]	—
(b) *Acer rubrum* 30 yr. old stem xylem	0.1 atm/meter	13×10^3 volt/meter [1]	—
PHLOEM			
H. mantegazzianum petiole phloem	1 atm/meter (10^{-3} (Joule cm^{-3})cm^{-1})	1.8×10^3 volt/meter [1]	5.1 molar sucrose [3] per *cm*
CELL WALL			
(a) *Nitella flexilis*	1 atm/cm (0.1 (Joule cm^{-3})cm^{-1})	1.5×10^{-3} volt/cm [1]	—
(b) *N. translucens*	1 atm/cm	—	77 molar sucrose [2] per *cm*

(1). Calculated from data in Table VI-3a.
(2). Calculated from data in Tazawa and Kamiya (1966).
(3). Calculated from data given by Fensom on volume flow under sucrose concentration gradients applied to excised phloem bundles 2.5 cm long. (Personal communication).

in phloem and xylem at the rate produced by physiological pressure gradients are excessively large. The largest potentials ever observed in living trees—*Ulmus americana, Pinus resinosa,* and *Acer saccharum*—are of the order of 0.2 to 0.4 volts/meter (Fensom, 1963; Burr, 1945, 1947), and the potentials observed inside the phloem of *Nymphoides* and *Heracleum* are of the order of 0.05 to 0.10 volts/meter, (Fensom and Spanner, 1969; Tyree and Fensom, 1970).

On the other hand, electrical gradients in cellulose cell walls may prove very significant in short distance translocation. One place where electrical gradients may prove important is in meristematic tissue where electrical gradients of the proper orientation are found on the order of 50 mV/cm (Tyree, 1969).

3. DETECTION OF TRANSLOCATION BY ELECTRICAL MEANS

It has been established that the electrical gradients observed inside trees can have little influence upon long distance translocation in phloem and xylem. However, this does not mean that electrical phenomena are not worthy of study. Indeed, the nonclassical phenomena such as streaming currents and streaming potentials afford new means for detecting sap flow in both phloem and xylem. In the following these techniques are presented in detail.

a. Detection of flow in xylem

It is, of course, possible to measure streaming currents inside the trunk of a standing tree by embedding electrodes into the tree and measuring the short circuit current on a low impedence ammeter. According to the Onsager relations, the streaming current should be linearly related to dP/dl and J.

However, for technical reasons, it is better to detect water flow by means of an externally applied test current. Recalling that there is a net flow of ions in the direction of positive current flow, it is easy to see that if a current is passed down through the xylem of a transpiring tree under a voltage v_0, it will encounter a greater frictional drag than current passed up the tree. This is due to the fact that when (positive) current is passed downward it must move *against* an upward water stream in the xylem and when the current is passed upward it will move *with* an upward water stream. So, under the same voltage v_0, the absolute values of the upward and downward current will differ by ΔI, and ΔI will be proportional to the water flux (and pressure gradient) inside the xylem.

In treating this technique quantitatively using the Onsager equations, it is essential to keep in mind that there are three different components of pressure inside the tree. The three components of pressure in xylem are: (1) The hydrostatic pressure gradient which is the pressure gradient resulting from the static column of water in the tree trunk; (2) the water tension or negative water potentials which occur when translocation in the stem lags behind the transpiration in the leaves; and (3) the hydrokinetic pressure gradient which is the "active" pressure gradient superimposed on the hydrostatic pressure and the water tension. The hydrokinetic pressure gradient, as the name implies, is that component of the gradient that actually causes flow. The pressure gradient term appearing in the Onsager equations dP/dl, is only the hydrokinetic component.

With this prelude completed, consider the xylem of a tree where there is a hydrokinetic pressure gradient dP/dl, driving water upward. Eq. VI-12 can be written for two states: (1) when an electrical gradient dE/dl is externally applied up the tree and (2) when the same electrical gradient—dE/dl is applied down the tree. Two different fluxes will result I_1 and $-I_2$ given by

$$I_1 = L_{EP} \frac{dP}{dl} + L_{EE} \frac{dE}{dl} \qquad \text{(Eq. VI-27)}$$

$$-I_2 = L_{EP} \frac{dP}{dl} - L_{EE} \frac{dE}{dl} \qquad \text{(Eq. VI-28)}$$

(It is assumed in Eq. VI-28 that the applied electrical gradient is chosen large enough such that $L_{EE}\, dE/dl$ is greater than $L_{EP}\, dP/dl$ (otherwise I_2 will not be negative as indicated). Adding these two equations and defining ΔI^* as the difference in the absolute values of the fluxes, one obtains $\Delta I^* = 2L_{EP}(dP/dl)$ or $dP/dl = \Delta I^*/2L_{EP}$. So dP/dl is a linear function of the difference in the absolute values of the current fluxes, ΔI^*, or for a tree with A cm^2 of active xylem $\Delta I^* = \Delta I/A$ where $\Delta I =$ the difference in the currents observed in the whole tree. So

$$\frac{dP}{dl} = \frac{\Delta I}{2A\, L_{EP}} \qquad \text{(Eq. VI-29)}$$

If then one substitutes Eq. VI-29 into Eq. VI-11 and neglects the very small influence that the applied dE/dl has on the volume flux, J, one obtains

$$J = L_{PP} \frac{dP}{dl} = \frac{L_{PP}}{2AL_{EP}} \Delta I \qquad \text{(Eq. VI-30)}$$

Since the total volume flow rate through the tree trunk is equal to the flux times the area of the sapwood the volume flow rate is

$$\text{volume flow rate} = AJ = \frac{L_{PP}}{2L_{EP}} \Delta I \qquad \text{(Eq. VI-31)}$$

Eq. VI-31 shows the linear relation between ΔI and the volume flow rate; this is the key to a new technique for measuring long distance translocation in trees. Figure VI-3 shows some typical values of I observed in *Eucalyptus tereticornis* (Tyree and Fensom, 1968).

b. Detection of flow in phloem

The detection of flow in phloem is more difficult than in xylem. The difficulty arises from the fact that streaming currents per cubic centimeter of phloem are smaller than in xylem, and also the cross-sectional area of active phloem in trees is small compared to the area of active sapwood.

Pressure gradients in phloem might be detected by measuring electrical gradients inside the phloem tissue. Extreme care is needed in this kind of mea-

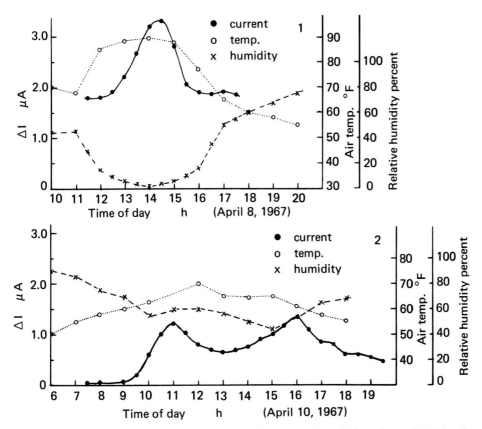

Fig. VI–3. Above and below are two typical examples of the observed ΔI in the stems of *Eucalyptus* trees on a warm-dry and cool-humid day respectively. Ambient temperature and humidity were recorded simultaneously with ΔI showing rough correlations between ΔI (presumably due to transpiration) and the prevailing weather conditions. From Tyree and Fensom, 1968.

surement, and the interpretation of the data is complicated by the possibility of metabolically maintained potentials inside the phloem. As a result, attempts at measuring flow of sap in the phloem tissue of *Heracleum* and *Nymphoides* by Fensom, Spanner and Tyree have met with only minimal success.

LITERATURE CITED

BEEVERS, Harry. 1961. *Respiratory metabolism in plants.* New York: Harper & Row, Publisher. 232 pp.—BURR, H. S. 1945. Diurnal potentials in the maple tree. *Yale Jour. Biol. & Med.* 17: 727–734.—BURR, H. S. 1947. Tree potentials. *Yale Jour. Biol. & Med.* 19: 311–318.

CANNY, M. J. 1960. The rate of translocation. *Biol. Reviews* 35: 507–532.

DAINTY, J., P. C. CROGHAN and D. S. FENSOM. 1963. Electro-osmosis with some applications to plant physiology. *Can. Jour. Bot.* 41: 953–966.—DAINTY, J. and B-Z. GINZBURG.

1963. Irreversible thermodynamics and frictional models of membrane processes, with particular reference to the cell membrane. *Jour. Theoret. Biol.* 5: 256–265.—DE GROOT, S. R. 1966. *Thermodynamics of irreversible processes.* Amsterdam: North-Holland Publishing Co.—DENBIGH, K. G. 1965. *The thermodynamics of the steady state.* London: Methuen & Co. Ltd.

FENSOM, D. S. 1963. The bio-electric potentials of plants and their functional significance. V. Some daily and seasonal changes in the electrical potential and resistance of living trees. *Can. Jour. Bot.* 41: 831–851.—FENSOM, D. S. and J. DAINTY. 1963. Electroosmosis in *Nitella. Can. Jour. Bot.* 41: 685–691.—FENSOM, D. S., S. MEYLAN and P. PILET. 1965. Induced electro-osmosis in root tissue. *Can. Jour. Bot.* 43: 453–467.—FENSOM, D. S. and D. C. SPANNER. 1969. Electro-osmotic and biopotential measurement on phloem strands of *Nymphoides. Planta* 88: 321–331—FENSOM, D. S. and I. R. WANLESS. 1967. Further studies of electro-osmosis in *Nitella* in relation to pores in membranes. *Jour. Exptl. Bot.* 18: 563–577.

GRIFFIN, J. R. 1967. Soil moisture and vegetation patterns in Northern California Forests. *U.S. Forest Service Research Paper PSW–46.*

KEDEM, O. and A. KATCHALSKY. 1958. Thermodynamic analysis of the permeability of biological membranes to non-electrolytes. *Biochem. et Biophys. Acta.* 27: 229–246.

LAKSHMINARAYANAIAH, N. 1967. Water transport through cation exchange membranes. *Desalination* 3: 97–105.—LEVITT, J. 1956. The physical nature of transpirational pull. *Plant Physiol.* 31: 248–251.—LORD RAYLEIGH (STRUTT, R. J.). 1873. Some general theorems relating to vibrations. *Proc. Math. Soc. London,* 4: 357–368.

ONSAGER, L. 1931a. Reciprocal relations in irreversible processes. I. *Phys. Rev.* 37: 405–426.—ONSAGER, L. 1931b. Reciprocal relations in irreversible processes. II. *Phys. Rev.* 38: 2265–2279.—ONSAGER, L. and R. M. FUOSS. 1932. Irreversible processes in electrolytes, diffusion, conductance and viscous flow in arbitrary mixtures of strong electrolytes. *Jour. Chem. Phys.* 36: 2689–2778.

SLATYER, R. O. 1967. *Plant water relationships.* New York: Academic Press.—SPANNER, D. C. 1964. *Introduction to Thermodynamics.* New York: Academic Press.—SPIEGLER, K. S. 1958. Transport processes in ionic membranes. *Trans. Faraday Soc.* 54: 1408–1428. —STAVERMAN, A. J. 1951. The theory and measurement of osmotic pressure. *Recueil Trav. Chim.* 70: 344–352.—STAVERMAN, A. J. 1952. Non-equilibrium thermodynamics of membrane processes. *Trans. Faraday Soc.* 48: 176–185.—STRUGGER, S. 1938/39. Die lumineszenzmikroskopische Analyse des Transpirationsstromes in Parenchymen. *Flora* 133: 56–68.

TAZAWA, A. and N. KAMIYA. 1966. Water permeability of a characean internodal cell with special reference to its polarity. *Aust. Jour. Biol. Sci.* 19: 399–419.—TYREE, M. T. 1968. Determination of transport constants of isolated *Nitella* cell walls. *Can. Jour. Bot.* 46: 317–327.—TYREE, M. T. 1969. The thermodynamics of short distance translocation. *Jour. Exptl. Bot.* 20: 341–349.—TYREE, M. T. and D. S. FENSOM. 1968. Methods of measuring hydrokinetic pressure gradients in the xylem of plants *in situ. Can. Jour. Bot.* 46: 310–314.—TYREE, M. T. and D. S. FENSOM. 1970. Some experimental and theoretical observations concerning mass flow in the vascular bundles of *Heracleum. Jour. Exptl. Bot.* 21: 304–324.—TYREE, M. T. and D. C. SPANNER. 1969. A reappraisal of thermodynamic transport coefficients in *Nitella* cell walls. *Can. J. Bot.* 47: 1497–1503.—TYREE,

M. T. and M. H. ZIMMERMANN. 1971. The theory and practice of measuring transport coefficients and sap flow in the xylem of red maple stems *(Acer rubrum)*. *Jour. Exptl. Bot.* 22: 1–18.

VAN RYSSELBERGHE, P. 1963. *The thermodynamics of irreversible processes.* New York: Blaisdell Pub. Co.

WEATHERLEY, P. E. 1965. The state and movement of water in the leaf. In Symposia of the Society for Experimental Biology, *The State and Movement of Water in Living Organisms.* New York: Academic Press, Inc. pp. 157–184.—WILLIAMS, E. J., R. J. JOHNSTON and J. DAINTY. 1964. The electrical resistance and capacitance of the membranes of *Nitella translucens. Jour. Exptl. Bot.* 43: 1–14.

CHAPTER VII

STORAGE, MOBILIZATION AND CIRCULATION OF ASSIMILATES

Martin H. Zimmermann

INTRODUCTION

After detailed discussion of the spectacular long-distance transport phenomena which enable plants to grow as tall as trees or vines, one should consider the organism as a whole to see how the two long-distance transport systems are connected.

Organization of multicellular plants is based upon the separation of the cells' activities in various compartments. Two major compartments in plants, namely the apoplast and the symplast, can be recognized whereby the latter is subdivided into many individual smaller compartments of tissue, cellular and subcellular size. Independent long-distance transport in the xylem and phloem is only possible if the two compartments (i.e. the sieve-tube lumen and the apoplast) are sharply separated. If this is the case, then by definition, there must be a transport mechanism, or mechanisms, for the transfer of molecules from one compartment into the other, because it is obvious that the plant can circulate substances (up through xylem and down through phloem) with the greatest of ease.

Short-distance transport from cell to cell across a cytoplasmic barrier involves secretion which is an active process requiring metabolic energy. As discussed in Chapter V, it is conceivable that secretion alone may be the driving force of long-distance transport in the sieve tubes. Nevertheless, it certainly plays a major role within tissues as well as in the cross transfer of materials from xylem to phloem and vice versa. This transport across membranes has been investigated mostly in unicellular organisms such as algae and yeast, and to a lesser extent in roots, in connection with mineral uptake. Present knowledge of this field has recently been summarized by Lüttge (1969).

Short-distance transport of substances in trees not only concerns transfer from xylem to phloem and phloem to xylem, but also transport into and out of storage tissues. Distances up to a few centimeters are thus involved. In this chapter no attempt is made to cover the vast amount of available data on when, where and what is stored in trees. Rather, a brief summary of a few relevant principles is given in order to describe how the two long-distance transport systems and storage tissues are linked.

1. DIURNAL STORAGE OF ASSIMILATES
IN THE LEAF

Photosynthesis in leaves occurs only during the daylight hours, whereas translocation of sugars out of the leaves goes on continuously day and night. Thus photosynthesis produces more carbohydrates during the day than the phloem can export. The excess is being stored in parenchyma cells of the leaves, in the form of starch. Plants are so well adapted to the diurnal cycle of light and dark that the total capacity of photosynthesis and translocation during a 24-hour period are approximately equal. Earlier botanists were well aware of the diurnal storage of starch in leaf parenchyma (e.g. Sachs, 1887). Demonstration of the phenomenon by staining the starch in cleared leaves with iodine at different times of day used to be a standard student exercise in plant physiology.

In his classical paper on phloem transport in apple leaves, Schneider-Orelli (1909) illustrated starch content of leaf parenchyma at different times of day in microscopic view (Chap. V, Sec. 2a). From this work two different types of transport are obvious: short-distance transport in leaf parenchyma, and long-distance transport in phloem. In the evening, when leaf parenchyma was "filled up", starch was located in the mesophyll, and not in the bundle parenchyma (see also Fig. V-4 and 5). In those leaf parts from which phloem export of sugars was prevented, starch had appeared in the bundle parenchyma by morning, while the mesophyll had become almost free of starch. Because carbohydrates are not transported in the form of starch, one must deduce from these results that mesophyll starch which had accumulated during the day had been broken down to sugars, transported to the vein parenchyma, and there redeposited in the form of starch.

A great deal of effort has been made by the Russian workers to analyze the nature of short-distance transport in leaf parenchyma (e.g. Brovchenko, 1965, 1967; Kursanov et al., 1961, 1967). It has become clear from this work that transport from mesophyll to veins is an active, ATP-dependent process, often occurring against a concentration gradient. Suggestions of transport mechanisms have been made, but one must be aware of the fact that they are based upon chemical analyses of rather crudely separated leaf tissues. The microscopic structure of leaves is such that a precise mechanical separation of mesophyll, bundle parenchyma, and sieve tubes is extremely difficult if not impossible. An interesting study about the relationship of translocation and structural details of venation in sugar beet leaves has been published by Geiger and Cataldo (1969).

2. STORAGE IN THE STEM

a. Annual storage in dicotyledons and conifers

STORAGE TISSUES.   Most types of living cells in woody axes function at times in the storage of reserve materials. Exceptions are specialized living cells in wood and bark in which storage would interfere with function. Storage does not occur to any appreciable extent, for example, in sieve elements and companion cells of dicotyledons, sieve cells and albuminous cells of conifers (cf. Ziegler, 1964). Whenever one stains microtome sections of wood and bark with iodine in late summer, the storage cells and tissue become very clearly visible because they stain darkly, almost black. In the bark, storage tissue consists mostly of ray and vertical parenchyma which is located in the living phloem between conducting phloem and periderm. In wood storage tissue is represented by vertical and ray parenchyma cells of the sapwood. The distribution of xylem parenchyma is characteristic for various taxonomic groups, and of evolutionary significance (Braun, 1963). The same is true, of course, for the phloem, but little taxonomic work has been done with phloem.

An interesting observation, pointed out by Ziegler (1964) is the fact that storage tissues must be continuous with the conducting phloem in order to survive. This is unquestionably the case in phloem as well as xylem of dicotyledons and conifers. Vertical xylem parenchyma also connects with the horizontal ray parenchyma to form a three-dimensional transport and storage system. In analytical motion-picture films of wood it is evident that all parenchyma, vertical and horizontal, forms a continuous network (Zimmermann, 1971).

SEASONAL SEQUENCE OF STORAGE AND MOBILIZATION.   The seasonal variation in quantity of stored material in woody plants, as well as the significance of this phenomenon, were recognized a long time ago. Many workers have investigated this seasonal phenomenon and much information is now available. The interested reader is referred to the recent review of Kozlowski and Keller (1966). This discussion will be restricted to only a few examples. Hartig published an unusually complete account of the problem in 1858. His observations concerned not only above-ground organs, but extended into the roots as well. He reported that reserve materials in early spring began to be dissolved first in twigs; mobilization then proceeded basipetally into the roots. In contrast, deposition began in the roots and extended distally up through the stem into twigs. His results are given in Table VII-1.

Another example, concerning above-ground organs (both phloem and xylem) of eight-year-old poplars, is illustrated in Fig. VII-1 (Sauter, 1966b). These observations indicate that starch content shows two peaks and two valleys throughout the course of the year. This observation has been made many times throughout the years. A third example, showing starch and sugar content in the bark of *Robinia* throughout the year, is given in Fig. VII-2. The early summer minimum shown in Table VII-1 and Fig. VII-1 and 2, is obviously the result of heavy

TABLE VII–1

Accumulation and dissolution of reserve materials in various parts of trees (from Hartig, 1858)

Tree species	Dissolution of reserve materials begins		Accumulation of reserve materials begins	
	in youngest twigs	in roots	in roots	in youngest twigs
Acer	early Feb.		May	early August
Quercus	mid-March		July	mid-September
Larix	early April	early May	June	early Oct.
Pinus	early April	mid-June	Sept.	mid-October
	Lasts about two months, shorter in roots than in stem and twigs		Lasts two to three months, longer in roots than in above-ground organs	

drain on reserves by the beginning of primary and secondary growth. The winter minimum seems to be a temperature effect, the result of starch-sugar conversion at low temperatures. This is suggested by the results of Siminovitch *et al.* (1953) which show simultaneously an increase of the sugar content and a drop of starch with the onset of cool weather (Fig. VII-2). Sauter (1967) looked into this question with three coniferous and five dicotyledonous tree species. He collected pieces of stem tissue during winter dormancy, subjected them to various temperatures and found starch synthesis between +5 and +10°C, and starch break-down below as well as above this range. There were differences among species and among tissues within single species.

Essentially then, woody plants store reserves during times of surplus production and utilize them as the demand arises. The demand arises regularly in the spring at the time of bud burst, but also in cases of emergency, for example when a tree is defoliated by insects. Spring mobilization of reserves must be of particular importance in ring-porous trees for reasons discussed in Chapter IV, Section 7c. The difference between ring- and diffuse-porous trees is quite striking when one walks through the forest at the time of bud burst. Diffuse-porous trees are ahead of ring-porous ones in leafing out and in shoot growth, but, if one measures diameter growth with dendrometers, one finds that ring-porous species are producing new water-conducting tissue to replace the previous year's xylem which had been thrown out of function by winter freezing and which has to be renewed before the new leaves emerge.

NATURE OF STORED FOODS.   Up to this point the implication has been that the main storage product in woody plants is starch. This is not entirely the case; there are other storage substances as well. Among the carbohydrates there are, besides various kinds of starch, oligosaccharides such as sucrose and the raffinose family of sugars, fructosans, various hemicelluloses, etc. For more information about this, the reader is referred to the appropriate chapters of the various textbooks (Pigman, 1957; Akazawa, 1965).

Besides carbohydrates, fats and oils play a certain role as storage products. This was recognized a long time ago, the suggestion to classify trees into the two

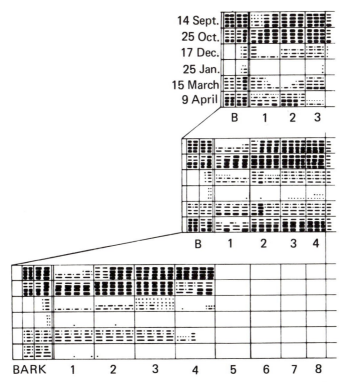

Fig. VII–1. Changes of starch content in the rays of eight-year-old *Populus* wood during the dormant period of 1962–63. The diagrams represent radial views of rays in the stem at the base of the tree (bottom diagrams), at the base of the crown (middle diagrams) and in the upper region of the crown (top diagrams). The number of horizontal rows of dashes within a ray indicates the percentage of starch-containing ray cells (1 row = 1–25% of the ray cells with starch; 2 rows = 25–50%; 3 rows = 50–75%; 4 rows = 75–100%). Boldness of the lines indicates average starch content (dotted lines = few starch grains; dash-dotted lines = cells $\frac{1}{5}$ to $\frac{1}{3}$ filled with starch; dashed lines = about $\frac{1}{2}$ filled; bold dashes = filled with starch). Rays are vertically subdivided into growth rings: B = bark, numbers = age of growth ring in wood. The horizontal subdivisions indicate the six collection dates. From Sauter, 1966b, slightly modified.

groups "fat trees" and "starch trees" was made in 1891 by Fischer. Sinnott (1918) surveyed many tree species in this respect, but it does not seem possible to find a clear-cut classification. Though most ring-porous trees are starch trees, representatives of the genera *Pinus Populus* and *Tilia* are fat trees; so there is no well-defined grouping along taxonomic or other lines. Nor do fat trees store lipids exclusively. One can merely say that some tree species store variable amounts of fats and oils in addition to carbohydrates.

The conversion of carbohydrates into fats and vice versa occurs easily (cf. Stumpf, 1965), and the process seems to be temperature sensitive. Low temperature favors conversion of carbohydrate into fat. Roots are less subjected to low temperatures during the winter than stems; so that even fat trees store mostly starch in their roots, except during especially cold winters (Ziegler, 1964). Fats

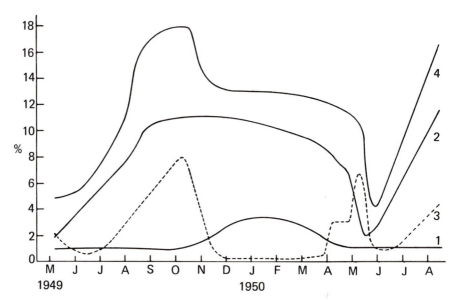

Fig. VII–2. Average seasonal variation as a percentage of dry weight of tissue in reducing sugar (1), sucrose (2), starch (3) and total reserve carbohydrates (4) in the living bark tissue of 12 *Robinia* trees during the period from May 1949 to August 1950. From Siminovitch *et al.*, 1953.

and oils are produced in large quantities in certain seeds, which often serve as sources for the commercial production of vegetable fats and oils.

b. Long-term storage in arborescent monocotyledons

Because most researchers have worked with trees of temperate regions, one tends to think in terms of annual storage and mobilization. However, there is a very large group of arborescent plants whose storage-mobilization cycle is very much longer. Some arborescent monocotyledons, notably some of the palms, produce surplus carbohydrates throughout their entire lifetime, storing it in the ground parenchyma of their trunk. This storage material, mostly starch, is of vital importance in those plants which flower only during a relatively short period at the end of their lifetime. *Corypha, Metroxylon* and other palms, as well as other monocotyledonous genera like *Agave*, produce a single terminal inflorescence when fully mature. Other palms, members of the Caryotoideae, flower basipetally after completing their vegetative growth. No more leaves are produced during this reproductive phase; flowering and fruiting causes the stored material in the stem to be mobilized. Enormous quantities of these carbohydrates (in some cases several hundred pounds) move into flowers and fruits within a relatively short time.

In some tropical areas, stored carbohydrates of palms which flower at the end of their lifetime, are harvested before flowering. The tree is cut down, the soft stem center is hacked up and the starch is washed out (Miller, 1964). Starch obtained in this way from the palm *Metroxylon* is available in the trade as sago.

Another method of harvesting palm sugar is by tapping inflorescence stalks. A sugary juice is thus obtained, which has shown to be phloem exudate (Tammes, 1933). Sugar or an alcoholic beverage can be made from it. For *Arenga,* the sugar palm, up to 10 ls of exudate per day can be harvested which might yield around 1 kg of sugar. Tapping palm inflorescences exhausts the storage carbohydrates in the stem, of course; therefore starch cannot be harvested from a tapped stem (Miller, 1964).

Other arborescent monocotyledons produce inflorescences periodically, although not necessarily annually. Among these are the Pandanaceae and members of the Agavaceae, as well as many palms. Green leaves are present during flowering; it is, therefore, not known to what extent storage materials are involved in the formation of flowers and fruits.

3. RADIAL TRANSPORT IN STEMS

a. Structure of rays in conifers and dicotyledons

Dicotyledonous and coniferous stems have relatively short-lived vascular tissues. The sieve tubes of the phloem, for example, function in most species for one year only, even though phloem parenchyma may remain alive for decades. The function of phloem parenchyma is primarily that of storage tissue. This means that much of the storage tissue in the phloem is not in direct contact with vascular tissue. A similar statement can be made for the xylem, i.e. xylem parenchyma stores assimilates, but it is not directly supplied by sieve tubes. This situation is in sharp contrast to that of stems of arborescent monocotyledons (cf. Sec. 3d). Dicotyledons and conifers have, therefore, acquired during the course of evolution specialized radial tissues, the rays. The first rays (primary or medullary rays) originate between the primary vascular bundles and are continuous with the pith when primary growth is complete. As secondary growth begins the cambial cylinder gains circumference and new ray initials arise in the cambium in various ways from the fusiform initials. Thus new secondary rays are constantly forming so that the ray density is approximately maintained (Bailey, 1923; Bannan, 1951, 1953). As a result secondary vascular tissues are thoroughly interwoven with radially-running ray tissue, through which, presumably, both water and assimilate transport takes place.

Because ray initials are part of the vascular cambium, most rays are continuous from xylem through the phloem. Their histological construction differs greatly from one species to another and is, therefore, of considerable taxonomic importance. Rays are a very useful feature in wood identification.

Xylem rays consist mostly of living cells in the sapwood. Special water-conducting (i.e. vascular) elements are not universally present, although some conifers have ray tracheids. In dicotyledons, ray tracheids and vessels are extremely rare, but do occur in *Banksia* and *Dryandra* of the Proteaceae (Chattaway, 1948) and *Lagunaria patersonii* G. Don of the Malvaceae (Chattaway, 1951). Ray parenchyma cells in the xylem commonly acquire a secondary wall, but may remain alive for long periods and store assimilates at certain times. Contact between vertical water-conducting elements and rays is of physiological importance. In conifers there are bordered pits between ray and vertical tracheids, obviously for the passage of water. Pits between ray parenchyma cells and vertical tracheids (in conifers) or vessels (in dicotyledons) are important for exchange of nutrients, whether it be for the transfer of previously stored carbohydrates from rays into the water-conducting channels in the spring, or for the uptake of solutes moving upwards from the roots. In dicotyledonous xylem, rays often contain marginal rows of "contact cells" with large pits to vessel elements and central rows of "isolation cells" without conspicuous pitting to vessel elements (Fig. VII-3). It is assumed that the former, which are often upright cells, are functionally specialized for the exchange of nutrients, the latter for radial transport (Braun, 1967; Sauter and Braun, 1968).

In the phloem the ray cells remain thin-walled as long as they serve a storage function. In many species, phloem ray cells proliferate to fill the space created by the continuous circumferential expansion of the phloem. This dilatation is very conspicuous in genera such as *Tilia*. Additional information may be found in the anatomy text by Esau (1965) and the literature cited therein.

The rays are presumably the tissues in which assimilates are translocated radially, from the sieve tubes into storage parenchyma of the sapwood and the living bark outside the conducting phloem. At the time of mobilization e.g. at the end of a period of dormancy during the onset of growth, assimilates move again radially back toward the cambium. This statement is based mostly upon

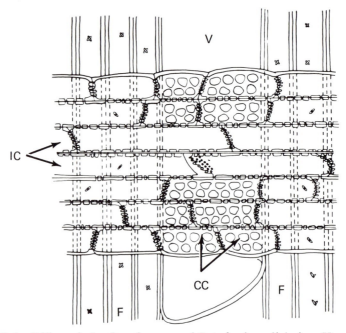

Fig. VII–3. Differentiation in xylem rays of *Populus* in radial view. Upper and lower rows of ray cells are "contact cells" (CC) which are connected with vessels (V) via large pits. Central rows of cells are "isolation cells" (IC). F = fibers. From Sauter, 1966b.

inference, because very little factual information is available on ray transport. Ziegler (1961, 1964) has pointed out the paucity of information on ray cell physiology and has gathered the small amount of literature relating to their function.

b. Movement of water and mineral nutrients in rays

Information about movement of water and mineral nutrients in rays is mostly derived from indirect evidence. In speaking about "water and mineral nutrients" one means xylem sap, in which many of the minerals are in organic form (Chap. IV, Sec. 9). The inner portion of the sapwood is supplied directly from roots via axial xylem, at least in many species; hence there is little need for radial movement. "Water utilization" of the inner sapwood and the heartwood consists primarily of a diurnal and seasonal fluctuation of water content. Water is pulled out during times of high tensions in the xylem; it re-enters when the tension relaxes (Gibbs, 1958; Sauter, 1966a) thereby acting as water storage tissues. The quantities involved in this water movement are probably quite small but may be very important in rehydration at night when transpiration is minimal. Of course, here one is not dealing with a diurnal replacement of water by air or water vapor, but with a daily dehydration and rehydration affecting volume which, in part, is responsible for the diurnal dendrometer fluctuations. The principle path of water movement in rays is through cell walls and through tracheary elements where these are present.

In the case of the bark one is probably not only dealing with a diurnal dehydration and rehydration or movement in and out, but superimposed upon this is a slow but constant movement from xylem to bark surface. It is known that the bark transpires, mostly through stomata in the epidermis of twigs and through lenticells in older barks (Geurten, 1950). This movement of a slight transpiration stream from the xylem to bark surface is undoubtedly beneficial for the mineral nutrition of the bark. The path of this radial movement can only be inferred, but it is most likely via cell walls of all the cells, and not restricted to the phloem rays.

c. Assimilate movement in rays

The assumption that ray cells transport assimilates is based mostly on indirect evidence. Rays are filled with starch during the summer, and this starch is mobilized again at the beginning of the new growth period when carbohydrates are needed. Furthermore, when the bark of a tree is removed in a small area, and the area is covered to prevent desiccation, tissue regeneration originates from rays, indicating that carbohydrates are supplied from ray tissue (Hartig, 1845). Still another piece of evidence is Bannan's (1951, 1953) observation that fusiform initials of the cambium (*Chamaecyparis* and *Thuja*) depend for their survival on ray contact. When ray contact is missing, initials are lost by shortening and differentiation, or by transformation into ray initials. Thus, new rays arise in even distribution as the circumference of the stem increases.

Ziegler (1964) suggested that assimilates do not pass directly from sieve tubes into rays, but do so via companion cells (in dicotyledons) and albuminous cells (in conifers). Little is known about the form in which assimilates move in the rays, and about the translocation mechanism, though there is evidence that the rate of movement exceeds that of simple diffusion (Ziegler, 1964). Sauter (1966c) speculated that movement of sugars across tangential walls of ray cells might take place in the form of sugar phosphates or a sugar complex. In a later paper, Sauter and Braun (1968) found that ray cells of conifers exhibit a distinct polarity in acid phosphatase tests during spring mobilization at the onset of cambial activity. The phosphatase reaction was distinctly concentrated inside on the cambium side of the cells, i.e. on the "wrong" side as far as Sauter's (1966c) earlier proposal was concerned. Whatever the meaning of this finding, the phenomenon of temporary polarity is an interesting one worthy of further exploration.

d. Monocotyledons

Radial xylem and phloem transport in monocotyledonous stems goes through leaf traces, which are connected, via bridges, with neighboring vascular bundles (Fig. IV-9). This is the case even in the lower parts of the stem where leaves have fallen off. Only the protoxylem and protophloem portions of the leaf-trace complex, i.e. the part of the bundle which leads directly into the leaf, goes out of function after leaf abscission (Parthasarathy and Tomlinson, 1967). The density of leaf traces is quite comparable with that of rays in dicotyledonous and coniferous stems. Even in a medium size palm, for example, there are hundreds of leaf traces going into each leaf base.

In monocotyledonous trees with secondary vascular tissue, the situation is very similar. There are no special radial secondary tissues. Leaf traces elongate within the secondary tissue as long as the leaves are alive. When the leaves die it is still not known if leaf-trace growth is discontinued and no further radial vascular tissue is produced (Tomlinson and Zimmermann, 1969). Radial structures may not be vital in the secondary tissue at the base of the stem, because there is vascular continuity between the crown and the basal vascular tissues.

In contrast to dicotyledons and conifers then, radial transport in monocotyledons is vascular transport, identical with transport in the axial direction.

4. CIRCULATION OF ASSIMILATES

a. Short-term circulation

The phloem and xylem of plants are in very intimate contact. Contact from functioning sieve tubes to outer portions of the living bark and to xylem parenchyma, the places of storage, is via rays. What little is known about ray transport has been discussed in the previous sections. With this three-dimensional arrangement of tissues the plant has a very efficient method of distribution of nutrients at its disposal.

Axial directions of transport are usually opposite in phloem and xylem respectively with the exception of growing shoot tips, flowers and some fruits where transport in both systems is distally unidirectional. Opposite transport

directions in phloem and xylem respectively has caused a great deal of misunder-
standing in the past. Many authors have "shown" upward transport of nutrients
in the phloem from the roots. If, for example, a tree is girdled, roots are deprived
of carbohydrates, reduction of nitrates in the roots is depressed, and the result is
a decreased nitrogen supply to the shoot system. Girdling, therefore, decreases
upward transport of nitrogen indirectly and not directly. Upward transport is
via xylem, rarely via phloem. Another easily misinterpreted example of circulation has been discussed in Chapter IV, Section 9c. Circulation of substances in
plants has deceived many workers, especially if they have used experimental times
of appreciable length.

It is quite obvious that the simultaneous bidirectional transport in phloem
and xylem offers the plant great flexibilities in nutrient distribution. Circulation
of substances by subsequent, and perhaps repeated, upward movement in xylem
and downward movement in the phloem can take nutrients to virtually every
part of the plant so that each can be utilized where and when needed. This is
borne out, for example, by investigations of Biddulph *et al.* (1958) who determined the circulation patterns of ^{32}P, ^{35}S and ^{45}Ca in bean plants from single
aliquots of tracer administered to the roots during a one-hour period. Calcium
moved initially in the transpiration stream and showed its well-known phloem
immobility. Some of the phosphorus displayed sustained circulation during the
four-day experimental period, while sulphur, initially retranslocated from mature
leaves via phloem, was captured and retained in young leaves. It is quite useful
to consider these circulation patterns in the light of the regulation mechanism
of phloem transport, described in Chapter V, Section 8.

An interesting, and for the plant essential, type of circulation, involving
nitrogen reduction in roots, has been investigated primarily by Kursanov and
his collaborators in a study of root metabolism (cf. the review by Kursanov,
1963, and the literature cited therein). These authors found that 18–50% (percent radioactivity after photosynthesis in a $^{14}CO_2$-containing atmosphere) of the
carbohydrates exported from leaves, entered the roots. About 60% of this was
incorporated in organic acids and amino acids most of which moved up in the
xylem. The flow of carbohydrates into roots was stimulated by mineral nutrition.
Nitrogen deficiency, on the other hand, resulted in a sharp, but reversible, decrease of sugar transport from leaves to roots. These detailed studies involved
mostly *Cucurbita* seedlings (not exactly trees!), but since tree species are well
known for organic nitrogenous substances in xylem sap (Chap. IV, Sec. 9b), they
illustrate principles which seem to be quite relevant here. Stimulation of ^{14}C
translocation to roots by addition of nitrogen to the nutrition solution has also
been found in *Pinus taeda* L. by Barnes (1962).

b. Seasonal circulation and its relations to growth

UTILIZATION OF RESERVES BY GROWTH. Annual circulation of carbohydrates
was recognized in the past century and early investigations are summarized in
contemporary textbooks (e.g. Hartig, 1878). The question of utilization of assimilates in primary and secondary growth and in flower and fruit production by

forest trees is of certain practical interest. The question particularly concerns the origin of these assimilates, whether they are transported directly from photosynthesizing leaves (and in conifers from generation of leaves) or from storage. A voluminous literature, recently reviewed by Kozlowski and Keller (1966), is devoted to this topic. The answer to this question is not a simple one; some shoot systems seem to draw primarily on current photosynthates, others, such as first emerging shoots in the spring, stump sprouts, etc. seem to depend more on reserves. Reproductive growth, i.e. flowering and fruiting, often draws heavily on reserve material, especially in cases where large quantities of fruits are produced at intervals of several years.

What has been said of food consumption in primary growth applies similarly to secondary growth. Ring-porous trees which produce their large earlywood vessels before the leaves emerge will certainly have to utilize storage material. It is equally likely that current photosynthates are chiefly involved in latewood formation in trees with a full set of mature, exporting leaves. One must be aware of the fact that the distribution between photosynthetic machinery, storage and utilization is controlled (or linked) by numerous enzymatic processes. This means that demand and supply are very flexibly interrelated and any sink may draw automatically from the nearest or most ample source of food (cf. Chap. V, Sec. 8). The entire food economy of a tree is so tightly integrated that clear-cut statements about the origin of carbohydrates can seldom be made. Numerous investigators have set up productivity balance sheets for entire trees, or even forest stands. Readers who are interested in these ecological aspects of tree physiology are referred to the reviews by Kozlowski and Keller (1966), Lyr *et al.* (1967), and Priestley (1962).

Attempts have been made during recent years to follow production and the seasonal changes in distribution of assimilated carbon with radioactive tracers (e.g. Nelson, 1964; Ursino *et al.*, 1968). This method is quite precise but difficult to use with fully grown trees. Food distribution in seedlings may be quite different from food distribution in mature trees.

In temperate tree species, or those of tropical regions which periodically shed their leaves, a periodicity of storage and mobilization exists. A vegetative period (i.e., a time of storage), is usually followed by a period of dormancy. The onset of new growth after the dormant period is then characterized by mobilization of storage material. Transport of this mobilized material is logically via rays towards the cambium. There is probably not much demand for longitudinal transport in the xylem because stored material is available more or less all along the axis. An exception are certainly the growing shoot tips which must be supplied with water and assimilates, i.e. by both xylem and phloem.

FLOW OF MAPLE SAP. Xylem exudate of some species (e.g. members of the genera *Acer* and *Betula*) contains dissolved sugar in late winter and early spring. The flow of sugary xylem sap in *Acer saccharum* Marsh. of Eastern North America is a notable example. When the xylem of *Acer saccharum* is severed in late winter, a sugar solution of a concentration around 2–3% (w/v) exudes under considerable pressure (of the order of 1 atm.). This sap was used as a source of sugar by the early Indians; it is still gathered today, supporting a maple-sugar industry of local economic importance. The mechanism of this sap flow is not yet fully understood. Unlike xylem exudation in *Betula* and *Vitis,* exudation in *Acer saccharum* is not directly caused by root pressure. It seems to be based upon the metabolism of sugar mobilization, and manifests itself as a diurnal xylem pressure fluctuation perhaps caused by a metabolically induced volume change of the stem. Generally speaking, xylem pressure rises above atmospheric levels when the temperature increases, and drops below atmospheric pressure during periods of cooling. When tapped, trees exude during the high-pressure phase and replenish their xylem water during the low-pressure phase from roots, whereby the wet walls of the severed vessels must act as valves, letting sap pass during the exudation phase but not permitting air to enter uninjured vessels during the replenishment phase (Chap. IV, Sec. 7b). Readers interested in this topic are referred to the paper of Marvin (1958) and the literature cited therein.

Occurrence of sugars in xylem sap at the end of the dormancy period gave rise to the idea that mobilized sugars move upwards in the xylem thus completing a regular annual sugar circulation (down in phloem and up in xylem). This idea was debated at length during the past century. Dissolved sugars will certainly be carried to points of transpiration, but it is doubtful whether the amounts of sugar transported upward in the xylem are very significant, except in a few species.

SUGAR TRANSPORT IN RELATION TO DORMANCY CALLOSE FORMATION.   Dormancy callose is formed in the phloem of all species (?) which go through dormancy periods, e.g. in *Fraxinus americana* L. approximately two weeks after leaf abscission (Fig. V-18). It is obvious that long-distance transport then ceases until sieve tubes are reactivated or new ones are formed. This period of change has been investigated by Hill (1962) with aphids whose feeding habits are an excellent indicator of sieve-tube activity. Obviously, complete closure of sieve tubes by callose makes feeding impossible. Callose seems to be dissolved at the end of the dormancy period (in southern New England in early March). Sieve-tube exudate can be obtained again at that time, be it with the incision (Zimmermann, 1964) or the aphid stylet method (Hill, 1962). It has been suggested that the signal for this reactivation is sent out by the swelling buds, for disbudding caused a considerably reduced exudation on detached branches (Hill, 1962). The onset of shoot growth evidently draws heavily from stored reserves; as the leaves begin to grow exudation ceases on the main axis and does not recommence until leaves are fully mature. Thus, there seems to be a period during shoot growth of little or no transport in the main axis. Local distal transport from older to young leaves must, of course, go on.

Seasonal fluctuations of amino acid and amide content in sieve-tube exudate are of particular interest. In *Salix* these substances increase from less than 0.03% (w/v) during summer and early autumn to about 0.12% at the time of leaf senescence. This relatively high concentration is evidently the result of protein break-down in senescing leaves and export from these leaves into the stem (Mittler, 1958; Ziegler, 1956; Zimmermann, 1958). A similar nitrogen export can be observed when leaf senescence is artificially induced by darkening (e.g. Schumacher, 1930). The interesting point is that these relatively high nitrogen concentrations can still be found during phloem reactivation in early spring, but they are then rapidly utilized by the growing shoots.

LITERATURE CITED

AKAZAWA, T. 1965. Starch, inulin, and other reserve polysaccharides. *Plant biochemistry.* J. Bonner and J. E. Varner, eds., pp. 258–297. New York: Academic Press.

BAILEY, I. W. 1923. The cambium and its derivative tissues IV. The increase in girth of the cambium. *Amer. Jour. Bot.* 10: 499–509.—BANNAN, M. W. 1951. The reduction of fusiform cambial initials in *Chamaecyparis* and *Thuja. Can. Jour. Bot.* 29: 57–67.—BANNAN, M. W. 1953. Further observations on the reduction of fusiform cambial cells in *Thuja occidentalis* L. *Can. Jour. Bot.* 31: 63–74.—BARNES, R. L. 1962. Glutamine synthesis and translocation in pines. *Plant Physiol.* 37: 323–326.—BIDDULPH, O., S. BIDDULPH, R. CORY and H. KOONTZ. 1958. Circulation patterns for phosphorus, sulfur and calcium in the bean plant. *Plant Physiol.* 33: 293–300.—BRAUN, H. J. 1963. *Die Organisation des Stammes von Bäumen und Sträuchern.* Wissenschaftl. Verlagsgesellschaft Stuttgart, Germany.—BRAUN, H. J. 1967. Entwicklung und Bau der Holzstrahlen unter dem Aspekt der Kontakt-Isolations-Differenzierung gegenüber dem Hydrosystem I. Das Prinzip der Kontakt-Isolations-Differenzierung. *Holzforschung* 21: 33–37.—BROVCHENKO, M. I. 1965. On the movement of sugars from the mesophyll to the conducting bundles in sugar-beet leaves. *Soviet Plant Physiol.* 12: 230–237 (translation).—BROVCHENKO, M. I. 1967. Some proofs of the splitting of sucrose during its movement from mesophyll into the fine bundles of sugar-beet leaves. *Soviet Plant Physiol.* 14: 352–359 (translation).

CHATTAWAY, M. M. 1948. The wood anatomy of the Proteaceae. *Austral. Jour. Sci. Res.* 1: 279–302.—CHATTAWAY, M. M. 1951. Morphological and functional variations in the rays of pored timbers. *Austral. Jour. Sci. Res.* 4: 12–27.

ESAU, K. 1965. *Plant Anatomy.* 2nd ed. New York: John Wiley & Sons.

FISCHER, A. 1891. Beiträge zur Physiologie der Holzgewächse. *Jahrb. wiss. Bot.* 22: 73–160.

GEIGER, D. R. and D. A. CATALDO. 1969. Leaf structure and translocation in sugar beet. *Plant Physiol.* 44: 45–54.—GEURTEN, I. 1950. Untersuchungen über den Gaswechsel der Baumrinden. *Forstwiss. Cbl.* 69: 704–743.—GIBBS, R. D. 1958. Patterns in the seasonal water content of trees. In *The physiology of forest trees.* K. V. Thimann, ed., pp. 43–69. New York: Ronald Press.

HARTIG, Th. 1845. Ueber künstliche Erzeugung neuer Holz- und Rindeschichten auf entrindeten Holzflächen durch Fensterung. *Allg. Forst- und Jagdztg.* 11: 165–169.—HARTIG, Th. 1858. Ueber die Bewegung des Saftes in den Holzpflanzen. *Bot. Z.* 16: 329–335.—HARTIG, Th. 1878. *Anatomie und Physiologie der Holzpflanzen.* Berlin: Springer.—HILL, G. P. 1962. Exudation from aphid stylets during the period from dormancy to bud break in *Tilia americana* L. *Jour. Exptl. Bot.* 144–151.

KOZLOWSKI, T. T. and Th. KELLER. 1966. Food relations of woody plants. *Bot. Rev.* 32: 293–382.—KRAMER, P. J. and T. T. KOZLOWSKI. 1960. *Physiology of trees.* New York:

McGraw-Hill Book Co., Inc.—Kursanov, A. L. 1963. Metabolism and the transport of organic substances in the phloem. *Adv. Bot. Res.* 1: 209–278.—Kursanov, A. L. and M. L. Brovchenko. 1961. Effect of ATP on the entry of assimilates into the conducting system of sugar beets. *Soviet Plant Physiol.* 8: 211–217 (translation).—Kursanov, A. L., M. I. Brovchenko, and E. P. Butenko. 1967. Transformation of sugars absorbed by the the leaf tissues of sugar beets. *Soviet Plant Physiol.* 14: 684–691 (translation).

Lüttge, U. 1969. Aktiver Transport (Kurzstreckentransport bei Pflanzen). *Protoplasmologia,* vol. 8. Wien und New York: Springer-Verlag.—Lyr, H., H. Polster, and H. J. Fiedler. 1967. *Gehölzphysiologie.* Jena: Gustav Fischer Verlag.

Marvin, J. W. 1958. The physiology of maple sap flow. In *The physiology of forest trees,* K. V. Thimann, ed., pp. 95–124. New York: Ronald Press.—Miller, R. H. 1964. The versatile sugar palm. *Principes* (Jour. of the Palm Soc.) 8: 115–147.—Mittler, T. E. 1958. Studies on the feeding and nutrition of *Tuberolachnus salignus* (Gmelin) (Homoptera, Aphididae). II. The nitrogen and sugar composition of ingested phloem sap and excreted honeydew. *Jour. Exptl. Biol.* 35: 74–84.

Nelson, C. D. 1964. The production and translocation of photosynthate-C^{14} in conifers. In *The formation of wood in forest trees.* M. H. Zimmermann, ed., pp. 243–257. New York: Academic Press.

Parthasarathy, M. V. and P. B. Tomlinson. 1967. Anatomical features of metaphloem in stems of *Sabal, Cocos* and two other palms. *Amer. Jour. Bot.* 54: 1143–1151.—Pigman, W., ed. 1957. *The carbohydrates.* New York: Academic Press.—Priestley, C. A. 1962. *Carbohydrate resources within the perennial plant.* Tech. Comm. No. 27, Commonwealth Agricult. Bureaux, Farnham Royal, Bucks, England.

Sachs, J. von. 1887. *Vorlesungen über Pflanzenphysiologie.* 2nd ed. Leipzig: Wilhelm Engelmann—Sauter, J. J. 1966a. Ueber die jahresperiodischen Wassergehaltsänderungen und Wasserverschiebungen im Kern- und Splintholz von *Populus. Holzforschung* 20: 137–142.—Sauter, J. J. 1966b. Untersuchungen zur Physiologie der Pappelholzstrahlen I. Jahresperiodischer Verlauf der Stärkespeicherung im Holzparenchym. *Z. Pflanzenphysiol.* 55: 246–258.—Sauter, J. J. 1966c. Untersuchungen zur Physiologie der Pappelholzstrahlen II. Jahresperiodische Aenderungen der Phosphataseaktivität im Holzstrahlparenchym und ihre mögliche Bedeutung für den Kohlenhydratstoffwechsel und den aktiven Assimilattransport. *Z. Pflanzenphysiol.* 55: 349–362.—Sauter, J. J. 1967. Der Einfluss verschiedener Temperaturen auf die Reservestärke in parenchymatischen Geweben von Baumsprossachsen. *Z. Pflanzenphysiol.* 56: 340–352.—Sauter, J. J. and H. J. Braun. 1968. Enzymatic polarity in ray parenchyma cells of conifers in spring. *Z. Pflanzenphysiol.* 58: 378–381.—Schneider-Orelli, O. 1909. Die Miniergänge von *Lyonetia clercella* L. und die Stoffwanderung in Apfelblättern. *Zbl. f. Bact.* 24 (II): 158–181.—Schumacher, W. 1930. Untersuchungen über die Lokalisation der Stoffwanderung in den Leitbündeln höherer Pflanzen. *Jahrb. wiss. Bot.* 73: 770–823.—Siminovitch, D., C. M. Wilson, and D. R. Briggs. 1953. Studies on the chemistry of the living bark of the black locust in relation to its frost hardiness V. Seasonal transformations and variations in the carbohydrates: starch-sucrose interconversions. *Plant Physiol.* 28: 383–400.—Sinnott, E. W. 1918. Factors determining character and distribution of food reserves in woody plants. *Bot. Gaz.* 66: 162–175.—Stumpf, P. K. 1965. Lipid metabolism. *Plant biochemistry.* J. Bonner and J. E. Varner, eds., pp. 323–345. New York: Academic Press.

TAMMES, P. M. L. 1933. Observations on the bleeding of palm trees. *Rec. Trav. bot. neerl.* 30: 514–536.—TOMLINSON, P. B. and M. H. ZIMMERMANN. 1969. Vascular anatomy of monocotyledons with secondary growth—an introduction. *Jour. Arnold Arb.* 50: 159–179.

URSINO, D. J., C. D. NELSON, and G. KROTKOV. 1968. Seasonal changes in the distribution of photo-assimilated ^{14}C in young pine plants. *Plant Physiol.* 43: 845–852.

ZIEGLER, H. 1956. Untersuchungen über die Leitung und Sekretion der Assimilate. *Planta* 47: 447–500.—ZIEGLER, H. 1961. Our knowledge of translocation in rays. In *Recent advances in botany.* pp 1229–1232. Toronto, Canada: Univ. of Toronto Press.—ZIEGLER, H. 1964. Storage, mobilization and distribution of reserve material in trees. In *The formation of wood in forest trees.* M. H. Zimmermann, ed., pp. 303–320. New York: Academic Press.—ZIMMERMANN, M. H. 1958. Translocation of organic substances in the phloem of trees. In *The physiology of forest trees.* K. V. Thimann, ed., pp. 381–400. New York: Ronald Press.—ZIMMERMANN, M. H. 1964. The relation of transport to growth in dicotyledonous trees. In *The formation of wood in forest trees.* M. H. Zimmermann, ed., pp. 289–301. New York: Academic Press.

INDICES

AUTHOR INDEX

Italic numbers indicate citations in one of the bibliographies.

SUBJECT INDEX

Italic page numbers indicate illustrations.